Computer Supported Cooperative Work

Springer
London
Berlin
Heidelberg
New York
Hong Kong
Milan
Paris
Tokyo

Also in this series

Gerold Riempp
Wide Area Workflow Management
3-540-76243-4

Celia T. Romm and Fay Sudweeks (Eds)
Doing Business Electronically
3-540-76159-4

Fay Sudweeks and Celia T. Romm (Eds)
Doing Business on the Internet
1-85233-030-9

Elayne Coakes, Dianne Willis and
Raymond Lloyd-Jones (Eds)
The New SocioTech
1-85233-040-6

Elizabeth F. Churchill, David N. Snowdon
and Alan J. Munro (Eds)
Collaborative Virtual Environments
1-85233-244-1

Christine Steeples and Chris Jones (Eds)
Networked Learning
1-85233-471-1

Barry Brown, Nicola Green and
Richard Harper (Eds)
Wireless World
1-85233-477-0

Reza Hazemi and Stephen Hailes (Eds)
The Digital University – Building a Learning
Community
1-85233-478-9

Elayne Coakes, Dianne Willis and
Steve Clark (Eds)
Knowledge Management in the
SocioTechnical World
1-85233-441-X

Ralph Schroeder (Ed.)
The Social Life of Avatars
1-85233-461-4

J.H. Erik Andriessen
Working with Groupware
1-85233-603-X

Paul Kirschner, Chad Carr and
Simon Buckingham Shum (Eds)
Visualising Argumentation
1-85233-664-1

Christopher Lueg and Danyel Fisher (Eds)
From Usenet to CoWebs
1-85233-532-7

Bjørn Erik Munkvold
Implementing Collaboration Technologies
in Industry
1-85233-418-5

A list of out of print titles is available at the end of the book

Kristina Höök, David Benyon and
Alan J. Munro (Eds)

Designing Information Spaces: The Social Navigation Approach

With 100 Figures including 16 in colour

Springer

Kristina Höök, PhD, PhLic, MSc
Swedish Institute of Computer Science, Box 1263, S-16428 Kista, Sweden

David Benyon, PhD
Department of Computing, Napier University, Canal Court,
42 Craiglockhart Avenue, Edinburgh EH14 1DJ, UK

Alan J Munro
Department of Computer Science, Strathclyde University, Livingstone Tower,
26 Richmond Street, Glasgow G1 1XH, UK

Series Editors

Dan Diaper, PhD, MBCS
Professor of Systems Science & Engineering, School of Design,
Engineering & Computing, Bournemouth University, Talbot Campus, Fern Barrow,
Poole, Dorset BH12 5BB, UK

Colston Sanger
Shottersley Research Limited, Little Shottersley, Farnham Lane
Haslemere, Surrey GU27 1HA, UK

British Library Cataloguing in Publication Data
Designing information spaces: the social navigation approach. – (Computer supported cooperative work)
 1. Human-computer interaction 2. Information technology – Social aspects
 I. Höök, Kristina II. Benyon, David III. Munro, Alan J., 1965–
 004.1'9
ISBN 1-85233-661-7

Library of Congress Cataloging-in-Publication Data
A catalog record for this book is available from the Library of Congress

CSCW ISSN 1431-1496

ISBN 1-85233-661-7 Springer-Verlag London Berlin Heidelberg
a member of BertelsmannSpringer Science+Business Media GmbH
http://www.springer.co.uk

© Springer-Verlag London Limited 2003
Printed in Great Britain

Typesetting: Gray Publishing, Tunbridge Wells, UK
Printed and bound at the Athenaeum Press Ltd., Gateshead, Tyne & Wear
34/3830-543210   Printed on acid-free paper   SPIN 10881474

Contents

Author Biographies

Rob Barrett
Rob Barrett (barrett@almaden.ibm.com) is a Research Staff Member at the IBM Almaden Research Center. He holds BS degrees in Physics and Electrical Engineering from Washington University in St. Louis and a PhD in Applied Physics from Stanford University. He joined IBM Research in 1991, where he has worked on magnetic data storage, pointing devices and web intermediaries.

David Benyon
David Benyon (d.benyon@dcs.napier.ac.uk) is Professor of Human–Computer Systems at Napier University. He obtained his PhD from the Open University in 1993 on the topic of Intelligent User Interfaces. His main research interests are in human–computer interaction (HCI), particularly in the application of knowledge-based techniques to HCI, and information systems design. David Benyon was actively involved with the EU's long-term research (LTR) intelligent–information–interfaces network of excellence, "i³-NET" and with project PERSONA (with Swedish Institute of Computer Science).
http://www.dcs.napier.ac.uk/~dbenyon

Monika Buscher
Monika Buscher (m.buscher@lancaster.ac.uk) is a research fellow at the Department of Sociology at Lancaster University. Her research interests include ethnomethodology, ethnographic studies of work practice, computer-supported cooperative work (CSCW), interdisciplinary theory and practice for systems design, theories of the information society. As a member of interdisciplinary research projects she carries out ethnographic studies of work, primarily in creative professions.
http://www.comp.lancs.ac.uk/sociology/mbuscher.html

Matthew Chalmers
Matthew Chalmers (matthew@dcs.gla.ac.uk) is a Reader in Computing Science at the University of Glasgow. Previously he worked at Xerox EuroPARC and UBS Ubilab. He is a principal investigator in Equator, a UK EPSRC Interdisciplinary Research Collaboration. His overall interest is the use of contemporary semiotics and philosophy to inform HCI theory and the design of information systems. One application of this work is City, a project in Equator that combines wearable computers, virtual environments and adaptive hypermedia in one

collaborative system. Other projects focus on information visualisation and recommender systems.
http://www.dcs.gla.ac.uk/~matthew

Rickard Cöster

Rickard Cöster (rick@sics.se) is a PhD student in the Machine Learning Group at the Department of Computer and Systems Sciences, Stockholm University. His research interest is in the broad area of information retrieval, information filtering and machine learning. He works part time at the Swedish Institute of Computer Science (SICS), and has developed systems for information retrieval and collaborative filtering that are currently used in a number of research projects at SICS.
http://www.dsv.su.se/~rick/

Andreas Dieberger

Andreas Dieberger (andreasd@us.ibm.com) is a Research Staff Member at the IBM Almaden Research Center. He holds a Masters in Computer Science, a PhD in Human Factors from the Vienna University of Technology, and a post-doctoral degree from a joint programme on environmental studies ("Technischer Umweltschutz") from the Vienna University of Agriculture and the Vienna University of Technology. He joined IBM Research in 2000 and works on supporting collaborative work and on visualisation tools with a focus on design.

Paul Dourish

Paul Dourish (jpd@ics.uci.edu) is an Associate Professor of Information and Computer Science at the University of California, Irvine. He has previously held positions at Xerox PARC, Apple Research Labs and Rank Xerox EuroPARC. His primary research interests are in the areas of computer-supported cooperative work and human–computer interaction. In particular, much of his research concerns the relationship between foundational aspects of software design and analytic perspectives on social action, especially ethnomethodology. This interest has led him to investigate such topics as the relationship between representation and action in workflow, the development of radically adaptive architectures for collaborative systems, and the integration of information with embodiments of activity, such as that implied by social navigation.
http://www.ics.uci.edu/~jpd

Thomas Erickson

Thomas Erickson (snowfall@acm.org) is a Research Staff Member in the Social Computing Group at the IBM T.J. Watson Research Center, where he works on designing systems which support network mediated group interaction. An interaction designer and researcher, his approach to systems design is shaped by work in sociology, rhetoric, architecture and urban design. He has contributed to the design of many products, and authored about 40 publications on topics ranging from personal electronic notebooks and information retrieval systems to pattern languages and virtual community.
http://www.pliant.org/personal/Tom_Erickson/index.html

Fredrik Espinoza

Fredrik Espinoza (espinoza@sics.se) is a researcher at the Swedish Institute of Computer Science. After receiving his Master's degree in Computer and Systems Science from Uppsala University, Sweden, he is now pursuing a PhD in the area of open environments for electronic services and cooperation between services. http://www.sics.se/~espinoza

Petra Fagerberg

Petra Fagerberg (petra@sics.se) received her Master's degree in Computer Science in 2002 from the Royal Institute of Technology in Stockholm. Her research interests cover social and ubiquitous computing. http://www.sics.se/humle/

Stephen Farrell

Stephen Farrell (sfarrell@almaden.ibm.com) holds a BA in History and Philosophy of Science, and an MS in Computer Science from the University of Chicago. He joined IBM Research in 1999 to develop systems that enhance the ability of people to work or collaborate. Some of his projects include personalisation of web experience, support for individual knowledge management and visualisation of collaborative groups.

R.H.R. Harper

Richard Harper (R.Harper@surrey.ac.uk) is Professor of Socio-Digital Systems and Director of DWRC (Digital World Research Centre) at Surrey University. He completed his PhD at the University of Manchester in 1989. He then became a research officer at the University of Lancaster, participating in research into the sociological aspects of air traffic control. Following this, he was senior research fellow on a project into the design of expert systems for the police force. In 1992, he moved to Xerox's European Research Centre in Cambridge. Here, he undertook numerous projects into the ways digital technologies change organisational life, working with BT labs in the UK, the IMF in Washington, DC, and Lloyds-TSB in the UK, amongst others. During this time he was also a visiting scholar at the University of Cambridge and a special lecturer at the University of Nottingham. His latest book is: *The Myth of the Paperless Office* with A.J. Sellen, MIT Press, 2002. http://www.surrey.ac.uk/dwrc/harper.html

John Hughes

Professor John Hughes (j.hughes@lancaster.ac.uk), graduated in 1963 with a degree in Moral and Political Philosophy from the University of Birmingham. He moved to Lancaster University in 1970. In a long, interminable career, John Hughes has published in the fields of political socialisation, political sociology, and research methods. His current interests, however, are in the field of computer-supported cooperative work which involves ethnographic studies of work activities to inform system design, and working with computer scientists at Lancaster. http://www.comp.lancs.ac.uk/sociology/jhughes.html

Kristina Höök

Kristina Höök (kia@sics.se) is the laboratory manager of the HUMLE laboratory at SICS (Swedish Institute of Computer Science). She also holds an associate professor position at Stockholm University. Her work includes work on social navigation, intelligent user interfaces, and affective computing. Most of her work has been directed towards the design and user studies of novel ways of interaction between system and user.
http://www.sics.se/~kia

Phillip Jeffrey

Phillip Jeffrey (phillipj@cs-club.org) is currently employed at Bell Mobility, a mobile and wireles communications company in Canada. He has a BA (Honours) in Information Systems and Human Behaviour from the University of Guelph in Canada. Previously, he has been a student researcher at Adastral Park, Ipswich, UK, and the GMD FIT (now Fraunhofer Institute), Sankt Augustin, Germany.

Wendy A. Kellogg

Wendy A. Kellogg (wkellogg@us.ibm.com) is Manager of Social Computing at IBM's T.J. Watson Research Center. Her current work involves designing and studying computer-mediated communication systems. Kellogg holds a PhD in Cognitive Psychology and is author of numerous papers in the fields of HCI and CSCW. She recently served as Technical Program Co-Chair for ACM's DIS 2000 ("Designing Interactive Systems") conference, and as General Co-Chair for ACM's CSCW 2000 ("Computer-Supported Cooperative Work") conference.

Joseph A. Konstan

Joseph A. Konstan (konstan@cs.umn.edu) is Associate Professor of Computer Science and Engineering at the University of Minnesota. His research addresses a variety of human-computer interaction issues related to filtering, comprehending, organising and automating large and complex data sets. He co-directs the GroupLens Research Group, and is best known for his work in recommender systems, multimedia and visualisation. In 1996 he co-founded Net Perceptions, a company that has since developed collaborative filtering recommender systems into a variety of commercial personalisation tools. He also works with a number of small and mid-sized businesses on issues related to web site design, user interfaces, and human–computer interaction. Dr. Konstan received his PhD from the University of California, Berkeley, in 1993.
http://www.cs.umn.edu/~konstan

Andreas Lund

Andreas Lund (alund@informatik.umu.se) is a graduate student and instructor at the Department of Informatics, Umeå University, where he is also a member of the Muse research group (http://www.informatik.umu.se/~muse). His general research interests include how computerisation brings about changed conditions for meaningful experiences in individual and social settings. He is

currently working towards the completion of his PhD thesis on the subject of how information visualisation design can be informed by recent theories of embodied meaning.
http://www.informatik.umu.se/~alund/.

Teenie Matlock

Teenie Matlock (tmatlock@psych.stanford.edu) is currently a post-doctoral researcher in the Psychology Department at Stanford University. She has a PhD in Cognitive Psychology from University of California, Santa Cruz, and prior to that studied linguistics and cognitive science. She has published in psychology, linguistics and human–computer interaction.
http://www-psych.stanford.edu/~tmatlock/

Paul P. Maglio

Paul P. Maglio (pmaglio@almaden.ibm.com) is a Manager and Research Staff Member at the IBM Almaden Research Center. He holds an SB in Computer Science and Engineering from the Massachusetts Institute of Technology and a PhD in Cognitive Science from the University of California, San Diego. He joined IBM Research in 1995, where he studies how people think about and use information spaces, such as the World Wide Web.

Gloria Mark

Gloria Mark (gmark@ics.uci.edu) is an Assistant Professor in Information and Computer Science at the University of California, Irvine. Previously she worked at the GMD in Bonn, Germany. Her main research interests are in computer-supported collaborative work (CSCW), particularly in understanding how collaborative technologies can support virtual collocation. She is currently working on projects with Intel and the Jet Propulsion Laboratory, studying distributed teams and technology use.
http://www.ics.uci.edu/~gmark

Andrew McGrath

Andrew McGrath (andrew.mcgrath@hutchison3g.com) is Head of User Interface group in Hutchison 3G, a mobile multimedia company that is one of five companies awarded licences by the UK Government in May 2000 to run third-generation mobile phone services. Prior to Hutchison 3G Andrew worked at BT Labs, Martlesham Heath, UK.

Rod McCall

Rod McCall (rodmc@totalise.co.uk) is currently writing up his thesis on navigation within electronic spaces at Napier University, Edinburgh. His thesis focuses on the development of navigational guidelines for two- and three-dimensional environments. In the past he has been a researcher into user interface design for offshore and maritime crisis management simulations and a member of the PERSONA project. At present he is a staff member at Runtime Revolution, Edinburgh, the authors of the user-friendly Revolution development environment.

David Modjeska

David Modjeska (modjeska@fis.utoronto.ca) is an assistant professor in the Faculty of Information Studies at the University of Toronto. He holds a PhD in Computer Science from the University of Toronto, an MS in Computer Science from Stanford University, and a BA in English from Harvard University. His research interests focus on information visualisation and human–computer interaction (HCI). Before joining FIS, he was an assistant professor in the Department of Computer Science at Chalmers Technical University/Gothenburg University in Sweden, and previously a guest researcher and instructor in the Department of Informatics at Umeå University in Sweden. Prior work experience includes six years as a software engineer in Silicon Valley. His teaching interests focus on information systems.
http://www.fis.utoronto.ca/faculty/modjeska/index.html

Alan Munro

Alan Munro (alanm@cis.strath.ac.uk) is a Research Fellow in the Department of Computer and Information Sciences at Strathclyde University in Glasgow. He has a MA and PhD in Psychology from the universities of Glasgow and Strathclyde respectively, and has done post-doctoral work in Oxford University Computing Laboratory, the University of Jyväskylä, Finland, and Napier University in Edinburgh, all in the broad area of support of collaborative activity and design of novel applications. His main interests are ethnographic fieldwork for the design and inspiration of new technologies, ecological psychology and novel interfaces for technologies. His current work is on the EU Disappearing Computer project Gloss where he is working closely with architects looking at the design of social navigational possibilities for different sorts of physical spaces using ubiquitous computing.
http://www.cs.strath.ac.uk/~alanm/

Per Persson

Per Persson (perp@sics.se) gained his PhD in Communication Studies from Stockholm University in 2000 with a dissertation on the spectator psychology of visual media. Since 1999, he has conducted research at the Swedish Institute of Computer Science on social computing, social navigation, ubiquitous computing and believable agents.
http://www.sics.se/~perp

John Riedl

John Riedl (riedl@cs.umn.edu) is Associate Professor of Computer Science and Engineering at the University of Minnesota. His research encompasses distributed and collaborative systems. His decade of research on recommender systems started in 1992 when he and Paul Resnick started to build the first automated collaborative filtering system. He continues to co-direct the GroupLens Research Group and has been a prolific author and speaker on the topic. In 1996, he co-founded Net Perceptions to commercialise collaborative filtering technology. After several years as the company's chief technical officer, he returned full-time

to research and teaching, though he continues to shape commercial use of the technology as the company's chief scientist. Dr Riedl received his PhD from Purdue University.
http://www.cs.umn.edu/~riedl

Anna Sandin
Anna Sandin (sandin@sics.se) received her Master's degree in Computer Science in 2001 from Uppsala University, Sweden. She performs advanced research in electronic services and personal service environments (PSE). She is presently affiliated with Swedish Institute of Computer Science, Kista, Sweden.
http://www.sics.se/~sandin/

Robert Spence
Professor Robert Spence (r.spence@ic.ac.uk) is currently at Imperial College in London, where he leads the Human–Computer Interaction Research Team in the Intelligent and Interactive Systems group. He conducts research into information visualisation, agent-based interaction design and the facilitation of Social Interaction through Information Technology. The IIS-HCI team specialises in the efficient and effective navigation of large information spaces using graphical display techniques.
http://www.ee.ic.ac.uk/research/information/www/Bobs.html

Martin Svensson
Martin Svensson (martins@sics.se) received his PhLic (2000) at Stockholm University. He has been at the Swedish Institute of Computer Science since 1996 and is currently finalising his PhD on how to design and evaluate systems that support social navigation.
http://www.sics.se/~martins

John Waterworth
John Waterworth (jwworth@informatik.umu.se) is Professor of Informatics and leader of the Muse research group at Umeå University in Sweden, and also Senior Researcher at the Interactive Institute Tools for Creativity studio. He has a PhD in Experimental Psychology and is a Chartered Psychologist of the British Psychological Society. John has worked on human–computer interaction for many years, at BT Labs in England (1980-88, on speech-based interaction), in Singapore (1988-94, on multimedia and VR) and in Sweden (from 1994). His research interests centre around the effects of technological mediation on consciousness, creativity and understanding. A current interest is how interactive art can be used as a vehicle for research on the effects of technological mediation on experience.
http://www.informatik.umu.se/~jwworth/

Alan Wexelblat
Alan Wexelblat (wex@hovir.com) received his PhD from MIT's Program in Media Arts and Sciences in 1999, where his dissertation work on interaction history was supervised by Dr Pattie Maes. He has worked in social navigation

and related areas such as virtual reality, multimodal interaction and information visualisation since the 1980s. His research interests currently revolve around time, history, memory and artefacts, particularly within a group or community context.

http://wex.www.media.mit.edu/people/wex/

Editors' Introduction: Footprints in the Snow

Kristina Höök, David Benyon and Alan Munro

Background

There are many changes happening in the world of computers and communication media. The Internet and the web, of course, have created this vast network of interlinked machines. Computers are becoming increasingly ubiquitous; they are "disappearing" into everyday objects. They are becoming increasingly small, so much so that they are now wearable. They are increasingly able to communicate with each other.

These changes have had a major impact on our understanding of how computer systems should be designed and on what people can and want to do with them. The discipline of human–computer interaction (HCI) has not really kept pace with the changes in technology, and much HCI education still takes the view that there is *a* person interacting with a computer. Courses on HCI will emphasise the cognitive difficulties that people might have in using large software packages. They will present guidelines on how to design screens and human–computer "dialogues" and will discuss methods of evaluating computer systems in terms of the "tasks" that people undertake and in terms of the "errors" that people might make.

In the mid-1980s and early 1990s a new discipline emerged out of HCI and areas of study related to people working together; computer-supported cooperative work (CSCW). CSCW looked at how software systems and communication technologies could support the work that people were trying to do. It shared many of the assumptions of HCI, but also introduced more socially-based ways of thinking. The importance of fitting technology into the workplace was emphasised, or *really* understanding what people wanted to do and of looking at what technologies were required in order to support and enable their activities.

During the 1990s a number of people were becoming dissatisfied with both these approaches. People were using computers for many purposes other than work. Computers were being used in different contexts such as households, and communities of people existed solely or primarily through computer-mediated communications. People were not simply interacting with a computer, they were interacting with people using various combinations of computers and different media such as video, mobile phones, animations, touching, gesturing and so on. The notion that we could see people as existing in an information space, or in multiple information spaces, grew and was offered as a challenge to the predominant "people outside the information" view of HCI (Dourish and Chalmers, 1994; Benyon, 1998a, 2001). Alongside this came the recognition that using computers needed to become a more enjoyable, social activity. The development of the Internet, particularly for leisure activities, and the emergence of Internet Service Providers that bundled news, chat rooms, web access with remote game playing, shopping and so on, resulted in designers looking outside of "traditional" CSCW and HCI for design principles and appropriate methodologies.

These developments have continued to grow into the twenty-first century informed by emerging theoretical frameworks such as distributed cognition (Hollan, Hutchins and Kirsh, 2002), social computing (Dourish, 2001) and experiential cognition (Lakoff and Johnson, 1999) and expressed through new design approaches such as holistic design (Maxwell, 2002), scenario-based design (Carroll, 2000). Recent times are also seeing a convergence of HCI, CSCW and interaction design that has its roots in the disciplines of creative design (Winograd, 1997).

Social Navigation is part of this movement. The chapters in this volume (and in the companion volume, *Social Navigation of Information Space*, Munro, Höök and Benyon, 1999) capture much of the debate and ideas surrounding social navigation. The chapters deal with concepts of social navigation, ideas of the nature of information, the impact of people working in new environments and with new media and design ideas coming from architecture, anthropology and social theories of interaction. In this introduction we aim to introduce many of the significant characteristics of social navigation and the backgrounds from which it has arisen.

A Short History

In March 1998 an international group of thirty researchers attended a workshop on Roslagens Pärla, a small island in the Swedish archipelago. The topic of the workshop was "Personal and Social Navigation" of Information Spaces. Although the researchers came from a wide variety of backgrounds – computer science, human–computer interaction, social science, psychology, information retrieval, computer-supported cooperative work – they shared an interest in exploring new ways of thinking about the relationships between people, technologies and information. In particular they were interested in the notion of social navigation: how to develop and enrich the experience of dealing with information within the electronic "worlds" provided by computing and communication technologies.

The idea for the workshop arose from discussions within the group working on a research project called PERSONA, a collaboration between the Swedish Institute of Computer Science (SICS) and Napier University, Edinburgh. David Benyon from Napier and Kristina Höök from SICS had developed the project after their experiences working with intelligent user interfaces. Attempts to get the computer to make sensible inferences about what people wanted to do, so that it could tailor the provision of information to their needs, had not been successful. The dream of having intelligent interface "agents" (Kay, 1991) was still a long way from becoming a reality because the techniques used to build agents and other "intelligent" user interfaces ignored a fundamental feature of people; people are social beings. The question for the workshop to consider was how to bring the social into information provision.

When people need information, they will often turn to other people rather than use more formalised information artefacts. When navigating cities people tend to ask other people for advice rather than study maps (Streeter and Vitello, 1985), when trying to find information about pharmaceuticals, medical doctors tend to ask other doctors for advice (Timpka and Hallberg, 1996), if your child has red spots you might phone your mother or talk to a friend for an opinion. Even when we are not directly looking for information we use a wide range of cues, both from features of the environment and from the behaviour of other people, to manage our activities. Alan Munro observed how people followed crowds or simply sat around at a venue when deciding which shows and street events to attend at the Edinburgh Arts Festival (Munro, 1998). We might be influenced to pick up a book because it appears well thumbed, we walk into a sunny courtyard because it looks attractive or we might decide to see a film because our friends enjoyed it. Not only do we find our ways through spaces from talking to or following the trails of crowds of people, we also evaluate the things we find in these spaces through understanding them in a social context. We put them in a framework of relevance.

During a break at the workshop a group of participants were standing in the winter sunshine. They were considering how the results of the workshop could be more widely disseminated and about where the ideas raised during discussions might ultimately lead. A line of footprints led across the snow and into the woods. As a metaphor both for social navigation and for the unknown destination of this work, it seemed perfect: footprints in the snow.

The outcome of the Roslagens Pärla workshop was published in a book *Social Navigation of Information Space* (Munro, Höök and Benyon, 1999).

3

In addition to papers from many of the workshop participants contributions were invited from others working in the area, resulting in fourteen chapters that explored various aspects of social navigation. At the Computer Human Interaction (CHI) conference in 1999 the issues of social navigation were debated in a panel organised by Alan Wexelblat. These activities resulted in a second workshop held in conjunction with the CHI 2000 conference. At this second workshop, a stronger emphasis on implemented social navigation systems and even user evaluations of these systems was made. Observing that social navigation happens in the world is, as it turns out, quite different from finding ways of designing for social navigation.

The first book was soon sold out and after much discussion a second version of the book has emerged. The emphasis on practical examples of implemented social navigation systems is stronger in this second book. For various reasons of space, focus, etc., some of the chapters from the original book were dropped, some have been retained in broadly their original form and others are completely new or have been completely revised.

The aim of the current volume is to make both the applications and the theories underlying social navigation available to a wide audience of practitioners and researchers alike. We hope that both groups will find a wealth of example systems, concepts and practical ideas. In order to help structure the work, we have organised the book into two parts. In Part I "Systems and Theories" the emphasis is on systems that have been built and on the rationale for the design choices made. Part II "Theories and Principles" puts the emphasis on the underlying, generic principles and theories that drive social navigation.

Mapping Social Navigation

The concept of social navigation was introduced by Dourish and Chalmers in 1994. They saw social navigation as *navigation towards a cluster of people* or *navigation because other people have looked at something*. Computer systems known collectively as recommender systems (Konstan and Riedl, this volume) have been developed that implement these ideas. By collecting the likes and dislikes of a large number of people, an individual can specify one or two things that they like or dislike and the system recommends others based on the data collected from other people. Later, Dieberger widened the scope (Dieberger, this volume). He also saw more direct recommendations of, for example, web sites and bookmark collections as a form of social navigation. Since then the concept of social navigation has broadened to include a large family of methods, artefacts and techniques that capture some aspect of navigation.

Social navigation can be seen from several different perspectives and in several different domains, both in the "real" world of human activities and in the "virtual worlds" of information spaces of different kinds. Collaborative virtual environments (CVEs) provide an area where people may interact with each other in various ways. Sometimes these environments will be textual, such as a newsgroup, sometimes they include video and sound, and in others people are represented by avatars. Work on social navigation brings together and occasionally critiques aspects of CSCW (computer-supported cooperative work), IUI (intelligent user interfaces), IR (information retrieval), and CVEs. Accordingly the underlying philosophies and disciplines come from work in cognitive and social psychology, anthropology, social theories of human action, human-computer interaction and artificial intelligence. The concept of social navigation brings some quite unique characteristics into our understanding of information, spaces, places, user interfaces, and the activities of those participating in these various worlds.

Social navigation does not have a narrow focus. Rather, its concerns range widely over "navigation" in different types of virtual worlds. Social navigation considers the creation of social settings and "places" in information space and behaviour in them, the sociality of information creation, people as members of groups and nature of information itself, its location, evaluation and use. We are seen not just as single users, but as members of many different types of information spaces both real and virtual. As is suggested by the term "navigation", many writers on social navigation draw upon work in architecture, urban planning, the visual arts and design.

The ideas of social navigation build on a more general concept that interacting with computers can be seen as "navigation" in information space (Benyon and Höök, 1997; Benyon, 2001). Whereas "traditional" human-computer interaction (HCI) sees the person outside the information space, separate from it, trying to bridge the "gulfs" between themselves and information, the alternative view of HCI as navigation within the space sees people as inhabiting and moving through their information space. Just as we use social methods to find our way through geographical spaces, so we are interested in how social methods can be used in information spaces. How could the ideas of social navigation change our view on design in this particular context?

Instead of imagining a "dead" information space, one aim of social navigation is to provide people with a lively space where (in some way) they can see other people moving about, can consult or instruct specialist agents and get advice and help from other people. These are examples of *direct social navigation*. Another aim of social navigation is to provide possibilities of providing information about what other people have done: pointing people to choices that, based on the preferences of other people, the system believes would be suitable; providing opportunities to peek at another's choice; showing which is the most popular choice. These are examples of *indirect social navigation*. Another form of indirect social navigation is for the designer of a space to enable effective navigation and choice-making through good sign posting, showing clear paths through the space or providing clear maps.

The form of social navigation chosen will depend upon an understanding of the properties of the space and people's activities in the space. Social navigation is not a set of ready-made algorithms; it is a philosophy of design. What we can do is to *enable* (make the world *afford*) social interactions and social trails to be revealed to others. We might direct people or point them to areas "off stage", making people aware of others (Dourish, this volume). Social navigation will often be a *dynamic*, changing, interaction between the people in the space, the items and the activities in the space.

A fundamental question which stems from social navigation concerns the methods we use in order to do research in this area, to inform our concepts. Within this book we find a diversity of answers. A number of chapters use ethnographic methods of different theoretical flavours, others more "traditional", cognitivist approaches, others from recent theoretical developments in psychology and cognitive science such as experientialism.

The fact that there are a wide variety of approaches and analyses is unsurprising. Social navigation does not have a single, underlying theoretical framework and we are all learning more about the applicability of different methods in different circumstances. This book is the outcome of an organic process, from the workshop, through the first volume, to the current book. The chapters represent in some ways the networks of researchers which have helped build this field.

It is true to an extent that a number of these researchers have similar concerns: ethnographic methodology and a shared philosophical acknowledgement of (the later) Wittgenstein (though exactly how his writings are interpreted does vary). There is often an influence from the work of the psychologist James Gibson (1986) on the importance of perception to thought, of George Lakoff (1987) and his approach to cognition, and of the sociologist Garfinkel (1967). There are also, as we mention elsewhere, shared concerns about architecture, the built environment and planning.

Design Possibilities

Using the idea of social navigation will thus bring about a view on information spaces and people's activities in them that enables a whole range of design solutions that are barely exploited in today's systems. With direct social navigation we shall be able to talk directly to other users and get their views on how to navigate, which will improve our navigation and understanding of the space. When we talk to someone else, the information we get back is often personalised to our needs. We are perhaps told a little bit more than exactly the information we asked for, or if the information provider knows us, the instructions may be adapted to fit our knowledge or assumed reasons for going to a particular place.

But direct social navigation can also be on the level of interpreting information based on how other people talk about or use information (Harper, this volume). We can judge to what extent the information given can be trusted depending upon the credibility of the information provider. Sometimes, even if it cannot be trusted, it still is of value as we know where it is from.

Social navigation is to an extent dependent on the modality in which one is able to operate, the affordances of it. A text only system can afford fewer social cues than one using graphics, sound or video. We also talk to one another through body language or through the collective visible actions of a group of people. We follow the crowd of people who leave the plane in an airport assuming that they are all heading for the baggage claim. In a virtual environment avatars may be used to express some simple forms of body language that can invite others to join the group, or to indicate privacy. The aura of the representation of a user can enable interaction with other people.

The possibilities for indirect social navigation also allow for aggregation of non-visible user behaviour. Designers can invent novel ways in which these things are displayed such as textures of items or trails of people, or it can be more direct instructions or recommendations: "others who bought this book also bought this one". We can also alter the way that data about people is collected, shown and mapped on the space in a dynamic way. The dynamics of this change is both good and bad: people shall have to adapt more quickly to new environments and the changed properties of the space. People are intrigued by spaces that do not behave as they expect them to, but they rapidly adapt and figure out new ways by which they can understand the space and the movements of people in them.

Both direct and indirect social navigation provide excellent opportunities to provide the seeker with a sense of security/safety: "since all these people have chosen this route, it must be the right one" or "if this is the way that my friend behaves with these sites, then I can probably do the same". Human beings are to a large extent behaving like flocks – we enjoy imitating other people's behaviours, body movements, use of tools, way of talking, etc. We use dialects, clothing, rituals as means to make our group distinct from the rest of humanity. We create a feeling of belonging – it makes us feel good! These mechanisms are efficient ways of learning and still they are largely excluded from spaces like the web (Dieberger, this volume).

Turn to Svensson and Höök, Persson et al., Erickson and Kellogg, Wexelblat, Maglio et al. and Konstan and Riedl (all in this volume) for concrete design examples of how the idea of social navigation can inspire the design process.

Shifting Perspectives

Social navigation does not just provide alternative design possibilities. It requires people to think differently about the nature of people and their interactions with computers and communication technologies. For example, Dourish (this volume) encourages us to view social navigation as a phenomenon of interaction. If we populate spaces they will offer users "appropriation and appropriate behavioural framing, distinguishing them from simple spaces, which are characterised in terms of their dimensionality". Dieberger (this volume) opens up the scope of seeing social navigation as a move away from the "dead" information spaces we see on the Internet today and in every way possible opens up the spaces for seeing other users – both directly and indirectly. His claim is that "future information systems will be populated information spaces". Users will be able to point out and share information easily, guide each other and in general open up our eyes for various ways by which we can "see" other users.

Ideas of social navigation naturally lead us to consider the concept of navigation in real and virtual worlds. We also need to change our view of information from being decontextualised, objective portions of the world, to socially interwoven subjective views of the world. The relationship between space and how it can be turned into "place" where meetings can happen and where social connotations constrain and afford activities is also significant. Finally, we need to reconsider the relationship between the modality of the space and interactions that can take place in it.

Social navigation is not a concept that can be unproblematically translated into a set of particular tools. Instead it encourages understanding of human activities in space and place – both virtual and "real". People are active participants in reshaping the space. There is a dynamic relationship between people, their activities in space, and the space itself. All three are subject to change.

Navigation of Information Space

Spence provides a model of navigation that focuses on how people form intentions, browse and evaluate alternatives and then decide which "direction" (or course of action) to follow. In this sense, Spence is quite close to the work of urban planners and architects who have used this cognitive view of spatial awareness. Lynch (1960) in particular has been very influential in identifying five features of urban environments – landmarks, nodes, edges, paths and districts – and their importance in the design of geographical space. Other influential work from the area of architecture is that of Alexander et al. (1977) who proposed a number of "patterns" for architectural features.

This work is not without criticism, however. The crucial thing missing from the traditional geographies is the failure to appreciate how environments are *conceived* by people as opposed to simply *perceived* by people. People play a role in producing the space, through their activities and practice (Lefebvre, 1991). So the social aspects of exploration and wayfinding need to be taken into consideration. Also important are the ecological aspects of navigation: how information is distributed throughout the people and artefacts in an environment and how that information is picked up and used by people as they navigate. The explorative, browsing behaviour of people needs to be part of our understanding of navigation (Spence, this volume; McCall and Benyon, this volume). It is one of the marks of social navigation and the chapters in this volume that the debate about how best to view navigational activities continues.

If we see the user as within the information space as opposed to outside it the job of the designer becomes one of providing graphical, auditory and haptic cues so that users will be better placed to understand, use and navigate within it; we need to "design for possible user experiences" (Waterworth et al., this volume).

From Space to Place

The recognition of the importance of the social construction of space leads to the important distinction between space and place; a theme picked up by several authors in this volume (particularly Dourish, Chalmers, Dieberger, Jeffery and Mark, Buscher and Hughes, and Waterworth et al.). Places are seen by a number of authors to be the settings in which people interact. People turn spaces into "places" where social interactions are encouraged and which are visible through the configuration of the space and how people conceive of the various interactions in it. Once again architecture is a significant influence on these ideas. Whyte (1980) in particular, is interesting; the photographic studies of various different configurations of space, showing in a very detailed way what configurations of space "work" and what ones do not, what ones lead to higher crime levels, what configurations lead to sociability. One of his main findings is that what attracts people is people. Something designers of information space should consider.

We must though be careful in our analysis. Particular physical configurations are associated with social situations. The consulting room is of course quite different from a lounge, and a pub. However we have to bear in mind that these are *reflexively* designed. It is the architect's knowledge of what goes on in these places which conditions how they were built. However it is not true that these places are not mutable (Dieberger, this volume). Whilst certain places encourage and afford behaviours, people can change the use of that place.

To what extent lessons from architecture and the social construction of spaces can be translated into the design of information spaces is something explored in several chapters in this volume (see particularly McCall and Benyon). The difference between information space and information place, however, is an important feature of social navigation.

From Decontextualised to Social Information

Just as the "space" concept of information space is important, so too is the "information" concept. Chalmers (this volume) aims to provide solid theoretical underpinnings for social navigation, meditating on its relationship to "conventional" approaches to HCI and informatics. He points at Wittgenstein's concept of a "language game" as a better way of understanding information. That is, language and its relation to the world it denotes is not a fixed thing, but something which is negotiated over and over in interactions between people. Information is a social artefact and we should design information systems from this viewpoint: the relevance of a piece of information is determined from its usage.

Harper (this volume) also looks at "information" as used by "information workers" who use it daily. In this setting, it is not just accuracy which is important. In fact, he shows in the context of these peoples' work, how sometimes "accuracy" is not as important as knowing where the information comes from. These people need to place information in a "framework of relevance" for the institution. Information which may be inaccurate and or biased can be more useful than more accurate and "factual" information. The "factual" information is not discarded, but rather for the moment placed aside until required.

There is a danger of taking an "objectivist" account of what information is; of seeing it simply as something in a database which has to be retrieved. The concept of social navigation goes beyond mining some information from large data sets like web pages. It is only when we look closer at information that as an entity it becomes strange. Through the careful study of various types of information work in a number of domains, such as Harper's work and in Chalmers' discussion on language games, we are coming toward a more problematic view of information. It is problematic, viewed as an objective, decontextualised entity.

Modalities, Affordances and the Physics of Spaces

A number of writers such as Jeffery and Mark, Buscher and Hughes, and McGrath and Munro discuss various types of virtual worlds in which people can see each other and perhaps informational objects of some type as well. In these worlds, people communicate in a number of ways, textually, visually, through audio channels and through "virtual contact". These different modes of interaction and the different representations of people and artefacts may have a significant impact on experiences within the information space.

Some suggest that textual or audio communication, because it lacks the cues of the real world, will be "depersonalised" and "antagonistic" compared to co-present communication. Whereas others put more emphasis on places and their influence on our behaviour, and the ways in which different virtual situations can have quite different ways of relating no matter what the modality might be. One newsgroup may require a strong constitution of its members because of the constant and rolling "flame-wars", whereas another will see such things rarely, if at all. When we regard the "effects of modality" in the encounter, we do so if at all in a way which acknowledges the strong influence of social situation.

The physical laws that the spaces run under may well determine affordances of the space in ways which are more complex than we might think (Buscher and Hughes, this volume). The ways in which media worlds work have an affect on the ways in which we have to communicate. For example, in the media space work (Heath and Luff, 1992b) we began to see how people would inhabit these spaces and orient to these various affordances. In the real world, for example, we might find it easy to get information quickly to a number of colleagues by shouting it, and in certain environments, for example, a City dealing room, this is entirely permissible. The shouted "outloud" is an efficient way to communicate with a number of people simultaneously. This can only be done given that there are certain physical laws which work to afford this. However, in many virtual worlds one only hears who is close to one. In contrast, anything said in a chat room is said to all, unless one explicitly messages someone.

The physical laws of spaces allow and afford certain ways of relating with others. A number of different elements of the navigational space work together. It may be that certain types of direct or indirect social navigation are particularly hard, that other types are afforded as to be effortless. Our creation of functionality in the space can help others, or conversely create systemic and recurring issues which members have to deal with. Just now, for example, it is difficult to know more about the other users of a web page other than the counter of "hits". On Internet relay chat systems, one can get an idea of the popularity of a channel, but know far less about whether they are attending as well as being online.

We can see therefore how modality of the interface is bound up with representation, how we can visualise others. All these elements are bound up with the social, for example, when we access the channel, the "physical" laws of that space mean that we have the equivalent of everyone shouting their interaction to everyone else. The only way to form a sub–group is direct messaging or explicitly inviting someone to another, sub–channel, and this may be regarded as over familiar and accountable.

The Future of Social Navigation

As put by Dourish: "The concept of 'social navigation' has come of age." Amazon.com uses the ideas of recommender systems. AOL.com provides a "buddy list" to show friends and colleagues are on-line As the reader will see when going through the chapters, the design idea(s) behind social navigation bears the potential of helping us to take a step forward from the prevailing interface culture of today's tool-based view to richer, more social-oriented spaces.

Since the field is new, there are of course numerous problems not yet dealt with. We do not yet understand how to design for social navigation in various different domains. The relationship between spatial metaphors and social navigation is discussed much in this book, but what about spaces that are not spatial in nature and their relationship to social navigation? Are there such spaces which we do not understand as spatial (Maglio and Matlock, this volume)? How do we deal with the issue of accountability and privacy (Erickson and Kellogg, this volume)?

Since social behaviours are by necessity closely tied to the culture of a community, we need to further our understanding of the new cultures we are building through applying the idea of social navigation. Even within western culture, for example, users with a lot of experience of on-line worlds will probably utilise them differently from those with little experience. How will the concepts extend to non-western cultures?

We are seeing more and more applications in the grey zone between tools and games: "infotainment", "edutainment", etc. Designers of information spaces have to think about issues such the natural "flow" of their designs, branding, the use of sounds to communicate "moods", and so on, much in the way that a garden designer, or interior designer considers such things. New applications may be designed to induce empathy, or use irony to enliven the space. They may encourage users to attribute intelligence and in general anthropomorphic qualities to the system (Reeves and Nass, 1996), they may allow for a more narrative, subjective, interactive experience (Murray, 1997), they may induce both negative and positive affective responses in the users, for example (Picard, 1997).

This is a whole new bag for the field of human-computer interaction, and so we turn to other areas where entertainment is in the focus hoping to borrow some of their principles, and learn from their successes and failures. At the other end of the spectrum, technology is making advances, creating completely new spaces that move us beyond the desk-top based "peep-hole" into some created virtual space. We now talk about ubiquitous computers that disappear into our furniture, walls and machines, shared soundscapes where we participate in work places through listening in on sounds of our fellow colleagues, and various augmented worlds where the reality is overlaid with information.

In the end this book is not necessarily going to be successful in answering questions, or giving ready solutions to building systems which will allow "social navigation". Rather, we wish that any success will be in the posing of interesting and foundational issues and in helping people see new paths to take, to follow the footprints in the snow.

Acknowledgements

There is no doubt that the book benefits from the long and interesting discussions from all those who contributed to and attended the Roslagens Pärla workshop: Kathy Buckner, Nils Dahlbäck, Andreas Dieberger, Mattias Forsberg, Leif Gustavson, Phillip Jeffery, Richard Harper, Michael Klemme, Ralf Kuhnert, Paul Maglio, Teenie Matlock, Luc Mertens, David Modjeska, Per Persson, Bas Raijmakers, Paul Rankin, Harald Selke, Robert Spence, Alistair Sutcliffe, John Waterworth, Romain Zeiliger and Shumin Zhai. The workshop was co-financed by the intelligent, information interfaces network of excellence i^3net and SICS. The work was done as part of the PERSONA project – one of the i^3 projects – funded by the EC through the ESPRIT programme. Discussions with all the members of the PERSONA project, particularly Nils Dahlbäck, Mattias Forsberg, Leif Gustavson, Rod McCall, Catriona Macaulay, Marie Sjölinder, Martin Svensson, have significantly contributed to the ideas.

Kristina Höök, Stockholm, Sweden
David Benyon, Edinburgh, Scotland
Alan Munro, Glasgow, Scotland
May 2002

Part I
Systems and Theories

Social Translucence: Using Minimalist Visualisations of Social Activity to Support Collective Interaction

Thomas Erickson and Wendy A. Kellogg

1.1 Introduction: The Ubiquity of the Social

As humans, we are fundamentally social creatures. From birth we orient to other people, and as we develop we acquire abilities for interacting with one another, ranging from expression and gesture through spoken and written language. As adults we are exquisitely sensitive to the actions and interactions of those around us. Every day we make countless decisions that are shaped by our social context. Whether it is wrapping up a talk when the audience starts fidgeting, or deciding to forgo the grocery shopping because the parking lot is jammed, social information provides a basis for inferences, planning and coordinating activity.

When we move from face to face interaction to digitally-mediated interaction, however, everything changes. The subtle social cues that we use to guide and structure our real world interactions are mostly absent. In the digital world we are socially blind, and our attempts to communicate can be awkward and labour-intensive. Although the web is used by millions of people, reading a web page is usually a solitary experience. Even when others are clearly present – as in a chat room or on a conference call – it is difficult to see who is present, who is paying attention, or who wishes to speak. Things that require little effort in face-to-face settings – taking turns when speaking; noticing when someone has a question; seeing who is responding to whom – require a lot of effort in on-line settings, if they are possible at all.

Our aim is to design systems that support deep, coherent and productive collaboration among large groups of people over computer networks.

We are particularly interested in the question of how to design such systems so that they allow groups to observe their interactions, and to steer them so as to make progress towards a shared goal. In this chapter[1] we describe our work towards this end. We begin by taking a close look at how people interact in physical, face-to-face settings, with particular attention to the ways in which they make use of socially salient cues to regulate their behaviour. Here we develop the notion of social translucence, an approach to designing digital systems that emphasises making social information visible to all participants. Next we describe how we map the concept of social translucence into digital systems. We do not try to imitate the real world (e.g. via virtual reality or video); instead, we use "social proxies", minimalist graphical representations of the online presence and activities of people. We illustrate this concept with several prototypes designed for different online contexts, noting how they provide the information that supports the social processes – such as imitation, norming and peer pressure – that underlie so much human behaviour. We then move on to describe Babble, an implemented system that uses two social proxies to support online conversation, and discuss what we've learned while studying its use over the last four years.

1.2 Foundations: Social Translucence and Interaction Architectures

As designers of communication and collaboration systems, we find ourselves taking inspiration from work in the areas of architecture and urban design. This is not surprising since, like architects and urban designers, we are concerned with creating contexts that support various forms of human-human interaction. What architecture and urbanism have to offer is long experience in exploring the interrelationship between physical spaces and social interaction – the interested reader should see Alexander et al. (1977), Gehl (1980), Jacobs (1961), Lynch (1990) and Whyte (1988a).

However, although we have learned much from architecture and urbanism, the fact is that designers in those domains can assume the existence of a consistent and unquestioned physics that underlies social interaction. There is no such constancy in the digital world, and so we need to go a bit farther than architectural discourse takes us. Our goal in this section is to look deeply at social interaction as it is embedded in physical space, and try to extract principles that are sufficiently abstract that they might be transposed to the digital realm.

---

[1] Sections 1.2, 1.3.1 and 1.4.1 of this chapter are reproduced with permission from Erickson and Kellogg (2000). © ACM 2000.

1.2.1 Visibility, Awareness and Accountability

In the building where our group works there is a door that opens from the stairwell into the hallway. This door has a design problem: opened quickly, it is likely to slam into anyone who is about to enter from the other direction. In an attempt to fix this problem, a small sign was placed on the door: it reads, "Please Open Slowly". As you might guess, the sign is not a particularly effective solution.

Let's contrast this solution with one of a different sort: putting a glass window in the door. The glass window approach means that the sign is no longer required. As people approach the door they see whether anyone is on the other side and, if so, they modulate their actions appropriately. This is a simple example of what we call a *socially translucent system*. While it is obvious why this solution works, it is useful to examine the reasons behind it carefully. We see three reasons for the effectiveness of the glass window:

- First, the glass window makes socially significant information visible. That is, as humans, we are perceptually attuned to movement and human faces and figures: we notice and react to them more readily than we notice and interpret a printed sign.

- Second, the glass window supports awareness: I don't open the door quickly because I know that you're on the other side. This awareness brings our social rules into play to govern our actions: we have been raised in a culture in which slamming doors into other people is not sanctioned.

- There is a third, somewhat subtler reason for the efficacy of the glass window. Suppose that I don't care whether I hurt others: nevertheless, I'll open the door slowly because I know that you know that I know you're there, and therefore I will be held accountable for my actions. (This distinction is useful because, while accountability and awareness usually co-occur in the physical world, they are not necessarily coupled in the digital realm.) It is through such individual feelings of accountability that norms, rules, and customs become effective mechanisms for supporting coherent social behaviour.

We see these three properties of socially translucent systems – visibility, awareness and accountability – as building blocks of social interaction. That is, we claim that social translucence is not just about people acting in accordance with social rules. In socially translucent systems we believe it will be easier for users to carry on coherent discussions; to observe and imitate others' actions; to engage in peer pressure; to create, notice and conform to social conventions. We see social translucence as a fundamental requirement for supporting all types of communication and collaboration. To see this, let's move on to a more complex example.

1.2.2 Translucence and the Power of Constraints

There is one other aspect of social translucence that deserves mention. Why is it that we speak of socially *translucent* systems rather than socially *transparent* systems? Because there is a vital tension between privacy and visibility. What we say and do with another person depends on who, and how many, are watching. Note that privacy is neither good nor bad on its own – it simply supports certain types of behaviour and inhibits others. For example, the perceived validity of an election depends crucially on keeping certain of its aspects very private, and other aspects very public. As before, what we are seeing is the impact of awareness and accountability: thus, it is not an accident that voting booths are designed so that observers cannot see who a person is voting for, but that they can see that the voter is alone in the booth; similarly, the ballot box is positioned in public view so that it is easy for observers to see that a voter puts one and only one ballot in the ballot box. The entire process and apparatus that supports elections is carefully designed to ensure that (a) the individual voter is accountable to no person or group with regard to his or her vote, and (b) both voters and the election administrators are publicly accountable for following the rules of the election process.

It would be a mistake, however, to think that translucence is only about the tension between privacy and visibility. Rather, translucence stands in more generally for the power of constraints. To see this, let's look at a more complicated example:

A group of thirty people – authors of the chapters of a forthcoming book – had gathered to mutually critique chapters. For three days, each author worked with a small group of about six others. At the end of the workshop the organisers decided to try to collectively create an organisation for the book. The authors, none of whom had read all the chapters, would decide on what the book sections should be and how the chapters should be ordered.

Everyone gathered in a room, each author with a copy of his or her chapter. To start the process, pieces of paper with possible section names had been placed on the floor and authors were asked to put their chapters near appropriate sections. After this, the procedure was simple: anyone could pick up any chapter and move it elsewhere; anyone could change the name of a book section; anyone could propose a new section by writing a name on a new piece of paper.

Although the ensuing process was characterised by a lot of milling about and simultaneous conversations, it was exceptionally effective. In half an hour the group had arrived at an organisation for a book of 30 chapters, with everyone participating in the discussion.

What is of interest here is how the spatial nature of the setting enabled what was, in effect, a process of social computation. First, as in the case of the door, the participants could see what was happening, and thus awareness and accountability came into play. For example, when someone went to move a chapter to another area of the room (i.e. move it to another section of the book), there would usually be one or more people around. Although not required by the rules, what happened was that the mover would politely offer a rationale for moving the chapter to those in the vicinity (hereafter the "on-lookers"), thus triggering a discussion about the purpose of that section and the point of the chapter. The consequence of this discussion was that either:

- the mover and the on-lookers would agree on the move
- the on-lookers would convince the mover that the chapter was indeed in the right place
- the mover and on-lookers would decide to change the name and definition of the section so that the chapter fitted the section better.

In each of these cases the result was that there was a greater shared understanding of the section names and definitions, the gist of each chapter, and the rationale for the chapter's inclusion.

In addition to the awareness and accountability brought into play by the visibility of the activity of moving chapters around in the room, another spatial property played an important role: physical constraints. Constraints shaped the way in which people could participate in the process of organisation. The fact that the chapters and section names were spread all over the room had an important impact: it meant that no one person could dominate the organisation of the book. Those who had strong opinions about where their chapters belonged tended to hover near their chapters, ready to "defend" their chapters' positions against would-be reorganisers. In contrast, those who had ideas about the arrangement of the book as a whole had to flit about from section to section, thus giving up any strong control over where their chapters (or any single chapter) were positioned. Similarly, people who stayed near a single section heading gained, over time, a detailed understanding of the rationale for the section as a result of repeatedly participating in the to-move-or-not-to-move discussions for its component chapters. This regulation of activity came as a side effect of the fact that the ability to hear and see in a crowded room decreases as distance increases; that is, the space is *translucent* (not transparent) to vision, speech and hearing.

Note that it was not simply the existence of the constraints that were important; in addition, as with the visibility of socially significant information, two other levels are of importance. First, it was important that *people were aware of the existence and nature of the constraints*. This awareness means that the participants were able to anticipate the ways in which the constraints structured the group's interaction and adjust their own actions accordingly. Thus, based on the amount of ambient noise, speakers adjusted the volume of their speech so that they could be heard by those to whom they spoke. Awareness of and experience with the physics of real world interaction enabled smooth interaction among the group. In situations where an awareness of certain constraints is lacking (e.g. if a participant has a hearing aid that doesn't cope well with high levels of ambient noise), the interaction may break down, with people's communicative acts failing unexpectedly and requiring joint action to detect and repair failures.

Second, it was important that *participants were aware of the others' awareness of the constraints*. Thus, in the situation described, there was a generally shared awareness that people on one side of the room were unable to see or hear discussions on the other side of the room. Everyone understood, by virtue of their common experience with the physics of human interaction, what was going on. Thus, while I might be held accountable for moving your chapter if you were standing nearby and could have easily been consulted, it was a different matter if you were on the other side of the room where you knew I could not have seen you. That is, not only do constraints serve to structure interaction, but the existence of a *shared awareness of constraints* is also a resource for structuring interaction.

These distinctions among the existence of constraints, participants' individual awareness of constraints, and shared awareness of constraints is important because, although these things are usually bundled together in physical environments, they are not necessarily coupled in digital ones. In digital environments it is rarely evident what the constraints are, nor whether the constraints are necessarily shared. The fact that I can hear you speaking over a speaker phone does not necessarily mean that you can hear me if I speak (half duplex lines), nor does my ability to send you email necessarily imply that you can reply to me. The assurances of communicative symmetry that arise out of our experience in unmediated physical reality are not automatically present in the digital realm.

1.2.3 Summary

We have discussed two dimensions of social translucence. First, a system that makes social information visible enables participants to be both aware of what is happening, and to be held accountable for their actions as a consequence of public knowledge of that awareness. Second, people also have a sophisticated understanding of the physics that underlie the visibility of their social interactions. The fact that physical space is translucent (and not transparent) to socially salient information is an important resource for structuring interactions. Neither of these dimensions of social translucence is a given in the digital domain.

1.3 Design: Embedding Social Translucence in Digital Systems

While the perspective we have developed – social translucence – is unique, we are certainly by no means the first to be concerned with making the activities of users of digital systems visible to others. First, in addition to our architectural examples, there are a number of ethnographic studies of transportation control rooms (e.g. Heath and Luff, 1991), offices (Bellotti and Bly, 1996) and other physical work places (see Heath and Luff, 2000) which reveal the crucial role of visibility and mutual awareness in supporting coordinated activity.

A concern for making other users visible in digital systems dates back to at least the Finger programme on UNIX. More recently, a considerable body of work begins with research in video-mediated communication (e.g. Finn et al., 1997), which has since been generalised and is often referred to under the rubric "awareness" (e.g. Dourish and Bellotti, 1992; Gutwin et al., 1996). A number of investigators have also explored ways of portraying socially-salient information in human–computer interfaces. Ackerman and Starr (1995) have argued for the importance of social activity indicators, particularly in synchronous CMC systems. Hill and his colleagues (1992) have discussed the creation of persistent traces of human activity, and a considerable number of researchers have constructed systems that attempt, in various ways, to provide cues about the presence and activity of their users (e.g. Benford et al., 1994; Gutwin et al., 1996; Hill et al., 1995; Isaacs et al., 1996).

1.3.1 Making Activity Visible: The Realist, Mimetic and Abstract Approaches

This brings us to the question of how social cues might best be portrayed in a digital system. We see three design approaches to answering this question: the realist, the mimetic, and the abstract. The realist approach involves trying to project social information from the physical domain into or through the digital domain. This work is exemplified in teleconferencing systems and media space research – see Finn et al. (1997) for many examples.

The mimetic approach tries to re-represent social cues from the physical world, as literally as possible, in the digital domain. The mimetic approach is exemplified by graphical MUDs and virtual reality systems, and uses virtual environments and avatars of various degrees of realism to mimic the physical world. Work here ranges from attempts to implement a virtual physics (Benford et al., 1994) to the considerably looser re-presentations of social information in the 2D and 3D avatars found in various graphical MUDs and 3D VRML worlds.

23

The abstract approach involves portraying social information in ways that are not closely tied to their physical analogs. Exemplars of the abstract approach include AROMA (Pedersen and Sokoler, 1997), the Out to Lunch system (Cohen, 1994), which uses abstract sonic cues to indicate socially salient activity, and Chat Circles and Loom (Donath et al., 1999), which uses abstract visual representations. This approach also includes the use of text to portray social information. Text has proved surprisingly powerful as a means for conveying social information, as can be seen in studies of MUDSs and MOOs (Bruckman, 1997; Cherny, 1999) and textual chat rooms (Danet et al., 1998).

We're particularly interested in the abstract approach. First, we believe that systems that attempt to leverage social processes need to be developed through a process of creating and deploying working systems, and studying their use in ordinary work contexts. This intent to deploy, in and of itself, is a strike against the realist and mimetic approaches, both of which face substantial pragmatic barriers (e.g. expense, infrastructure, support) to deployment outside of research institutions. Second, and more importantly, we believe that the abstract approach has not received sufficient attention from designers and researchers, particularly with respect to graphical representations. Text and simple graphics have many powerful characteristics: they are easy to produce and manipulate; they persist over time, leaving interpretable traces (helpful to those trying to learn the representation); and they enable the use of technologies such as search and visualisation engines.

1.3.2 The Concept of a Social Proxy

A social proxy is a minimalist graphical representation that portrays socially salient aspects of an online situation. Typically, a social proxy shows participants in the situation, and some of their activities with respect to it. As should be evident from the previous section, we are not in favor of making all aspects of activity visible: the choice of which aspects of activity are to be visible, and which are to remain private, depend on the particulars of the situation.

Social proxies have four basic characteristics:

- *Figure-ground.* A social proxy typically consists of two components: a relatively large geometric shape with an inside and an outside and sometimes other features that represent the online situation or context (e.g. a circle), and much smaller shapes positioned relative to the larger shape (e.g. small coloured dots) that represent participants.
- *Relative movement.* The presence and activities of participants in an online context are reflected in the location and movement of the smaller shapes relative to the larger one. Most often, the relationships

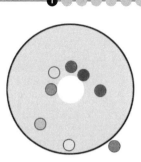

Figure 1.1 The Babble Cookie (*see also* colour plate 1).

and movements of the proxy's visual elements have a metaphoric correspondence to the position and movement of people's bodies in face-to-face analogs of the on-line situation.

- *Public not personal.* Social proxies are public representations. That is, everyone who looks at a social proxy for a given situation, sees the same thing. It is not possible for participants to customise their views of a social proxy. This is important because it is what supports mutual awareness and accountability: I know that if I see something in the social proxy, that all other viewers can see it as well.

- *Third-person perspective.* Social proxies are represented from a third-person point of view. When I look at a social proxy, I see myself represented in it in the same way that other participants are represented. This opens an important avenue for learning. As I act within system, I can see how my actions are reflected in my personal representation, and thus I can begin to make inferences about the activities of others.

This is rather abstract, so let's take a look at an example. Figure 1.1 (see also colour plate 1) shows a social proxy from the Babble system (discussed in section 1.4), that we refer to as "the Cookie". The purpose of the Cookie is to reflect the real time presence and activities of participants in a multi-channel chat-like system. The large circle represents the "current" conversation (i.e. the one being viewed by the user). The small coloured dots (called "marbles" – see colour plate 1) represent people who are logged onto the Babble system, including the user from whose viewpoint we are seeing things. Marbles that appear inside the circle depict participants who are looking at the current conversation; marbles outside the periphery represent people who are logged on to the chat system but in a different chat. Finally, when participants are active – meaning they either "speak" (i.e. type), or "listen" (i.e. click or scroll) – their marbles move to the inner part of the circle, and then, when activity ceases, drift back out to the edge over the course of about 20-minutes.

Thus, the Cookie shown in Figure 1.1 shows that "something is happening". The tight cluster of five marbles around the centre core of the circles shows that those participants are engaged (they are either typing, or clicking and scrolling as one often does when participating in the chat). Two other users, depicted by marbles at six and seven o'clock, are also viewing the same conversation, but have not been active. Possibly they are away from their computers, or possibly they are working on other things and ignoring the conversation. The eighth marble (at four o'clock) depicts a user who is logged onto the system but viewing a different conversation; that user may or may not be active – all we can tell is that he or she is connected to the system. Thus, the Cookie shows people are either here or "around", and if here, how recently they have done something; it also shows when people arrive or depart, in that new marbles appear or disappear (if logging on or off) or move into or out of the bounds of the circle.

We will discuss the Babble Cookie and how people make use of the cues it provides in the next section. However, before we do that, we will present some other examples of social proxies to provide a glimpse of the power and generality of this technique.

1.3.3 The Lecture Proxy

A common situation in the face-to-face world is that one person will speak to an audience which, by and large, remains quiet. Class room lectures, professional talks, and business presentations are all examples of this. Suppose that we have an on-line analogue of this situation. Perhaps the talk or lecture is being delivered via audio as part of a large conference call; we can imagine that members of the distributed audience are in their own offices, where they have access to desktop computers, or perhaps they are mobile users who have screen phones.

The social proxy shown in Figure 1.2 assumes that we have some way of identifying who has spoken. As with other social proxies, the large containing shape represents the situation, in this case the lecture, and the small coloured marbles (see colour plate 2) represent the participants. The horizontal positions of the marbles reflect a running average of the number or length of comments during the last five minutes. The "lecturer" starts out on the left, the members of the audience on the right, and the proxy is dynamically updated.

The aim of the Lecture proxy is to provide a visible representation of the interaction that foregrounds the interactive expectations that define it. As long as the lecture follows its canonical interaction pattern, with the lecturer speaking and the audience being silent, it retains its initial form. However, if a person interrupts with a question or a comment, his or her dot will move a bit to the left, and if the interruptions continue, that person becomes, quite literally, "out of line" (as shown in Figure 1.2). Because the proxy is seen by everyone, everyone knows (and knows that everyone knows) what is happening. How the group makes use of this information

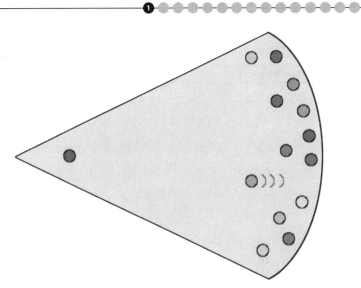

Figure 1.2   The lecture proxy (*see also* colour plate 2).

is up to it. The Lecture proxy may serve to enforce norms about how to behave during a lecture; or it may be used as a signal that people are getting restless and that it is time to shift to a more open discussion (in which case we might imagine that the proxy could shift back to the circular form of the Cookie). The basic point here is that one role that social proxies can play is to make interactive expectations visible, and to highlight how the group is behaving relative to them. We believe that this is an interesting alternative to the technical solution, sometimes employed in conference call situations, of making it impossible for anyone but the speaker or moderator to talk.

1.3.4 The Auction Proxy

Social proxies are not just for conversation, though conversation is certainly one of the most prevalent forms of on-line interaction. To look at some different cases we turn to the realm of e-commerce and auctions. In the face-to-face world, auctions are dramatic and intensely social events. People arrive before the auction begins to look at what's for sale; and they not only look at *what* is for sale, they also look at *who else* is looking. Auctions are not just about bidding *for items*, they are also about bidding *against other bidders*. In fact, they serve a wide variety of social ends (Smith, 1989).

However, when we look at online auctions, the social cues that make their face-to-face counterparts such rich and engaging experiences have vanished. The social proxy shown in Figure 1.3 (see also colour plate 3) is

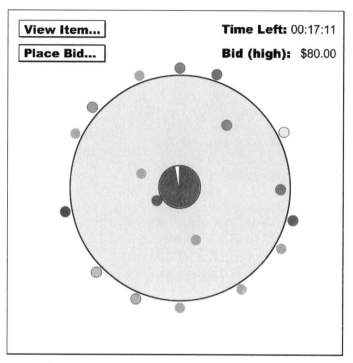

Figure 1.3 The auction proxy (*see also* colour plate 3).

an attempt to restore some of these cues. The auction itself is represented by the large circle, and participants are represented by coloured marbles. The inner core of the circle is a clock, that fills in as the auction's time runs out; the next ring out is the "bidding room", where the marbles of people that have placed bids are shown; and those marbles shown around the outside of the circle are those who have showed up to look, but have not (yet) bid. Because on-line auctions may last for days or even weeks, this proxy is designed to be asynchronous. The way the Auction proxy works is that participants who have downloaded the web page in the last three minutes have their marbles shown in colour; after three minutes pass, their marbles gradually fade to grey, but they remain for the entire duration of the auction. Thus, in Figure 1.3, we see the number of people who have showed up to look or to bid for the entire duration of the auction. The other thing that the Auction proxy shows is the bidding spread: that is, the closeness of a marble to the centre of the circle represents the magnitude of the bid. The innermost marble is the current high bidder, and when another outbids them, the other bidders' marbles are pushed out towards the edge.

Like the other social proxies we've shown, the Auction proxy creates a public representation of a collective experience: it shows how many people are present, and to what extent they are participating in the activity. Note, as well, that the Auction proxy does not show certain things (for example, the identity of the bidders, or the number of times an individual has bid). Depending on the circumstances, it may or may not be desirable to show this. As with the Lecture proxy, the Auction proxy makes some of the interactive expectations visible: it foregrounds the bidders, particularly the high bidder; and it relegates those who are only watching to the periphery. The Auction proxy also highlights some new aspects of social proxies. First, social proxies need not represent only synchronous activity, but can represent activities extended over considerable periods of time. Second, the Auction proxy is being used to create a sense of drama: the clock in the centre shows that time is running out; the colour of the clock is the same as that of the current high bidder, something which symbolises the high bidder's current dominance; and the use of colour to indicate that someone has connected recently reminds participants that some of the viewers are "present" and may choose to enter the auction at the last minute with a new high bid.

1.3.5 The Queue Proxy

Auctions are a special case of commercial interaction. For a different example of supporting non-conversational interaction, let's turn to the most ubiquitous hallmark of commerce-oriented interaction: the line or queue.

As experienced users of queues we understand a lot about them. We understand the implications of their length; we make estimates of their speed; we mutter when someone with a problem slows the queue; we become irritated when others "cut" in front of us; we feel elation if extra personnel show up to handle a lengthy queue. We may decide to postpone a transaction if the queue we are in appears to be moving slowly, only to change our minds if we notice that the growth of the queue behind us has accelerated. However, when we leave face-to-face interaction, the queues have vanished; there appear to be no lines, on-line. But, as anyone who has listened to the "your call is important to us please remain on the line and your call will be answered in the order in which it was received" message knows, "vanished" doesn't mean that they're gone. They have simply lost most of the cues that transform a really annoying experience into a mildly annoying, or very occasionally, a mildly interesting experience.

Figure 1.4 shows a social proxy designed for on-line situations where customers are, for example, waiting to chat with a technical support person or a customer representative. The proxy shown in the figure conveys information about the length of wait (in this case the colour of the marbles encodes estimated wait time – see colour plate 4), the number of customer service representatives present (shown as triangles), and the

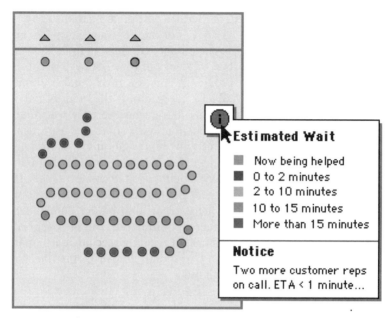

Figure 1.4   The queue proxy (*see also* colour plate 4).

length of queue, showing both those in front and those behind the user (shown with a gold "halo").

Queues differ from the other situations we've discussed – chats, lectures and auctions – in that we neither seek them out, nor view them as an end in and of themselves. Nevertheless, providing a visible representation of an on-line queue can support a variety of ends. First, it enables those in the queue, or considering joining it, to engage in the sorts of reasoning about the questions to which we we've already alluded: Should I join the queue? Should I come back later? How much longer will it be? Second, it provides a potential foundation for social interaction. That is, while face-to-face queues are certainly not necessarily convivial occasions, in some situations, as at a sporting event or a Grateful Dead concert, shared enthusiasms may provide a foundation for opportunistic conversation. Thus, an on-line queue of people waiting for technical help might benefit if they were able to chat with one another: perhaps some members might have the solutions to others' problems, or, perhaps the complaints and associated remarks of disgruntled users of a product might serve as a sort of naturalistic focus group for the vendor. Finally, the ability to monitor an on-line queue can lay the foundations for new types of behaviour. Thus, it would become possible to wait in multiple queues at once, and perhaps, if one reached the head of two queues simultaneously, it might be possible to allow someone else to go ahead of one without losing one's place.

1.3.6 Summary

That's a look at an array of social proxies. The purpose was to make it clear that the concept of social proxy is quite general. Social proxies can be designed to support a wide range of on-line interactions, whether they involve conversation or not. They may be synchronous or asynchronous, and they may be associated with activities which are an end in themselves (e.g. auctions), or activities which are simply a means to an end (e.g. waiting in queues). We believe that by providing a shared representation of the activity in which participants are involved, social proxies can help create shared expectations, shared experiences, and can serve as a resource which participants can use to structure their individual and collective interactions. That is, at least, our claim. However, it is important to note that, except for the first, the proxies described so far are concept pieces, meaning that they haven't been implemented and deployed to real situations. Now, however, we will turn to an implemented system, and look at a real example.

1.4 Experience: The Babble System

In the previous section we introduced the concept of social proxies and discussed examples illustrating the wide range of situations to which social proxies can be applied. In this section, we focus on our experience in designing, implementing and studying a social proxy in the context of an on-line system called Babble. We begin by describing the vision behind Babble, which provides a further illustration of the importance and utility of making social information publicly available to a system's users.

1.4.1 The Vision: A Social Approach to Knowledge Management

What might it mean to have social translucence in a digital system? How might making social information more visible actually change the way digital systems are used? Why might this be a desirable thing? To answer these questions, let's look at knowledge management from a socially translucent perspective.

Knowledge management is a currently popular term for the attempt to provide organisations with tools for capturing, retrieving and disseminating information about their own activities to their own employees. In a sense, it is an attempt to make organisations self-conscious, to enable them to tap their own experience in solving problems rather than having to reinvent solutions to recurring problems. Knowledge management is often seen as a problem of putting useful information into databases and providing schemes for organising and retrieving the information. This perspective leads people to think in terms of data mining and text clustering and databases and documents. This isn't wrong, but it is only part of the picture.

The production and use of knowledge is deeply entwined with social phenomena. For example, one of us once interviewed accountants at a large accounting company about how they would use a proposed database of their company's internal documents. A surprising theme emerged: the accountants said that they'd love to access the documents so that they could find out who wrote them. As one explained, "Well, if I'm putting together a proposal for Exxon, I really want to talk to people who have already worked with them: they'll know the politics, the history, and other information that usually doesn't get into the reports." Of particular importance was the fact that someone who had worked with the prospective client could give referrals, thus saving the accountant from having to make a "cold call". The ability to say "so-and-so said I ought to call", was of great value to the accountants (and illustrates yet another function of accountability). Having a referral, however tenuous the connection, is a valuable *social resource* that can only be directly conveyed from one person to another: saying "I found your name in the corporate knowledge database", is not the same. It was only through the people – and the social networks they were part of – that the accountants could get the knowledge and social resources they needed. (See Erickson and Kellogg (2002) for a more lengthy analysis of the social aspects of producing and using knowledge.)

This sort of situation – the production and use of knowledge in a social milieu – is not the exception; it is the rule. A variety of research programmes – social studies of science, critical theory, the sociology of knowledge, and ethnographies of the work place – all point to the deep connections between knowledge and social and cultural contexts. Knowledge, whether it be of bugs in the Java Virtual Machine or of how to begin negotiations with an executive from another culture, is discovered, shared and used in a social context, not just for its own sake, but to construct the identities and advance the agendas of the individuals, groups and institutions involved. Having the information in a database isn't as useful as we would hope, unless it also provides an *entrée* into the social networks that produced the data. It is from the social networks – not from the information itself – that social resources can be recruited.

Imagine a knowledge management system that was designed from a social perspective, a system predicated on the assumption that knowledge is distributed throughout a network of people, and that only a small proportion of it is captured in concrete form. As the above vignette suggests, such a system would, along with its data and documents, also provide a rich set of connections back to the social network of people who produced the information. But, if we think in terms of making socially significant activity visible, considerably more possibilities suggest themselves. Imagine that the knowledge management system provided access not only to authors, but to people who were accessing and using the knowledge. Suppose that – just as we look for crowded restaurants, eye fellow shoppers, or look for engaging conversations – we could see similar traces of those making use of information in a knowledge management system. After all, some of the knowledge users might have to go to considerable work to apply the knowledge to their own ends, thereby developing an understanding of its shortcomings and particularities, as well as building on it. If we could capture traces of this knowledge work, others with similar needs might find as much value in talking with users as with the original authors. Such a system would not be just a database from which workers retrieved knowledge, it would be a *knowledge community*, a place within which people would discover, use and manipulate knowledge and could encounter and interact with others who are doing likewise.

Making this sort of activity collectively visible serves one other role. In addition to laying the foundation for a variety of activities that aid in the production and sharing of knowledge, it also has the potential to answer a question that Grudin (1989) has raised with respect to collaborative systems in general: why should those who end up having to do extra work to support collaboration actually do so? The answer is that by making such activities visible, a system of this sort makes it more likely that an organisation can see and value such work.

1.4.2 The Babble System

The Babble system (Erickson et al., 1999) represents our first step towards such a knowledge community. Our goal was to be able to support active, conversationally-based communities that could function as part of the business environment. Our hope was to the blend the spontaneity and opportunistic nature of "water cooler" or "hallway" encounters and conversations with the possibilities of deeper, more focused talk that might be expected to emerge in a business environment. While there are other requirements for supporting a knowledge community, these aims seemed sufficiently ambitious given that social proxies were untried and the viability of chat-like environments in business situations was unknown (this was before the advent of instant messaging as a workplace phenomenon).

The Babble user interface is shown in Figure 1.5 (see also colour plate 5). Starting from the upper left corner, its components are: the user list (all users currently logged on to Babble); the social proxy (as described in section 1.3.2); the topics list (all conversations in the system); and, in the bottom half of the screen, the textual conversation. It should be noted

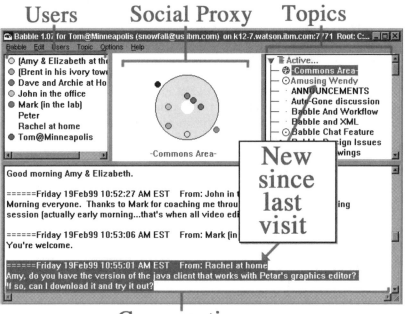

Figure 1.5   The Babble user interface (*see also* colour plate 5).

that although we describe Babble as "chat-like", the conversation model is not quite the same as ordinary chat. It is what we refer to as persistent conversation (Erickson, 1999), or blended synchrony. The basic idea is that Babble conversation may either be synchronous, like chat, or asynchronous, as in bulletin board and netnews systems. Like chat, the conversation accumulates utterance by utterance; like bulletin board systems, the utterances persist across sessions. So that a single conversation in Babble may proceed at a rapid, near real-time pace when many people are around and active, but may then slow and become asynchronous, with people continuing to contribute, but at a much slower pace of a comment per hour, day, week, etc.

A few other features of the Babble user interface are worth noting. First, Babble provides user-specific cues about what has changed recently. Thus, the reverse highlighted text in the conversation pane indicates that that comment is recent; the topic name ("Amusing Wendy") shown in red in the Topics list indicates that it has content that has appeared since the user was last there. Also, just to the left of the topic names are spaces where "mini-cookies" – miniature social proxies – appear, providing an indication of how people are distributed through the conversation space. Finally, Babble has a number of features that are not on the "surface" of its user interface. Thus, menu commands allow

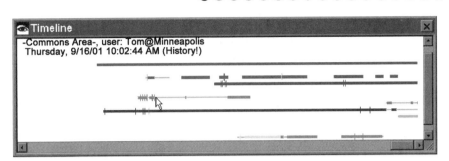

Figure 1.6   The Babble timeline proxy (*see also* colour plate 6).

users to create, rename and modify conversations. Right clicking on a user's marble provides access to user-specific commands, such as setting preferences and engaging in a private one-to-one chat. And, last, but not least, a menu command also brings up a second social proxy called the Timeline.

The Timeline proxy (Erickson and Laff, 2001) was added because many Babble conversations are asynchronous. The Timeline (Figure 1.6 – see also colour plate 6) works as follows: each user is represented by a row in the Timeline; when they are logged on to Babble, they leave a flat trace or line, and when they "speak" they leave a vertical mark or blip on the line. If the line/blip is in colour, it means that that user was present/ speaking in the conversation currently being viewed by the user of the Timeline; if they were in a different conversation, the line/blip is shown in grey (and the line becomes thinner). As the user mouses over the Timeline proxy the name of the conversation and the user and the time is shown in the upper left corner of the proxy; the user can scroll back through as much as one week of activity. The Timeline proxy also provides access to other functionality via a menu accessed via a right-click on another user's row (e.g. private chats). For example, in Figure 1.6, we can see that nine people have logged onto Babble (shown by the presence of lines), and that all of them have spent some time in the current conversation (shown by the colour/increased thickness of the lines), and that many but not all have "spoken" (shown by the blips). The line being indicated by the cursor shows that the user "Peter" logged on around 11 a.m., made a couple of comments in the "Commons Area" conversation, switched to another topic, and then switched back to the Commons Area about 1 p.m., and then logged off.

1.4.3 Experience with Babble

Babble was implemented as a client-server system in SmallTalk. It was first released and used by its developers in the fall of 1997 (see Erickson et al., 1999); and the year 1998 saw its first deployments, some of which were studied in depth (Bradner et al., 1999). As of this writing, Babble has been deployed to over 20 groups, most though not all of them within IBM (see Thomas et al., 2001, and Erickson and Kellogg, 2002, for recent summaries of deployment experience).

In this section we will focus on our experience with Babble's social proxies. This is not an easy task, because it is difficult to isolate the effect of Babble's social proxies from its other functionality (such as the persistence of its chat, or the use of its private chat as a back channel). So, what we will do is report on our observations of how people make use of the social proxies, and on their comments on the value of the social proxies (in response to several surveys that we conducted).

The Cookie

One phenomenon, originally reported in Bradner et al. (1999), is called waylay. Waylay refers to the practice in which a user monitors the Cookie for signs of another person's activity (i.e. their marble moving into the centre of the circle), and then initiates contact. Contact may be carried out through Babble (entering a comment in a topic or opening a private chat), or through another medium (e.g. the telephone). The Babble Cookie facilitates waylay because, since simply clicking or scrolling triggers the movement of a person's marble, other participants can tell that a person is "looking at" Babble, even if they "say" nothing. The indication of "looking at" is quite valuable; it not only means that the person is at their computer, but it implies that because they are interacting with Babble that they are likely to be receptive to group communication. (After waylay was initially observed, the Babble Cookie was redesigned so that it had a visible centre core – this enabled people to see whether someone was touching the centre (meaning they'd been active very recently), or whether they had drifted out a little.)

Another way in which the Babble Cookie is used is to spot new users. When a person first logs on to Babble, the system assigns their marble a default colour: black. As a consequence, black marbles are generally taken to be the sign of a new user, and (depending on the customs of a particular Babble deployment) the user may be greeted, welcomed, or offered help (either in general, or told how to change their marble colour). Although we don't know whether the following instance was provoked by a "black marble", this user's comment conveys the idea:

> I really like the babble a lot! There is a very friendly and helpful atmosphere. … What triggered me to actually respond at first was however that people had seen me logged in, and welcomed me! The got me over the first hinder of contributing to the chat.

Another user also observed that Babble seemed to do a good job of supporting first-time users:

> I have been impressed with how easily people have been able to parachute into the community. … I strongly suspect that elements like the cookie subconsciously help us to relate to each other more easily and make this a more friendly medium than the typical chat.

More generally, users report that the Cookie is a useful resource for supporting synchronous interaction. Often this has to do with seeing whether there are dots clustered around the centre; if so, people often assume that they will get a reply to a question or comment. Here are comments in this vein from two other users:

> The cookie has a definite use for me in indicating how active team members are. It really eases the social interactions knowing whether an immediate reply is likely.

> The cookie is what makes the difference. … The cookie makes me feel connected when seeing others read stuff in the same room. Babble without the cookie would be like "being blind". Not knowing if it's worth to stay and wait for someone to post a question.

Finally, users comment that the cookie helps create a sense of place.

> The cookie is what make Babble useful to me – it gives me a sense of "place" which I don't get with [instant messaging, asynchronous discussions, web sites or email].

> Ah, the cookie … we love the cookie … the cookie is good – our coloured dots circulate around to "make room" when someone new joins the conversation – that's fun. And when someone's connection dies, they rather dissemble into the ether, angelic like. Which is sort of fun to watch. … Also, when I'm wondering whether my comments have fallen on deaf ears, I can tell when a response may in fact be on its way when someone's dot moves back to the centre (happens as soon as someone starts typing). So, yes, we like the cookie – it makes me feel like there are actually people in a room with me …

The Timeline

The Timeline proxy also serves as a resource for users, although it is generally less successful. In part this is due to problems with its user interface, and in it part it may be because the Timeline must be called up with a menu command, rather than being always visible as the Cookie is. Nevertheless, some users find it useful. The most common use is as an indicator of who has been around:

> ... I wanted to see if [R—] was on Babble at a particular time [and just not writing anything].

People also use the Timeline to see if someone has read something that was posted (technically, it is only possible to see that someone has *been* in a topic; however Babble users typically infer that that means someone has *read* the topic's new content).

> ... after a week or so I was able to tell that most people had not read the material I posted ...

Finally, users commented that the Timeline was useful for seeing patterns of usage. It is easy to see when people tend to come on in the morning, and when they tend to depart at the end of the day. Depending on the make up of the community, one may see waves of users arriving, with the Europeans preceding the North Americans by five to eight hours. It is also possible to see whether there are particular patterns of conversation (often people are quite talkative in the morning, and turn their attention to other activities in the afternoon); other events may be visible as well (the most obvious being system crashes, where all traces terminate simultaneously). One user expressed the role of the Timeline with particular eloquence:

> It's a little like reading an electrocardiogram, the heartbeat of the community. I noticed that I missed [S—] by an hour on Monday morning. ... [P—] comes in every so often as a blip. [L—] jumps from space to space ...

While the Timeline is not as generally successful as the Cookie, it nevertheless serves as a resource for those who use it, enabling them to see who has been present or absent, and as the basis for inferences about individual activity ("who has read what I posted?") and collective activity.

1.4.4 Summary

Babble is our first step towards designing a knowledge community, an on-line collaborative system that takes a deeply social approach to supporting the production, elaboration and dissemination of knowledge. There is a lot that remains to be done. One layer of functionality that is needed has to do with making Babble conversations easy to browse. That is, within an active Babble, it is easy for an energetic group to generate several thousand words a day. This adds up, and the ability to simply scroll and skim or conduct keyword searches of conversations is not adequate. As a consequence we are exploring ways of creating conversation visualisations, where it is easy to see both their content and structure. A second layer of functionality we are investigating has to do with supporting communities of communities. One of the reasons Babble works well is that Babble communities are small enough that people know and trust one another. Thus, Babble participants can offer friendly critiques, off-the-cuff suggestions and wild ideas that would be less appropriate (and less likely ventured) in a larger, more formal situation. Yet, the *raison d'être* of a knowledge community is to support widespread knowledge sharing. The approach we are currently exploring to resolve this tension is to provide ways in which statistical summaries (but not detailed excerpts) of discussion content might be allowed to "leak" out of (or perhaps undergo a monitored release from) a Babble, and that an outsider who came across hints of an interesting discussion would have to go through the normal social protocols (e.g. talking to a contact, or perhaps an official "gatekeeper" within that Babble) to find out more.

Even though Babble is more effective at supporting the exchange of knowledge among a relatively small group than serving as a long term organisational repository of knowledge, we regard it as a successful experiment. Our experience of the last several years has convinced us that social proxies are effective and engaging mechanisms for signaling the presence and activities of participants in online interactions. In particular, it is clear that that the relatively abstract cues produced by social proxies are easily learnable and interpretable by participants, and that we need not be constrained by the requirement to try to mimic familiar cues from face-to-face interactions.

1.5 Summary and Conclusions

In this chapter we've described an approach to designing online systems that we call "social translucence". Its central tenant is that making information about the presence and activity of online participants mutually visible can support social processes – such as peer pressure, imitation and norming – that help groups interact coherently. However, it is not *just* about making information visible: the word "translucence" signals that we do not propose to reveal all social information; rather, we recognise that there is a subtle interplay between privacy and visibility (as in elections) that shapes interactions in fundamental ways. In face-to-face situations, individuals and groups exhibit sophisticated understandings of the extent to which the cues they give and give off are visible (as in the "table of contents" example), and use that to adjust their actions. Thus, part of the social translucence research programme involves how to create systems in which participants can understand which of their activities are visible, and the extent and duration of that visibility. To the extent we succeed, we believe that we can design on-line systems that enable groups to self-organise and otherwise steer their collective interactions.

Babble represents our first steps towards supporting such self-organising groups. It has proved quite successful in supporting interactions among small communities within IBM (Erickson and Kellogg, 2002; Thomas et al., 2001). Furthermore, our experiences with the Babble Cookie and Timeline indicate that Babble's social proxies serve as useful group resources. The sorts of uses participants report making of the social proxies – seeing when people are around, making inferences about who is listening, noticing and welcoming newcomers, and getting a feel for the overall activity of the group – are just the sorts of behaviours that we want to support. That is, by making the presence and activities of individuals mutually visible to everyone, we create a foundation on which richer social interaction can be built.

To conclude, let us return to the tale of the door with the glass window. Although we have focused on designing systems for communication and collaboration, the contrast between the opaque door with its sign and the door with its glass window seems an apt metaphor for a very general problem with technological systems today. In the first case, the system creates a barrier between users; the remedy requires that they do extra work – noticing the sign, interpreting its words and adjusting their actions just in case. In the second case, the system reveals the presence of those using it, enabling already-established social rules and mechanisms to come smoothly into play.

From our perspective, the digital world appears to be populated by technologies that impose walls between people, rather than by technologies that create windows between them. We suggest that understanding how to design digital systems so that they mesh with human behaviour at the individual and collective levels is of immense importance. By allowing users to "see" one another, to make inferences about the activities of others, to imitate one another, we believe that digital systems can become environments in which new social forms can be invented, adopted, adapted and propagated – eventually supporting the same sort of social innovation and diversity that can be observed in physically based cultures.

Acknowledgements

This work is highly collaborative. Thanks to our colleagues at IBM: David N. Smith for originally creating the Babble prototype; Mark Laff and

Peter Malkin for work on the Babble client and server; Cal Swart for supporting Babble deployments; and the members of the Niche Networking and Social Computing groups, and several generations of summer interns, for conversation, inspiration and general support.

2

Collaborative Filtering: Supporting Social Navigation in Large, Crowded Infospaces

Joseph A. Konstan and John Riedl

2.1 Introduction

The advent of the web has made possible the publication of vast amounts of new information. Information spaces have become more and more crowded with information. Web users are faced with the daunting task of sorting out from among all of the available information that which is most valuable to them. Social navigation systems have emerged as a broad array of techniques that enable people to work together to help each other find their way through the crowded spaces. In a social navigation system, each user who visits a web site does a small amount of work to untangle which of the paths from that web site are most valuable. Early users leave information signposts that help later users make sense of the wealth of alternatives available to them. Later users benefit from the signposts, because they are able to direct their attention to the parts of the site that are most valuable to them.

Some forms of social navigation are very closely related to collaborative filtering, the topic of this paper. For instance, Munro, Höök and Benyon (1999) discuss ways in which the passage of users through an information space can leave footprints that help other users find their way more readily through that same space. As information spaces become more crowded with users, we may find it important to have automated systems that show us only those footprints that are most useful to us. Harper (1999) argues based on fieldwork, that information becomes relevant based on how it is used in an organisation, and that the information is eventually socially organised. Current information tools largely ignore the social relevance of information. Collaborative filtering is a technology that offers hope in remedying that ignorance.

Many other forms of social navigation extend beyond the recommender applications considered in this paper. For instance, Dourish (1999) discusses social navigation techniques that are based on awareness of what others are doing in synchronous collaborative systems. Rankin and Spence (1999) consider how computer systems may support navigation in virtual worlds based on human experience with that navigation in the physical world. They specifically consider navigation in a cocktail party and in home hunting – both arenas that have so far not been successfully tackled by collaborative filtering. Systems like these are clearly social navigation systems, but are not collaborative filtering systems. Our hope is that these researchers may find some valuable ideas in the collaborative filtering systems we discuss in this chapter, and may be able to use some of the advanced techniques that have been invented for recommender systems, though their research focus is in other areas of social navigation.

Many social navigation systems build systems of signposts that are the same for all users. These systems are like the street signs in a city, helping both familiar and unfamiliar users make their way around more readily. In some cases, though, different users may have very different tastes. How can we build social navigation systems in which each user is directed to the information she, individually, will find most valuable?

Collaborative filtering has emerged as a form of social navigation system that is dedicated to presenting each user with the most individually relevant information. It works by taking advantage of patterns of agreement and tastes between users. These patterns are often consistent across time, so users who agreed with each other yesterday will often agree with each other today. Collaborative filtering (CF) systems leverage that agreement by recommending to each user information on the site that was valuable to past visitors to that site who have similar tastes. Some CF systems form their recommendations by having users explicitly identify other users who will benefit from specific information, while other CF systems automatically observing agreement among users have transformed that agreement into automatic recommendations. In either case the premise is the same: users who agreed with each other in the past are likely to agree with each other in the future.

As information spaces become more and more crowded with both information and users, collaborative filtering offers another benefit to social navigation systems. On a very crowded site, the social cues may themselves be overwhelming. What will happen when every single alternative has been valuable to thousands of users? How will new visitors to that site make sense of the cacophony of social cues? Collaborative filtering-based navigation systems will be less overwhelming, because they will present each user with precisely those social cues that are from people who are most like him or her. Two ends of the spectrum are illustrative. In a very sparsely visited information space, collaborative filtering-based social navigation will turn into classic social navigation in which cues from all of the visitors to the site are used. In a very densely visited information space, collaborative filtering-based social navigation will produce about the same number of social cues as in the sparsely visited space, but those cues will be based only upon the experiences of previous visitors who are most similar to the current visitor.

In some systems the early users are rewarded just by knowing they are part of the solution to the complexity of these crowded information spaces. In some CF systems, early users are also rewarded by knowing that the system is learning more about their tastes in information. These systems are building a profile of each user, and automatically making the profile richer by observing the user's interactions with information contact of web sites.

Collaborative filtering has reached prominence because of its successful application on many Internet sites in recommender systems. *Recommender systems* suggest specific interesting alternatives to every visitor to the site based on his past interactions with that site. Nearly all successful e-commerce sites have recommender systems, and they are becoming commonplace in information sites as well. Collaborative filtering is one of the technologies that are being used to implement recommender systems. In this paper we will use the term recommender systems generically, to refer to any system for providing recommendations to users, while reserving the term collaborative filtering for the specific technology explained below.

This chapter presents an overview of collaborative filtering research, along with its relationship to social navigation. The chapter includes a range of topics from collaborative filtering, including past research, ongoing research problems and likely directions for future systems. In each case the presentation includes an overview of the idea, one or more motivating examples of systems that are using the idea, and analysis of the important design decisions in the area. The nine collaborative filtering issues discussed are organised into three categories: lessons learned from early CF systems (sections 2.2 and 2.3), ongoing experience with automatic collaborative filtering (section 2.4) and advanced issues in collaborative filtering (sections 2.5–2.10). The nine sections, numbered as in the chapter, are:

2.2 Pull-active collaborative filtering: systems in which the users "pull" the information they want by formulating queries. The queries can be based on characteristics of the items, such as keywords, or based on the reaction of previous users to those items.

2.3 Push-active collaborative filtering: systems in which users "push" items to other users based on their understanding of the other users' information needs.

2.4 Automated collaborative filtering: systems that automatically analyse the relationships between users and form recommendations based on correlations among the behaviour of different users.

2.5   Implicit interest measures: measurements of user interest that do not require explicit interactions with the user, but that are instead based on implicit observations of behaviours that the user would have exhibited independently of the recommender system.

2.6   Situational recommendations: recommenders that are able to form recommendations based on a combination of the user's long-standing interests and a specific short-term interest that the user is exploring right now.

2.7   Recommending for groups: recommenders that explicitly recognise that a group of people may be navigating together, and that form recommendations that are appropriate for the entire group, not just for individuals in the group.

2.8   Manual override: a feature of the recommender that makes it possible for users to control the operation of the recommender. Manual override enhances the feeling of control of the users, and can help them obtain better recommendations from the system.

2.9   Confidence and explanations: features of recommenders that enable them to give more information to the user about not only what the recommendations are, but about why these recommendations were formed, and about how accurate these specific recommendations are likely to be.

2.10   Beyond humans: recommenders that are able to include non-human agents in addition to humans in forming their recommendations. As these agents become a larger part of information sharing communities, their inclusion in recommender systems will enhance the functioning of the systems, and of the community as a whole.

This chapter should be valuable to social navigation researchers because it surveys collaborative filtering as a social navigation system and lays out a set of solutions that has proven valuable in collaborative filtering, and that may prove useful in other social navigation systems. For instance, group awareness has proven useful in collaborative filtering and is likely to add value to any social navigation system in which multiple people are sometimes interested in navigating together. It should also be valuable to recommender system researchers who are interested in understanding how they can apply their techniques to a broader range of social navigation systems.

2.2 Pull-Active Collaborative Filtering

As computer-supported communication blossomed in the 1980s and early 1990s, new information distribution channels such as e-mail lists and bulletin boards evolved to enable widespread distribution of information. The dual-problem of easy distribution, however, is information overload; information users quickly moved from starving for information to drowning in it. Fortunately, the same communication technology that "caused" information overload could be applied to alleviate it.

The key innovation was to tap the power of a community of people to help filter the flood of information. Pull-active CF systems give each member of a community the opportunity to publish their own evaluations of information or products. Potential consumers can consult these evaluations to determine which information or products to consume. These systems are referred to as "pull-active" because they require the user of evaluations to take an active role in pulling evaluations from the published set.

Pull-active CF systems are an early example of using social navigation techniques in information filtering applications. The collection of published evaluations represents the experiences and opinions of the community of information navigators. Each community member is responsible for identifying which evaluators and evaluations are relevant to her, either from her experience with the evaluator or the content of the evaluation.

2.2.1 Motivating Example: Tapestry

The Tapestry system (Goldberg et al., 1992), developed at Xerox PARC in the early 1990s, is considered the first modern CF system (see Figure 2.1). It was developed to help alleviate the overload associated with e-mail lists. The Tapestry system augments basic information filtering by providing users with a query language that can express filters based on both message contents and associated annotations. For example, a user could request messages on the topic "social navigation" that were marked as "important" by Goldberg. In addition to supporting explicit annotations, Tapestry provides access to implicit evaluations specific to e-mail discussion lists. For example, a user could request any messages that his boss has replied to, since those are presumably messages that his boss found interesting.

In practice, Tapestry was designed to operate in a mostly automatic manner. Users were expected to have a set of standing queries (filterers)

```
m.sender = 'Joe' AND m.subject LIKE '%recommender%' AND
EXISTS (a: a.type = vote AND a.owner = 'John' AND a.msg = m)
```

Figure 2.1 Tapestry's query language, TQL, supported queries over both direct message attributes and annotations. This query returns messages from Joe, about recommenders, for which John has entered a vote.

that would select a set of candidate messages. A separate appraiser would prioritise these items. Only if the user discovered that the filtering no longer met his needs (e.g. was not appropriately specific or no longer represented the right content) would he need to update the queries.

2.2.2 Analysis

The pull-active collaborative filtering model is particularly applicable in smaller communities where people know each other. A system such as Tapestry may be effective for a workgroup, but it is hard to extend to larger systems with more anonymous and rapidly changing user sets.

An advantage of the pull-active model is the control it gives to the user – she can choose exactly which information she considers to be relevant to her decision. Such control may be very valuable when the system is used to make important decisions, or when established rules remain valid for a long time. On the other hand, exercising such control requires knowledge and effort – perhaps too much for many low-value applications such as filtering Usenet News.

Applications of pull-active collaborative filtering are often found in informal situations. A person planning to buy a car may select a few car-expert friends to recommend or evaluate choices. Tapestry added a new level of automation – opinions are captured and stored so they can be accessed when the user needs them without the delay and overhead of contacting community members each time a recommendation is needed. Web-based review sites, such as epinions.com, collect databases of reviews and allow users to identify the reviewers and reviews they find useful, even rewarding valued reviewers with status or money. So far, such systems have not replicated Tapestry's integrated evaluation-based filtering and information filtering.

2.2.3 Summary

Pull-active CF systems provide social navigation of information spaces by allowing individual users navigating the space to consult the evaluations left behind by other users. Effective use of these systems requires both that users leave behind evaluations for others and that users be able to judge which evaluations are worth using and considering. Point-of-consumption feedback and implicit evaluations (e.g. Susan printed this message) can ease the evaluation load for users. Pull-active CF systems have been most successfully applied in close-knit communities, where users know each other and can accurately judge which evaluations to consider from which community members. Such systems can also be effective in communities with members of longstanding and well-known reputation. In such communities, however, the burden of evaluation may fall on a small number of respected community members, and may result in a reduction in the level of personalisation possible for ordinary users. Some applications attempt to give incentive to members to provide high-quality evaluations in the hopes of building a larger and more diverse set of respected members, and thereby greater diversity of available recommendations.

2.3 Push-Active Collaborative Filtering

Push-active recommender systems are a modification of pull-active systems in which the person who writes the recommendation directs the system to deliver the recommended item to specific users. These systems are related to the web browser function that enables users to e-mail web pages to other users, but offer more sophisticated support for recommending across many types of documents, for annotating the recommendation and for rating the expected interest of the recipient for the document.

Push-active recommenders are different from other social navigation systems in that the "pusher" leads the navigation. This person takes the active recommendation role, selecting other users who should see items while separated from those users by both time and space. On the other hand, these systems are fundamentally a form of social navigation, because the recipient of the pushed items uses the included social cues to guide her navigation.

2.3.1 Motivating Example

Dave Maltz and Kate Ehrlich built a push-active recommender system inside of Lotus Notes (Maltz and Ehrlich, 1995) – see Figure 2.2. Their Notes-based system was centred on the concept of "pointers", which are a combination of a hyperlink with contextual information explaining why this document was recommended to this user. A user who wants to push a recommendation creates a pointer and distributes it, either by publishing it in a shared Notes database for a group of users to browse, or by e-mailing it to a user or a distribution list. When the users later view the pointer, they see the contextual information and can click through to the recommended document.

In their user studies, Maltz and Ehrlich discovered that many of the pointers that were sent were sent by just one member of each group. This member had informally taken on the role of information intermediary, spending a significant amount of time browsing through potentially interesting items and forwarding them to people who might find them valuable.

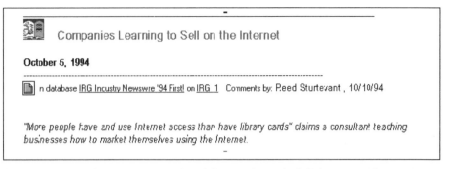

Figure 2.2 A sample pointer. (Reproduced from Maltz and Ehrlich, 1995, with permission. © ACM 1995.)

2.3.2 Analysis

The many different approaches to push-active recommendations derive from choices in the recommendation method, the selection method, and the delivery method. The recommendation method can be either to recommend items to any of a group of people who might be interested, such as the Notes databases used in the Maltz and Erlich approach, or to recommend items to a specific set of people. The first approach is in some ways a hybrid of push-active and pull-active, since the recipients must still discover the recommended items in the database. The second approach is a pure push-active approach, often using direct e-mail to the select recipients. In addition, the recommendation may just be a hyperlink to a document, or may include a description, numerical rating, or text comment on the document.

The selection method is the technique used by the recipient to select which of the recommended items should actually be read. The simplest selection method is to just read all recommended items, but this may be impractical for people at the top of an information hierarchy who may find many hundreds of items recommended to them every day. Alternately, the recipient may choose to read all documents from selected individuals, all documents with numerical ratings above a threshold, or a fixed number of documents each day, perhaps sorted in ratings order. One challenge in selection methods for push-active systems is that there is no explicit feedback loop based on the experience with the quality of recommendations from different pushers. For instance, a CEO might discover that all documents rated 3 or higher by her VP of Engineering are critical, while only documents rated 5 or higher by her VP of Sales are important.

Delivery of the selected documents may be through e-mail, the web, or other information browsers. The delivery method is relatively unimportant, especially as the types of information viewable through different delivery methods converge. However, push-active methods work best with a push delivery method, and currently most desktop users receive push information through e-mail.

2.3.3 Summary

Push-active recommenders are useful in similar environments to pull-active recommenders: small communities of shared information interests where everyone knows everyone else, and knows what everyone else is interested in. A benefit of push-active recommenders is that they do not require the recipient to guess when documents of interest are available, because the documents are pushed to the recipients. Further, push-active recommenders do not suffer from the cold-start problems that slow usefulness of other recommenders, since documents can be pushed effectively from the first day the system is deployed. Push-active recommenders have the disadvantage that users cannot get information on a particular theme of interest, except perhaps by letting the information intermediaries know of their interest.

Push-active recommenders do rearrange the costs and benefits of recommendation: the cost to the sender is the cost to review the document, select a recipient, and direct the document to the recipient. The cost to the recipient is the time to review the documents received. If the sender would have reviewed the document anyway, the costs are low to push it to other users. If the recipient finds the document valuable the cost is low, since search costs are paid by the sender not the recipient. On the other hand, if the recipient is the target of too much pushed information, the cost of searching through the received information for the information worth reading may be high. By contrast, the costs in the pull model are mostly paid by the recipient, who searches only for information he wants to read.

2.4 Automated Collaborative Filtering

Automated CF systems build a database of user opinions of available items. They use the database to find users whose opinions are similar (i.e., those that are highly correlated) and make predictions of user opinion on an item by combining the opinions of other like-minded individuals. For example, if Sue and Jerry have liked many of the same movies, and Sue liked *Hoop Dreams*, which Jerry hasn't seen yet, then the system may recommend *Hoop Dreams* to Jerry.

Automated CF systems are like push and pull CF systems in that they use the opinions of a group of people to help other people find items that might be of interest to them. Unlike the push and pull CF systems, automated CF systems determine the relationships between people and items algorithmically. While Tapestry (Goldberg et al., 1992), the earliest CF system, required explicit user action to retrieve and evaluate ratings, automatic CF systems such as GroupLens (Resnick et al., 1994; Konstan et al., 1997) provide predictions with little or no user effort. Later systems such as Ringo (Shardanand and Maes, 1995) and Bellcore's Video Recommender (Hill et al., 1995) became widely used sources of advice on music and movies respectively.

Automated CF systems are social navigation systems in the same way as push and pull systems. The algorithms look through the footprints left by previous visitors to a web site, and create signposts not only to paths that are most heavily trodden by all users, but to paths that are most heavily trodden by the users who are most similar to the current visitor. As social navigation systems become more and more heavily used, the signposts directing users to previously visited parts of the site will become so dense that nearly every alternative will be recommended to the user. By automatically filtering all available social navigation signposts to just those that are most useful for the current visitor, automatic collaborative filtering extends social navigation to systems in which the number of users and the number of visits to each site is so large that just seeing which paths have been travelled is no longer sufficiently helpful. Further, automatic collaborative filtering reduces the effort required from the users to get benefits from the CF system. In push CF systems, the recommenders must put in the effort to select which users should read each message. In pull CF systems, the readers must put in effort to select the information they want to read. In automatic CF systems, the CF system puts in the effort to match the recommenders and the readers with little effort from either.

2.4.1 Motivating Examples

We consider three motivating examples of automatic CF systems: GroupLens, Ringo and Video Recommender.

Usenet, one of the earliest and largest bulletin board systems, was originally a valuable source of information. However, as the number of users grew rapidly, the system became overloaded with articles. It reached the point where most users found only a few useful articles in a group filled with dozens or hundreds of articles a day.

The GroupLens recommender system (Resnick et al., 1994; Konstan et al., 1997, Miller et al., 1997) made Usenet useful again by providing personalised predictions on the quality of the messages, pointing out the gems among the stones (see Figure 2.3). Of course what is a gem to one, might be a stone to another. To understand the quality of messages in light of these differing tastes, the GroupLens system asked each user to

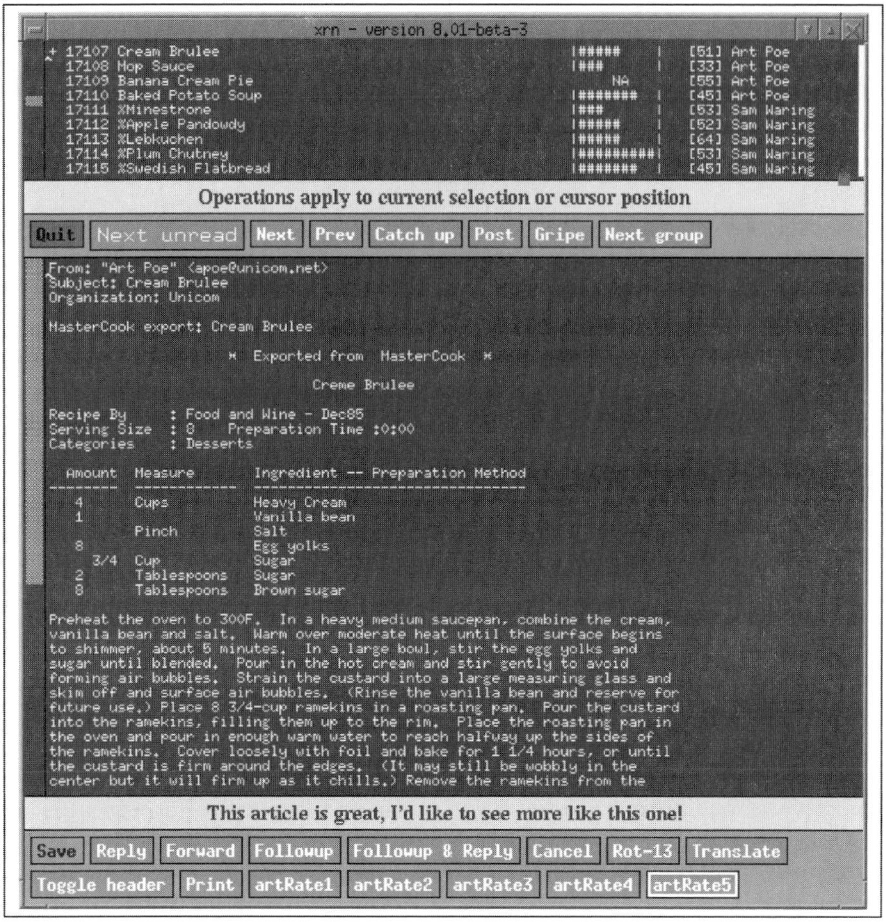

Figure 2.3 A news reader adapted for the GroupLens system. Users rate articles using keyboard shortcuts or the buttons at the bottom; they see predicted ratings for articles in the newsgroup listing at the top.

enter a 1 to 5 rating after reading an article. GroupLens collected and compared these ratings to find users who shared similar tastes. When you needed a prediction for a new unread article, GroupLens would see how the other users who shared your tastes had rated the article. If they liked it, chances are you would too, and GroupLens would give you a high prediction for that article. These other users became your colleagues down the hall or your personal movie reviewers, helping select the information of value to you.

GroupLens created a new model of recommender systems that extended Tapestry in several ways. The small Tapestry communities were limited to reading and evaluating only a small set of messages; a large community was needed to generate recommendations across a large stream of information like Usenet news. GroupLens created a large virtual community, where users could share recommendations without actually knowing each other. Surprisingly, the virtual community of GroupLens allowed this personalisation at the same time it assured privacy and anonymity; you did not need to know the identity of those you correlated with to gain the benefit of their recommendations, unlike Tapestry where the benefits came directly from your personal relationships with the recommenders.

GroupLens showed that predictions from an automated recommender system can be meaningful and valuable. Predictions generated by the GroupLens engine correlated well with the users' actual ratings and were more accurate than average ratings. Highly rated articles were more likely to be read and rated and users were more likely to rate if they got predictions – they see the value of the predictions and so want to rate.

Several other systems developed at about the same time followed the GroupLens model. Ringo was an e-mail and web system that made recommendations on music (Shardanand and Maes, 1995). It experimented with variations on the core algorithms and verified that predictions improved as more ratings were collected.

Video Recommender (Hill et al., 1995) made recommendations on movies. It found a middle ground on the trade-off between lots of work and lots of value (the Tapestry model) and no work and little value (ratings by movie critics). In exchange for submitting ratings on a selected set of movies, the system generated personalised predictions. The personalised recommendations were more accurate than the recommendations of movie critics. Video Recommender's predictions correlated at .62 with the users' actual ratings of the movies, while the movie critics achieved only a .22 correlation.

Both systems showed that collaborative filtering applies to all media, even domains like music and movies where content analysis was not feasible. They showed collaborative filtering allows serendipity where content based systems might not. If you've shown interest in only country and western music in the past, a content filter will only recommend more country and western. In a recommender system, users who correlated with you on country and western might lead you to discover rock or blues albums of interest.

Ringo and Video Recommender extended the virtual community to a real connected community by allowing users to post textual comments for others to read, and by revealing e-mail addresses of correlated users who had volunteered to reveal their identity. People wanted to get to know others who shared their tastes – they even requested a Video Recommender singles club! And this knowledge made them more confident in the recommendations they received.

2.4.2 Analysis

Approaches

Many different approaches have been applied to the basic problem of making accurate and efficient automatic CF systems, ranging from nearest-neighbour algorithms to Bayesian analysis.

The earliest recommenders used nearest-neighbour collaborative filtering algorithms (Resnick et al., 1994; Shardanand and Maes, 1995). Nearest-neighbour algorithms are based on computing the distance between consumers based on their preference history. Predictions of how much a consumer will like a product are computed by taking the weighted average of the opinions of a set of nearest neighbours for that product. Neighbours who have expressed no opinion on the product in question are ignored. Opinions should be scaled to adjust for differences in ratings tendencies between users (Herlocker et al., 1999). Nearest-neighbour algorithms have the advantage of being able to rapidly incorporate the most up-to-date information, but the search for neighbours is slow in large databases. Practical algorithms use heuristics to search for good neighbours and may use opportunistic sampling when faced with very large populations.

Bayesian networks create a model based on a training set with a decision tree at each node and edges representing consumer information. The model can be built off-line over a matter of hours or days. The resulting model is very small, very fast, and essentially as accurate as nearest-neighbour methods (Breese et al., 1998). Bayesian networks may prove practical for environments in which knowledge of consumer preferences changes slowly with respect to the time needed to build the model but are not suitable for environments in which consumer preference models must be updated rapidly or frequently.

Clustering techniques work by identifying groups of consumers who appear to have similar preferences. Once the clusters are created, predictions for an individual can be made by averaging the opinions of the other consumers in that cluster. Some clustering techniques represent each consumer with partial participation in several clusters. The prediction is then an average across the clusters, weighted by degree of participation. Clustering techniques usually produce less-personal recommendations than other methods and, in some cases, the clusters have worse accuracy than nearest-neighbour algorithms (Breese et al., 1998). Once the clustering is complete, however, performance can be very good, since the size of the group that must be analysed is much smaller. Clustering techniques can also be applied as a "first step" for shrinking the candidate set in a nearest-neighbour algorithm or for distributing nearest-neighbour computation across several recommender engines. While dividing the population into clusters may hurt the accuracy or recommendations to users near the fringes of their assigned cluster, pre-clustering may be a worthwhile trade-off between accuracy and throughput.

Horting is a graph-based technique in which nodes are consumers, and edges between nodes indicate degree of similarity between two consumers (Wolf et al., 1999). Predictions are produced by walking the graph to nearby nodes and combining the opinions of the nearby consumers. Horting differs from nearest-neighbour as the graph may be walked through other consumers who have not rated the product in question, thus exploring transitive relationships the nearest-neighbour algorithms do not consider. In one study using synthetic data, Horting produced better predictions than a nearest-neighbour algorithm (Wolf et al., 1999).

Dimensionality reduction techniques such as singular value decomposition can be applied to reduce the sparsity of the user x rating matrix and thereby improve efficiency. Sarwar et al. (2000) showed that dimensionality reduction not only provided a smaller and more efficient collaborative filtering system, but it also could produce more accurate recommendations. Intuitively, this is accomplished by mapping both users and items to a smaller-dimension "taste space". For movies, fewer than 20 dimensions were needed. This reduced space is densely populated, and it is therefore easier to find and exploit agreement.

Interfaces

The results of automatic CF systems can be presented to the users through several different interfaces. The simplest is to keep the interface unchanged, and merely add the results of the automatic collaborative filtering algorithm as the score on each item as it is presented to the user in the original way. These interfaces are called *prediction interfaces*, because they augment the information provided with predictions of the value of each item to the user.

An alternative interface is to restructure the set of alternatives presented to the user by providing a sorted list of suggested items in the order the user is likely to value them. These systems are called *recommendation systems*, because the interfaces are structured around the list of recommendations. Recommendation interfaces simplify the set of choices for the user, perhaps at the cost of limiting the alternatives she considers.

A hybrid interface includes a set of recommendations, sometimes ordered, sometimes not, associated with each item the user has selected. These systems are called *item-based recommenders*, because their recommendations are structured around items specifically selected by the user. Item-based recommenders have the advantage that they augment the usual navigation paths for the user. The recommendations just become new paths that are likely to be valuable to the user.

Finally, recommendations may be used to create a semi-custom or fully-custom interface that presents recommended items without explicitly labelling them as "recommended". These subtle interfaces, sometimes referred to as "organic" interfaces, allow the user to experience a personalised information space without being explicitly aware of the recommendations. For example, a custom newspaper may rearrange stories to place ones with high predicted interest at the front (Bharat et al., 1998). Similarly, an e-commerce storefront may personalise its offerings to users it recognises through cookies or logins. Designers of personalised interfaces must balance the benefits of personalisation against the disorientation that occurs when different users have different views of the same "space". Custom newspapers and storefronts, in particular, may undermine other forms of social navigation as users directed to the "front-and-centre" content find something different than expected.

2.4.3 Summary

One key advantage of automatic collaborative filtering is that it works in large anonymous communities. Other forms of collaborative filtering explicitly leverage the relationships between users to form their recommendations. In a push system like Maltz and Ehrlich (1995) items are recommended to specific users based on specific, personal knowledge of their tastes. In automatic CF systems on the other hand, the users who are the most valuable recommenders for each other may not even know each other at all. This advantage can be a disadvantage too. The automatic CF systems neither leverage nor strengthen interpersonal relationships. Ringo and Video Recommender users both wanted extensions to the system to make it possible for them to build personal relationships with the other users who were the most effective recommenders for them.

One key advantage of push, pull and automatic collaborative filtering is that they *do not* consider the content of the items being recommended. Rather than map users to items through "content attributes" or "demographics", collaborative filtering treats each item and user individually. Accordingly, it becomes possible to discover new items of interest simply because other people liked them; it is also easier to provide good recommendations even when the attributes of greatest interest to users are unknown or hidden. For example, many movie viewers may not want to see a particular actor or genre so much as "a movie that makes me feel good" or "a smart, funny movie". At the same time, collaborative filtering's dependence on human effort can be a significant drawback. For a CF system to work well, several users must evaluate each item; even then, new items cannot be recommended until some users have taken the time to evaluate them. These limitations, often referred to as the *sparsity* and *first-rater problems*, cause trouble for users seeking obscure movies (since nobody may have rated them) or advice on movies about to be released (since nobody has had a chance to evaluate them).

More recently, a number of systems have begun to use observational ratings; the system infers user preferences from actions rather than requiring the user to explicitly rate an item (Terveen et al., 1997). Observational ratings have the potential to even further reduce the effort required by users of automatic CF systems. Users just take the actions they would have taken in the absence of any recommender system, and the system learns their preferences transparently from their actions. These systems are particularly well suited to automatic collaborative filtering, since no effort is required to process the ratings either. In such a system, the user might not even be aware that recommendations are happening. She just notices that the navigational aids on the site appear to be particularly well suited to her tastes. Little does she know that the set of navigational aids she sees is different from the set of navigational aids that any other user of the site would see!

Another solution to the startup problem is filterbots (Sarwar et al., 1998; Good et al., 1999). Filterbots are robots that analyse characteristics of the items in a system and rate the items according to those characteristics. Because filterbots are robots they are willing to rate all of the items in a system. By the time the first user arrives at the system, all of the new items may have been rated by dozens or even hundreds of filterbots. Collaborative filtering can be an effective way to combine the ratings of filterbots into recommendations for users (Good et al., 1999).

Hybrid systems that combine the benefits of several different recommender systems are likely to be a fruitful area for research. For instance, automatic CF systems will be blended with push and pull systems to create filtering systems in which users leverage their existing external relationships with other users, and even create new relationships with other users they've never even met.

2.5 Implicit Interest Measures

One of the challenges facing implementers of CF systems, both active and automated, is getting enough participants to evaluate, recommend or rate the items being filtered. In automated CF systems in particular, users may be tempted to rate just enough items to build a useful profile and they may then take advantage of the continued ratings of others to filter items for them. Of course, if everyone adopts this strategy, the system fails as too few users evaluate new content and the availability and quality of recommendations becomes poor. This problem is commonly studied in economics as the "free rider problem" in public goods.

The free rider problem is evident in a wide range of social navigation systems. Not only is it easier to navigate without spending "effort" (leaving information for others), but it may also be worth confining your navigation to "well-worn" paths where others have already done the hard work. In CF systems, as in other social navigation systems, the problem can be addressed in two ways: increasing the value to users of entering ratings or decreasing the associated cost (i.e., effort). We examine each in turn.

Increasing the value of ratings can be done intrinsically or through external recognition. In domains where tastes change frequently, a user may find that recommendations are only accurate if she continues to rate new items, increasing the value of rating; this approach is less likely to work in domains where collaborative filtering is commonly used since CF systems work best when tastes are stable. Alternatively, the system can externalise the value of ratings by directly compensating users for ratings, by according status to users who provide many ratings, or by requiring users to pay for their recommendations by providing ratings. All of these have been tried in systems, with several successful review systems according status to raters (e.g. Amazon.com's book reviews) and even directly paying raters (e.g. Epinions.com's compensation system). Thus far, we are unaware of any studies that indicate the degree to which compensation systems skew the ratings database or affect rating behaviour. In particular, we do not know the effect on personal prediction quality of using primarily compensated ratings.

Decreasing the cost of rating items can done by simplifying the rating interface (e.g. simply requiring a single click or keystroke), but that simplification does not eliminate the needed mental effort to decide upon a rating. Our experience with the GroupLens system for Usenet News suggested that, even when rating articles required no extra keystrokes, the majority of articles that user read still went unrated. Instead, many systems observe the actions taken by users and interpret these as implicit ratings. This section reviews research and systems using explicit ratings in CF systems.

Tapestry (Goldberg et al., 1992) was the first system to directly use implicit ratings for collaborative filtering. The system stored annotations corresponding to user actions such as replying to a message. Other users could query these annotations thereby interpreting the act of replying as a rating. The GroupLens project experimented with time-spent-reading as an implicit rating for Usenet News articles (Miller et al., 1997; Konstan et al., 1997). Building on the work by Morita and Shinoda (1994) that showed that users spent more time reading articles they preferred, the GroupLens project was able to show that collaborative filtering was able to predict ratings for substantially more articles by using time-spent-reading and that the ratings predicted were of similar quality to explicit rating-based predictions.

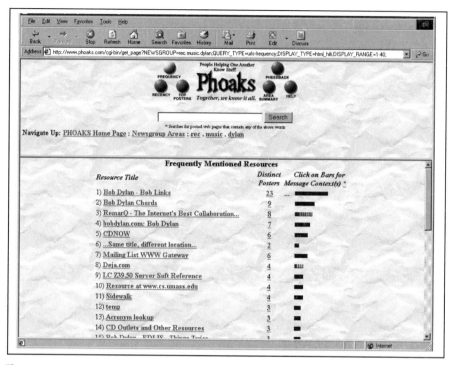

Figure 2.4 A recommendation page from PHOAKS. Resources are shown with the number of distinct endorsements as well as direct access to the messages from which the endorsement was mined.

2.5.1 Motivating Examples

Three other systems expanded the use of implicit ratings more broadly.

PHOAKS

The PHOAKS system (Hill and Terveen, 1996; Terveen et al., 1997) mines Usenet News postings to identify web sites of most value to the participants in a newsgroup (see Figure 2.4). The system identifies URLs in news postings, determines whether they were likely "recommendations" by examining the context of appearance (e.g. discounting signatures), surrounding words and apparent relationship to the posting author. PHOAKS then provides a web site identifying the most highly recommended web sites for a newsgroup (discounting repeated recommendations by the same author). Hill et al. found not only that they could identify recommendations with high accuracy, but that this method did a good job of identifying the same type of well-liked pages that appeared in manually edited FAQ postings. PHOAKS uses recommendations that were explicitly created for one purpose and repurposes them to create a collaboratively constructed map guiding people to sites deemed useful in a particular community.

Link Mining

Web links, in addition to providing direct access from one web page to another, represent the web page author's endorsement of the target page as useful and relevant, at least in context. Terveen and Hill (1998) found this data to be useful in classifying sites – specifically for identifying authoritative sites and information hubs. The Google search engine employs a similar technique to rank results returned from a search in an attempt to present the most important sites first; sites that are linked to from many other authoritative sites are considered more important than sites that are sparsely linked to. Both Terveen and Hill's system and Google use only information already created by web page authors for another purpose, benefiting from both the availability and the relative objectivity of implicit ratings.

Usage Mining

Linton's OWL system (Linton et al., 2000) is a recommender system that performs collaborative filtering on word processing commands to help users discover commands that could simplify their word processing tasks. The system monitors command usage without any user intervention, and then analyses the usage data to determine "norms" of word processing behavior and to identify deviations from those norms that might be the result of a user being unfamiliar with a particular command. OWL relies entirely on implicit measures of command usefulness, that is actual use, to support social navigation of an interface.

2.5.2 Analysis

Implicit ratings, and more generally ratings not explicitly created for the collaborative filtering system, are widely used as inputs to research and commercial collaborative filtering recommender systems. Many commercial recommender systems use page visits or purchase records as a measure of product interest. Implicit data is often noisy; users may purchase a product they personally dislike as a gift or may seem to spend a long time on a page when they actually lost interest and were talking on the phone. But implicit data also has the benefit of being more available, and potentially more honest. It is no surprise that a implicit data has also become the most prevalent source of "ratings" in more general social navigation systems. Usage tracking through footprints, awareness triggered by navigation, and other social navigation techniques may require users to sign into a system, but afterwards the user's navigation is followed automatically, freeing the user to focus on her task rather than on being a source of data for others.

2.5.3 Summary

The availability of implicit measures of user preference make it possible to construct CF systems, and more generally social navigation systems, without depending on users to consciously evaluate and provide feedback on the options they consider. While implicit ratings address the problem of a ratings database being a public good, they do not completely solve the problem. Some users will still find it more valuable to wait and only navigate through explored space. But the increase in ratings and the decrease in effort needed to rate can go a long way towards solving this problem – perhaps far enough so that other user motives, including altruism and adventure, will produce enough ratings to allow the system to guide users through new content as well as old.

2.6 Situational Recommendations

Automated CF systems form a model of user taste from that user's ratings, implicit or explicit, and then use that model, together with the ratings of all other users in the system, to recommend items that match that user's taste. This approach works well when users have consistent tastes, but it does not adapt to situational changes in taste. For example, the user of a movie recommender might want different recommendations depending on his mood. If he is feeling depressed, he may want a "happy" movie, while if he is ponderous, he may want a thoughtful one. Similarly, situational preferences exist in other domains. A user may want to hear a recommendation for "work appropriate" music vs. music for driving home. Or a user seeking recommendations for news may want to distinguish his desire for a quick overview from an interest in deeply learning the topic. All of these domains exhibit a trade-off between long-term tastes and short-term situational interests.

Many recommender systems address this trade-off by providing a separate mechanism for selecting the set of items from which the recommended one will be drawn. MovieLens, for example, allows the user to request recommendations for a comedy. This is a good first step, but syntactic filtering is often insufficient for representing mood and other complex constraints.

Interestingly, CF systems are more likely to experience this problem than most other current social navigation systems. Because collaborative filtering automates much of the process, recommendation decisions are made without much user intervention. Other social navigation systems may present less data at one time, giving the user an opportunity to steer in directions that she perceives as more likely to meet her current, as well as persistent, needs. As social navigation systems are applied in domains where filtering is required, situational recommendation becomes increasingly necessary.

2.6.1 Motivating Examples

Herlocker's Ephemeral Recommender

Herlocker (2000) designed and tested an extension to MovieLens that allowed users to select a subset of the movies they'd already rated to reflect their current short-term interests. For example, a user interested in an "intelligent Sci-Fi" film could show the system examples of other such films, and even save and name the category for future use. To produce a recommendation based on these ephemeral interests, the system would first use item-to-item ratings correlation to identify movies that the user community treated similarly to the specified movies. These are movies that tended to elicit agreement among the same set of users. This subset was then evaluated using standard collaborative filtering using the user's long-term interests. User studies showed wide interest in the feature, though many users felt they would better be able to describe their ephemeral needs by specifying negative examples along with positive ones.

MetaLens

Ben Schafer's MetaLens system integrates collaborative filtering recommendations with other situational requirements (see Figure 2.5). For example, users can request recommendations for movies starting after 9 p.m. at theatres near their house, and at a very minimal charge. MetaLens users can assign relative importance to each criterion, including the MovieLens collaborative filtering recommendation. MetaLens allows different objectives to be combined to form a single list of recommendations that factor in multiple objectives, some of them situational.

2.6.2 Analysis

It is important for recommender applications to strike a balance between long-term tastes and short-term interests. Traditional collaborative filtering

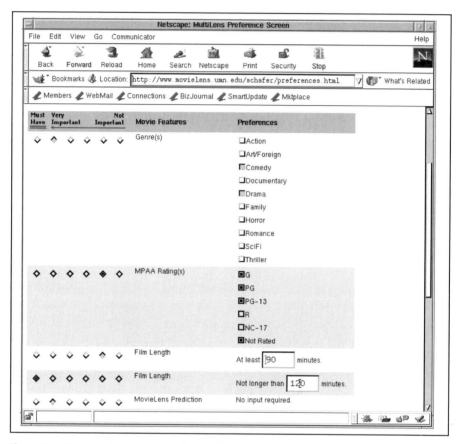

Figure 2.5 User preference screen from MetaLens. Users assign importance to different movie attributes. In this example, it is very important that the movie be a comedy or drama, essential that it be less than two hours, and very important that it come highly recommended by collaborative filtering. It is less important that it not be rated R or NC-17 and that it be at least 90 minutes.

systems focus entirely on long-term tastes. Query and browsing interfaces focus mostly on short-term interests. The examples above are just two of many ways of combining these interests. Temporal weighting of ratings has been proposed as a means for representing tastes that evolve over time. Others have proposed assigning weights to ratings in the neighbourhood selection process to identify different neighbourhoods depending on mood (perhaps as a variant on Herlocker's system). Herlocker suggests a second dimension of rating: explicit similarity ratings that could be used to better identify themes and patterns among consumption.

Currently, these techniques are most urgently needed in social navigation systems that provide filtering of information or products. It is easy to see, however, how this need can be extended to information browsing, rather than filtering, interfaces. Annotations that highlight well-travelled links on a web site, for example, may be situational. Users may want to distinguish between links that were well travelled by people who were able to spend a lot of time looking vs. those travelled by people who needed quick answers. And, as social navigation systems serve increasingly large communities, situational factors may be used to determine which subcommunity is most prominent in navigational roadmarks.

2.6.3 Summary

The guidance a user needs in finding her way through a content space may depend on short-term situational factors. A variety of techniques can be used to incorporate these factors into a collaborative filtering recommender system, as well as into other social navigation systems. Such systems may use situation factors to pre-filter a set of candidates (perhaps using an additional social filtering step); they may merge a variety of information together into a single recommendation set; or they may use other techniques to strike a balance between long-term and short-term user tastes.

2.7 Recommending for Groups

Most automated CF systems have focused exclusively on recommending items to individuals. In some domains, such as Usenet News (Resnick et al., 1994; Konstan et al., 1997; Miller et al., 1997), this limitation is understandable. Few users read articles collectively. In other domains such as books or music (Shardanand and Maes, 1995), it is common both to enjoy the media alone and in groups. Moreover certain items, among them board games and movies (Hill et al., 1995), are more commonly enjoyed in groups. Recommender systems that identify items such as movies for individuals do not address the user's key question, which is not "what movie should I see?" but rather "what movie should we see?". Recommendations can be provided to a group either by extending the automatic recommender to automatically recommend for the group, or by creating a new interface that displays individual recommendations for each member of the group, so the users can form their own group recommendation. In either case, the problem requires extending existing recommendation algorithms.

Group recommenders are a special form of social navigation system in which the group is navigating together. Group social navigation can be as simple as a group obtaining a recommendation together at a movie site. More sophisticated systems might include group web browsing systems in which a group of people use a multi-browser with windows on individual workstations to navigate the web together. On a micro scale, such a browser is itself directly a form of social navigation, since the group dynamics direct the navigation. On a macro scale, a recommender system can be providing guidance to the group about which links are likely to be most fruitful for the group as a whole to explore, based on past browsing behaviour of other individuals or groups.

Another example of a group social navigation system is the MultECommerce system, which supports a group of shoppers visiting a virtual store together (Puglia et al., 2000). A recommender system in such a store should be integrated into the group experience, perhaps providing recommendations of items for individuals in the group, but basing the recommendations in part on the taste of the entire group. For instance, the recommendations of clothing shown to a group of teenage girls shopping alone might be very different to the clothing recommendations shown to one of the girls shopping with her mother.

2.7.1 Motivating Examples

We built such a group recommendation interface for our MovieLens research web site. We call the group interface PolyLens (see Figure 2.6). PolyLens encourages users to form groups of other MovieLens users, using either the e-mail address or MovieLens pseudonym of the other users. Once a group is formed, each user in the group can get lists of recommended movies with the PolyLens prediction of how much that user will like the movie, and a separate prediction of how much the whole group will like the movie. To preserve privacy, only the current user's individual predictions are displayed, and join requests can be refused. We discovered that 95% of the users were very satisfied with the group recommendation features, and 77% found the group recommendations more useful than individual recommendations in choosing a movie to see. However, 94% of the users would have preferred seeing the personal recommendations prepared for other group members, and 93% of the users would have preferred to reduce their own privacy by permitting other users to see their personal recommendations. Overall, the results demonstrate that users are enthusiastic about group recommenders, and that group recommenders would help users make choices.

MusicFX is another system that supports group formation, though without using collaborative filtering (McCarthy and Anagnost, 1998) – see Figure 2.7. MusicFX was designed to address the challenge of selecting music for the often-large groups of people using a corporate gym.

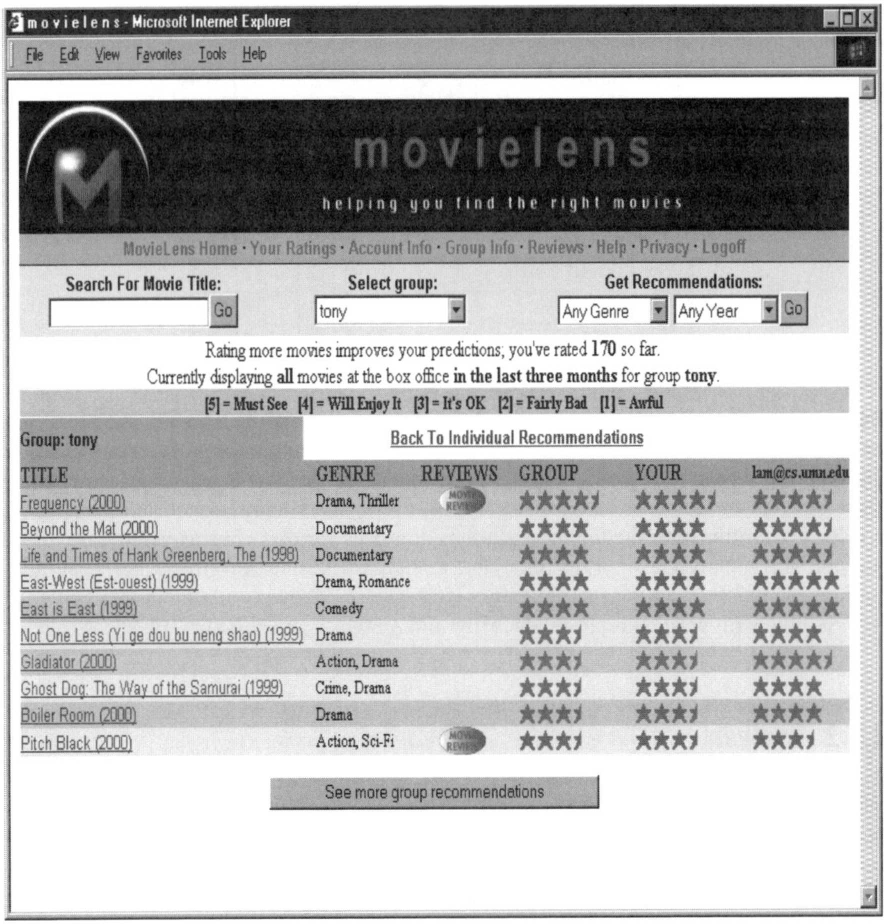

Figure 2.6 *Composite* interfaces display a list of recommended movies with both group and individual member predictions. Depending on the privacy policy of the system, particular group members may be omitted from the listing. These interfaces allow group members to balance the system's estimate of group welfare with the predicted happiness of each group member. This example shows a simple composite interface for a two-member group.

Each person filled out a taste profile describing their music preferences. The computer that tracked who was in the gym also kept track of what type of music would be most appropriate for the current group of people who were working out. Over time, some people changed their work habits to arrange to be at the gym when other people, often strangers, with similar music taste were there.

67

i	Genre	Person	A	B	C	D	E	GP$_I$	Pr$_I$
1	Alternative Rock		2	2	0	2	2	68	0.48
2	Hottest Hits		1	1	2	0	-2	38	0.27
3	New Music		1	1	1	0	0	35	0.25
4	Hot Country		2	0	0	0	-2	28	0.00
5	Dance		2	-1	1	-1	-1	28	0.00
6	World Beat		0	1	-1	1	-2	23	0.00
7	Traditional Country		1	0	0	-2	-2	17	0.00
8	50's Oldies		0	0	0	-1	-1	14	0.00
9	Heavy Metal		-1	-1	-1	-1	-2	4	0.00
10	Polka		-1	-1	-2	-2	-2	2	0.00

Figure 2.7 Example preferences from the MusicFX system. Users A–E are the five users currently in the gym. Each of the users A–E has specified her preference for each radio station that could be chosen to be played in the gym. MusicFX has computed an aggregate preference score for each of the radio stations for the five users. The stations are sorted by agregate preferences. In this case, the top three stations dominate for these five users, so those three stations will be played most of the time. Note that MusicFX is not a winner-takes-all system: stations with lower aggregate preference will still be played, though less frequently. (Reproduced with permission from McCarthy and Anagnost, 1998. © ACM 1998.)

2.7.2 Analysis

The differences between single-user recommenders and group recommenders make possible changes in three areas: recommendation algorithms, recommendation interfaces and group formation.

Recommendation algorithms for groups can either be entirely new algorithms or can be novel applications of existing individual recommenders. Existing recommender algorithms can be extended to groups either by transforming the group into a representative user with characteristics of all of the group members, or by merging the outputs of the individual recommender algorithms into a group recommendation.

Group recommendation interfaces must balance the needs of the group for details about individual preferences with limited screen real-estate and the need of individuals for privacy. The range of possibilities goes from recommenders that show individual ratings and predictions for every member of the group, to recommenders that show only the recommendation for the group as a whole, with no individual information.

Group formation also involves the issue of privacy, because adding someone to a group may give me information about that person's preferences. The crucial questions are: Can a user put another user into a group? Can a user see existing groups? Can a user join any existing group?

Privacy can be protected by requiring opt-in on operations that might expose a user's information.

2.7.3 Summary

This section discussed how group recommenders comprise a new form of social navigation, to support a group of people navigating through a shared space together. We saw how emerging social navigation paradigms, such as virtual malls that support groups of shoppers, will require group recommenders. We looked at the PolyLens and MusicFX experience with group navigation, and briefly reviewed design alternatives for each of the three areas in which group recommenders are different from individual recommenders. Note that this discussion of group recommenders only includes the most immediate: a group of people who are all planning to consume the recommended items together. Other forms of group navigation may include navigation with information robots (Good et al., 1999), or obtaining recommendations for a group of people of a set of items that each should consume separately so they will be able to work or play together more efficiently. For instance, a research group might each want to read a subset of the literature in a new area to ensure that the group has covered all of the relevant papers with the least effort.

2.8 Manual Override

Some recommender systems make it possible for users to directly control the way the system works. Although these recommenders usually have manual components too, users are able to control many of the functions of the recommender. For instance, the user might select which other users are used to produce recommendations for her, or precisely how the opinions of other users are combined to form her recommendation. Many of these systems provide help to the user in choosing which of the possible other users might be the best neighbour for her.

In some ways these systems are a form of meta-social navigation system. Such a recommender is not only a social navigation system to help the user navigate among documents, but is also a social navigation system that lets the users navigate among the other users, selecting which of them are most valuable as thought leaders. The choices the user makes in the meta-social navigation system influence the paths that are shown to her by the recommender system space in the underlying social navigation system. Most social navigation systems in the past have been either entirely automatic or entirely user controlled. Manual override recommender systems are a hybrid, offering the convenience of automatic

69

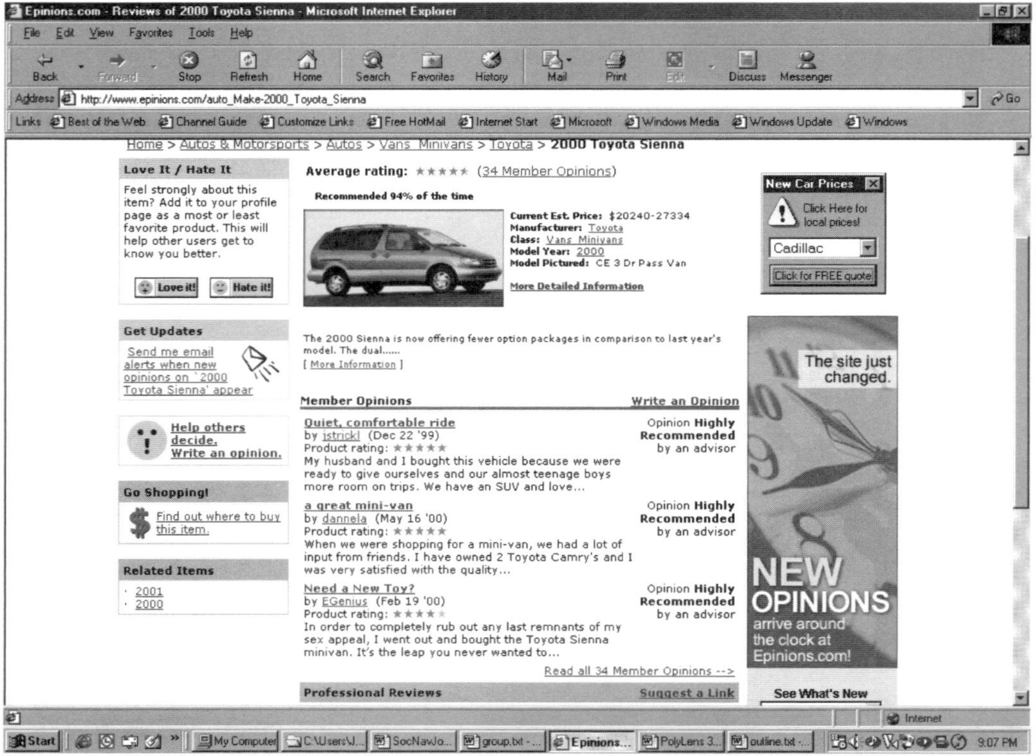

Figure 2.8 Epinions provides a forum for members to share opinions about products they have tried. This page shows a product recommendation page for a Toyota Sienna. The recommendations on this page are generic, but the user can personalise them by creating a "web of trust" of other users whose opinions he likes.

recommendations, along with the flexibility of user control of the recommendation process.

2.8.1 Motivating Examples

Launch.com creates a personalised Internet radio station that streams audio selected specifically for each listener. To jump-start Launch users select other users, well-known artists, and local radio stations that are representative of their musical tastes. Launch then begins selecting music for the user based on their profile and streams it to them over the Internet. While listening to the music users then rate the individual pieces of music and select other users with whom they share musical tastes. Over time, Launch tunes the music it selects for each user according to their ratings of the music that is played for them and the other users they identify as similar to them. All of the individual decisions that Launch makes about what music to play for each user must be made using automatic algorithms that simulate a DJ for each user, to satisfy Launch's contractual obligations to the holders of the copyrights for the music. However, users exercise a form of manual control over the DJs through their ratings of music and their selections of other users.

Epinions is a web site that has created a marketplace for user opinions about products (see Figure 2.8). Users come to Epinions to write reviews about products they have owned or used and to read the reviews of other users about those products. One of the unique features of Epinions is that it pays its users a small fee every time one of their reviews is liked by another user. The unique social navigation feature of Epinions though, is that each user creates a "web of trust" for himself. As the user reads reviews from other users, he may choose to place some of them into one of two different categories. Some he places into the category of trusted users whose opinions are weighed heavily by Epinions in forming recommendations for him. Others he places into the category of untrusted users whose opinions are ignored by Epinions in forming recommendations for him. Over time, Epinions personalises its recommendations for each user according to the web of trusted individuals he has selected for himself. Although users control the structure of the web of trust, Epinions uses an automatic algorithm to convert the web of trust into specific recommendations for the user.

2.8.2 Analysis

Many different parts of the recommendation process can be controlled manually by users, including which other users are considered for possible neighbours, how the opinions of those neighbours are combined to

71

create opinions for the new users, and which opinions of other users are used in forming opinions for the selected user. Users might select neighbours based on their perceived agreement in the past, based on external measures of the user's authority such as whether they are doctors or lawyers, or based on their feelings about the user in the real world. Users might control the algorithm that combines the opinions of neighbours by directly specifying combining rules. For instance, one such rule might say "if Betty likes the movie then I'll like it". Another rule might say about a restaurant "if Joe likes it and Ben likes it but Nathan does not like it then I'll eat there". Users might have preferences about which opinions of other users to trust. For instance, a user might trust a doctor's opinions about medical questions, and a lawyer's opinions about legal questions.

2.8.3 Summary

To date, relatively few recommender systems give users choices about how the recommendations are formed. Over time we can expect to see more and more of these systems created as the number of alternatives for recommender algorithms increases, and as user sophistication increases. Recommenders with manual control offer significant benefits to users because they can incorporate the user's preferences to achieve more accurate recommendations. On the other hand, manual control can be challenging to manage and understand, so we are also likely to see continued use of automatic systems. Over the long-term, hybrid systems are likely to emerge, such as those at Launch.com and Epinions. In these hybrids, users get an initial recommendation based on aggregate data and purely automatic algorithms, and over time the users manually tune the automatic algorithm to their personal preferences.

2.9 Confidence and Explanations

CF systems produce recommendations from large sets of data representing both the preferences of the target user and of the larger community of users. The amount, consistency and quality of data, however, vary on a recommendation-by-recommendation basis. In the movie domain for example, the quality of recommendation depends on how much data the system has about the target user (i.e. the number of movies rated), the number of other users identified with similar tastes (i.e. the number of neighbours), the consistency of agreement with these neighbours and the number of common ratings on which that agreement is based (i.e., the quality of neighbours), the number of neighbours who rated the movie being recommended, the consistency of opinion on the recommended movie among the neighbours, and many other sources of variance.

In some domains, users are willing to accept recommendations as given, either because they face little risk in following them or because they confirm the recommendation with other sources. Launch.com listeners for example, do not vet each song recommended – it is easier to listen to it and react if they dislike it. MovieLens users often read reviews or watch movie trailers to help decide whether to follow a recommendation. In other domains, however, users are less likely to take a chance on a recommendation of unknown quality – few prospective vacationers accept a recommendation for a destination without asking "why?".

Confidence measures and explanations are two approaches to helping users determine which recommendations to follow. Confidence measures are estimates of the likely error distribution of a recommendation. While systems might want to represent an accurate confidence interval, the complexity of the weighted, normalised, k-nearest-neighbour algorithms used in collaborative filtering systems has thus far prevented analytic confidence measures. Instead, some systems display a general confidence level; moviecritic.com, for example, uses a bulls-eye display to help convey how "spot-on" the predicted rating should be. These general confidence displays can represent an ad hoc combination of the quantity, quality and consistency of data used in the recommendation. They can be computed as part of the collaborative filtering process, allowing efficient display alongside the recommendation.

Explanations can provide more general information to a user to aid in her decision-making process. Four common models of explaining collaborative filtering recommendations are process, recommendation data, track-record and external data. Process explanations address the manner in which recommendations were produced, helping users determine whether that manner is appropriate for the decision being considered. Recommendation data can be explained generally, through summarisation, or it can be presented or visualised in greater detail. The recommender system's track record for the user or in similar cases may help users gauge how well the system is likely to perform for them. Finally, external data, while not used in the recommendation process, can provide an additional input to help users determine whether to follow a particular recommendation. These explanation models can be combined to create more elaborate recommendations. Additional explanation models can be used to address social navigations systems with data other than ratings.

2.9.1 Motivating Example: The Explain Experiments

Herlocker et al. (2000) designed and tested 21 different explanations for movie recommendations. These explanations included all four models and conveyed different levels of detail. Example interfaces included

73

textual descriptions of the process without data, summaries of the number of neighbours found, summaries of neighbours' opinions of the recommended movie, charts showing movie ratings vs. historical agreement with the user, statistics including the average correlation with neighbours, an assertion about the percentage of past recommendations that were successful, external data about actors and awards, and a self-described confidence level.

User studies showed that such explanations could both increase and decrease user acceptance of a recommendation for which there was substantial supporting data. Complex displays and explanations based on statistical terms made users less likely to consider the movie. Simple summaries, track records and some external data (i.e. actor data) made users more likely to consider the movie (see Figure 2.9). "Content-free" process descriptions and confidence levels did not significantly affect user actions.

2.9.2 Analysis

Social navigation systems, particularly those that recommend a course of action, can better serve users if they can answer the question "why?" in a way that leads users to the solutions they seek. Confidence measures are often included implicitly in social navigation systems; markers of recency and frequency of navigation help users judge the relevance of historical trails. The explanations used in CF systems can also be extended to other social navigation systems. A user looking at footprints, for example, might ask why they are there. The system could explain process – they are there because people followed this link – or data – the following six users followed this link. The system could also reflect on how often following those footsteps led in the correct direction or add corroborating evidence such as "the destination page is very popular."

Work on explanations in social navigation interfaces is still just beginning. Herlocker's work showed that explanations can be created and that they have an effect. Further work is needed to explore how to create effective decision-support recommendations that not only increase confidence when warranted, but also decrease confidence when warranted.

2.9.3 Summary

Users of social navigation systems are often presented with advice. Confidence measures can help users understand the quantity and consistency of data behind the advice. Explanation systems can provide further information to help a user decide whether a piece of advice should be followed.

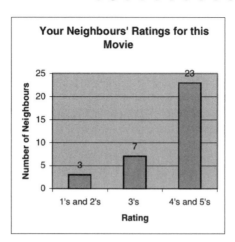

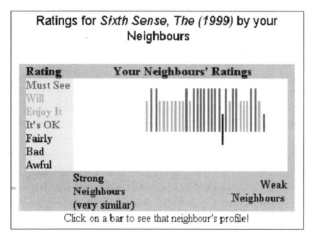

Figure 2.9 Two explanation displays. The 3-bar summary display was one of the most effective displays, while the chart showing rating vs. neighbour similarity contained more information, but was less effective. (Reproduced with permission from Herlocker et al., 2000. © ACM 2000.)

2.10 Beyond Humans

Human opinions and actions form the basis for collaborative filtering and all types of social navigation systems. At the same time, in certain domains, it is hard to get enough human ratings to accurately model individual tastes, cover the wide span of content, find agreement among pairs of users, and still meet the goal of protecting people from bad content. Furthermore, as new content is added to a system, no recommendations for it can be made until some people have chosen to see it – without it being recommended.

Usenet News contains newsgroups where both conditions are true. In our study of the newsgroup rec.humor, for example, we found that the vast majority of articles were considered worthless by most users. Not only were they not funny – they weren't trying to be funny. To protect most of us from the "dreck" in such domains, we would need a set of self-less, consistent, round-the-clock raters. Since humans lack such attributes, we found it useful to employ "trained agents" to read articles and rate them on our behalf.

Agents have long had a role in information navigation systems. Systems such as Tapestry had "standing queries" that differ from filtering agents only in name. Lieberman's Letizia (Lieberman, 1997) browsed ahead of a user on the web, looking for pages of relevance to the user's current navigation. Animated agents have also played the role of guide in several systems. In social navigation systems, agents can take on roles normally fulfilled by humans, particularly in navigating sparsely explored spaces. In collaborative filtering systems, this role-playing is accomplished by entering ratings.

2.10.1 Case study: Filterbots

The GroupLens Research Group completed two different studies of automated filtering agents. Sarwar et al. (1998) found that simple ratings agents for Usenet News articles correlated with some users, increasing the quality and coverage of their predicted ratings. These agents used very basic text analysis techniques, looking at the length of the articles, the percentage of new content, and the quality of spelling within the new content. Results showed that different newsgroups and users benefited from different agents, but that overall the agents could be used to improve the recommender system.

Good et al. (1999) extended this work by testing a variety of personally-trained movie-rating agents (as well as non-personalised ones). The agents were trained using rule-induction systems, TFIDF information filtering systems, and basic linear regression; they used a variety of data including genre information, cast lists and descriptive keywords. In experiments using data from a small user community (50 users), the best agents outperformed collaborative filtering using users, but the combination of users and agents in a CF system outperformed all other combinations. Later results suggest that as communities get larger, they reach a cut-off point at which agents stop adding much value.

2.10.2 Analysis

Trained agents provide many benefits to CF systems. In addition to providing more ratings, they can help build bridges between users with similar tastes but non-overlapping experiences. In those cases, a user might agree with another user's agent, and thereby be able to benefit from that other user's experiences. More generally, providing a source of ratings to decrease the sparsity of the ratings space, especially for new items, helps ensure that users can get recommendations for all items.

Social navigation systems can apply the same techniques. Synthetic users can either learn a goal from user behaviour and scout out paths to those goals, or learn actual user behaviour patterns and attempt to lay tracks through an information space as a user might lay them. Recent work on information scent (Chi et al., 2000) may be one mechanism for training such agents. Agents may also be programmed with behaviours that anticipate users who do not already exist, as may be useful in providing social navigation support in an entirely new site.

2.10.3 Summary

Social navigation techniques rely on the availability and activity of a community of users. In domains where user experience still results in sparse coverage of all or part of the space, trained agents can supplement user data. Experiments in collaborative filtering have shown that even simple agents can help users in noisy spaces. Slightly more elaborate, personal agents can help users in smaller communities and in domains where sparsity is high or there are many new items.

2.11 Discussion

Nearly a decade of research into recommender systems has yielded both extensive knowledge about recommendation techniques, algorithms, interfaces and a variety of practical systems (Schafer et al., 2001). While recommender systems research initially focused on directly augmenting information filtering approaches, it has become clear that these efforts resulted in much broader social navigation systems. Substantial future work remains; we discuss three particularly relevant thrusts: (1) using recommender systems within other social navigation systems, (2) applying the lessons of social navigation in recommender systems research and vice versa, and (3) general open research problems in recommender systems.

2.11.1 Using Recommender Systems in Social Navigation Systems

As social navigation systems grow in popularity, simple knowledge of "who went where" becomes overwhelming and perhaps useless. Current systems have several ways of avoiding this problem. Most research systems avoid the problem by having a small enough user base so that the current (and even historical) behaviour of each user is still meaningful. Other systems aggregate user behaviour (e.g. by assigning trails a colour or symbol based on total traffic), implicitly assuming that the quantity of usage is sufficient for a user to determine whether a path meets her interests. Larger social systems, such as on-line game venues and chat centres provide two solutions: they usually divide the space into smaller rooms, so that it is possible to examine all of the other users in a room, and they provide a mechanism for members to identify, page, or "message" their friends (often called a buddy list), to provide specialised awareness.

While these ad hoc systems work for small communities, homogeneous infospaces and places where people already know each other, they provide little support for either infospaces that serve heterogeneous users or communities where users generally do not know each other. A shopper in a virtual mall, for example, cannot use any of these techniques to see what paths are taken by people with her shopping taste, unless she happens to have mainstream tastes. Similarly, a newcomer to a chat or game centre will have a hard time finding compatible partners when faced with dozens or hundreds of rooms, all seemingly alike.

Recommender systems can provide a solution to this problem. When adequate preference information is available (from behaviour, ratings, or other personal profile data), social navigation interfaces can use recommender systems to identify the most valuable set of people to use to help a particular user. The mall shopper could see not only where people go in general, but which stores and paths are favoured by people like her. The game centre can help newcomers find suitable partners. Of course, these social interfaces can still support existing approaches – buddy lists and aggregate user behaviour may still add value for users. We are thus far unaware of any non-recommender social navigation systems that personalise the presentation of a navigation space by limiting the set of users to those identified as similar by a recommender system. Further research needs to be done to validate and evaluate the approach.

2.11.2 Applying Lessons Across Research Models

Research on recommender systems has yielded several lessons that could well be applied to more general social navigation systems. In particular, recommender systems have shown both the importance of and the algorithmic opportunities for efficient scaling to large numbers of users and large information spaces. Nearest-neighbour collaborative filtering algorithms, combined with clever sampling approaches, have been scaled to applications with millions of items and hundreds of thousands of users. Newer algorithms that reduce the dimensionality of the recommendation problem have improved upon these algorithms, promising to efficiently serve virtually unlimited numbers of users and items (Sarwar, 2000). Similarly, recommender systems have taken great steps to incorporate other machine learning models as surrogates for actual user behaviour (e.g. filterbots), an approach that could help social navigation systems avoid the cold-start problem. Recommender systems have also demonstrated the value of personalised assistance. While most social navigation systems present essentially identical views to all users, recommender systems address the specific needs of particular individuals and even groups of fellow travellers. Finally, recommender systems research has shown the value of designing and evaluating interfaces for specific decision-support tasks. Explanations and situational recommenders demonstrate the importance of matching the information and interface to a specific user's need.

Social navigation research also provides several lessons that inform recommender systems researchers. One of the strengths of most social navigation interfaces is the degree of transparency in their underlying mechanism. Users can directly see not only the aggregated behaviour of others, but also the effect of their own actions. Today's recommender systems lack that transparency, leading to mistaken user models and lower user confidence. Social navigation systems also provide a mechanism for taking advantage of less-travelled spaces. While most recommender systems either provide low-reliability recommendations, or simply refuse to recommend items with few ratings, social navigation systems instead provide users with the information that, for example, a particular data path has not been viewed (at all, or perhaps recently), allowing the users to draw their own conclusions about whether the path is therefore likely low value, or perhaps in their context high value since it is unexplored. More generally, general social navigation systems are more successful than recommender systems at providing users with information, but allowing the users to interpret that information in the context of their own tasks and interests. One user may seek recently-updated content, while another may seek stable content, both in the same social navigation system. Recommender systems rarely provide that level of flexibility to users.

2.11.3 Open Recommender Systems Research Problems

The recommender systems research community has identified a wide range of open research problems. We limit our discussion here to four of the problems we find most relevant and interesting.

Integrated Content/Collaborative Filtering Solutions

Pure collaborative filtering is impractical in many domains because of the rate of new items (that arrive unrated) and because of the high sparsity

79

(and high desired sparsity) of the domain. Domains where items are created frequently but have a short useful life span are particularly problematic, limiting the effectiveness of recommender systems for news, live discussions and live or scheduled entertainment. Several researchers are examining approaches to better integrate content filtering with collaborative filtering to take better advantage of the strengths of each. The filterbots work described above is one example. Other examples include Claypool et al.'s on-line newspaper project (1999) and Baudisch's TV-Scout system (1998). The key challenge is to develop a system that uses the best information available, relying more heavily on collaborative filtering when there is a lot of data from reliable predictors, and falling back to content filtering otherwise.

Human Interface Issues: Complexity vs Control

Automated CF systems provide a very simple user interface – the user enters ratings and receives recommendations. As more specialised features are introduced, users are given more insight into and control of the recommendation process, but in turn face increased complexity and effort. Manual recommendation, for example, allows users to fine-tune their neighbourhoods, but at a substantially greater effort than automated CF. Herlocker's ephemeral experiment similarly allowed users to better express their current mood, but in doing so increased the required amount of introspection. We find it useful to model these interfaces as a trade-off between the amount of "magic" a user is willing to accept and the amount of effort the user must put forth to use the system. Automated CF is highly "magical", explanations can reduce the magic somewhat, and purely manual systems, including pull- and push-active systems, can nearly eliminate the magic. Research is needed into both the perceived and real value of expending extra effort to gain understanding and control, into user confidence and satisfaction, and into interfaces that reduce the added effort needed to understand or control aspects of the recommendation process.

Moving Beyond Individual Item Quality and Relevance

Like information filtering, collaborative filtering systems have been primarily concerned with identifying high-quality, relevant items from within a larger set of generally lower-quality, irrelevant ones. As the overall quantity of good content available increases, it is becoming increasingly important to address the next question of information overload: what do I do when faced with more good, relevant items than I can possibly consume? Recommender systems can respond to this challenge by identifying not just individual items, but collections of items that, taken together, maximise the user's utility. For example, even a fanatic sports fan might wish to forego the fifth or sixth high-quality article about his favourite team for a good (if less perfect) article about economics, politics, or the arts. Recommender systems can incorporate a model of "diminishing returns" if they can discover the degree to which content overlaps, either by examining the behaviour of other consumers of that content or by analysing content. The question of how much diminishing returns and overlap differ from user to user remains to be studied.

Beyond Content to Communities

Recommender systems have often focused on "navigation" while ignoring the potential to be "social". While some early recommender systems recognised the value of building communities, most of them simply provided recommendations to unknown users without making as much as a simple introduction. As the Internet becomes increasingly used for communication purposes (Kraut et al., 1998), we see an increasing need to help people find *other people*. Content recommenders have the information they need to form communities of common interest, and recommender technology can be used to help people find others who share their tastes, or even others who disagree, but are otherwise compatible and able to engage in stimulating discourse.

2.12 Conclusions

Substantial research progress has been made on recommender systems. The evolution of recommenders from active to automated, and then to special-purpose interfaces and algorithms reflects the increasing complexity of navigation tasks in infospace. Recommender systems employ social navigation to help users carry out these tasks, and new interfaces provide better decision-support tools, better mapping of sparsely-navigated spaces, and new interfaces and algorithms to support situational, group and other specialised tasks. Recommender systems themselves can be used to help social navigation systems deal with high user and data volumes, while the research results from recommender and social navigation systems can be used to develop more robust and usable solutions in both domains.

Acknowledgements

We gratefully acknowledge the contributions of the students who are members of the GroupLens Research Group at the University of Minnesota, without whom this work could not have been done. This work was supported by the National Science Foundation under grants IIS 9613960, IIS 9734442, IIS-9978717, and DGE 9554517. Support was also provided by Net Perceptions Inc., a company that we co-founded that sells an automatic collaborative filtering system.

3

Screen Scenery: Learning From Architecture and People's Practices of Navigation in Electronic Environments

Monika Buscher and John Hughes

3.1 Introduction

Three-dimensional on-line electronic environments allow people from globally distributed locations to "meet" (e.g. Activeworlds, Cyberworlds, see also Drozd et al., 2001). The character of such meetings can be anything from casual encounters between strangers in public spaces, through on-line games, to interactive TV or drama. The environments themselves differ with regard to the visual and physical qualities of the "material" structures they provide, the embodiments or avatars that users can employ, and the means of communication that are available: video, audio or textual chat.

The potential use of such environments outside of entertainment is still a matter for discovery, but there are commercial interests. Some, for example, seek to transform websites "into a growing online community, enabling highly interactive real-time communication" (http://www.blaxxun.com/). Creating such a "home" for customers reflects the fact that "corporate site owners have recognised that by creating a community around their products, they are able to greatly increase … the loyalty of the customer for their company" (Rockwell, 1998). A more abstract approach makes it possible to visualise "information" in three dimensions. The contents of databases and archives, and people's movements in this "infoscape" (Benford et al., 1997a) – whether at work or for entertainment – could develop into "inhabitable" information spaces. Moreover, the concept of inhabited information spaces can also be extended to encompass *several* single environments.

Over recent years there has been a proliferation of 3D on-line environments which has resulted in a great number of systems whose insularity and diversity causes both technical and orientational difficulties (Trevor et al., 1998). Different standards mean that software has to be downloaded and machine settings have to be configured before a user can enter a world for the first time. This is awkward because there are few other means of finding out about a world without entering it. In effect, users might go through time consuming preparations only to find themselves in a place that does not match their expectations, or whose structure and appearance they find confusing. Standardisation is one solution to allowing users to move between worlds that is being pursued by the virtual reality community (most notably in the case of VRML). Another possibility is to support translation between environments. eSCAPE, an EU i[3] research project (eSCAPE, http://escape.lancs.ac.uk/) envisages and develops an "electronic landscape" (e-scape) as a collaborative virtual environment (CVE) that provides a container – a landscape or universe – where translation across a diversity of worlds can take place. We can consider an e-scape as a technical common ground and, at the same time, a "physical" space where people can move around and gauge some information about a world before entering it. This information may include world-specific information such as the quality of display available from the user's respective platform, the structure and appearance of worlds, and the current population of, and activities in, different worlds. It could also include information about the relationships between different worlds (expressed, for example, through their position relative to each other in the e-scape) and the orientation of people inspecting these worlds. Such information provides users with a sense of overview and transition and improves on the current abruptness of teleporting between environments.

However, there are some difficulties involved in the design of CVEs of this kind. First, "community", is not, as it is sometimes tacitly assumed, an automatic corollary of providing a place where people can meet – neither in the physical world nor in an electronic environment. The "material" arrangements in an electronic environment – whether they exist for their own sake or represent informational content – have to be, above all, legible. It is here that principles of real-world urban design can be useful. The complex links between material arrangements, time, and people's practices that have to be considered in making physical environments legible and conducive to specific social uses have long been a focus of attention for architects, artists and urban planners (Lynch, 1960; Alexander et al., 1977; Whyte, 1980; Hillier and Hanson, 1984; Kaplan and Kaplan, 1989; Arnheim, 1996; Hillier, 1996). If we want to create three-dimensional information spaces that can be "inhabited"; that provide a socially and aesthetically rich, intuitive and pleasurable experience, the insights gained by an examination of the way people interact in and with physical spaces may be a source of inspiration.

Yet, however useful such an exploration of work concerned with "spatial grammars" may be, it cannot yield a catalogue of principles that can be literally translated into the electronic medium. Current theoretical and experimental approaches to the design of electronic environments almost univocally (cf. Bridges and Dimitrios, 1997) suggest that legibility can be achieved through ever more sophisticated "realism" with regard to the way things look and "feel" in electronic environments (Benedikt, 1992; Heim, 1993; Jenison and Zahorik, 1998; Slater, 1998). However, there are serious limitations to this kind of realism. There are, firstly, technical limits. Secondly, a consideration of the "physical" character of electronic environments suggests that realism is not the only option. There is, for example, no topography, no natural light, no gravity and no friction in the electronic medium unless it is artificially introduced. How and in what combination such factors could and should be introduced is a matter of investigation.

This chapter is based on research undertaken with a focus on the design of "electronic landscapes". It begins with a brief introduction to an ethnographic study of people's engagement with a number of interactive multi-media art installations. The study suggests that people orient towards visual and narrative strategies of organising electronic environments. Such strategies can be found in the fine arts, but also in film, architecture and urban planning. We present a selection of architectural and urban planning approaches to understand and achieve spatial legibility. Bearing these in mind, we examine two examples from the ethnographic study. Against this backdrop, we explore design avenues for more intelligible, enjoyable "inhabitable information spaces" or e-scapes.

3.2 The Ethnographic Study

One means of informing a creative approach to designing CVEs that allow people to experience a sense of presence and navigate effectively within them are empirical studies of the strategies people employ in moving around physical spaces. However, such observations in physical space settings do not suffice. Mediating technologies, while in many respects extending the possibilities for human interaction, inevitably alter and impoverish the richness of interactionally relevant information we take for granted in everyday face-to-face interactions. Therefore, it is necessary to observe people's interactions in and with electronic environments. But despite the emergence of on-line electronic environments these still remain a specialist concern and are seldom used by general citizens – there are few opportunities to observe real-world situations in which people begin to inhabit electronic spaces (but see, for example, Becker et al., 1998). To overcome this problem, we undertook a series of studies at the ZKM, an internationally renowned centre for art and media technology in Karlsruhe, Germany.

The ZKM was founded in 1985 as a new type of institution that brings together art and technology. It combines two research institutes (the Institute for Music and Acoustics, and the Institute for Visual Media) with a Media Library and three museums: the Museum for Contemporary Art, the City Gallery, and the Media Museum. After 12 years in temporary accommodation, the ZKM moved into a new building and opened to the public in October 1997. Permanent and temporary exhibitions at the Media Museum now contain around 30–40 works.

The ethnographic study was carried out over a total of 9 weeks, covering the whole of the ZKM's opening, and 3 weeks of "normal" opening time in December 97 and March 98. Field notes and transcripts of people's engagement with the artworks in audio and video recordings were analysed. In this paper we explore a set of issues that emerge from our observations. Essentially, video, audio and observational data suggest that a sense of presence is not an individually owned, private quality, but embedded in the sociality of our existence in the world (Büscher et al., 2001). What is more, people adapt familiar practices and interpretations to the affordances of electronic environments. Everyday practices of orientation, movement and interaction in space are drawn upon, but *transposed* rather than transplanted in order to fit in with the affordances of the environment. Thus, and in addition to the limits to realism outlined above, such transpositions suggest that a more creative, symbolic approach to structuring electronic environments could be useful. However, once we turn our back to realism as an organising principle, the question of what other structuring principles could be employed becomes crucial. The ethnographic study provides insight into lived practices of orientation in electronic environments. It may guide a more creative approach towards exploiting theories and insights from architecture, art and urban planning. In the following we will examine two concrete examples from the ZKM. However, before we do so, a brief overview of "spatial grammars" is required.

3.3 Spatial Grammars

According to a number of design theorists, the design of material arrangements in physical spaces is, and should be, rule governed. A brief critical foray into some of their arguments can help us to identify important "grammatical" features of spatial design in physical space. There are studies that try to define the elements of spatial design and rules for their combination, ranging from algorithmic approaches (Stiny and Gips, 1978), through Alexander's universal pattern language (Alexander et al., 1977), to Kevin Lynch's observations of structures of urban agglomerations as they feature in people's mental image of the city (Lynch, 1960). Another approach is to place an emphasis on "natural" generative laws of spatial configurations, such as the relationship between strangers and inhabitants and its expression in the permeability or restrictiveness of buildings and cities (Hillier, 1996). A third perspective focuses on the detail of features that make material arrangements legible (Lynch, 1960; Whyte, 1980; Kaplan and Kaplan, 1989). Due to constraints of space, the review presented here is selective and tightly focused. The emphasis lies on issues related to the legibility of large-scale spatial configurations.

3.3.1 Some Elements of Spatial Design

Christopher Alexander's *Pattern Language* is a hierarchical, networked list of 253 components of material arrangements in the environment (Alexander et al., 1977). The individual patterns are arranged in clusters. The highest order pattern is *independent region*, the smallest one is *things from your life*. Each pattern is structured to incorporate links to higher order patterns, a formulation of the problem it addresses, an analysis of the problem, the essential features of the pattern and the solution it provides, and links to lower order patterns. The first 94 patterns are of such high order that no individual or group could build what they describe in one sweep. They are to be understood as principles that must be *shared* in order to create coherent large scale structures in a piecemeal manner. One example is *identifiable neighbourhood*. Based on the premise that a neighbourhood must provide some opportunity for people to organise to participate in local politics, Alexander draws on anthropological and other empirical studies to specify a maximum number of inhabitants (500) and a maximum area (not more than 300 yards across) (p. 82). Further, he argues that there has to be some protection from heavy traffic. Through his patterns Alexander attempts to describe how the physical constraints and possibilities that our environment provides, social and cultural conventions, and the qualities of different materials can be combined in a way that "can make people feel alive and human" (p. xvii). However, his theory of what exactly it is that constitutes such architecture is based on his own world view which may be seen as somewhat "dogmatic, vitalistic, and nostalgic" (Stiny, 1981). Thus, while the basic ideas are useful, Alexander's actual suggestions are in need of review .

Kevin Lynch (1960), in contrast, grounds his work more firmly on people's experience of space. He identifies large-scale structures and their characteristics with reference to empirical studies. His research is based upon people's "mental images" of three different American cities. Interviews, sketches, and the researchers' own explorations of the cities are combined in order to gain insight into the structure of large-scale urban agglomerations. The distinctions people make allow Lynch to specify five elements and to suggest ways in which they could be enhanced in order to improve the overall legibility of cities:

- *Paths*. Roads, bridges, tunnels, etc. that link different parts of the city. Since people tend to perceive a path as "going towards something", the designer could respond by providing directional indicators: "a progressive thickening of signs, stores, or people may mark the approach to a shopping node; there can be a gradient of colour or texture of planting as well; a shortening of block length or a funnelling of space may signal the nearness of the city centre" (p. 97).

- *Edges*. Linear boundaries that impede, divert, or require a change in the mode of, movement. For a pedestrian, for example, a major road can be an edge, whereas the motorist would find the beginnings of the pedestrian zone an edge. There are also "softer" edges that are like seams that visually divide and hold together different areas. An edge may be improved by giving it continuity and lateral visibility (p. 100).

- *Districts*. Areas with a common, identifiable character. Homogeneity can be achieved through "a continuity of colour, texture, or material, of floor surface, scale or facade detail, lighting, planting, or silhouette. ... It appears that a 'thematic unit' of three or four such characters is particularly useful in delimiting an area" (pp. 101–2).

- *Nodes*. Points at which paths cross or converge, or a change of transport takes place, but also public squares, street corners, and other points at which people gather. Apart from giving a node a clear identity through the means already outlined, it can be more clearly defined "if it has a sharp, closed boundary, and does not trail off uncertainly on every side; more remarkable if provided with one or two objects which are foci of attention" (p. 102).

- *Landmarks*. Objects that stand out from their surroundings and can typically be seen from many different positions. The "contrasts with its context or background" is where the designers' efforts to enhance a landmark's features should focus (p. 101). Moreover, it is "stronger if visible over an extended range of time or distance, more useful if the direction of view can be distinguished. If identifiable from near and far, while moving rapidly or slowly, by night or by day, it then becomes a stable anchor for the perception of the complex and shifting urban world" (ibid.).

Lynch's work provides a repertoire of structures, but his work also indicates that the legibility of the elements that make up a large-scale material arrangement and the intelligibility of the whole lie in the *detail* of the design. While Lynch takes an interest in people's perceptions of a city with a view to orientation, the detailed design of material structures is also related to the fit between the design and its use.

3.3.2 Sociability, Mystery and "Visual Gravity"

William Whyte (1980) studied the use of public squares in New York to find out what it is that makes one place popular and another deserted. Through time-lapse photography and observation they specified some factors that could be incorporated in the zoning regulations for the creation of public space. Perhaps not surprisingly, the majority of these relate to the embodied experience of physical space. The role of light, warmth, sounds, seating arrangements, or the provision of food are some examples that proved to be significant for the success of a space. However, there are also some insights that could be more easily seen to be relevant for the design of electronic spaces. One example, is the fact that "what attracts people most … is other people" (Whyte, 1980, p. 19). The favourite places to sit or stop for a conversation were those that were close to a flux of passers-by (p. 21). Evidently, there is pleasure in sociability – in seeing others, being seen, and taking part in even fleeting encounters. In fact, enabling people to watch the "show" of other people's movements and activities is one of the main factors for the success of a space: "The activity on the corner is a great show and one of the best ways to make use of it is, simply, not to wall it off. A front row position is prime space; if it is sittable, it draws the most people" (p. 57). Whyte's studies also reveal that allowing people to use a space flexibly – through, for example, moveable chairs, had a favourable effect. Against this backdrop, Whyte argues that planning regulations should be more rather than less specific (p. 30). Rather than specifying merely *that* sitting space should be provided and leaving the detail to the respective architects and builders, Whyte suggests that what counts as valuable sitting space should be specified in detail.

Sociability is an important aspect of spatial design, but there are other experiential factors. Rachel and Stephen Kaplan, for example, point to *mystery* as an informational factor that draws a person towards a point in the landscape. Through the promise of further information if one ventures just a little further, *mystery* attracts attention and directs movement. The means of achieving mystery "include the bend in the path and a brightly lit area that is partially obscured by foreground vegetation" (p. 56). Rudolf Arnheim (1996) takes a similar approach to the study of paintings, sculptures and architecture. He identifies a visual "force field" whose balance can be manipulated to communicate meaning. One particularly powerful feature of this force field is "visual gravity". Arnheim argues that given our constant exposure to gravity, we perceive it not only through our muscles, but also visually. Essentially, our visual perception

Figure 3.1   Visual gravity.

is weighted. Objects "will carry more weight when placed higher up. Therefore, balance in the vertical direction cannot be obtained by placing equal objects at different heights. The higher one must be lighter" (p. 30). Arnheim uses the numeral 3 to illustrate this (Figure 3.1). At a casual glance, the two halves appear virtually equal and "comfortably poised". However, if the figure is turned on its head, the top half can be seen to be considerably smaller.

3.3.3 The Relationship between Material Form and Forms of Sociability

In *The Social Logic of Space* (1984) Bill Hillier and Julienne Hanson address the question of how certain material arrangements foster certain forms of social interaction. Their work forms the basis for Hillier's *Space is the Machine* (1996). The logic examined through space syntax is not so much one of design detail but, rather, addresses the larger underlying logic of spatial design. Hillier and Hanson outline a complex theory and provide analytical tools for the measurement and definition of the factors they find to affect this relationship. One of the main characteristics is the permeability or degree of restrictiveness of spatial arrangements to movements of inhabitants and strangers. Axial and convex elements of spatial design have their equivalent in people's movements along axial lines and the spatial extension of interactions between people which take the form of convex spaces (Hanson, 1994, p. 676). Very crudely, the number of access points to a spatial element, and the nature of its relationship to other spaces (e.g. whether one can get to it directly or whether one has to pass through another space), express and have an impact on social characteristics such as a sense of community (Hillier and Hanson, 1984, p. 108; Hillier, 1996, p. 376). There is no direct correlation between "integration" (a high degree of interconnectivity) and positive social forms such as neighbourliness. Yet, the right kind of integration in the right place – for example a public space constituted through the fact that a number of houses open towards it – can foster "good" social relations.

3.3.4 Discussion

This brief glimpse into attempts to map social practice and material form, and to achieve legible configurations, serves as a repository that we will return to after descriptions of two examples from ethnographic fieldwork at the multimedia art museum of ZKM. However, a few remarks about the spatial grammars delineated here are in order before we proceed.

There are, firstly, considerable epistemological differences that underpin these studies. While some take an empirical, almost ethnographic approach (Whyte, 1980; Lynch, 1960), others build upon a substantial – albeit at times implicit – theoretical edifice (Hillier and Hanson, 1984; Alexander, and, in a different way, Arnheim, 1984 and Kaplan, 1987). This is not the place to debate the intricacies of these positions. However, it must be made clear that there is more overlap between Lynch's and Whyte's findings and the ethnographic approach we take towards informing system design. Ours is an ethnomethodologically informed ethnographic study. Rather than being guided by a "theory" or interested in developing a "theory", ethnomethodology takes an interest in the activities involved in creating, understanding and maintaining the order of social life. Careful observation provides insight into the orderly organisation of everyday action (see, for example, Garfinkel, 1967, and Wittgenstein, 1953/1997). Within the field of computer-supported cooperative work (CSCW) ethnographic studies of work like this have been used very successfully to inform the design of collaborative systems (Luff et al., 2000), and we undertake ethnographic studies of the social organisation of space in physical and electronic environments to inform the design of an electronic landscape. From this point of view Lynch's and Whyte's studies are more easily adapted than more theoretical approaches.

Secondly, the examples chosen are neither representative nor exhaustive of research undertaken with a view to visual and narrative strategies employed within architecture, let alone the fine arts, film, or other forms of expression that combine aesthetic concerns with a desire to communicate meaning or facilitate use. There is a huge body of literature which has only been tapped into at the surface here. However, what this brief exploration makes clear is that there is potential for such approaches to sensitise us to issues of great importance in the design of electronic spaces. It also begins to delineate the dimensions that we need to consider:

- *Landscape elements.* The material environment is inter alia structured through an arrangement of distinctive man-made structures or clusters of such structures that dissect spaces into distinguishable "areas" with different uses and practices associated with them. Kevin Lynch's *Paths, Nodes, Edges, Districts, Landmarks*, are one way of categorising such elements.

91

- *Quality*. Some of the qualities of such structures (e.g. the exact height of "sittable space"), as well as their visual appearance impact on how they are perceived and used. *Mystery* and *Visual Gravity* are examples.
- *Composition*. The composition of structures also relates to their perception and use. Alexander, Lynch, and Hillier and Hanson formulate "rules" that can improve this relation.
- *Action and environment*. Human action is entwined with the material environment. *Sociability*, for example, seems to be a pervasive feature of the use of public space. There are ways of fostering, as well as controlling such tendencies (Whyte, 1980; Hillier and Hanson, 1984).

Bearing these considerations in mind, we now turn to two examples of interaction in and with electronic spaces.

3.4 Presence and Orientation in Electronic Environments

The main questions for an ethnographic study that is intended to inform the design of CVEs are "How is presence in electronic environments experienced?", "How do people find their way around in such environments?", and "How can interaction between people and between people and the environment be supported?". We present two examples from the field work at the ZKM. The first is concerned with the legibility of "material" arrangements in the electronic environment, while the second example looks at people's interactions in the space.

Example (1): Reading the City

In *The Legible City* (Jeffrey Shaw) a single visitor can (literally) cycle through representations of three cities (Figures 3.2–3.4): Amsterdam, Manhattan and Karlsruhe. Each is displayed on a large screen and based on a street plan of the respective city, but the buildings are made up of letters and words. An LCD display of a street map with a red dot indicating the user's position is mounted onto the bicycle. The following excerpt from the field notes describes how a succession of people (A, B, C, …, N) take turns over the space of 30 minutes to explore the Legible City. They clearly orient to visible, but also to "physical" features of the electronic "cities" and begin to formulate rules for appropriate behaviour in this environment:

> A is cycling. His friends B, C at the back laugh when he can't stay on the street. A: "where am I?" – he checks on the plan. Two women (D & E) look over his shoulder onto the display. B, C leave. A evades letters, then gets off the bicycle and leaves, too. D & E take over,

Figure 3.2 The Legible City.

Figure 3.3 Reading between the lines.

Figure 3.4 Discovering a different way of travelling.

D cycling, E checking where they are on the display. F and a boy (G) enter. F explains the installation to the boy, referring to what a friend told her yesterday. Another couple with a boy enter (H, I & J). The boy wants to try, but his father (H) gets to the bike first. He cycles really fast, switches to Manhattan, cycling. F comments: "there's going to be a storm" ((referring to the gloomy sky)). I: "it's not raining" F: "mhm seems to just stay the same". H cycles up closely to letters, then goes through. ... Another boy (K) gets on, goes through letters carefully, then backwards, then through them again. ... a girl (L) follows. The audience laugh when she goes through letters. When she comes to a row of red letters, she can't get through. She turns round on her bicycle and goes through the blue letters opposite, then tries the red ones again. Her parents look over her shoulder. A small girl and her father (M & N) take over. The father is doing the pedalling for the child whose legs won't reach the pedals. He guides their movement, too: "No not there it doesn't go anywhere, don't go through letters, stay on the road. This is Karlsruhe now, lets go to the castle, past the tax authorities."

Several issues relevant to the experience of presence and practices of orientation can be drawn out from this extract. Firstly, people are concerned with finding answers to the question "where am I?", which in the course of movement through the city turns into "where have I been and where am I going?". Visual and physical features are employed as orientational aids. They range from urban infrastructural elements such as roads, junctions, buildings and landmarks, to natural characteristics such as the sea or the weather, to physical laws such as the solidity of materials. In our everyday interaction with the material world, such material features are mainly understood and interpreted tacitly. Some of the features in the *Legible City* give rise to surprise and thus draw to our attention, not only what kinds of material features form part of our tacit interpretation of the physical world around us, but also point us in the direction of how such features are employed differently within electronic environments.

- *The urban metaphor.* The combination of the bicycle as an interface and the roads and buildings on the screen that adjust to the cyclist's moves in real-time allow the user to travel through the cities. People readily recognise this as the function of the installation. Whether people recognised the cities as based on the ground plans of real cities or not, the urban metaphor allowed them to see *at a glance* what the rudimentary workings of this piece of art are. Most carried an urban interpretation further by initially trying to stay on the roads. This is sanctioned by the audience. The father instructing his daughter not to go through the letters but to stay on the road makes public just how strong this interpretation is. Similarly, the laughter that greets the difficulties people have in staying on the roads indicates that there is something "wrong" in deviating from these paths "meant" for traffic.

- *Collision control.* Most people inevitably overshoot junctions and pass through a row of letters sooner or later. Thus the lack of collision control within the Legible City is discovered as the result of "accidents" (Murray, 1998). It proves a source of enjoyment: after having crossed through letters once, people clearly enjoy doing it again. It is evidently fun to do, but it also has practical consequences: roads are no longer the only routes. Different types of journeys become possible (Figure 3.4). While slow movement allows people to read the text alongside the roads, they can now also decide to "just go" or use the street plan to steer towards an interesting destination regardless of the "buildings". The degree to which the immaterial character of the letters comes to be taken for granted once it has been established is illustrated through the fact that when a row of letters is discovered that is impenetrable, people react with disbelief. L tries several times before she accepts that *this* row of red letters (which is the end of the model) is not penetrable like the others.

- *Landmarks.* People's use of landmarks is most pronounced where visitors who are familiar with the ZKM's home city Karlsruhe choose it in the *Legible City*. N, for example, locates the castle, the main architectural focal point of the city, with the help of other landmarks.

- *Weather.* F states "there's going to be a storm", as H is proceeding along a broad road towards a vista of dark clouds on the horizon. However, the fact that the "weather" does not worsen even though they should be getting closer and closer to the centre of the storm, exposes it as governed by unfamiliar physical laws. In this case the everyday practice of reference to large-scale orientation clues in the sky fails, because the way the storm follows the cyclist makes it unusable as such a resource.

Example (2): The Hunter's Perspective: Labyrinthos

Labyrinthos (F. den Oudsten) is a collaborative environment. It is a game that allows eight players to move through a model of the real museum and "shoot" each other. Each player controls a coloured sphere through a simple control. The terminals have different colours that correspond with the colours of the avatars (Figure 3.5). If an avatar is repeatedly hit, its face changes expression. Eventually it becomes transparent and immobile. The successful "hunter" on the other hand gets a crown. In the transcript of a short and fast exchange, three boys are hunting in a "pack". Yves is sitting at the yellow terminal and thus has a yellow avatar, Oliver has an orange avatar at the terminal to Yves's right, and Tom is moving from one to the other:

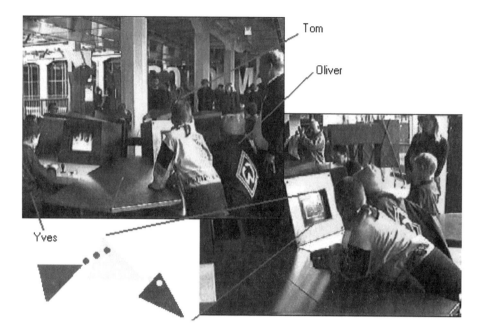

Figure 3.5 Yves, Thomas and Oliver at their terminals and the plan view showing Yves being attacked by Red.

The transcript is translated from German. Some expressions and overlaps ([   ]) do not exactly correspond with the original, others are approximations from talk that was difficult to hear (in brackets). Double brackets contain comments about significant non-verbal actions.

1	O:	hey I'm alive again!
2	T:	eh cool (d'y' know)
3 →		[where you are right now?]
4 → Y:		[eh? Where are you?] (0.4) eh ((glances across)) where are you?
5	O:	I don't know either I'm back at (the square there)
6 → Y:		WHERE?
7	O:	there comes purple
8	T:	ah!
9	O:	eh!
10 → Y:		((bends across and back while saying)) I I'm coming where are
11		you? Oh there
12	T:	blue!
13	Y:	((spoken very fast)) I've got re- I see red I SEE RED I I'm coming to help you I've

14		got green under attack ((starts shooting))
15	O:	me too I'm shooting=
16	Y:	=eh? (but you said)
17	O:	shit
18	T:	he!
19	Y:	die you (damn)
20	?:	attention!
21 →T:		eh! Red is behind you
22 →O:		red is behind you (0.4)
23 →		Y: where? (.) ni- attention (.)

At the beginning of this excerpt, Oliver's avatar suddenly responds to his manipulations of the control after a period of immobility. Immediately, he makes public that he is once more an active player in the game. Now his position in the space becomes important. In order to "attack" their opponents effectively, the three have decided to "pack up" and pursue them. They need to assume strategic positions and coordinate their actions, and it is therefore crucial to know *where* they are with respect to each other, possible targets, and other hunters. In their approach they take advantage of the fact that they are distributed across a large distance in the electronic space, yet co-located in the physical space. Tom and Yves ask "where are you" (lines 2–4), but the answer is too vague to find Oliver. Yves's third request "WHERE?" (line 6) is cut short by the fact that Oliver discovers "purple" and is put on the spot (line 7). Shots are exchanged and help seems required. Yves, in one move, bends across, and glances at Oliver's screen (line 10). Having seen what Oliver sees, Yves is able to work out where he is. However, on his way he encounters first "red", then "green". He attacks "green" (line 14). What he fails to realise is that while he is busy shooting "green", "red" has moved behind him and is attacking him. Looking at a plan view on Oliver's screen the others notice and warn him (lines 21–23).

3.4.1 Analysis: Everyday Practices of Orientation and Spatial Grammars

Within physical environments, objects and people, and the environment itself, provide ample information about themselves. What we usually orient to in this informational field are their *affordances* (Gibson, 1986), that is, the things that we could do with, in or through them. The term refers to physical and interpretative constraints and possibilities that arise in our engagement with people, animals, objects and spaces. A door, for example, affords opening, but also leaning on (although we must be prepared for someone trying to open it from the outside). Which affordances we perceive at a certain moment in time depends on the situation.

97

The fact that the letters in the *Legible City* are permeable and afford passage, for example, is taken for granted when people steer by orienting to the LCD display of the map, while it is disregarded when they focus on reading the words made up by the letters.

With regard to interactions between people, face-to-face situations are also characterised by a rich array of interactional information that allows us to gauge information about other people's activities. Sociability can be discursive, but it is also an embodied phenomenon. Through our position in relation to others, our posture, movements, the direction, intensity and duration of our gaze, and other finely tuned embodied actions, we occupy a place in the encounter, where we make available to others what actions they can reasonably expect us to take (e.g. Ciolek and Kendon, 1980; Heath, 1986; Kendon, 1990; Robertson, 1997). Face-to-face situations thus afford the dynamic and flexible display of, for example, the degree of our involvement in the interaction, how we understand others' actions and our own in its context, whether we are listening or want to say something. This information also applies at a larger scale. Moving in public places, we routinely gauge information about who else is there and what their activities are, and weave our own actions into the flow – to avoid collisions, but also to see who we could talk to, how long we would have to wait for our turn if we were to join a queue, or where there is something to see (Sacks, 1992; Sudnow, 1972). Usually we have a whole host of clues that indicate *at a glance* "what sort of people" there are and "what they are doing", reaching from clothing to movements, gestures and facial expressions. We use this information to interpret and categorise what we see (Sacks, 1992). Sacks delineates the rules that govern this activity. For a person there are a number of categories that might apply. She can be a "female", "mother", "teenager", the "head of a queue", the "captain of a rowing team", and so on. How we choose categories depends on the context and the cluster of categories that apply in a particular situation. These clusters of categories are, in Sacks' terms, "membership categorisation devices" or MCDs. In an MCD – for example "family" – the different categories "mother", "father", "grandfather", etc. are mutually exclusive. Moreover, there is a "consistency rule" that implies that once a category and its MCD is chosen we tend to hear or see the surrounding talk, activities, or features as belonging to that MCD (unless explicitly stated otherwise). In mediated encounters, such as those in *Labyrinthos*, the range of information relevant to our interaction with others and the environment is considerably impoverished and altered. Yet people manage to conduct orderly encounters. An examination of how this is achieved in *Labyrinthos* and the *Legible City* can provide some insight into which features of interaction between people should be represented in a more symbolic approach to visualising electronic environments.

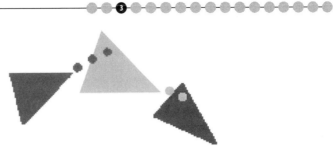

Figure 3.6   An attack on Yves.

3.4.2 The Hunter's Perspective: Transpositions of Everyday Practices

In bending across to see Oliver's screen in line 10 of the transcript, Yves rightly assumes that the space of the game is the same for everybody involved and thus projects a principle we routinely apply in our everyday actions into the electronic space. As a "hunter" in the game, Yves does, and in fact, needs, to take for granted that views from different positions in the game are interchangeable. The space *must* be the same for everyone, otherwise one would not be able to aim at targets. "Reciprocity of perspective" – the fact that if I were to change place with you, I would see what you see (Schutz, 1962, p. 183) – is necessarily reflected in the visual display of one's position in the space on the respective screens of the players. Yves exploits this fact. He bends across, and seeing what Oliver sees allows Yves to locate him on his own screen. If the game took place in physical space, Yves would not be able to put himself in Oliver's place so easily. Here he makes use of the affordances of the situation and transposes his knowledge of the interchangeability of perspectives without hesitation.

This "reciprocity of perspective" is one aspect of a more general principle of *intersubjectivity* that underpins interactions between people and between people and their material environment. What we say, perceive, or do is part and parcel of a world known in common (Schutz, 1962). In our actions, we assume that others know the world and the situation at hand in ways that are similar to how we know them. This includes people's distribution, appearance and activities in space. In the context of *Labyrinthos*, position, colour, shooting or not shooting are the only clues available to categorise people's activities within the frame of the game. However, this information is sufficient to allow the players to monitor the state of affairs. In lines 21–23, where Oliver and Tom spot Yves being attacked by Red, competence is enacted in a way that mirrors everyday practices of seeing. Oliver and Tom have switched to plan view and see that Yves (in the middle of Figure 3.6) is being attacked from behind his back.

Such an abstract, animated, real time plan view is a device usually unavailable to us. It is an affordance that exceeds everyday environmental conditions. Oliver and Tom transpose and combine competencies of categorising people ("hunter", "target", "us" and "them") drawing on a minimal and abstracted set of clues, and their knowledge of real-world plan views to fit in with the environmental affordances of the game.

The example of Yves's, Thomas's and Oliver's use of different screens and abstract, animated, real-time plan views illustrates how everyday practices of seeing and categorising people's activities can survive in an environment where only a fraction of the interactional information usually available is present.

3.4.3 The Legible City: Grammars of Perception

Practices of categorising people and their activities have their equivalent in practices of categorising the material arrangements that we encounter. The urban metaphor employed in the design of the *Legible City* provides a frame for categorisations that people initially transplant quite literally to guide their movement and orientation within the "cities". People stick to roads and look out for familiar landmarks. However, through the (accidental) experience of some of the physical and structural laws in the cities, and the letters' invitation to literally read "between the lines", this categorisation framework is altered to fit the engagement with the altered affordances of the *Legible City*.

In practice interpretation and perception are *one, situated* activity (Wittgenstein, 1953/1997; Gibson, 1986; Coulter and Parsons, 1991). To see and act, people draw upon the resources provided within the electronic environment and its artistic context to develop a "grammar" for perception (Wittgenstein, 1953/1997). Transpositions of everyday practices of movement and orientation – such as cycling through letter-buildings – reveal the creativity that is inherent in people's efforts to make sense of/perceive the affordances of a new environment.

The design of structures or objects is inextricably tied to such practical perceptual grammars. In ways that are similar to the intelligibility of texts, the legibility of the material world is "both a feature and an outcome of a set of practices inscribed and evident in, and relied upon" by designers of the material environment (Jayussi, 1991). The categories that we employ with regard to the material world are intersubjective – albeit in a mediated fashion. Living in the physical world we assume that architects, landscape designers, and urban planners are members of the world known in common and likely to have imbued their designs with features that are known to us all. They, on the other hand, may apply their creativity, but part of their professional skill is to know, for example, what features make a door recognisably a door, and when those limits are exceeded, leading people to mistake a glass door for air and hurt themselves, for example (Gibson, 1986, p. 142); or when people are likely not to see a door at all but a continuous wall. The designers of objects and spaces provide legible affordances and thus act at a distance (by anticipating and inscribing certain forms of engagement with these affordances). Together, the situated interpretative freedom we have with respect to the objects and spaces that we encounter, and the well-trodden trajectories of everyday practice that both designers and users rely upon, make for both the intelligibility and the flexibility and creativity of our relationship with the world.

3.5 Conclusion: Creating Intelligible Spaces

The observation of the actual use of electronic environments clearly illustrates that realism with a view to visual appearance, but also physical laws, and sensory access is not as critical as the "realists" within the virtual space designers' community suggest. The examples illustrate that the affordances of the electronic environment – with a view to both "material" structures, and people's activities within them – are interpreted with reference to the physical "world known in common" but submitted to review and learnt about in light of the experience of moving around in the environment. The crucial issue with regard to an exploration of architectural principles is that people need very little persuasion to adopt an urban metaphor or to extrapolate from what could potentially be seen from a physical world real-time plan view for their approach to the space. The letter-buildings in the *Legible City* are based on the original street plans of the respective real cities. But this is all there is that really is urban or "realistic". Equally, the perspective of the plan view in *Labyrinthos* may be similar to a real-world aerial view, but what is seen *in* it, is very different. Yet people readily applied and adjusted these metaphors. Given that so many of the rules of a perceptual grammar that one would expect to be part of these activities are relaxed, what is it about the *Legible City* or the plan view in *Labyrinthos* that makes it possible for people to transpose everyday practices of orientation to these environments? Spatial grammars provide some insight into this question and some inspiration for features that could be used to enhance the legibility of electronic environments. They indicate some possible avenues with a view to the design of large-scale electronic landscapes. E-scapes are likely to attract people who want to search for a world that suits their current interests. They therefore need to display some rudimentary information about a world that can be gauged at a glance, and/or some more detailed information on closer inspection. What would this information be and how could it be visualised? Some possible answers can be delineated by combining spatial grammars with the ways in which people creatively discover and define appropriate behaviour through reference to an environment's features:

- *Sociability.* If "what attracts people most ... is other people" this should motivate the visualisation of other people's movements in an e-scape. In order to make an e-scape that contains multiple different worlds a "place" itself, people's tendency to seek out the company of others suggests that it is not enough to display the number of people that have already entered a particular world. In order to make available how visitors distribute their interest in different worlds, it would be desirable to also visualise their movements around them. By making embodiments directional, visitors could see where other people are heading, where there is a crowd of people taking an interest in a specific world, or where there are some special interest worlds that only attract a small group of people. Allowing people to choose or create an individual avatar could increase the amount of information available in a way that is similar to how we express aspects of our identity through clothing.

- *Reciprocity of perspective.* In order to be able to coordinate actions, people need to be able to assume that others see the same space and the same objects as they do. But this does not mean that the principle must not be relaxed under any circumstances. It can be relaxed – as long as this is made available as a feature of the environment – or provided for in ways that deviate from familiar strategies. Based on the transpositions of everyday practices that build on the interchangability of perspective, it could be possible to provide:

  - an abstracted, animated, real-time plan view
  - a screenshot of "this is what I see from where I am"
  - a vehicle into which others can be invited to share a particular perspective onto a joint space (Murray, 1998).

- *Intersubjectivity.* Some of the spatial grammars outlined here explicitly draw upon commonsense knowledge of, for example, large-scale urban structures and seek to enhance their design by extrapolating from and refining already existing and commonly known features. These elements could be used to structure an electronic landscape. There have been attempts to introduce Lynch's structural features into the design of visualisations of information (Benford et al., 1996). Benford et al. introduce, for example, edges (a plane that separates two areas). However, because these are introduced as *additional*, separate features, rather than emergent characteristics of the overall structure, this clutters the environment rather than contributes to its legibility. In order for Lynch's (or Alexander's) patterns to be useful in the visualisation of information, they have to emerge from the distribution and appearance of information in the space.

More generally, there are two different ways in which an electronic landscape could be realised. The first is static – the number of worlds, their appearance, and the visualisation of information about them would be determined before construction, and people would be allowed in after completion. The other possibility is to provide a space that could be incrementally populated with worlds. The "metaverse", invented by Neal Stephenson in his novel "Snow Crash" (1992) is a fictitious cityscape that grows in such an organic fashion. In order to ensure the legibility of an environment based on the "metaverse", metaphor planning principles would have to be inherent in the tools given to people to add their own "buildings". Alexander's patterns and Lynch's structures could be a starting point for such principles. Equally, Hillier and Hanson's "Social Logic of Space" can be and has been used to build planning principles into the tools that generate an electronic environment (Bowers, 1995).

4

Navigating the Virtual Landscape: Coordinating the Shared Use of Space

Phillip Jeffrey and Gloria Mark

Collaborative virtual environments, such as multi-user domains (MUDs), chatrooms, or three-dimensional graphical environments, provide a common space for people to interact in, independent of geographical location. In this chapter we examine how the different metaphors used to represent two- and three-dimensional environments might influence interpersonal behaviours. We focus on behaviours related to navigation and positioning: (1) proxemics – the maintenance of personal space, (2) the signaling of private space and (3) the effects of crowding. We discover that the design of the three-dimensional space offers sociopetal spaces that encourage interaction, make clusters of actors easily visible and provide cues so that people maintain a sense of personal space. In both environments, adverse reactions to crowding occur. We suggest that differences in interpersonal behaviours may be influenced by embodiment (avatar) design features of the space and the number of other actors present. In a three-dimensional environment, these factors appear to influence navigation and positioning in the environment.

4.1 Introduction

Collaborative virtual environments (CVEs) have been attracting interest for their potential to support communication, collaboration and coordination of groups. We are already seeing cases where such environments are proving effective as shared information spaces for collaborative tasks, e.g. multi-user domains (MUDs) (Bruckman and Resnick, 1995) and graphical virtual worlds (Neal, 1997). A special case of CVEs employ a three-dimensional graphical representation of space in which users are represented as a figure (i.e. avatar). Examples of diverse approaches to these types of CVE designs includes the DIVE system (Fahlén et al.,

1993), MASSIVE (Greenhalgh and Benford, 1995b), and Active Worlds (http://www.activeworlds.com).

The advantage of using such systems is that group members located in different geographical places can therefore occupy the same virtual space, and thus have a common frame of reference for collaboration. Many CVEs, whether text-based or graphical, are synchronous, which offer actors the advantage of receiving immediate feedback; one can present one's position, field questions, and receive immediate answers. Such immediate feedback is useful for clarification of an issue and, it has been argued, may lead to group cohesiveness (Gomez et al., 1998). Users' interaction and navigation within a virtual space may be influenced by a variety of factors, among them, how the space is designed, the presence of other users, and the positioning of artefacts. This result was found in an empirical study involving the rearranging of artefacts in a virtual CVE room; the choice of targets was to some extent determined by other participants' behaviours (Hindmarsh et al., 1998).

The purpose of this chapter is to examine the question of how a three-dimensional representation of space in a CVE might, if at all, influence interaction among the participants. To answer this question, we observed interaction in two CVEs distinguished by how their space is represented; we contrasted interaction in a text-based chat environment that employs a three-dimensional representation of space, with a purely text-based chat environment. In this exploratory study we were particularly interested in how the design of space and the presence of others affect navigation and positioning. Our selection of interpersonal behaviours to observe was motivated by choosing those that concern spatial positioning and navigation among actors. This led us to choose behaviours that show how personal space is maintained, how privacy is indicated, and reactions to crowding. In the following, we provide a framework in which to understand the relevance of such types of social interaction in a CVE.

4.2 Shared Information Spaces

A CVE is a kind of shared information space. Bannon and Bødker (1997) describe that shared information spaces are characterised not only by the information present, but also by the interpretation and the meaning derived from it by the users who inhabit the environment. A digital library, chatroom, or even graphical virtual world must provide a meaningful context for collaborative and cooperative work. We view an information space as an environment such as the World Wide Web (WWW) that presents information to be interpreted to the user and that can be extracted or previewed based on how one navigates through the space. Enhancements to CVEs already enable the capability to link to web pages

(Fuchs et al., 1998), share virtual workspaces (Huxor, 1998), and even physical places (Benford et al., 1996).

4.2.1 Spatial Metaphors and Connotations

How the information is found and interpreted in such a space is important. Spatial metaphors have been shown to be valuable devices to aid navigation in virtual environments. The experience of the WWW has been described using the metaphor of a mansion, filled with rooms, continually expanding (Goldate, 1997). People have been found to use spatial metaphors while navigating the WWW for information, perceiving it as a landscape that they move through physically, or as navigation towards information (Maglio and Matlock, 1998). Maglio and Matlock (this volume) found in a later study that experienced and inexperienced users differed in their descriptions of their web experience. Both experts and novices used language representing physical movements and actions towards information (e.g. "go", "went") rather than simply passively receiving it. However, when language usage involved trajectory movement, experts perceived themselves as an active agent, navigating through the information space (i.e. "I *went into* this thing called Yahoo"). In contrast, beginners were more likely to see the web as the agent, with the information moving toward them (i.e. "It *brought me* to the Anthropology page"). Maglio and Matlock (this volume) suggest that these results indicate that WWW users view the virtual space within the familiar context of a physical space.

Other metaphors used in CVEs include a city metaphor applied in a MUD environment (Dieberger and Frank, 1998) and the results suggest that spatial metaphors can be helpful tools for navigation. Some chatroom environments use metaphors from the physical world such as a house or extended hallway, with different rooms having different functions or purposes. A "homepage" represents a personal location on the WWW, further reinforced with its location marker as an "address". Language associated with the WWW such as "surfing", "explorer", and "navigator", and with CVEs such as "teleporting" all convey the notion of movement and traversal through a virtual landscape. Dieberger (1995a) describes navigation in the information spaces of graphical-user interfaces and WWW hypertext in terms of "magic features" which provide shortcuts for increased efficiency. If the source of a metaphor is something in the physical world, then features such as teleportation that disrupt this metaphor may be seen to originate from a magical world.

The contextual cues of a place may suggest appropriate behaviour within that space. Dieberger (this volume) refers to these cues as social connotations. Certain behaviours that may be appropriate within the privacy of one's bedroom are forbidden in a public workplace. In addition, the nature of navigation may also be influenced by the social connotation conveyed by a place (Dieberger, this volume). The same space in fact may connote different interpretations of appropriate behaviour at different occasions, such as a community hall that may be used for a music concert, a wedding or for a local sports event. Spaces that don't provide what Harrison and Dourish (1996) refer to as a *sense of place* may adversely affect conversations and the participants' behaviour. Thus, it appears that the design of a CVE, and the cues it contains, can influence the nature of the interaction and movement through that space.

This idea is intuitively obvious when we think of physical environments, such as workplaces, which have different spatial layouts. Architects and interior designers have long been concerned with the spatial positioning of offices, interiors and public areas in designing environments for work. Not only can the interior layout influence the degree of interaction between employees, but it can also define the hierarchy within the workplace, and distinguish areas for work from those for socialisation. Even the placement of shared artefacts is crucial since they can provide peripheral awareness information about other people's activities (Heath and Luff, 1992a). Osmond (1957) classifies space as being sociopetal or sociofugal. Sociopetal spaces (i.e. a cafeteria) encourage interpersonal communication. Sociofugal spaces, such as a lobby waiting area, are designed to restrict or discourage social interaction. A working environment where people perceive the space as sociopetal should have expectations that social communication will take place.

Although we may exist in *space*, we actually refer to artefacts and architecture within the context of a *place*. Tuan (1977) believes that we navigate through space until we pause, at which point an awareness of our positioning with respect to artefacts transforms our location into a place. This perception is similar to that proposed by Altman and Zube (1989) who state that as individuals become more familiar with a space, they learn to associate meaning with it, and thus through experience, a space is perceived as a place.

4.2.2 Social Navigation

It may be that the perception of a space as a place is facilitated as interacting partners develop a shared understanding of the environment (Dieberger, this volume); this creates a dynamic process as interaction within a space fosters meaning. Social navigation has been described as navigation through collected information that is enabled due to the activity of others. Dieberger classifies social navigation as being direct or indirect. Direct social navigation involves active and direct interaction between users such as pointing out information required. Indirect social navigation is more passive and may involve recognising and identifying navigational cues left by users found in the information space.

In our definition, we believe that navigation within an information space such as a virtual environment could be considered "social navigation" when the presence of others within the shared space influence one's direction of movement or choice of position. Social navigation involves an awareness of other users who are currently present or who have been there in the past. This may involve the process of recognition of others; cues such as a username or unique personal identifiers signal familiarity. The user who is navigating within the environment is completing a goal-oriented task – finding others to interact with or seeking information from others. This view is similar to that proposed by Dourish and Chalmers (discussed in Harrison and Dourish, 1996) who describe that clusters of individuals serve as focal points to where people navigate. The type of environment may determine the type of questions asked, the behaviour that is appropriate, and how users will respond (Dieberger, this volume).

Many virtual environments are designed as spaces primarily intended for socialisation and interaction; in this context, navigation serves to find others. In the physical world, public spaces such as local pubs or neighbourhood parks are used as areas for meeting new people and reacquainting relationships with friends. Similar places may also be provided within virtual space. Thus, the process of socialisation with others in a shared space may involve both communicative as well as navigation behaviours.

4.2.3 Social Norms for Shared Spaces

Thus far we have discussed the notion of how one's perception and behaviour in a shared information space is affected by the presence of others. As the level of interaction increases, shared norms, values and expectations emerge in a group. Expectations about behaviour during interpersonal interaction exist as social guidelines. This is to ensure that group members behave in a regulated manner as participants within the group specifically, and more broadly, as members within an organisation or society (McCormick and Ilgen, 1987). Shared expectations of behaviour also have sanctions, which lead to uniformity in the behaviour of group members. These standards of behaviour can be commonly referred to as norms (Field and House, 1995).

Group norms are informal regulations that are usually unwritten and implied (Feldman, 1984). They have two main purposes: to create a frame of reference for understanding within the group, and to identify appropriate and inappropriate behaviour (Vecchio, 1997). Norms are not static but rather dynamic. Determinants such as the environment, one's culture, and the composition of the group will influence the emergence, acceptance and effectiveness of norms by the members (Goodman et al.,

1987). The existence of group norms is an important part in helping members feel a sense of integration within the group.

Carry-over behaviour, according to Feldman (1984), is one method that enables social conventions to develop within a workgroup. Individuals, through past experience as participants in other groups or similar working environments, are believed to transfer those previously learned conventions into their current group. Violations of social norms may produce conflict between the violator and the other group members, increase the level of interpersonal communication directed at the violator about appropriate behaviour, or result in dismissal from the group (Field and House, 1995).

Thus, social norms regulate behaviour within society as well as one's social group and play an important role in guiding one's own behaviour as well as shaping expectations about the behaviour of others. The members of a workgroup or social group have dual roles as societal members in the physical environment. Therefore, it is expected that conventions are not only transferred from group to group, but also are transferred from society to a group. It seems reasonable then that interpersonal behaviours and social conventions might transfer from experiences with the physical use of shared space to a virtual shared space. In fact we may view CVEs as "social spaces" as an awareness of other users may produce conditions that foster social conventions in order to regulate interactions. Virtual environments are still a novelty compared with face-to-face interaction. With any technological invention, users develop new usage conventions that are appropriate for the new technology by transferring over and modifying familiar metaphors (Carroll and Thomas, 1982). However, familiar norms such as when to answer a telephone call must be modified when using mobile phones, due to the often public nature of such conversations. Dix et al. (1998) suggest that success with a new media environment may be dependent on the success of transferring these norms.

Behavioural research on social interaction in CVEs has suggested that social conventions are formed and used as common communication systems in text-based MOOs (Dieberger, this volume; Bruckman, 1992; Raybourn, 1998), newsgroups (Baym, 1995), as well as in graphical environments (Becker and Mark, 1999; Jeffrey and Mark, 1998; Kauppinen et al., 1998). In the following, we introduce a set of interpersonal behaviours which people use to coordinate interaction in physical shared spaces. We then examine how they function in virtual environments.

Personal Space

Proxemics is the study of personal space, a field founded by Edward T. Hall (1966). It focuses on the societal use of space to attain comfortable conversational distances and obtain preferred levels of interpersonal involvement. The study of proxemics focuses on theories related to the distances expressed during social interaction. In this sense individuals are regarded as active participants within their environment, rather than passive observers. Personal space may be defined as an area with invisible boundaries surrounding an individual's body which functions as a comfort zone during interpersonal communication (Aiello, 1987; Knapp, 1978). Violations may result in adverse and emotional reactions (Altman and Vinsel, 1977).

According to the principle of proximity, individuals who are physically closer develop a stronger attraction to each other than when they are further apart (Vecchio, 1991). According to Hall (1996), one's preferred distance for comfortable communication has societal (contact vs non-contact), social (stranger vs friend) and conversational intimacy (business vs casual) determinants. Face-to-face communication is often seen as the ideal setting that computer-mediated forms of communication strive to emulate (Dix et al., 1998). Therefore, the question of whether a sense of personal space might also exist in CVEs, as it does in face-to-face interaction, was examined, keeping in mind that a sense of personal space in a CVE may be a function of the nature of the embodiment and degree of immersive experience.

Private Space

In social interaction, privacy is the selective control by individuals or groups, of personal information, the degree of interpersonal communication, and the level of social interaction (Altman, 1975; Westin, 1970). An imbalance results when one's perceived level of social interaction differs from one's optimal level. The need for group and individual privacy and its related social conventions are common throughout physical world societies, with studies showing that the preference for privacy, disclosure or social interaction is cultural and situation-dependent (Westin, 1970). This desire for private spaces for interaction is reflected in the design of CVEs, which provide password-protected private rooms or whisper commands, which create a private, shared communication space. Following this idea, we investigated how behaviours indicated a desire for a private space in a CVE.

Crowding

Crowding is a psychological perception characterised by feelings of personal space violations if one's current level of social interaction is higher than preferred (Altman, 1975). Stokols (1972) refers to social crowding as feelings of being crowded due to the presence or awareness of others, which can lead to stress. However, stress due to crowding was found to be lower when individuals received positive group feedback (Freedman et al., 1975) and where groups were in an atmosphere of getting to know each other rather than evaluating one another (Stokols and Resnick, 1975).

The feeling of crowding in virtual environments has been intentionally simulated to help people to overcome phobias (Strickland et al., 1997) which suggests that such a simulation can provoke genuine feelings of being crowded by others. A technical solution to support crowds in CVEs has been implemented in MASSIVE-2 (Benford et al., 1997), although the psychological effects have not been examined. We examined here how users react to crowding in CVEs.

The commonalities linking personal space, private space and crowding are related to people's shared use of space. Each of these social norms involves physical spaces that may be perceived as personal although interaction occurs within public environments. We now examine these behaviours within virtual space.

4.3 Methodological Approach and Research Setting

To examine the relationship of users in shared virtual spaces, we have explored two contrasting online, virtual environments: Active Worlds (AW)[1] and WebChat (WBS)[2] in order to examine social conventions that may exist in interaction and navigation. All environments are multi-user and are accessible from the Internet. The environments differ in terms of their means for navigation and their representation in space, which enabled us to detect differences that might be due to the design of the virtual space.

WBS is designed in a flat two-dimensional space using the spatial metaphor of a house, each with different "rooms" serving as a different chat environment (Figure 4.1). Together the rooms form what is called "a community". Communication is text-based.

AW is designed using the spatial metaphor of a three-dimensional physical world or landscape. Navigation occurs within and between "worlds" where users communicate with text and use graphical representations (i.e. avatars – see Section 4.4.3).

The basic functionality available for navigation, communication and representation in these virtual environments is:

- WBS: Communication is text based in an input box. All public messages appear in a large text area and individuals can alter their size and

---

[1] Copyright © 1997–2002 Activeworlds Corp. http://www.activeworlds.com
[2] Copyright © 1995–1998 Infosek Corporation, Inc. http://wbs.net

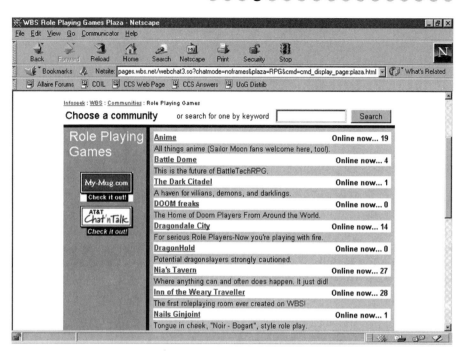

Figure 4.1   WBS: role-playing games chatrooms.

colour. Individuals are represented with user names and can attach pictures, images or WWW links to messages. Private messages can be sent using an internal e-mail message system or directly to the desired user during conversation. Private rooms can be created for private conversations. Socialising occurs within a room and individuals can easily navigate within and between rooms using the mouse.

- AW: Full-bodied avatars can walk and exhibit movements dependent on the particular world visited and one's membership status (i.e. citizen or tourist). Possible movements include waving, dancing, and fighting activated by mouse clicks. Avatars can navigate in three dimensions by using the arrow keys or the mouse. Communication is text based from the keyboard. All public messages appear in a scrollable window and may also appear above the avatar's head with the avatar's name for 30 seconds or until the next typed message appears, if this functionality is desired. Citizens can send private messages by clicking on the telegram icon to access the internal message system.

Approximately 50 hours of time was spent observing the two different online environments. The observations were performed in a period spanning September 1997 through November 1998, although not continuous. Online recording occurred in AW in order to ensure accurate data.

We were interested to what extent notions of space in the physical environment might transfer into a three-dimensional graphical virtual environment, and whether references to these notions also appear in a text-based chat environment. We coded the following behaviours: (1) Is a certain personal distance kept? (2) What happens when this distance is violated? (3) When people navigate through the environment, do they disturb others' personal space? (4) Does personal space exist in a primarily textual environment? (5) How do people express privacy? (6) How do people respond to environments that they perceive are crowded?

4.4 Observations

In comparing our observations, we find differences in how the social behaviours we examined are expressed within each virtual space. In each environment, such behaviours appear to be influenced by the available functionality for representation and communication. We describe our observations as follows.

4.4.1 Personal Space: Social Positioning

In the text environment of WBS, instances were rarely observed that indicate that users behaved as though they had a sense of personal space. The following is one example that occurred in a role-playing chatroom called "Inn of the Weary Traveller".

Steven: *edges closer and closer to DAYNA [another user] until within talking distance*hello … *Grin*

In contrast, behaviours involving personal space were regularly observed in AW. During interpersonal communication, avatars maintained a distinct personal distance. In areas with open spaces, such as the landing point in each world, which also functions as a common meeting place, the avatars of a number of users were present. Invasions of personal space occurred when the Observer (O) moved the avatar from a comfortable personal distance and positioned it face-to-face close to another (Figure 4.2). Reactions to personal space invasions were generally expressed through verbal or non-verbal behaviour and were observed to signal discomfort, as in the following example.

O met Laracat in the AlphaWorld supply dock getting building materials. O moved face-to-face and immediately Laracat moved back maintaining a slightly larger distance than had been previously observed and remarked:

Laracat: Actually … It's funny … but it does make me uncomfortable when another avatar gets "too close" in my avatar's face.

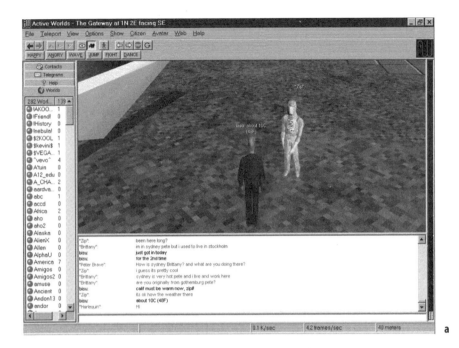

Figure 4.2 **(a)** Comfortable personal distance. **(b)** Personal space invasion.

O: [moves forward] Why?

Laracat: [moves back] Just does.

Laracat: This is a nice distance to keep ...

Laracat: [I backed up] the same way I'd back up if a "real" person got up that close ... someone I don't know very well.

On several occasions in AW, O experienced a personal space invasion. When O was teaching a user named *"trooper"* to fly, *"trooper"* passed through O's avatar and then apologised.

"trooper": Sorry about that ... you sure do speed up with the ctrl key!

Having an avatar navigate into one's personal space was unappreciated, as the comments below suggest:

Wepwawet: Something about personal space ... we carry the conventions of [real life] into AW.

22much: ... I need my personal space here.

Geophrey: Netiquette will be amended to include "personal space" in [virtual reality] I'm sure.

Dizzy: I try to walk around [avatars]. Courtesy you know.

Danaidae: [avatars] need [their] personal space too.

Blade: ... it feels wrong/strange like we stare at each other if we are [too] close don't you think?

Thus, we observed that within the three-dimensional graphical environment AW, individuals preferred to maintain a comfortable personal distance during conversation. When the O removed the personal distance and moved face-to-face in close proximity to another avatar, behavioural reactions indicated that the other participants realised their personal space had been violated. Individuals preferred to navigate around rather than through other avatars.

As AW uses a metaphor of three-dimensional space, it appears to produce a place conducive for behavioural conventions such as personal space to emerge. The AW observations parallel those found in physical shared spaces. Physical proximity plays a significant role in how workgroups communicate, collaborate and coordinate tasks (Citera, 1998). In face-to-face interpersonal communication, people change their positioning to maintain their personal space (Hall, 1966), and use non-verbal communication such as gestures and turn-taking for assistance in regulating conversation (Okada et al., 1994). Reactions to personal space invasions have been perceived in mediated environments as threatening (Persson, 1998; Meyrowitz, 1986).

There may also be a practical reason for adverse reactions to personal space invasions in AW. Participants used the first person perspective for communication and viewing the immediate surroundings. During face-to-face personal space invasions, one's viewpoint is obscured if using the first person perspective. This may explain negative reactions towards personal space invasions, namely, that standing in front of an avatar will block the viewpoint, similar to real life. Personal space may then affect people differently depending on their avatar perspective (i.e. first or third) or where their vision is primarily focused (i.e. viewscreen or text window).

Geophrey: ... when you stand in someone's face, you're taking up most of their viewing area.

We attribute the low referral to spatial behaviour in WBS to the text-based nature of the system. This behaviour may be due to the lack of a distinct spatial location provided for participants of textual environments such as chatrooms or MUDs (Dieberger, pers. comm.). A perception of personal space may also be due to the result of avatar embodiment. What it may mean is that personal space, as a non-verbal cue for communication, may not have an equivalent in a purely textual environment such as WBS. According to Fletcher (1997), non-verbal behaviours such as personal space and gestures complement one's communicative message and are ineffectively transferred in computer-mediated communication such as e-mail, the Internet or chat groups. This should not be surprising. In MUD studies of non-verbal communication (Masterson, 1996; Turkle, 1997) personal space seems to be redefined in terms of private places rather than the proxemic definition defined by Hall (1966) for physical world spaces. Therefore, it may be that personal space does in fact exist in text-based WBS, when we redefine it in terms of private areas of the metaphorical rooms.

4.4.2 Private Space: In the World but Not of It

In WBS, messages are typed into a chat-input window and appear immediately on the message screen. Functionality exists to send private messages and images to other users instantaneously, to leave messages in users' personal WBS e-mail box, or to create a private room. Often more people were present than those participating; this could be due to using ICQ, a private real-time chatting system simultaneously with WBS, or they may have been passive observers rather than active participants. Sometimes people would express in their tagline attached to their message, or through a public message, whether private messages are desired, as the following user's tagline indicated.

Lizabeth21: (no PMs [private messages] please!!!): I dislike private messages. Because there's nothing that anyone can say to me that can't be said in public

Lizabeth21: Plus in my experience, I only get nasty messages in PM ... not many have the guts to be crude, rude, crass in public

Similar to WBS, functionality in AW exists for citizens to send private messages to each other, but avatar positioning sometimes also indicated that a conversation was private. Avatars were observed positioned high above others watching the avatars below or two avatars were positioned face-to-face in close proximity. Other examples that may also be indications of privacy markers include avatars that were observed separated from the main gathering points either above ground or on the same plane. Attempts at communication usually resulted in non-responses or the avatars leaving to another location.

Our observations indicate that a desire for private spaces exists in virtual environments. In both environments, people used functionality to engage in private conversations and to create privacy markers. Westin (1970) classifies privacy into four different definitions: solitude, intimacy, reserve and anonymity. Solitude and intimacy may be most relevant to the environments observed. Westin defines solitude as choosing to separate oneself from observation by other people. In both environments this behaviour, referred to in CVE vernacular as "lurking", occurred as individuals observed the social interaction of others without participating themselves. In WBS, this was noticeable, as the population of the world was usually higher than the number of active participants:

vista-958: Thirty-five people in here and only 15 are talking.

Intimacy is commonly associated with close-knit friends or small workgroups. Personal messages in WBS and telegrams in AW provided a means for more intimate conversations. In AW, dyads and groups were observed face-to-face sometimes during conversation, creating, perhaps, a privacy marker by their avatar positioning. Thus people create private spaces in three-dimensional environments.

One reason for this privacy behaviour that we observed may be that people, especially new users, are trying to understand appropriate behaviours from watching others. By removing oneself from the main activity centre, one can become an observer, without the social pressure to interact with others.

4.4.3 Crowding: Navigation and Design Constraints

In each environment there was a limit on the number of users that could comfortably communicate, and in AW, navigate. Reaching these upper limits created technical and social problems. If the environment is perceived as crowded, individuals have a number of options available. They could remove themselves from the environment, limit the numbers of conversational partners in order to minimise the number of messages missed, or use direct, private methods of communication such as telegrams or personal messages.

Indicators in WBS list the most populated public rooms that can be immediately accessed. Communities are listed by current population, e.g. Thirtysomething, 61 or Inn of the Weary Traveller, 26. Communication is often disrupted due to crowding. Crowding is not only related to the number of people but also the size of messages or pictures that are sent. When there are too many people present in a room the server may be affected causing messages to first stall and then to rapidly speed past. This requires extra effort for the user who must scroll back to read missed messages.

In other instances, a large number of users made it difficult to be "heard". In a WBS chatroom with 137 users present, O repeatedly tried to initiate conversation with others present for 45 minutes without one reply. In both WBS and AW, individuals expressed displeasure when ignored, such as:

SneakinSam: I dont know what it is, but it happens all the time … WHY IN THE HECK DOES EVERYONE IGNORE ME?! oh well, i'll never know, adios.

In AW, users must not only attend to the flow of the text as in WBS, but must also be aware of the positioning of other avatars. Functionality exists that enable people to communicate with either the 12 or 50 nearest avatars. A large number of avatars concentrated in one's immediate vicinity led to a number of observable difficulties. The ability to effectively navigate without violating the personal space of others decreases significantly as the density of avatars increases. Again, it is extra effort for the users, some of whom report strategies on where to focus their attention:

Lixx Array: It's a two way thing for me … either chatting, or exploring/building … where my focus on the screen is.

Geophrey: When it's slow like it is now the chat window can be narrower. But when it gets busy I stretch so there's only a sliver for viewing.

When text was displayed above the head of each avatar (an option), then crowding of avatars made the text difficult to read since it overlapped. Monitoring one's own conversations, understanding the thread of other conversations, or maintaining conversations with more than one person became quite difficult with crowding. Concerning the central interaction area, one user expressed that she never stays there since it is too crowded.

In WBS, pictures that consumed a large area of the screen would cause difficulties for some users whose computers were unable to handle the increased bandwidth. In AW, some individuals would maximise the text screen and minimise the viewer screen in order to view more messages at one time in crowded environments.

Figure 4.3   Group conversation in AW.

The effect of crowding, a type of information overload, may have cognitive, technical, and visual implications. Messages streaming too fast are difficult to read; it is easy to miss personal messages. In both virtual worlds, a high volume of users and messages combined with a low baud modem or slow Internet browser resulted in a system slowdown or users being disconnected, which disrupted social interaction. Therefore, crowding made both navigation and communication within the environment more difficult:

Darrs: Bob don't know how those people talk in those crowded rooms.

4.4.4 Group Space: Positioning and Movement Within a Group

In WBS, group membership was indicated by a common thread of conversation. Similarly in AW, group membership was also indicated through common threads of conversation as well as sometimes the positioning of avatars (Figure 4.3). However, it was also observed that moving together or using the same motions conveyed group membership in the environment, e.g. simultaneously flying up and down in rhythm (i.e. bobbing vertically), walking together, dancing, or teleporting together. Such simultaneous movements served to create a weak "social boundary", separating this group from others.

Common language also created a form of social boundary. In AW, when O was speaking to *Stine*, a native Norwegian speaker, another disrupted the conversation by speaking to *Stine* in their native language. The shape of the group changed from a dyad to a triad, although O could not participate in the Norwegian conversation.

The face-to-face positioning of avatars indicated visually a group formation. We observed also in AW that when the avatars were positioned face-to-face, the relative distance between them would increase as group size increased. The physical shape was determined by group size: two avatars formed a line; three, a triangle; four, a diamond; and larger groups adopted a circle-shaped form. As additional members navigated into a group, group members would reposition, expanding the social space and relative personal space of the group.

Was this lack of embodiment in WBS compensated for in any way by the text medium? The answer seems to be that to some extent, users tried to portray embodiment through text. For example, participants created a form of virtual embodiment using self-portraits, filling out their user profile, or attaching links to homepages. And as mentioned, in role-playing chatrooms, users took on identities consistent with the themes.

4.4.5 Movement Through Space

In each virtual environment, users must first determine which particular world to enter. In WBS, worlds are grouped into categories, which contain related themes. Either one navigates through categories and themes to reach a room, for example, destinations and travel, or the user navigates directly to a community using a menu command. Users can also navigate room to room. Individuals sometimes would leave the room temporarily to navigate to another's homepage or to temporarily view pictures sent to them.

Although seldom occurring in WBS, using text to describe navigation occurred occasionally in role playing rooms. For example, in the WBS "Star Trek: Nexus Bar", text descriptions which were encased in asterisks indicated navigation, thoughts, and gestures.

Lady Milldorf2: … decides to leave the bar *walks along the wall towards the door*.

In AW, in contrast to using the first person view during communication and when scanning the surrounding area, third person view was used more for navigation and situations where it was important to see one's avatar, e.g.

"trooper": Talking is better in 1st and moving is better 3rd.

Danaidae: Only use third when checking out avatars or trying to position myself precisely.

Seeing oneself during navigation helps minimise personal space and group space violations of other avatars and provides a better view of what personal and group space boundaries are. In other words, it enables one to navigate around invisible boundaries rather than pass through other avatars. From user comments, it appears that they see this as impolite behaviour, and in fact a violation of personal space.

4.5 Summary and Conclusions: Coordinating the Shared Use of Space

Virtual information spaces are being designed along physical world spatial metaphors, e.g. digital libraries (Nilan, 1995), CVEs (Munro, 1998), and information spaces such as StackSpace and InfraSpace (Waterworth, 1997). They enable the user to visualise information and can provide an immersive environment for collaboration of work activities as physical objects are represented as virtual artefacts, as people become virtual embodiments and representations, and as workplaces become virtual landscapes. A key to the effective use of these spaces should therefore be that the information space is designed to be both meaningful and logically organised for the task.

Familiar spatial concepts may not be sufficient to guide navigation within these new forms of shared information spaces, even though they are found to be used (Goldate, 1997; Maglio and Matlock, 1998; Maglio and Matlock, this volume; Dieberger and Frank, 1998). Consistent with the spatial metaphor of a physical world, users walk through AW. However, the ability to teleport within and between worlds may represent navigation that deconstructs this spatial metaphor (Dieberger, 1995a). In WBS, it can also be argued that the teleport functionality in chatrooms, and the ability to navigate through the WWW and back is also inconsistent with a spatial layout of rooms.

The design of the two- and three-dimensional CVE spaces, in our opinion, helped guide the nature of the interaction. Navigation in WBS occurred mostly between chatrooms and the WWW rather than within a particular chat community. Information artefacts, such as user profile icons, contain selective personal information which enable others to immediately access and navigate to someone's personal home page or send e-mail. The degree to which this information was meaningful and navigable may have assisted users in developing a mental image of others that enriched conversation and facilitated social interaction. We observed users coming back after visiting another user's homepage or requesting others to accompany them to another room. Navigation often relied on the assistance of others, suggesting it was a collaborative effort (Waterworth, 1997).

The design of the virtual space in AW also influenced interaction by offering sociopetal spaces conducive for interaction (Osmond, 1957). In most worlds (i.e. divisions of the virtual space), the highest concentration of individuals was found in the landing point in each world, called "Ground Zero". Similar to communicative behaviour associated with a courtyard, individuals would congregate there. We also observed examples of worlds having a meeting place other than the "Ground Zero" location such as in a beach bar, which may also offer specific connotations for interaction.

In the two-dimensional space WBS, rather than providing an embodiment through visual forms, usernames and linked images seemed to provide a degree of embodiment. But we also see differences with respect to the portrayal of space. In contrast to the flat two-dimensional plane, a three-dimensional graphical environment conveys a landscape for interaction. As the user navigates through the space, the environment and artefacts change as one passes by. Also, one can change perspectives, from first person for communication purposes to third person for navigation. Distance perception exists: a small avatar or a small house is far away. Thus, in AW, the three-dimensional metaphor offers certain cues that influence users to behave and interact in a virtual space in ways that are different to how people interact with a two-dimensional virtual space metaphor.

These similarities to a real environment may translate into navigation playing a stronger role in a three-dimensional space for social interaction. In a two-dimensional space, conversation rather than movement is the primary focus. In the three-dimensional space, movement and conversation both play a role and differ in relevance depending on the user's task (e.g. house building vs group interaction). The visualisation of the three-dimensional space provides a visible awareness of others; a sense of their presence is not only based on conversation but also on their movement and positioning. Each user then maintains a visible location within the three-dimensional world. From a cognitive viewpoint, one can easily grasp the information of who is interacting with whom (within a close distance) simply by observing the clusters of avatars. In a two-dimensional chatroom, gaining this information requires more effort; one must observe the conversational threads. However, this ease of awareness breaks down when the avatars do not change position as they change conversation partners (Becker and Mark, 1999).

In a three-dimensional space, proximity of avatars may be a factor in determining who one converses with and whether others may enter a conversation (i.e. by signalling privacy). In a two-dimensional space, conversational partners are not linked by proximity. In addition, the three-dimensional landscape influenced specific behavioural actions (i.e. groups collectively viewing houses or dancing) and often entered into the conversation (e.g. speaking together about the view while suspended in space). In contrast to the more varied landscape, the rooms in WBS are fairly uniform.

In each environment, social conventions involving the use of the space exist. This was observed in AW from the personal distance separating interacting avatars, the reluctance of avatars to invade another's personal space, especially during navigation, the positioning of an avatar in the environment to indicate privacy, and in the adverse reactions towards avatars when their personal spaces were violated. In WBS, the conventions were less obvious, but some references in conversation were made by users concerning navigation and the personal space of other users. In addition, reactions to crowded environments occurred, illustrating the cognitive difficulties of interacting with large numbers of users.

The existence of social conventions may support Harrison and Dourish's (1996) notion of place. They consider *placeness* as an evolved social understanding of the type of behaviour and actions that are appropriate within a space. The architecture and inhabitants may have collectively functioned to enable conventions to emerge. Without the particular concept of place that developed, we would not have expected some of the conventions in AW to exist, such as personal space. Similarly, the theme chatrooms of WBS also appear to promote an idea of place, since conversations appropriate to the theme occurred in them. While both AW and WBS also have conventions that are more of a linguistic nature, such as the use of acronyms, AW appears to have additional conventions associated with an idea of a three-dimensional space.

Although we cannot draw strong conclusions from this exploratory study, we can suggest that such interpersonal behaviours may be influenced by factors such as the presence of an embodiment (avatar), expectations about the space, design features, and the presence of others. But as new forms of shared information spaces continue to emerge, corresponding new notions of placeness and appropriate behavioural conventions will also need to develop. Our basic results that shared virtual environments are regarded as social spaces, with corresponding socially acceptable behaviours, is also consistent with results found from studies of other virtual environments (Bruckman and Resnick, 1995; Turkle, 1997; Curtis, 1996). CVEs are an exciting new form of virtual communication, and we hope that our results can stimulate further research into their behavioural aspects.

Acknowledgements

We thank Andreas Dieberger, Kaisa Kauppinen, Alan Munro and Mike Robinson for their useful feedback during earlier drafts of this chapter. We thank Deborah Stacey for her generous support at the University of Guelph.

5

Experiential Design of Shared Information Spaces

John A. Waterworth, Andreas Lund and David Modjeska

5.1 Introduction: Bodies in Space

This chapter outlines an approach to designing information spaces that we call experiential design, and illustrates the approach with examples of our recent work. The main virtue of this approach is that it claims to draw on universal primitives in the way people understand things, events, relationships – and information. And because of this virtue, it naturally supports social navigation of information spaces. The basic idea of experiential design is that, because we are embodied beings, meaning ultimately resides in bodily experiences. We have evolved to act in the physical world, and how we are able to understand abstract information is derived from that capacity. If we design for embodiment, understanding comes free; this is the first major benefit of the approach.

The second major benefit of the experiential approach is this: since we all share the same evolutionary history and hence, bodily structures and potential for experiences, we share the same primitives for understanding information. This is what makes social interaction – and social navigation of information spaces – possible. If we design for embodiment, the potential for shared understanding comes free.

A third benefit of the approach is that it is also applicable to the design of mobile – or wearable – computing, a line of research currently being followed here in Umeå by Daniel Fällman (see Fällman, 2001). However, that aspect of designing for embodiment will not be discussed in detail here.

We experience the physical world as a three-dimensional space, with gravity holding our bodies, other people and things onto horizontal surfaces. To benefit from these characteristics, the most obvious idea is to create three-dimensional, spatial visualisations of information. The World Wide Web (web) is by far the most popular shared information space around, and an increasingly popular approach to the representation of information on the web is to use 3D rendering techniques to convey a sense of space and apparently solid structure. This means that information explorers can bring their innate skills for spatial navigation into play, in addition to those few sensori-motor abilities utilised by the familiar direct manipulation (WIMP) interface. However, because no one is designing the web, and because of the simple linking mechanisms underlying its evolution, there is no way to make sense of its structure as a whole. There can be no 3D representation capturing its whole structure which, as is implied by our approach, means that people simply cannot make sense of its structure as a whole.

However, space is powerful as a means of representing the structure of designed environments, such as personal file systems and the intranets of organisations. Personal environments can be happily represented as Personal Spaces – 3D structures apparently containing stored and current items of interest to the individual user (e.g. StackSpace; Waterworth, 1997).

In the following sections, we describe work to design information spaces that capitalise on the embodied nature of cognition. The virtual worlds constructed for these studies were based on the general approach to information spaces described by Waterworth (1996), which allows for alternative virtual realisations at three architectural levels:

- *structure* – the underlying information organisation
- *world model* – the interaction model or UI metaphor
- *user view* – the customised presentation for a particular audience or task.

5.2 Information Cities, Islands, Vehicles and Views

About 13 years ago, the idea of a virtual 3D Information City – a world model for presenting sets of information to tap people's skills in urban navigation, was raised in Singapore, itself a highly "wired" city aiming to deal largely in information in the future. A later development of the basic Info City idea was the "Information Islands" model for the Singapore National Computer Board's National Information Infrastructure Project; this work was carried out in 1993/94 and aspects of the model were published soon after (Waterworth, 1995, 1996; Waterworth and Singh, 1994). Again, this was a natural idea to arise on the self-styled "Intelligent Island" in close proximity to the giant archipelago of islands that is Indonesia.

Under the "Information Islands" world model, the world (through which the structure of a set of information is presented) is seen as a group of Archipelagos, each composed of Information Islands. Each Archipelago represents a set of broadly related entities, providing a clear, top-level classification of what is available in this world and where it is to be found – an overall orientation that is easily accessible to both the

Figure 5.1 Store Directory and Information Counter.

novice and the experienced user. Each major class of service or application exists as an Archipelago. Examples might be Entertainments, Government Services, Information Services, Communications, Medical, and Financial Services. Archipelagos are collections of Information Islands. The size of an Archipelago depends on the number (and size) of the Islands of which it is composed.

Each Island generally contains only one subclass of service. Users will become familiar with this world mostly by learning the location of Islands with the kinds of services they use or are interested in. Each Island contains one or more Buildings. Some Islands may be representations of the services offered by particular providers – Provider Islands. An example might be a particular information provider's Island located near other Information Services' Islands.

Each Building contains a set of information sources or services related to a particular topic or application focus. Examples might be Weather Building, Sports Building, Stocks and Shares Building. Buildings on a particular Island will have a distinctive appearance (shape, colour, graphics, text). All Buildings have common features including a Store Directory and an Information Counter (see Figure 5.1). The Store Directory allows users to browse and select from what is available in a Building. The Information Counter is a public agent that searches for information in response to requests from users.

An important part of interacting with this world of information is the exploration, selection and collection of items of interest to the individual user. These items may be services, information or particular configurations of applications. One common way of catering for this need for a personal selection from a public world (a set of public places) is to demarcate part of the world as personal, and allow the user to collect items and configure that private area. This is one of the key ideas behind the well-known Rooms concept (Henderson and Card, 1986). However, such an approach is limiting. Users must navigate to their own area frequently, bringing back items they want to collect, then venture out again into the world-at-large. In such a case, the disadvantages of a spatial metaphor can outweigh the advantages: because the users' personal space is part of the global information space, they frequently have to move around to switch between their own perspective and the higher levels of organisation. Use (which always involves a user) is confounded with level of structural organisation (which includes a user level). Use should be possible at any level, at any time. A private area at a particular location in the informational world may not be the best way of supporting individual customisation.

5.2.1 Vehicles with Views

To overcome these problems, the concept of private Vehicles was developed; these can be thought of as transparent, mobile, personal workspaces. They combine the idea of a private collection of information and configuration of services (customised workspace) with that of multi-level navigational device and customised information viewer. The user is always in his (or her) Vehicle, and therefore always has access to both public and private worlds. Items can be transferred between these two without navigating space. A key aspect of the model is that the user has a filtered way of looking at the same spatially-arranged world that occupies public space. The private "world" is actually a manipulable way of viewing rather than a specific place (cf. Nagel, 1986). It assumes that there is no one true view of the world, but always many possible ways of looking at things.

In the original Information Islands model, the user in his Vehicle had two Views of the world outside – a public "God's Eye" View that includes everything that is available, and a personal View showing only those items that the user has selected as of interest or use (see Figure 5.2). Although there are two Views, there is only one world. The private View and the God's Eye View are different perspectives on the same world; the former is filtered and limited, the latter is a complete display at the level of detail on which it is focused. The user can choose to have a split screen showing both Views simultaneously, or alternate between the two. Views

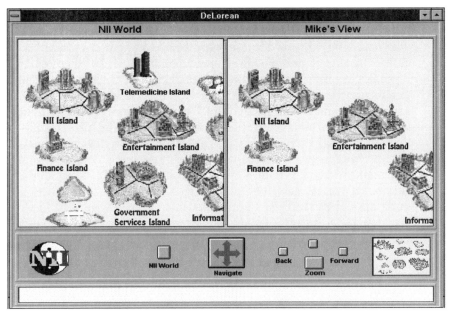

Figure 5.2 Two views of the same part of the world.

have some similarities with the idea of "Magic Lenses" (Fishkin and Stone, 1995). However, a key aspect of Views is that the 3D structural integrity of the world model is always maintained (the philosophy of "one world, many views").

Views become more interesting when applied in the social sphere. I may want to see only items visited by members of my research team recently. Or I might want to compare one View I have (or my agent has) compiled of interesting sites, with the View a colleague (or his agent) has collected. My View is a way of looking where only things of interest to me exist, and the same applies to him and his View. We can combine these two into another View that shows only those items that are of interest to both of us, or we can create a difference View that shows only those things chosen by only one of us. So the collection of public places that currently comprises cyberspace is filtered to give a socially-shareable and customisable View. This is arguably quite close to the way different groups and individuals hold different views of places such as cities in the physical world.

5.2.2 Parallel Worlds

Research on navigation in virtual spaces could be said to have begun with studies conducted by urban designers in the physical world. Classic research (Lynch, 1960) on urban legibility (imageability) concluded that the efficiency and enjoyment of residents can be enhanced by certain design elements arranged in a strongly hierarchical pattern – landmarks, paths, districts, nodes (focal points), and edges (boundaries). Psychological research confirms that people use hierarchical representation for spatial data (Chase, 1983; Stevens and Coupe, 1978). Later work analysed wayfinding – the conceptual aspect of navigation – into three iterative stages: mental mapping, route planning and plan execution (Passini, 1984). Lynch's work concerned primarily strategies to increase the effectiveness of mental mapping. Recent research has concluded that wayfinding design principles from the physical world often apply to large-scale virtual environments (Darken and Sibert, 1996a). In this work, global structure was recommended to support good wayfinding. We have used the Information Islands concept as a basis for several experiments examining a range of factors related to information visualisations based on such principles from urban design.

In developing a VR landscape to visualise hierarchical information, a large range of initial possibilities exist. In particular, there is always a discrepancy between semantic and spatial structure that must somehow be reconciled (McKnight et al., 1991). Our initial hypothesis was that varying the strength of spatial cueing would significantly affect searching performance and environmental perception. More specifically, we expected that more spatial cueing would result in better understanding of the spatial structure of the environment and its information objects. That is, spatial cues would aid navigation and prove more enjoyable. Accordingly, a series of three virtual worlds was designed, taking key points on a design continuum between text- and object-based representation of information structure. Each design applied the idea of Information Islands to visualise a filtered subset of a web index. The three worlds were maximally isomorphic in features (e.g. locations, sizes and text labels). The data set was chosen for general interest to experimental users and the research community. This data included about 1500 information items over seven levels of hierarchy, which allowed for both rich detail and computational tractability.

The first design was the most naturalistic, with coloured objects and greyscale labels. This design featured strong colour and lighting cues, and it was called the *Day World* for reference purposes (Figure 5.3 – see also colour plate 7). Virtual objects were laid out to maximise imageability according to Lynch's guidelines: islands, cities, neighbourhoods, and buildings ("districts"); mountains and rivers ("edges"); rivers, roads, and bridges ("paths"), and geometrical objects ("landmarks" or "nodes"). Objects at each level of scale were clustered around landmarks, according to sibling groups in the data hierarchy. Colour assignment grouped virtual buildings in neighbourhoods with common palettes, while ground and water objects had naturalistic colour. Text labelled each virtual

Figure 5.3   The Day World (*see also* colour plate 7).

object. To avoid information overload, the distance from which a text label was visible varied inversely with the label's depth (unimportance) in the data hierarchy. In general, the best point from which to survey a virtual data region was its centre. Avoiding indirect navigation, users were permitted to fly freely throughout the virtual worlds, or to use a shortcut gesture to fly directly to interesting objects. Navigationally indirect features such as elevators and hallways were avoided.

At the midpoint of the design continuum between object- and text-based representation of information structure, the *Dusk World* resembles the Day World with changes in colouring (Figure 5.4). In the Dusk World, virtual objects are desaturated 90% (as in twilight) and semi-transparent. Text labels, however, are shown in bright, saturated colours (like neon signs), and grouped according to sibling relationships in the data hierarchy. The design is intended to offer the benefit of some optical illusions, where perception varies between modes of perception, here object- and text-based.

At the textual end of the design continuum lies the *Night World* (Figure 5.5). This world is like the Dusk World without virtual objects. Here, the user moves in an abstract information space without absolute location or distance. This design was inspired by recent prototypes, including HotSauce and others, that draw on Rennison's work with *Galaxy of News* (Rennison, 1994). The Night World has no directional lighting, only brightly coloured text on a black background.

131

Figure 5.4   Dusk World.

Figure 5.5   Night World.

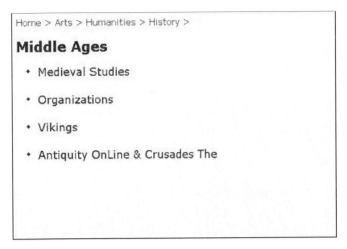

Figure 5.6 The hypertext interface.

In a first experiment, participants were first trained in the user interface in a sample world for 15 minutes. In each experimental world, participants then explored freely for a couple of minutes. They then performed a 20-minute "scavenger hunt": a participant received a series of paper cards, each showing the context and name of an information item in the virtual world. Participants were to find as many of the ten targets as possible in the available time. A participant could skip difficult targets. The hunt tested search performance, as well as serving to focus attention on the model worlds.

In general, self-reported sense of presence, ease of use, and enjoyment were highest for the Day World, and comparably lower for the Dusk World and the Night World. But world design did not affect search performance on the test task.

A second experiment compared the Day World with an equivalent hypertext interface (see Figure 5.6). This time, both self-reported ease of use and search performance were significantly higher for the hypertext interface, although the Day World was rated as more enjoyable. This surprising result led to a redesign of the Day World, as described in the next section. Performance with this improved 3D world was not significantly worse than with the hypertext interface. For more details of the study and results, see Modjeska and Waterworth (2000).

5.2.3 Bird's-Eye versus Fly-Through Views

Navigation can generally be viewed as purposeful movement, or transformation (Zuberec, 1994), using the metaphor that "information occupies 'space' through which readers 'travel' or 'move' ..." (McKnight et al., 1991, p. 67). The study reported below was designed to explore how user assets such as spatial ability affect navigation in a virtual world. Virtual worlds can be three-dimensional (3D) or they can be implemented as a series of two-dimensional (2D) birds-eye "snapshots" that can be traversed as if they were in 3D using operations such as panning and zooming interactively (i.e. 2.5D). Thus the study also sought to examine how the relationship between user assets such as spatial ability, and outcomes such as information exploration performance, are moderated or modified by the extent to which the virtual world is fully three-dimensional (i.e. 3D vs 2.5D).

Two different interface designs of the same world were used, one providing "fly-through" views and the other "map" views (see Figure 5.7 – see also colour plate 8; and Figure 5.8). Both applied the idea of Information Islands (Waterworth, 1996) to visualise a filtered subset of a web index. The two worlds were isomorphic in all features (e.g. object locations, sizes and labels). The data set was similar to that used in the early study, described in the previous section. The world was an abstract, urban, daylight landscape, with coloured objects, directional lighting and grey-scale labels. This design had strong colour and lighting cue; Lynch's (1960) guidelines were represented with more salience than in the earlier parallel worlds, partly as a result of applying the the CityScape algorithm (Keshkin and Vogelmann, 1997) for laying out hierarchical data nodes in a plane. See Modjeska (2000) for more details.

As in our previous experiments, users could navigate in either discrete or continuous fashion. A user could point-and-click to navigate up or down the data hierarchy, and between sibling data nodes. Users could also navigate continuously between items of interest, even if these items were separated by one or more levels of data hierarchy, or were not located on the same branch of the hierarchy.

The map-view design (Figure 5.8) used the same 3D world as the fly-though design. In the map-view, however, user navigation was restricted to zooming into and out of the model, as well as 2D translation or "panning" with reference to the ground plane. As in the studies described above, participants performed a search task and also gave subjective ratings of their experiences. This time, we also tested each participant's spatial ability before the trials.

The results showed that search performance was significantly better with the map-view than the fly-through design, as was self-rated efficiency. People with low spatial ability performed poorly with both designs. Taken together with our earlier comparison with hypertext, this study raises questions about the benefits of 3D interfaces for information visualisation. People with low spatial ability may be selectively disadvantaged when performing tasks within virtual environments. Nevertheless, where virtual environments are used, simplified movement using panning

Figure 5.7   The fly-through design (*see also* colour plate 8).

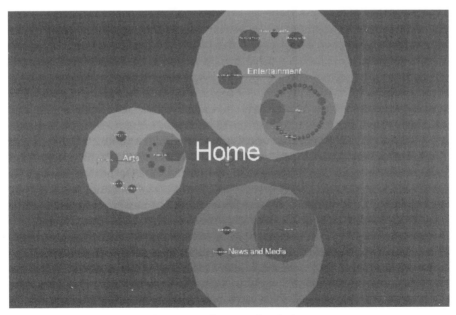

Figure 5.8   The map-view design.

135

and zooming in a 2.5D environment seems to assist people regardless of their level of spatial ability.

5.3 Evolution and Experiential Realism

The work with various versions of Information Islands attempted to capitalise on the kinds of man-made landscape that people find understandable. There is also much evidence that people prefer certain sorts of natural landscape (Zube et al., 1982), specifically, the African savannah. A prevalent explanation for this is that people evolved successfully in similar environments, and so find them intrinsically pleasing at an emotional level. Support for this evolutionary explanation comes from results showing that young children, wherever they live in the world, choose savannah-like landscapes in preference to all others. Adults, on the other hand, will also choose landscapes considered in their culture to be attractive – such as a panorama of Swedish forests and lakes – but will also retain a fondness for savannah-like landscapes (Balling and Falk, 1982). An implication is that cognition is guided by emotional responses to the environment; we find those environments pleasing in which we could function effectively as animals – that is, survive and reproduce successfully – and we also find them relatively easy to navigate and explore.

There is also evidence from evolutionary psychology that these two distinct activities, navigation and exploration, are facilitated by somewhat different collections of environmental features. Navigation would seem to require coherence and legibility (Lynch, 1960), whereas exploration is more of a response to complexity and mystery. How people react to mystery depends on what causes it – a degree of physical mystery raises preference scores for an environment and invites exploration, but social mystery usually reduces preference and tends to be equated with danger (Hertzog and Smith, 1988). The experiments described in the previous section looked only at navigation, and suggested that while some features of 3D spaces can aid navigation, 3D may not be optimal for navigation – even for people with good 3D spatial skills. Preferences for natural landscapes seem to reflect some combination of these factors. We are currently investigating the extent to which we can design information spaces to capitalise on evolutionarily-determined cognitive biases in particular types of environment.

Research in evolutionary psychology, relating the information processing characteristics of people to their evolutionary significance (see, e.g., Kaplan, 1987), is one strand of evidence supporting the overall claim that the evolutionary nature of our embodiment produces specific regularities in the way we tend to deal with information. In several publications over the last twenty years or so, linguist George Lakoff and philosopher Mark Johnson have presented a theory of meaning they call "experiential realism", which also suggests that the way humans make sense of their experiences is largely dependent on basic, bodily interactions with physical environments, as well as on social and cultural interactions with other humans (see for instance Lakoff, 1987; Johnson, 1987; Lakoff and Johnson, 1999). More specifically, they argue that abstract concepts are processed in terms of metaphorical relationships to experiences in physical environments.

Consider for instance the concept of relevance. Although relevance is an abstract concept in the sense that we never can see it, hear it or touch it, we think and talk about relevance without difficulty. The main thrust of Lakoff and Johnson's argument is that we can do so because humans have a capability for unconsciously making sense of relevance – and other abstract concepts – by means of conceptualisation in terms of other less abstract concepts. Consider for instance the following sentences: (1) 'A central issue concerns the role of inheritance.' (2) 'Of peripheral interest for our purposes is the recent development in China.'

These sentences are examples of how we actually talk and think about relevance, and seem unremarkable. However, a closer examination shows that relevance in these sentences is construed as something spatial, something that can be more or less central in relation to an observer. This is just one example of metaphorical projection, where we project unconsciously from that of which we have concrete experience, to concepts of a more abstract kind. Similar projections are pervasive in everyday language and thought.

The capacity for doing this kind of projection is, according to Lakoff and Johnson, based on our recurrent bodily and perceptual interactions with the physical and social world that surrounds us. Our constant bodily interaction with the physical world is embodied as image schemata, which are recurrent structures of our experience, based on the evolutionarily-determined nature of our bodies.

5.3.1 Designing Experientially-Real Information Landscapes

One of our recent approaches to information landscape design (Lund and Waterworth, 1998; Lund and Wiberg, 2001), based on this experiential realist account of meaning rather than the usual objectivist cognitivism of the traditional "mental model" approach, rests on the fundamental premise that *to design HCI is to design the conditions for possible users' experiences*. Taking an experiential realist view of interface design suggests that a meaningful interface is one that is experienced in a way that supports the metaphoric projection of image schemata. If the experientialist designer is primarily a creator of user experiences, the traditional interface designer is primarily a communicator of mental models, using metaphor as a useful device.

We are not arguing that all traditional interface metaphors should be replaced, but we do suggest that for several application areas – and these are areas that are at the forefront of current HCI research and development – an experiential approach to HCI design may be more appropriate. A notable example is that of information visualisation and exploration. If we revisit the Information Islands interface wearing our experiential realist sunglasses, we see that what matters is not so much the metaphor itself, as the experiential features we chose to take from the real world and incorporate in the virtual.

In adopting the experiential realist approach, a valuable source of design insights is that of language. How do users talk about their experiences? Utterances can be gathered at two stages of the design process: user requirements analysis early on and, later, as corroboration that a particular design is producing the kind of experiences the designer intended. It could be argued that we cannot effectively describe experiences with words, but, as Samuel Beckett remarked, they are all we have. The approach to understanding these words is somewhat akin to psychoanalysis; we are looking for the unconscious structures (image schemata) that lie behind the chosen way of describing an experience.

The traditional approach to HCI design uses metaphor to communicate the functionality of the system to the user. The designer draws on users' experiences in another domain to assist their understanding of the system. As Erickson (1990) has pointed out, this implies that designers know what the system really is. Despite its problems this approach has been successful in encouraging the widespread use of computers, at least for certain classes of application. The experiential realist approach to design also draws on users' prior experiences, but there are several fundamental differences. Firstly, for the traditional perspective, metaphors are useful (usually) but not essential. A traditional user interface metaphor can always be paraphrased into a literal interface. From the experiential realist perspective, however, metaphoric projection is essential to the way people make sense of the world, including a user interface. Secondly, that metaphoric projection is essential to sense-making does not mean that we live in a world of metaphors. If we design from an experiential realist perspective, this does not mean that the interface need be a virtual world of metaphoric objects. Such a world is more likely to be the outcome of the traditional approach. Experiential realism can, however, provide the basic elements of a natural and flexible HCI design pattern language (cf. Alexander et al., 1977).

This approach has its critics. Although he recognises some merits of experiential realism, Coyne (1995), for example, claims that Lakoff and Johnson put too strong an emphasis on the primacy of bodily experience and that there are non-embodied and non-spatial uses of concepts like containment and balance. However, Coyne's criticism seems to illustrate, rather than contradict, Lakoff and Johnson's main point; that is, that we project our spatial experiences (embodied as image schemata) to abstract, non-spatial domains of experience.

5.3.2 SchemaSpace: An Experiential Realist Environment

How should a personal information space (Waterworth, 1997) be designed? If we try to answer the question from an experiential realist point of view we first have to reformulate the question as: *what kind of experiences does the user want to get from the interface*? By posing the question this way we put emphasis both on the designer's role as a creator of meaningful experiences and on the role of the user interface as a source of meaningful experiences.

The intention of SchemaSpace was to design a personal information space in such a way that it allows the user to have four different kinds of experiences that each informs the user about different qualitative aspects of the information:

- *Distinctiveness* – which of the information references belong together, for example, fall under the same subject or category?
- *Quantity* – how does the number of references in a subcollection compare to other subcollections found in the information space?
- *Relevance* – given that a collection of information references belong together, of what relevance is each individual reference in relation to the subject or category?
- *Connectedness* – how do different subcollections of references relate to each other?

A vital step in the design process is to identify image schemata that are associated with the qualitative aspects of the information space we want the user to experience. This identification is by no means arbitrary: on the contrary, it ought to be informed by empirical enquiries.

Distinctiveness Through Containment

In the particular instance of SchemaSpace pictured here, we have about three hundred different web-references to information on very disparate subjects, ranging from modern literature, via architecture, to computer graphics. Even such a relatively small collection calls for some kind of categorisation, a way to organise and order the information in subcollections consisting of references belonging to the same category. Put differently, we have to provide for the possibilities of experiencing *distinctiveness*, that is, an experience which informs the user that some information references are in some respect different from other references. In order to provide such an experience we have to identify an image schema that is

139

involved in our general understanding of ordering objects and activities in our everyday life.

Our encounter with containment and boundedness is one of the most pervasive features of our bodily experience. We are intimately aware of our bodies as three-dimensional containers into which we put certain things and out of which other things emerge. Not only are we containers ourselves, but our everyday activities in general – and ordering activities specifically – often involve containment in some respect: we live in containers (houses, shelters, etc.), we organise objects by putting them in different containers. We travel in containers, often in the company of others. Our frequent bodily experiences of physical boundedness constitute an experiential basis for a *container schema*.

One plausible way of providing for the experience of distinctiveness is to present the information references that belong together in a way that encourages metaphoric projection of the container schema. There are countless ways of visualising containment, and folders and rooms are probably the most familiar user interface containers. However, in our design of SchemaSpace we have as much as possible avoided elements which are – like folders and rooms – heavily metaphorically laden, in order to stress the experiential realist features of SchemaSpace. The elements of SchemaSpace consist largely of simple geometric shapes not closely associated with a specific source domain. We have chosen to visualise containment by means of semi-transparent cones (see Figure 5.9). A cone contains information references visualised by stacks of slices (based on StackSpace; Waterworth, 1997) each with a descriptive textual label. By using semi-transparency it is possible to see that a cone actually contains information references, and it is also apparent that they are bounded by the cone and are thus distinct from other references.

Quantity Through Verticality

Each cone contains a subcollection of the information references in SchemaSpace. Some of the subcollections will contain more or fewer references in comparison to other subcollections. Even though the cones are semi-transparent, viewed from a distance in the three-dimensional environment it will be difficult to judge the quantity of each cone. In order to provide for a meaningful experience of the quantity of each cone's contents we have to identify an image schema which is involved in our general understanding of quantity. Our basic experiences of quantity are closely associated with verticality (examples from Johnson, 1987).

Whenever we add *more* of a substance – say, water to a glass – the level goes *up*. When we add more objects to a pile, the level *rises*.

Figure 5.9   Distinctiveness through containment and quantity through verticality.

> Remove objects from the pile or water from the glass, and the level goes *down*.

Spatial experiences of the this kind constitute an experiential basis for a *verticality schema*, a schema which by means of metaphoric projection plays an important role in our understanding of non-spatial quantity. Our tendency to conceptualise quantity in terms of verticality reveals itself in everyday language used to talk about quantity:

> The crime rate kept *rising*. The number of books published *goes up and up* each year. The stock has *fallen* again. You'll get a *higher* interest rate with them. [...].

In our design we have tried to exploit this verticality aspect of quantity. As shown in Figure 5.9 the cones in SchemaSpace vary in height. The larger cones have a larger number of references inside compared to the shorter cones. Our intention has been to combine the container and the verticality schema in order not only to express quantity, but also to strengthen the experience of cones as containers of information references.

Degree of Relevance Through Centrality

As already mentioned, one of our goals has been to provide for the experience of distinctiveness. Even if a subcollection constitutes a unity by virtue of belonging to the same category or subject, different references within a subcollection may be of different importance or relevance in relation to that particular subject. As pointed out by Johnson (1987):

> our world radiates out from *our bodies* as perceptual centers from which we see, hear, touch, taste and smell our world.

We also have very basic spatial and physical experiences of centrality as a measure of importance and relevance. Not only is that which is near the centre (the body) within our perceptual reach, but we also experience our bodies as having a centre and periphery where the central parts (trunk, heart, etc.) are of greatest importance to our well-being and identity (Lakoff, 1987).

For a potential user of SchemaSpace to experience some references as more important and relevant in relation to other references within a cone, we exploit a *centre-periphery schema*, which has its experiential grounding in perceptual experiences of centrality mentioned above. As shown in Figure 5.10, stacks of information references are organised along an arc. In those cases where there are a lot of references within a cone, the arc will eventually be closed and form a circle centred around the vertical axis of the cone. Information references can, however, be placed at varying distances from the centre; that is, some references will perceptually be closer to the centre and some will be more peripheral (see stack to the right in Figure 5.10). Our goal with this arrangement is to invoke a metaphoric projection – on the part of the user – of the centre-periphery schema in order to experience those references that are perceptually central as conceptually central.

Connectedness Through Linkage

Finally, we want the user to experience that some subcollections of references are related to each other, even though they are distinct from each other. The link schema is often involved in our understanding of relations and connections of different kinds, not only physical connections, but also more abstract, non-physical connections like interpersonal relationships.

In SchemaSpace cones are connected with a path-like link if the subcollections contained in the cone are connected in some abstract way (see Figure 5.11). As with the centre-periphery example above, our goal with this arrangement is to provide the user with perceptual cues that

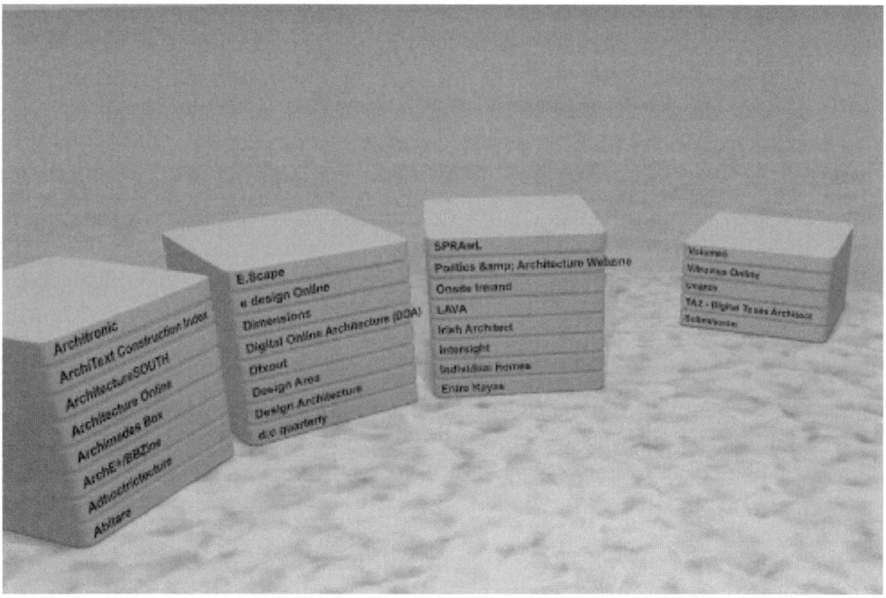

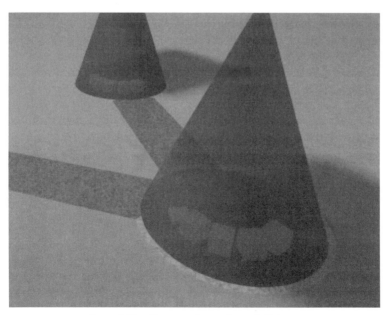

Figure 5.10 Degree of relevance through centrality.

Figure 5.11 Connectedness through linkage.

allow for structuring by means of projection of a certain schema, in this case the link schema. Of course, linking to show connectedness depends on some knowledge of what is connected and why, knowledge which is often lacking in constructing information spaces.

5.4 Experiential, Shared Visualisation of Events

Social navigation of information is often useful, as when someone directs us to information relevant to our current interests or needs. But when is it necessary? When do even contentedly-introverted and excessively self-reliant individuals find they must navigate information spaces with others? Perhaps only when scheduling of resource-dependent events is needed, for a work-related project schedule, for example. An understanding of the dynamic development of a project calls for a visualisation of events in the project (primarily meetings), resources related to events (people, documents, notes, etc), and event relationships. How should these be visualised?

5.4.1 Experiential Understanding of Time

I am *looking forward* to the summer vacation. Stop *looking back* and concentrate on what's *ahead* of you.

These linguistic expressions reveal the spatial-perceptual nature of everyday conceptualisations of time. Lakoff and Johnson (1999) refer to this conceptualisation as "The time orientation metaphor" (ibid., p. 140). As shown in the examples, time is spatially orientated in relation to an observer so that the future is in front and the past is behind. Consequently, the present is at the location of the observer. How is it that this particular orientation is the case in many languages and cultures rather than, say, an orientation where the future is to the left and the past to the right? The experiential realist explanation is that this particular way of conceptualising time is grounded in embodied, concrete interactions that pertain to temporal aspects of experience. For instance, what someone will encounter is typically in front of the person; what someone has encountered is typically behind the person; what someone is encountering is typically in the closest proximity to the person (ibid., p. 152).

The time orientation metaphor provides structure to make sense and talk about the temporal location of events and also to compare the immediacy of different events. However, orientation alone does not provide enough structure to account for the change of time. Lakoff and Johnson present two major metaphorical conceptualisations of time that surface in linguistic expressions: the moving time metaphor and the moving observer metaphor. Consider for instance the following two sentences:

(1) *The deadline is approaching.* (2) *We are approaching the deadline.* The sentences are very similar in that they both describe the decreasing distance between observers and an event (the deadline). However, a striking difference is that in the first sentence it is the time – or rather the event – that is moving in relation to the observer, whereas in the second sentence it is the observer that moves in relation to the event. Thus, both ways of conceptualising time involve the structure of spatial motion with the same time orientation, but differ in terms of what is figure and what is ground.

As is the case with time orientation, the reasons for conceptualising time using the structure of these two metaphors can – according to Lakoff and Johnson – be explained by the embodiment of recurrent experiences of what they refer to as "motion situations". For instance, the conception of time as a moving agent in relation to a fixed observer is partly grounded in recurrent experiences of moving objects in the visual field that approach the observer. Similarly, the conception of time as something spatially fixed that the observer moves in relation to correlates to the experience of moving the body in relation to fixed objects. In both types of conceptualisations, motion of – or in relation to – external objects stands for the "passage of time".

5.4.2 RoamViz: Visualising Sustained and Dynamic Projects

Mobile workers especially may benefit from a shared visualisation of events that occur in ongoing projects. In this context, we are primarily interested in events such as meetings. Meetings may be physical in the sense of face-to-face meeting but may also be virtual in the sense of being mediated by communication technology and involving physically remote participants. Events may also have explicit relationships through association with certain documents or other resources. And events have relationships by virtue of being temporally situated in relation to each other. In this section we present a design for event visualisation based on the experiential realist framework.

Our design, called RoamViz, is influenced by a recognition of the importance of co-location even in the context of mobile work. Consequently, it is intended to serve as a physical meeting place for making sense of otherwise dispersed meetings and events that occur in mobile project work. We have chosen a table-like device for our visualisation prototype. As shown in Figure 5.12, events are depicted as clusters of objects, laid out on a tabletop. For more details of RoamViz, see Lund and Wiberg (2001).

In the illustration in Figure 5.13, there has been an event at some point in time in the form of a presentation. A number of people (Jun, Bruce and Natasha) are connected to this event. Also linked to the event are a video

Figure 5.12   Conceptual design of RoamViz.

Figure 5.13   Events in RoamViz.

recording and some slide materials. The notion of linkage is also applied to visually express relations between events. Presentation clusters of event related objects are also linked to another cluster of event objects. This cluster represents an event that occurred some time prior to the presentation event and is related to the presentation by being a meeting to plan an agenda for the presentation.

Following the experiential realist account of different time conceptualisations, our visualisation design embodies the notion of time orientation. By introducing the chevron stripes at the margins of the interface we suggest a spatial direction for the events in order to make temporal order distinguishable.

RoamViz is based on the moving observer metaphor requiring an active user to "travel" across a project landscape of related events in order to experience time segments of the project. In addition to its value as an artefact for planning and conflict resolution, a table may be arranged in ways to invite and encourage social interaction (see Borghoff and Schlichter, 2000, for a discussion of the social role of different table arrangements). Our intention is to make the RoamViz table a computer enhanced, physical meeting place where project members can interact socially and navigate information that pertains to their work.

Of course, the mobile workers who might gather around the table from time to time would not want to carry a table with them on their travels! But the same shared visualisation could just as easily be displayed on a laptop PC, or even a PDA. The tabletop visualisation can be seen as an attempt to transform an abstract and cognitively demanding information navigation task into a concrete, perceptually rich and shared activity. This focus emphasises our view of embodiment as the foundation for shared signification.

In this first attempt to incorporate the dimension of time, we have not included other image schematic elements to convey the non-temporal relationships between displayed items. An obvious next step is to create a landscape akin to SchemaSpace on the tabletop, and include a representation of time passage as already described.

5.5 Conclusions

According to the experiential approach, the design of information landscapes and features can be based appropriately on notions of meaning as experience, rather than ideas of meaning as functionality conveyed through traditional HCI models. This is partly because we can never fully know what the function of shared information landscapes might be. But such a situation is biologically natural for us, since we don't know what the function of the natural world is.

Information spaces are a powerful way of presenting collections of information because they allow people to explore virtual worlds of information using cognitive processes similar to those with which they explore the real world, whether this is an individual activity or in groups. These cognitive processes have developed to be run unconsciously and to interfere minimally with conscious attention. The landscapes that encourage them are pleasing to us.

Views of spaces can serve as a powerful mechanism for social interaction because they can be compared, contrasted, shared and exchanged. Groups interacting in real time probably require a sense of co-presence in a shared space, and groups interacting asynchronously required a shared world of information to navigate (and explore). For coordinated activities, time must also be represented within a navigable information space.

Although we have all evolved with similar bodies and emotional responses to environments – responses that are indicative of their likely navigability – we are not all equally competent navigators. People in the lowest quartile of spatial ability have serious trouble navigating in 3D environments, including 3D virtual worlds. Even so, we believe that investigations of the influence of our shared evolutionary background on preference and performance in different environments may provide a rich seam of knowledge for our future work with the experiential design approach.

An argument is sometimes heard, along the lines of "if bodily experience guides our understanding, how can we ever not design experientially?". One answer is that we don't know what our bodies know; there are different types of knowledge. What "we" know is explicit, conscious, externalisable and individual. What our bodies know is implicit, often unconscious, not easily externalisable in words, and universal. If a theory claims to explain everyone's behaviour, that doesn't mean that everyone knows the theory and can apply it in design. We all know instinctively what makes a pleasant dwelling, but architects still design buildings in which nobody would like to live – and sometimes win prizes for them.

Experiential design captures basic, unconscious, animal reactions to physical environments and introduces them to shared virtual landscapes. We can design appropriate tools and environments, just as we can design churches, cinemas and houses, but we do not design societies or social behaviour, just as we did not design our own bodies. We are social (and spatial) by nature, not design. Having a body means that things, and information, can have meaning for us. We all have the same types of body, designed by evolution, and this allows us to share meanings. Bodily experience is the only universal medium for understanding.

Acknowledgements

Mark Chignell of the University of Toronto has contributed in many ways to this chapter, especially the experimental comparisons of alternative virtual worlds and views, without knowing it. Mikael Wiberg of Umeå University worked closely with Andreas Lund on the RoamViz concept. Eva Lindh Waterworth made several valuable suggestions to improve the chapter, many of which we have adopted.

6

GeoNotes: A Location-Based Information System for Public Spaces

Per Persson, Fredrik Espinoza, Petra Fagerberg,
Anna Sandin and Rickard Cöster

6.1 Introduction

The basic idea behind location-based information systems is to connect information pieces to positions in outdoor or indoor space. Through position technologies such as Global Positioning System (GPS), GSM positioning, Wireless LAN positioning or Bluetooth positioning, the system keeps track of where a terminal (and its user) is located in space. Via his terminal, the user is allowed to enter/upload information, to which the system automatically allocates a latitude–longitude coordinate. Later, the same user, or some other user, can access that information (again via their wirelessly connected terminals) when they enter the place. Although the digital information is stored on a remote server away from the actual location, the position technology and the mobile terminals give users the impression that information is actually "attached" to the place where the user is. In this way, location-based information systems create user experiences similar to those of Post-its, graffiti and public signs and posters. In both cases, an information space is "superimposed" on indoor/outdoor space.

Quite a few systems have been working with this basic concept over the last five years within the fields of augmented reality, wearable and ubiquitous computing (Abowd et al., 1997; Broadbent and Marti, 1997; Burrell and Gay, 2001; Cheverest et al., 2000; Caswell and Debaty, 2000; Leonhardi et al., 1999; Marmasse and Schmandt, 2000; Pascoe, 1997). Some have used goggles as access medium (Rekimoto and Ayatsuka, 1998). Most, however, work with hand-held devices that may not provide the same stunning and spectacular visual effects, but still preserve the basic functionality.

All the same, none of this research has directly addressed the social and navigational implications of location-based information systems. If we allow all users to author and access others' digital annotations without restriction, a rich information space will be created, but information overload will become a problem. In similar ways to the World Wide Web, we must design navigational tools to search, filter and sort information according to users' information needs. In contrast to the web, however, location-based information will be superimposed on the real, physical world. Authoring and accessing information will not take place in offices and homes, but rather in *public spaces*, including streets, squares, pubs, public transportation, churches, cafés, galleries, malls and libraries. Potentially, the ways in which information is produced and consumed will be transformed by the spatial context. Equally true, peoples' understanding of (public) space will be affected by the overlaid information. We will describe a fully implemented system – GeoNotes – that takes a step in this direction.

First, we describe the functions of analog location-based information systems such as post-its, graffiti, signs and posters. Then we describe the interaction design of GeoNotes.[1] Finally, we explain the technical implementation of the system.

6.2 Analogue Location-Based Information Systems in Public Spaces

Location-based information systems are not a new phenomenon. Since the cave-paintings 30,000 years ago, humans have annotated space with imagery, figures and text, and human societies have developed technologies to support this, for example, graffiti, posters, billboards, neon signs and paper post-its. Although digital location-based information systems need not slavishly replicate the features of their analog counterparts, they may offer design inspirations.

On a *physical* level, analog annotation technologies adhere to surfaces in varying degrees. Glue, pins, fridge magnets, ink and paint are perhaps the most common ways of accomplishing this, with different endurance performances. Some stay put for centuries (paint and carvings) while others wither and disappear quickly (messages on a sandy beach or ink in the rain). Some surfaces are somewhat resistant to annotation. Textile materials, for instance, are not well compliant with post-it notes. In order to impede annotations, some public space surfaces such as house façades, metro wagons and buses are even manufactured in anti-graffiti, easy-to-clean materials.

---

[1] In Persson et al. (2001) and Espinoza et al. (2001) we describe earlier versions of the system.

Analogue annotation systems support different forms of media. Paper-based annotation systems, for instance, allows for text and still imagery. Neon signs and screen-based annotation systems support moving imagery in addition to that.

Sizing is pivotal since it determines the exactness of the placement of the annotation. A big poster, for instance, can be placed on a wall, but hardly on a mug or a piece of paper (cf. post-it notes). The smaller the annotation, the more exact its position in space.

On the other hand – and now we enter the *communicatory* dimensions of location-based information systems – large-scale annotations have a perceptual salience that attracts more attention in public environments. Size at daytime and neon lighting at night, augment the "sensory radius" within which an annotation is perceptible to passers-by. Small signs require careful attention to be detected. In some cases, a headline or an image captures our attention, but we have to approach the poster or sign in order to access its full content. In extreme cases, the overwhelming perceptual salience of a billboard or outdoor neon sign makes it difficult to steer clear of: it "pushes" itself onto the passers-by not unlike spam e-mails and directed marketing.

Since author and reader share the same spatial context, the message can refer to that context without loss of understanding, so called spatial *deixis*. For instance, attaching a Post-it note to a piece of paper with the text "Peter, would you please make 10 copies of this?/Angie" is perfectly comprehensible since the position of the annotation clarifies the reference of the word *this*. The more exact position of the annotation, the more authors can rely on deictic expressions. This, of course, also makes messages shorter and more economical.

It is also essential to point out that location-based annotations have many functions. Posters and signs may *inform* about events, activities, facts and authorities' decisions, but they may also *persuade* people to change ideologies or rethink their lives. Image- and text-based graffiti often makes political and philosophical statements. Commercial billboards and marketing encourage people to consume more or differently than they normally do. And classified advertisements connect buyers and sellers. Some annotations fulfil *aesthetic* functions, such as public art, paintings and some graffiti. Finally, location-based annotations also operate as effective *reminders* to oneself and others. In many cases, it is more efficient to direct reminders to places than to points in time (via, e.g., calendars and alarm clocks). A Post-it note on the door, for instance, reminds me to bring my keys in the exact right moment (exiting the apartment before I slam the door locked).

In addition to the physical and communicatory dimensions, *social* aspects determine how people annotate space and how those annotations are produced. The assumed reader affects the contents of an annotation. Post-it messages between peers, family members and colleagues take place in a shared understanding of one another's preferences, sense of humour, personality, tasks and daily routines. By exploiting and alluding to this shared context, messages can be short and yet expressive. In public spaces, the potential reader of the message may not be entirely clear, which forces the author to deal with more general subjects. Still, many places are assumed to attract a certain clientele. In Stockholm, billboard producers can expect a Swedish audience; in a mall, one can expect shoppers; and on a university campus, students and teachers will be the most likely reader of your message. In addition, since many places *physically* restrict access to large groups of people, target audiences can be clear (only family in my house, only students in the university library, only Nokia employees in Nokia facilities, only males in the gents' room). For sure, the placement of the annotation affects the subjects chosen and the opinions expressed.

To maximise visibility, annotations are often placed in passageways where it is known that many people (of the appropriate target audience) have to go through. Examples include entrances/exits of malls, stores and metro stations, as well as traffic-intense gateways and portals into and out of cities.

If the author's understanding of the reader affects the annotation, the opposite is equally true. In particular, the degree of the author's *anonymity* plays a role here, that is the extent to which readers can trace (or not trace) the unique identity of the author (Erickson and Kellogg, 2000). If an author is reassured that her identity will be maintained secret, she will not be morally or legally accountable for opinions expressed or statements made. Such situations can be liberating for many annotators since one can express what one feels, bring taboos and political incorrectness to the surface, joke about forbidden phenomena and criticise authorities – all without social reprimands. On the other hand, yielding accountability may also encourage racist and sexist statements, invoking social stereotypes and leading the way for criminality and abuse of power. For what it is worth, anonymity tends to unleash the society's "unconscious".

A softer form of anonymity involves anonymous signatures, in which the unique identity of the author is unknown but its repeated occurrence in several messages indicates the same source ("Mokaby was here").

With increasing risk of discovery – for example, through witnesses and handwriting analysis – turf taggers, graffiti writers and anonymous poster publishers will presumably become less daring and subversive. In a fully non-anonymous situation, the author's identity is clearly recognised which makes him subject to potential public criticism, counterarguments or even legal charges. One may need to defend statements made and beliefs expressed.

Of course, making one's views, attitudes, personality and preferences known in a public setting is not something people generally avoid. On the contrary, it is striven for. Humans are social animals with deep-going needs to show personal and social identity to others, and become recognised, accepted and respected for it. By articulating our attitudes to others, we "become" someone. By exhibiting what we think and are, we mark our group-belonging in terms of ethnicity, gender, religion, class, social status, sports clubs, communities, interests groups, political parties, music taste, etc. (Willis, 1990). Political demonstrations, manifestations, performance, public posters, information flyers or "legal" graffiti are ways in which people express their views not anonymously, but in a fully transparent and open way. In these cases, the author *wants* to be identified and recognised as something, in order to heighten the public's awareness concerning some issue. This relates not only to individuals but also to organisations, authorities, commercial players and interest groups. Public space is the most prominent arena to express what we are and stand for, not only through annotating space, but also through behaviour, clothing, hairstyles, jewellery and other consumer goods. By indulging in such "social exhibitionism" we hope not only to be recognised, but also that other people will give feedback in all sorts of ways, acknowledging our presence, identity and beliefs. Without some form of social feedback, opening up to the socio-public space will be a waste of energy. As we shall see shortly, allowing *all* users to express themselves in public space – as well as supporting feedback mechanisms on those expressions – have been leading design principles in the GeoNotes application.

If humans are social, this means not only that we express ourselves, but also that we are inquisitive about other people's lives, personalities and background. Private and celebrity gossiping is one expression of this *social curiosity*. Sometimes this urge is channeled through voyeurism (e.g. illicitly glancing at people in a street café), sometimes not (e.g. approaching people in bars and starting to talk to them). We are curious of other people and public annotations provide a window into the lives and world-views of others. A local bulletin board, for instance, may tell quite a lot about the neighbourhood and its inhabitants. Much of the attraction and pleasures of public spaces stems from the reciprocal tension between social exhibitionism and curiosity: one can see and be seen at the same time (Goffman, 1963).

Finally, the growing commercialisation of public space is a hotly debated political issue (Klein, 2000). There is concern that public space is taken over by commercial interests through messages and logos on billboards, buildings, streets, clothes, cars, and even in schools. *Branding* public space has become a multi-billion pound industry. To become visible in public space requires a substantial amount of marketing resources. Why are some allowed to "tag" the urban environment, but not others? Who and what forces are to decide about images, messages, logos and architecture in public space? What is the right balance between buyable and non-commercial public space? How can we provide space

155

for alternative players and messages? Underlying this political discussion is the assumption that public annotations affect not only our preferences and beliefs, but also the ways in which we act and behave. Although GeoNotes is certainly not the single answer, it provides a technology that puts the question under new light. It may even offer a balanced compromise between commercial players and organisations like *Reclaim-the-Streets*. Let us see how.

6.3 GeoNotes: Interaction Design

6.3.1 Mass-Annotations vs Professional Content Providers

Most digital annotation systems built so far, rely on content created by professional providers such as art institutions, museums, tourist organisations and business interests (Abowd et al., 1997; Broadbent and Marti, 1997; Cheverest et al., 2000; Caswell and Debaty, 2000; Marmasse and Schmandt, 2000). Relying on professional content providers, these systems run the risk of making the information formal, official and impersonal. Although some users are great fans of museums and art galleries, these domains are not part of the fabric of everyday life, and they do not involve friends, families, (potential) acquaintances or other interpersonal relationships. Moreover, professionally created information often tends to be "serious" and "utility oriented" in ways in which post-its, graffiti, tagging and posters are not. In those systems, the social, expressive and subversive functions of analog annotation technologies – described above – tend to be overlooked.

Another problem with professional content is that information easily becomes static. With large information spaces, maintaining and updating information is expensive and time consuming when relying on a few content providers. Since many users (and many information seeking situations) insist on information freshness, such an approach will eventually become untenable.

An alternative to this is to let information space free, allowing it to grow, expand and develop with its users. Usage will change the organisation of information space (Dieberger et al., 2000). Instead of making location-based information systems a vertical (one way) channel for information, by allowing and encouraging "ordinary" users to provide, update, remove and comment information, the information space will become more of a horizontal communication medium between users. In this scenario, all users can leave highly expressive traces in the system (and in the geography) for others to see, which will create *social awareness* (Dourish and Belotti, 1992). The information space overlaying physical space will become more social, reflecting the lives, concerns and social reality of the users in that space, rather than reflecting the views of some organisation or authority (cf. Klein, 2000).

This idea fundamentally affected the design of GeoNotes. All users are allowed to author as much content as they want. All content is accessible to all other users. There is no mechanism by which the author can restrict reading access to oneself or others. It is fully transparent system. Thus, it differs from systems such as GPS enabled *ComMotion* system (Marmasse and Schmandt, 2000) and the goggle system of Rekimoto and Ayatsuka (1998). Although both of these systems allow and encourage users' annotations, these are mainly directed to oneself as reminders and documents. The social aspect is lacking.

This radical transparency is not only a way to create more social user experiences. It is also a highly politically design decision, allowing digital information space to channel voices of anyone in a fully democratic way. In contrast to urban space, which is commercially and legally regulated as to who is allowed to annotate, GeoNotes grants all users equal status. GeoNotes is thus the equivalent of legalising graffiti, tags and posters, as well as forbidding anyone to make money on private property billboards. If you have access to a GeoNotes equipped mobile terminal, you have the same right to digitally "tag" your neighbourhood as any multi-billion pound transnational company. In physical urban space, such anarchy would devastate the architectural space of the city, leading to decadence, vandalism, wreckage and violence. With GeoNotes the anarchy – which is digital – can co-exist with the regulated and ordered city space – which is physical. In their experience of urban space, citizens can choose the one or the other (or, preferably, both).

This anarchic approach to information space sets heavy design requirements on the GeoNotes system. As the responsibility to structure GeoNotes information space is transferred from the information providers/authors to the information readers, readers will have to be provided with powerful tools in order to find information that is meaningful, up-to-date and relevant to their situation. Before outlining our solutions to this (section 6.3.4), we need to describe how authors create content in GeoNotes.

6.3.2 Authoring and Placing a GeoNote

In order to promote (en masse) annotations, a basic user requirement is that authoring and placing should be quick and easy. A GeoNote should be neither difficult nor time-consuming to produce, and the interface has to allow such spur-of-the-moment authoring in ergonomically uncomfortable and noisy mobile circumstances (cf. the Post-it note). At the same time, it should be filled with content that is meaningful and somewhat

Place Label: Coffee machine

This machine never works! Who is responsible for maintenance? If nothing happens soon, let's boycott and buy our coffee somewhere else!

Signature: per

Cancel   Place It

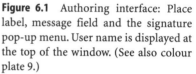

Figure 6.1 Authoring interface: Place label, message field and the signature pop-up menu. User name is displayed at the top of the window. (See also colour plate 9.)

structured, in order to support readers' navigation of them. We settled for three fields (Figure 6.1 – see also colour plate 9).

The message field contains the content. Although sound files, images, and multimedia – in principle – could be part of the annotation, GeoNotes' current version supports text input only. GeoNotes makes use of the available text input mechanism of the terminal (keyboard on PCs, or pen-based input modes of PDAs).

In addition, the user has to choose a signature (below the message field). As mentioned, the anonymity/identity recognition of the author is an important regulator in public spaces. We wanted to support the same kind of processes in GeoNotes. On the one hand, users can choose to be anonymous to other people in the system. If the user, via the signature pop-up menu, chooses 'Anonymous' other users cannot trace him back to his GeoNote (see discussion below, section 6.3.4). On the other hand, users are allowed to create their own signatures in order to regulate their anonymity to the readers. In some cases the identity and contact information of the author is essential, for example in advertisements ("www.hem.passagen.se/anna", or "Anna Sandin, telephone 070-633 15 07"). In others, for example digital graffiti, the identity of the creator needs to be recognised but not identified (e.g. "SkateGirl"). These signatures, which can be easily created via the signature pop-up menu, are preserved in the system and available every time the user authors a new GeoNote.

The final action of the author is to allocate a specific position for the GeoNote. In the ultimate system, users would just hold their device in vicinity of a door, bookshelf, bench, tree or even a mug – and press "place here". This would be equally exact as attaching post-it notes to small-scale objects, and the users' understanding of *here* would be automatically understood by the system. For several reasons this is not likely to happen.

First, the accuracy of the author's positioning technology may be rather low. In the current version of GeoNotes, for instance, our W-LAN positioning gives quite rudimentary positioning data (even if refinement technologies such as base-station triangulation are employed) – see section 6.4. The radius of "here" is rather large. Even if the author had a millimetre-precision positioning system, we have to expect other users to be less fortunate depending on their terminals, type of wireless connection, software, etc. (In fact, as a full-fledged product, GeoNotes should allow the user to chose her positioning technology independent of the service.) In these cases, even if the author has accurately placed the GeoNote at, for instance, the handle on a door, a passing-by reader of that note may be equipped with a positioning technology with an accuracy as bad as 20 metres. Without some – by the reader understood – "connection" between the author's intended place and the GeoNote, its message may become incomprehensible and meaningless (e.g. words referring to the spatial surrounding like *this*, *here*, and *that*).

For these reasons, a *place label* is required for each GeoNote. Place labels provide a *semantic* coupling between the message of the GeoNote and the place where the author intended it to be attached, more or less independent of the positioning technology. Even though authors and readers carry crude position precision, the place label describes – in natural language – where the GeoNote is thought to rest. Position technology acts as rangefinder; the place label as a focuser.

A place label system could be implemented in several ways. José and Davies (1999) can be said to represent the formal approach in which the system creators systematise and organise space in addition to providing natural language labels (see also Burrell and Gay, 2001; Caswell and Debaty, 2000). By labelling rooms, corridors, elevators and buildings and specifying their spatial relations, the system administrators create a (formal) model of space. For instance, by defining inclusiveness, such a model can infer that "Engineering building" is found within "South Area", which in its turn is situated on "University Campus". Employing such tree-like, location-within-location model, the GeoNotes system would know the spatial surroundings of an annotation.

In the context of GeoNotes, there are two major problems with this approach. First, the effort and work required to categorise and maintain such a structure is enormous (imagine describing street corners, bus-stops, park benches, doors and desks on a global scale). Even more

Figure 6.2 Choosing a place label. (See also colour plate 10.)

troublesome, however, is that place labels express the system administrators' view of space, not the users'. A description of a location in space can be quite subjective, depending on the users' situation, activity and even socio-cultural-personal background. Thus, to the greatest possible extent, users themselves should be able to provide the place labels.

In GeoNotes, place labels are provided by the author (before entering the authoring interface – Figure 6.2 and colour plate 10). She can define a new place label in any way she likes in order to provide the maximum clarity in connecting the GeoNote to its intended position. We expect users to create all sorts of place labels, formal as well as personal (e.g. "the ugly blue door").

In addition to creating new place labels, GeoNotes supports *label sharing*. Label sharing means that labels for a given place are stored in the system and may be reused by other authors of GeoNotes. When a user begins to author a GeoNote, the system collects all place labels that earlier authors have created (for that position) and displays them in a list (Figure 6.2). Although authors are free to create their own place label, they may save time if they can find an appropriate ready-made place label. Label sharing also allows users to get a sense of how other users appreciate and interpret a given place. How such traces of others influence authors' behaviour and annotation activities is an interesting research problem that will have to be addressed in user studies.

Place label recycling also allows the system to sort out well-formulated and useful labels, from not-so useful or very personal labels. The list of available place labels will be sorted according to the number of times each label has been chosen (actually, only the top 10 labels will be displayed). This system encourages people to formulate useful place labels and creates a dynamic world of place labels that updates "automatically" if the physical place changes.

This system also allows place labels to become more exactly positioned over time. By letting the user choose only among the 10 most used labels, poorly positioned labels will "disappear" or be recreated again by another user at a more exact location to gain new popularity. A well-positioned range of place labels will therefore grow dynamically. In addition, place label sharing could enhance the positioning precision of a user's device. If Mr. Good Position authors a GeoNote and creates a new place label, Mrs. Bad Position can later place her GeoNote on that place label. Since the position of that place label has a precision by far exceeding the capabilities of Mrs. Bad Position's device, she is able to "take advantage" of Mr. Good Position's excellent position equipment.

Even more interestingly, the place label system is distinct from GeoNotes. Since place labels code real places that are not specific to the GeoNotes service, this means, in principle, that any location-based service can make use of them. The more usage the system is subjected to – through "global" label sharing across services – the more likely it is that the place labels it contains will be relevant, accurate and to the point for all services.

After these three steps, the author places the GeoNote (the "Place-it" button in Figure 6.1). It should be noted that the system does not allow the author to restrict reading access to his GeoNote. As an analogy with public space posters, his annotation is fully visible to all passers-by.

Finally, it is worth pointing out that the author and the GeoNote must share position at the time of placing. Users can only place GeoNotes "here". Supporting authoring from remote sites was discarded for one major reason: we wanted this to be a *location-based* annotation system. A major purpose of GeoNotes is to investigate how location-based information differs from non-location-based information, for example, the World Wide Web. Although a remotely authored GeoNote would have a position coordinate attached to it (chosen by the author via some map interface?), it would be difficult for the author to relate to the spatial context without being there. Instead, we wanted to investigate the consequences of a situation in which authors and readers of a message share the same space (but not time).[2]

---

[2] Instant messaging systems such as SMS and ICQ can thus be said to be the opposite of GeoNotes, In GeoNotes, authors and readers share space but not time, whereas SMS authors and readers share the same point in time (more or less), but not the same space.

Figure 6.3 GeoNotes reading interface. This GeoNote has received no comments. (See also colour plate 11.)

6.3.3 Social Feedback: Comments and Number of Readers

GeoNotes provide a channel of expressing one's views, opinions, and concerns in public space. As mentioned above, however, it is equally central to get implicit or explicit feedback on one's presence in public space: Was one's message received? How many received it? Was it recognised? Did it have the intended effects on the readers? Did people agree or disagree with the message?

We argued that if users of GeoNotes received answers to questions such as these, they would not only get a richer social experience from the system, but would be encouraged to author many GeoNotes and fill the system with information. We provided a number of feedback mechanisms.

GeoNotes allows users to comment other people's GeoNotes. Figure 6.3 shows the reading interface of a GeoNote (see also colour plate 11). Below the message and signature is indicated how many comments the note has and by clicking on the button the user is able to read those comments and contribute with a new one. The comments interface operates in similar ways to normal discussion group windows, with the signature and a time stamp attached to each comment. As with any GeoNote, all comments are publicly accessible and commentators can choose signature and/or anonymity. The author can choose to receive notifications every time a comment is placed at one of her GeoNotes. The comment function allows dialogues between users similar to those of toilet graffiti discussions. In order to avoid removing other users' comments, GeoNotes authors are not allowed to remove their GeoNote if comments are attached to it.

Other feedback mechanisms are more implicit. For each GeoNote, the system allows the reader to give button-based feedback at the bottom of the view interface (Figure 6.3). "Add to Favorites" means that the user "picks it up", stores it locally on the client and has instant access to it even though the client is not connected to the GeoNotes server. It implies that the reader finds this information piece interesting. "Blocking" a GeoNote means that the note will not again be visible for that reader. "Blocking the author" means that all GeoNotes created by its author will become invisible to the reader in the future. These three feedback mechanisms are primarily tools for the reader to regulate information overload and filter out "spam" GeoNotes as well as the senders of such spam. However, they are also used to promote social feedback to the author. GeoNotes allows users to access information about whether invited friends blocked their GeoNotes or added it to favourites (discussed in 6.3.4).

More implicit and anonymous feedback mechanisms are related to number of readers. Like any other user, authors can see how many readers any given GeoNote has had in the past (or per day).

6.3.4 GeoNotes Access

If we allow users to annotate digital space en masse and without restrictions, we may achieve a socially rich environment, but information space will become cluttered with unstructured information. How will users be able to find relevant and timely information in a system that has no central information designer? At a location with 5000 GeoNotes, how will the user be able to sort, filter and navigate this information space? If we allow GeoNotes to be 'pushed' to the mobile device when a user passes a place, how do we avoid irrelevant and disturbing notifications, and yet provide valuable and interesting GeoNotes? No location-based information system has addressed these navigational issues. For instance, the *Graffiti* system – based on Wireless LAN positioning with laptop computers as access terminals – enables users to annotate a university campus with virtual notes directed to friends and fellow students, but it provides little support for navigation (Burrell and Gay, 2001).

GeoNotes supports both *content-based* and *socially-based* access. In the content-based approach, the user focuses on the information content; words in a document, images in a film, the meaning or the topic of a book. In socially-based access, users search information based on the social context in which a given information piece is placed. Information seeking is then guided by questions such as:

- Who is the creator of this information?
- In what context was it created? Purpose? Genre? Organisational context? Cultural and historical context?
- Do I share taste, preferences, situation or world-view with the author?
- Is the author considered an authoritative, influential or otherwise powerful person?
- Has this information been recommended by someone whose expertise I trust?
- How many have read/seen this information and do I share taste, preferences, situation or world-view with these readers?
- ...

Such socially based information methods are much more common than we usually expect, not only in personal affairs but also in professional, commercial, cultural and academic life.

For content-based access, GeoNotes includes a search engine (Figure 6.4).

The search engine supports full text search of all GeoNotes fields and provides instant index updating. In order to support socially based access, GeoNotes employs techniques of social navigation and collaborative filtering. Automatically capturing the behaviour, actions and choices of unique users and then making this context information available to other users was an important requirement of the system. GeoNotes captures the following parameters:

- The identity of authors and commentators (unless their anonymous signature is used)
- The unique identity of readers
- The time stamp of reading, authoring and commenting
- The unique identity of readers adding a GeoNote to favourites, blocking a GeoNote or blocking a sender in the reading interface (Figure 6.3).

Although this information is available to the system, it is not, of course, immediately available to all users. As will be described in the following, GeoNotes balances carefully between promoting socially based access methods and social awareness on the one hand, and privacy and integrity

---

[3] For a technical description of how and where this information is stored, see section 6.4.

Figure 6.4 GeoNotes search interface.

on the other. Suffice to mention one general principle which governs some of the distribution of context information, namely that of *friends*. In general, the ways in which friends access films, music, documents, books, places, clubs, museums, events, etc. are pivotal in our navigation in everyday life since *we know their preferences, habits, and sometimes their intentions.* Irrespective of whether a person shares the same taste as his friend or not, the ways in which the friend has authored and accessed information are crucial since he can relate his own preferences with those of his buddy. If I share the taste of my friend, I can imitate his access behaviour. If I know that I do not share the taste of my friend, I know what information to stay away from. In both cases, the knowledge about the friends' preferences makes information about their access behavior valuable in the constant negotiation between me and information space.

In addition, since friends are *trusted*, users can be relatively sure that the context information made accessible to them will not be misused or taken advantage of. In similar ways to instant messaging systems such as ICQ, GeoNotes employs an invitation procedure in which each user accepts or declines requests from other users to become a friend. Only accepted users will have access to intimate information of my behavior in GeoNotes. The next section will describe exactly how this is solved in the system.

In addition to the parameter of content-based/socially-based access, GeoNotes also supports a number of *access modes*. Since the situation and information needs of a mobile user will shift abruptly, it is important to provide "pull", "push" as well as mixed modes of access. In an active search, the user formulates his information need, enters a search string and retrieves matching GeoNotes. Here the user actively "pulls" information. At the other extreme, "push" systems "throw" information at the user without any explicit request from the user's part. Notification-based systems such as telephones, messaging applications or reminder systems, force the user to interrupt his present activity and shift attention to the incoming message/information. If the information pushed is less relevant than the present activity, then disturbance is experienced. If the information pushed is experienced as more relevant than the present activity, the notification is experienced as efficient, making the user aware of something interesting that he otherwise would not have known. Such notifications may even create experiences of happy surprise.

In a mixed push/pull access mode, the user is paying attention to the search situation (he is not attending some other task), but he may not be actively searching. Since he may not be able to exactly formulate his information need, he *explores* the information space (Benyon and Höök, 1997). In this more "open" information search, the user is trying to come to grips with what he is looking for, and tends to be open for "suggestions" from the environment. For instance, shopping for clothes initially tends to be a rather open question, but by browsing stores, shelves and prices, consumers' understanding of their needs becomes more focused.

GeoNotes, we reasoned, required navigation tools that would allow the user to shift easily between "pull", "push" and "mixed" access mode. It is to the interfaces supporting these various access modes that we now turn.

Mixed Access Mode: Main Window

The primary purposes of GeoNotes' main window are to provide the portal to reading, writing, searching and profile functionalities of the system (Figure 6.5 – see also colour plate 12). Equally important however, is to provide the user with an at-a-glance overview of GeoNotes in space so that he can take "a closer look" if something appears interesting ("mixed" access mode). The main window lists all GeoNotes attached to the user's present position (except blocked GeoNotes – see above). The list of GeoNotes automatically updates as the user shifts location. The definition of "location", and thus the number of GeoNotes displayed in the list, is dependent of the precision of the position technology carried by the user. In the current version of GeoNotes, which relies on Wireless LAN positioning, a location shift will occur when the user shifts base-station access.

Each GeoNote is listed as a header, containing the compressed version of its content (signature, the beginning of the message, place label and

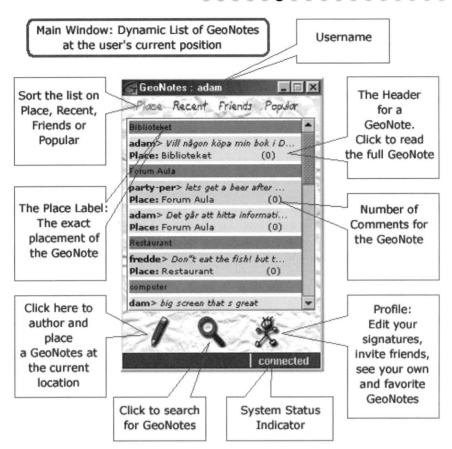

Figure 6.5 GeoNotes main window. (See also colour plate 12.)

number of comments it has received). If something feels interesting, clicking on a header in the list brings the user to the view interface of the individual GeoNote (Figure 6.3).

Due to its expected length (we expect a great number of GeoNotes for each location), the list of GeoNotes needs sorting mechanisms in addition to mere scrolling. Sorting mechanisms, available at the top GeoNotes main window, determine the order in which the GeoNotes are to be displayed in the list.

- *Place* (red tabs): Sorts all GeoNotes at current location according to place labels in alphabetical order. Good to use when entering a place and wanting to find GeoNotes on a particular object at the location.
- *Recent* (green tabs): Sorts the list according to when the GeoNotes were created. Recent GeoNotes appear first in the list.

167

- *Friends* (yellow tabs): Sorts the list with friends' GeoNotes first in the list. Each friend gets a tab. Then the users' own GeoNotes get listed, and then all others' GeoNotes.
- *Popular* (violet tabs): Sorts the list according to popularity. This is defined as total number of readings, divided by the number of days since the GeoNotes was authored. In order to prohibit authors to boost the popularity of their own GeoNotes, his own readings are excluded in this statistics.

Pull-Access Mode: The Search Window

When users come to a location with hundreds or even thousands of GeoNotes, scrolling and browsing through the Main window list will not be a meaningful way to find things of interest. Even though sorting is employed, the number of GeoNotes may be overwhelming. Besides, users may be searching for kinds of GeoNotes not supported by the sorting buttons.

The search interface allows users to perform advanced searches by combining a text string ("Text Search") with one of several "Search Options" (Figure 6.4).

- *Signature*: This search retrieves GeoNotes with a signature defined by the searcher.
- *Friends*: If people have agreed on becoming GeoNote friends with a user, that user can search for GeoNotes that one or several friends have written, read, added to favourites or commented.
- *Popular*: This search retrieves GeoNotes with high readings per day statistics.
- *Comments*: Retrieves GeoNotes with more than 5, 10 or 20 comments.
- *Recommended*: This search retrieves GeoNotes' recommended by GeoNotes recommendation system. If we allow the system to keep track of how unique users behave, the system will be able to automatically cluster users with the same behavioural profile. If two users have read more or less the same GeoNotes, rejected the same GeoNotes and saved the same GeoNotes, we can expect them to share preferences even though they have never met. Within such a preference cluster of users, the system can recommend new GeoNotes on the basis of the actions of other users. The recommendations are thus based on automatic "matching" of the usage history of users. This is the core feature of collaborative filtering techniques and recommendation systems (Konstan et al., 1997; Svensson et al., 2001). Since our system keeps track of usage data (reading) and provides channels for positive and negative feedback via "save GeoNote", "reject GeoNote" and "reject author", it is well suited for collaborative filtering. Storage of user data

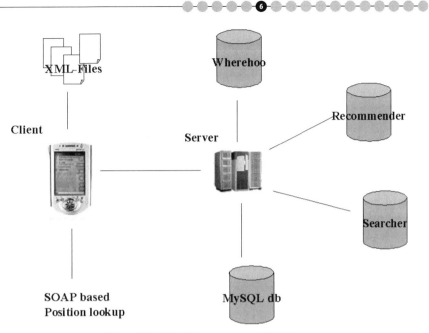

Figure 6.6 GeoNotes system architecture.

and the clustering take place in the recommender module (see Figure 6.6).

- *Date*: Get GeoNotes with a certain age (Written Today, Written the last 7 days, Written the last 30 days).

The user is allowed to choose only one of these search options, but he may combine it with a text string. When the user has filled out the search fields, clicking the "Search here" button retrieves the matching GeoNotes and displays them in a list (under the tab "Search Results"). This list has the same structure as the list in the main window. In the future, we could also expect the results to be displayed on a fine-grained map.

In the design of GeoNotes, we had several heated discussions of whether or not we should allow searches independent of the location of the user. Users could, for instance, generate global searches for GeoNotes or perhaps restrict searches to regions (via, e.g., some map interface). In both cases, the user would be allowed to search for GeoNotes outside his perceptual space. For similar reasons as we discarded remote authoring of GeoNotes (see above 6.3.2), we finally settled for "here-searches" only: we wanted to promote a spatially sensitive search paradigm, in which author and information seeker are positioned at the same place. Although GeoNotes are connected to a lat-long (latitude-longitude) coordinate, global searches tend to promote a system experience similar

169

to that of the spatially contextless World Wide Web. In contrast, we wanted to profile GeoNotes as a *location-based* annotation system.

Push-Access Mode: Queries

In a mobile setting, we cannot expect the user to stare at the GeoNotes' main window as she moves through space. In contrast to a stationary user who pays attention to the computer screen all the time, the attention of a mobile user is typically occupied by other phenomena. The ergonomics of mobile usage makes it difficult to visually monitor a screen (walking in a busy urban environment, driving a car, paying a bus ticket). More importantly, however, the mobile user typically enters activities and situations in which there are so many more interesting things to do than monitoring GeoNotes' information space: Sunday picnics with family, club-hopping with friends, skateboarding, shopping, observing street life, talking on the phone, admiring/studying urban and non-urban landscapes, tourism. In situations such as these, typically, the terminal will be placed in pocket or bag.

At the same time, many mobile users are still open for suggestions from the physical and social environment on how to enrich and improvise the present activity. GeoNotes' notification system allows the user to be notified of GeoNotes when he or she enters a new place. The notification consists of a sound signal and a pop-up window.

However, in order to avoid disturbance effects (discussed above), users must be able to create filters that only let through relevant GeoNotes. Since the situation and information need of the mobile user shifts abruptly, such a tool has to be easily configurable. At the same time, it has to be powerful enough to strike a balance between filtering out too little and too much.

GeoNotes allows the user to create such filters through the search interface. Instead of "Searching here", however, the user is able to save his search as a "Query" (Figure 6.4). The user is asked to give his query a recognisable name, after which the query ends up in the user's query list (Figure 6.7). Queries have the same scope as searches, but *constantly and continuously perform their search as users move through space*. Whenever the user shifts location, the query scans the new location for appropriate GeoNotes and notifies the user if there is a match. All results are displayed in a list under the "Query Result tab". In this way, queries operate like a mobile search engine, always "accompanying" the user.

The user can add as many queries as she likes to her list. Via a checkbox she can deactivate any query (without deleting it) and quickly activate it again. She can also choose to deactivate the notification signal. With this box un-checked, results will be listed under "Query results" as normal, but no notification signal will be given. At the end of the day, the user may check if her movements through space "collected" any matched

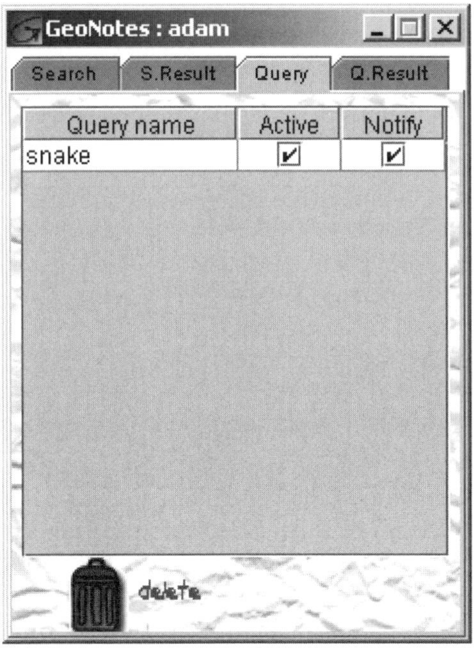

Figure 6.7 The list of queries.

results, and she will be able to read those GeoNotes, even though she is off-line and on another location. (Besides one's own GeoNotes and saved GeoNotes, this list is the only possibility to read GeoNotes remotely.)

6.4 Technical Implementation

The GeoNotes implementation has partly been affected by the constraints of a forthcoming user study in the campus Wireless LAN network of the Royal Institute of Technology (KTH) in Kista. Since a meaningful study of GeoNotes requires a great number of users, utilising the system over a longer period of time (at least a month), the KTH campus network provided a doable setup: at our disposal we will have 300 students equipped with Wireless LAN-ready laptops. Although the area covered by the approximately 35 access points is limited, it is a neighbourhood in which many students work, attend lectures, go for lunch, have coffee breaks, read, and study on a daily basis, often in accompany of their semi-mobile terminals. With little investment, this setup will, we hope, provide us with valuable, real-usage data of GeoNotes. We will encourage students to download the application and have the GeoNotes main window (Figure 6.5) on their desktop during their time in school. In fact, the interaction design described in the previous sections, was guided by a small-window approach, which would fit GeoNotes onto people's desktops beside their

171

normal applications (like instant messaging software). This also enables us to run GeoNotes on Wireless LAN-equipped PDAs, such as Compaq's iPAC.

Despite small area coverage and relatively crude positioning, Wireless LAN provides wireless access and position data in the same package. Measuring and cataloguing the physical lat-long coordinates of the access points will provide each client with its position since the system keeps track of client-access point connections (via a configuring tool built by John Sevy at Drexel University).[4] Technically, the lat–longs of each access point are stored in a MySQL database (Figure 6.6). When the client connects to a new access point, the system detects its mac-address and gets its lat-long from the MySQL database. If this position data turns out to be too imprecise, we will have to experiment with triangulation or other refinement techniques (Castro et al., 2001; Nord et al., 2002).

Content and usage data for each GeoNote is stored in various databases. "Searcher" stores message content, the comments, signature and number of readings. It also keeps track of when a GeoNote was authored and the last time it was read. Searcher database hosts the content-based search methods described above.

"Recommender" stores users' actions in the system. The ways in which users save or block GeoNotes, block authors, read (others') GeoNotes or make comments, will affect the ways in which the Recommender generates user profiles. In principle, any action can be recorded. These profiles are used in two ways. On the one hand, they allow users to search for friends' actions in the search interface (Figure 6.4). On the other hand, Recommender matches user profiles and generates clusters of users with the same preferences (also described above).

Searcher is a full text search engine that implements the Boolean and Vector Space models of information retrieval (Witten, Moffat and Bell, 1999). The text is indexed into an inverted file structure for fast query computation. Recommender is a general package for memory and model-based collaborative filtering. GeoNotes uses a variant of memory-based collaborative filtering described in Breese et al. (1998), implemented using the nearest-neighbour search algorithm. Both Searcher and Recommender have been developed by Rickard Cöster. Since they are general engines, GeoNotes is one of several information domains to which they have been applied. Both packages are implemented in Java.

The client keeps track of the position and stores XML-files containing the user's profile information. This involves signatures, blocked GeoNotes, and GeoNotes friends. Since friends' lists are mutual, there could be problem if one client suddenly was deleted or uninstalled. For this reason, the server also keeps copies of users' friends-lists.

---

[4] http://gicl.mcs.drexel.edu/sevy/airport

The server database stores information about passwords, friends and messages between users. Messaging could relate to inviting a user to become a friend, or accepting a request to enter the user's friends-list. If the user is not on-line, the server will store the message and forward it as soon as he comes on-line. The message function is also used for delivering messages to all users, for example, invitation to upgrade to a new GeoNotes version. In addition to this, the Server handles all requests from the client to the different databases. For instance, when a user enters a new location, the Server retrieves the place labels and GeoNotes IDs for the present position from the MySQL database. With the ID in hand, the Server then asks the Recommender and the Search databases for content and usage data.

As soon as GeoNotes users are equipped with more precise positioning technology, we will need a module that can scan an area for GeoNotes. *Wherehoo*, a location database developed at MIT Media Lab, provides precisely this functionality (Youll and Krikorian, 2000). In *Wherehoo*, strings of text can be stored on lat-longs. It is possible to search over a range of lat-longs. In the future, GeoNotes IDs and place labels will preferably be stored in this database instead of the MySQL database.

To enable clients to access the GeoNotes server over the Internet and through firewalls we implemented the communication between client and server using *Simple Object Access Protocol* (SOAP). This protocol carries XML encoded remote method invocations over HTTP. Another advantage of using SOAP is that we ensure that GeoNote clients can be implemented on any platform in any programming language. As long as the client sends the right SOAP messages to the server, the system will function correctly.

Acknowledgements

The authors would like to express their deep gratitude to Damien Bailly, Joanna Drapella, Tommy Gunnarsson, Tobias Larsson, Adam Lindström and Pawel Wiatr at Royal Institute of Technology for their work in the deployment of GeoNotes in the StockholmOpen.Net Wireless LAN. Most people at the HUMLE lab at SICS have provided fruitful and well-founded critique since GeoNotes' inception a couple of years ago. In particular, we would like to mention Elenor Cacciatore, Martin Svensson, Hanna Nyström, Markus Bylund and Kristina Höök. Jim Youll (MIT, Boston) has been generously helpful with our requests concerning *Wherehoo*. Kåre Synnes (CDT, Luleå) and Mikael Nehlsen (SICS, Kista) offered assistance in situations when it was most needed.

7

Footsteps from the Garden: Arcadian Knowledge Spaces

Andrew McGrath and Alan Munro

This chapter describes work in progress on a new way of approaching *social navigation* (Dourish and Chalmers, 1994; Benyon and Höök, 1997) through the use of populated, growing, *knowledge gardens*. These shared virtual landscapes provide an online space where people communicate and information can be "tended" through the affordances of an ecological metaphor. If we define social navigation as "finding things or going to places via, or with, other people", and take that the whole process of categorising and finding information is a largely social process, then these Arcadian landscapes can provide a useful approach to social navigation in cooperative information applications.

7.1 Introduction: Personal and Social Navigation in Shared "Organic" Landscapes

> *All our progress is an unfolding, like a vegetable bud. You have first an instinct, then an opinion, then a knowledge as the plant has root, bud, and fruit. Trust the instinct to the end, though you can render no reason.*
> Ralph Waldo Emerson (1803–1882)

In the century since Emerson wrote the lines of our opening quote we have seen a change in the relationship between humankind and nature. We are now entering the biological age. Our leading "public" technologies are biochemical, our sympathies are with organic products and our relationship with nature is becoming more complex; one of custodian rather than exploiter. This profound change in our perception of the world could change the nature of the systems we build to make sense of our information rich society, and the work we do. Organic metaphors are now being used to *explain* technology to us, the ecological view is one we are beginning to use to examine our processes and their effectiveness. What if such a view was used to make sense of our information, of our collective knowledge, what if such a view became the backdrop to our social navigation systems? In the following pages we attempt to show how the rich, mysterious nature of spatio-social collaboration/navigation might be mapped through the affordances of ecological information spaces.

7.1.1 Helping People Who Cannot be Together to Work Together

Chance meetings, recruited conversations, seeing what people are doing or reading, seeing when people are available, unplanned, unforced, social interaction, the ability to ignore people politely when passing them in the corridor – our work-lives are made up of these things. We might view these things as "by-products" of co-location. They are often difficult to support, or even absent in systems given to flexible workers. There is a whole genre of papers on this theme, of which we will mention but a few. In many cases these "by- products" would not be described as the actual *work* of the people concerned. The "desktop" metaphor of the computer is pervasive. It may reflect an element of our understanding of work as well; that it is something done at the desk, isolated from sociality, from others; planned, and done according to procedures and schedules. The field of computer-supported cooperative work (CSCW) has been concerned to look closely at work, the artefacts, practices and everydayness of it, looking at the things which slip by the wayside in our normal understanding.

The desktop metaphor is, of course, not only pervasive in the work place. We can look at the normal desktop and its effect in our early ideas of what an "Internet leisure environment" might be, the cybercafé. As one commentator points out, often what we here is very little "clatter and din" which is normally associated with café-society, rather "there is a hushed silence broken only by the mouse-clicks of customers silently roaming their own private corners of cyberspace" (Naughton, 1999). This is not to say that there are no applications which support sociality and which do not help us work. What we are arguing is that often these applications do so in a way which supports either the "meeting" or the "social chat" but does not have the multiple possibilities for action of real space. It is hard to "bump into" appropriate people in these spaces. There have been various attempts to do this, but often they rather violate the methods of approach which we have in the real world (cf. CRUISER). What is interesting is the possibility to bump into others, have a social chat, then be able to act on the discussion in the space, sharing information or navigation or indeed simply ending the conversation and continuing with our activity.

How we work is still quite a mysterious business (Suchman, 1987; Harper, 1998). There has been a significant body of research over the past ten or so years in the field of CSCW and general sociology looking at the ways in which work happens (Moran and Anderson, 1990), in particular at the ad hoc and situated nature of work. Moran and Anderson note the importance of the informal, the meetings in the corridor, around the coffee machine, which might not normally be termed as "work". They make a persuasive argument for these to be considered, despite their informal and loose nature, despite being unplanned and "just happening", as somewhat central to what goes on in an organisation. They are ways in which organisational issues get raised, where information is disseminated, where things are brought to one's attention. This sort of activity has been increasingly studied in this field and a rich picture emerges of its usefulness in the work environment.

Button and Harper (1996) have demonstrated how we can easily be misled by a cursory look at what people do in the workplace. The partial picture we get is likely to be one which relies too much on organisational ideas of what people do (as well as their own "glosses" of what they do) rather than seeing the ad hoc, everyday work-arounds which make up real work. These work-arounds can be often seen as messy and inelegant. For example, they may involve the everyday flaunting of accountancy procedure in order that a thing gets done quickly and efficiently, rather than in the "right" way. In the case of a furniture factory studied by Button and Harper, the way in which we might be lead to believe that the work is done can often be far from what we find after a more contextual analysis. It seems as if the work goes as follows: an order comes in to the office, a price is then negotiated, and work proceeds through the various parts of the factory. It is then delivered with an invoice. A computer system is designed to support this procedure, and it does so, following through the various stages, one after the other, and quite defensibly from this analysis, it does not allow the stages to be done any way around. This seems entirely natural; the stages being done any other way would not make sense. For example, it would be odd to start devoting work and material resources to an item without negotiating a price and assigning an order number. But a close look at the every day "messy" reality of the factory reveals that this sort of thing actually happens. A job is begun for certain established clients without a formal contract or agreed price. The actual negotiation and paperwork is done retrospectively. These everyday work-arounds can be time saving, and generally useful, but they are also "messy" and often to outsiders made invisible. They often rely on informal, personal contact and informal practice. In this case, the new system, embedding in it an "accounting" view of the work, becomes a problem which has to be overcome, rather than a resource.

It is easy, therefore, to miss these informal elements of work practice, and discount them as legitimate parts of the work, though they have been

177

demonstrated to be effective and useful. It is precisely these elements which may be missed in a more "mediated" encounter. Thus it is vitally important that these elements are not overlooked in an account of work which is incorporated into the design of any given system for remote working, that the parameters of a given set of design possibilities are sufficiently wide enough to include these aspects. It is not just enough to include issues of usability; it may be in a much wider dimension that the system succeeds or fails, for example in the arena of organisational politics, (cf. Star and Ruhleder, 1994). For example, much work is not just about doing. It is also about being seen to be done. Some recent work (e.g. Harper, 1998; Hinrichs and Robinson, 1997) discusses this. Hinrichs and Robinson (1997) discuss the "work done" in a phone call from one small organisation to another larger organisation. The larger organisation acts in a number of roles: as a funding body, as an information provider. The phone call, they argue, does not only ask for information (which could perhaps be done more "efficiently" via the web). A cursory analysis might assert this. Rather, the phone call also can work as a "marker" that organisation X is interested in the area of Y. It can also re-establish relationships, taking them up from where one left off, allow for gossip to happen, etc. These "by-products", are as much part of the "work" of that call. Coming back to copresence in working environments, Boden says:

> The flexibility and multidirectionality of copresence allows seemingly irrelevant (but actually important) talk to occur on occasions otherwise dedicated to prescribed topics ... in ways that provide formative updates on colleagues' activities and moods ... These strips of talk provide interactional biographies as they provideorganizationally relevant information.
>
> (Boden and Molotch, 1994)

This chapter describes one attempt to create a system which attempts to embody some of the aspects of work as we do it today; our various and many encounters with others whether planned or unplanned, with informational artefacts. Essentially, it could be viewed as one of a number of attempts to bring sociality into our encounters with different types of informaton artefacts (cf. populated information terrains). It is at an early stage, but is heuristic in generating some new ways to think about work and information representation, which we will discuss further below. Principal of these are *organic metaphors* for these represented virtual spaces. In particular, we utilise a set of *arcadian* metaphors, that is, metaphors utilising various ideas of the garden. In the next section, we will go on to look at information as it is used by people, and argue for the centrality of a social navigation approach. We will then discuss aspects of these organic metaphors, ending with an illustration of some of these concepts in a system which has been constructed at BT Labs.

7.2 Information Finding, Memory and Social Navigation

In our information world, we might not understand the need for sociality. Might we not be better with decent search tools, information interfaces? With the volume of information in the world, there is surely little need for consulting others. There is a cornucopia of information from all corners, at which we can look, or perhaps get some device to filter it. Perhaps this is part of the answer, but we would like to argue it is most certainly not all. We will now go on to look at the nature of information as it is used by people. We argue that information searching and use in our everyday worlds can be profoundly social in a number of different ways. This for us is the crux of the *social navigation* approach.

"Recorded" information in the work place once consisted simply of hard copy "paper" document in physically located storage systems. We are now seeing more and more of this "recorded" information being kept on the intranet or the web. In addition the quantity of information is growing and is beginning to appear in a number of media formats. The need to find information on these networks has given rise to a number of tools. These range from the "finder" on the desktop and the "recent documents" menu to the search engine or the portal. The effectiveness of these in particular circumstances is clear. These tools do help us to find information. What is not clear is that we have always found the *right* information or indeed where we might start to search for it. The concept of social navigation acknowledges that we may begin to look for information by using others to help us, either directly or indirectly. Information may be found directly, by asking other people, and indirectly by perhaps watching where others go, following trails like footprints in the snow. Information can be "actively" sought, or "passively", by information being sent by others because they know one is interested. The notion of "active" and "passive" is a problematical one, as we will see later.

Benyon and Höök (1997) discuss the kind of information we tend to get from recourse to other humans. The information tends to be personalised (to the other's situation), for example, route navigation might be radically different whether one is a pedestrian or road user. It tends also to be embedded in social interaction and perhaps even further in a weave of personal relationships.

Star, Bowker and Neumann (1997) discuss the relationship between our social worlds and the information artefacts we use. In particular they focus on the differences between the ways that professors "keep up with their field" and the way that undergraduates find information for their various types of assignment. There are telling differences between the two groups. They particularly focus on the concepts of "transparency" and "ease of use": "transparency and ease of use are products of an alignment of facets of information resources and social practices; each of these facets are interrelated and in motion". Notice here there is an explicit connection made between the social practices of individuals and their information resources. This is very evident in the two groups' differing ways of getting and "accessing" information. Note here, that we use "accessing" in inverted commas. In fact in the case of the senior academics, what is often happening is that information is often "at hand". Senior academics are often very much part of the community from whom they might wish to seek information. Papers, journals, preprints often come to them unasked for, as the result of membership of editorial committees, conference programme committees, etc. Here the information is often quite inextricably linked to the social worlds in which they work. Here we come back to what is problematic about the terms "active" and "passive". It may well be the case that an academic, being sent information could be seen as being a "passive" recipient of the information. However, one can look at the "active" way in which the academic maintains a manageable weave of social relationships, friendships and acquaintances, "tending" his or her social world.

As Star, Bowker and Neumann (1997) go on to say:

> the sharing of information resources is a dimension of any coherent social world – be it the world of homeless people in Los Angeles sharing survival knowledge via street gossip, or the world of high energy physicists sharing electronic preprints via the Los Alamos archive. On the other hand, any given social world itself generates many interlinked information artefacts. The social world creates through bricolage (a loosely coupled yet relatively coherent) set of information resources and tools … put briefly, information artefacts undergrid social worlds, and social worlds undergrid these same information resources.

We see that in the case of the senior academics, the concept of information access is often a complete misnomer. Rather we could talk about the information world "at hand". This is because the information artefacts that the senior academic uses are almost in complete convergence with their social world. Latour (1987) states quite categorically that "an isolated specialist is a contradiction in terms". Specialism is very much bound up with membership of communities, and the resources that they reflect. In the case of undergraduates, it is very much a case of "information access" of having to actively "find" information. Their concerns and informational resources may be more to do with organisational realities, the paucity of books and journals, the everyday problems of finding these articles. In their case, this reflects themselves in the information they use, taking perhaps local irrelevant articles over relevant ones. As Star and Bowker point out, this is not the result of apathy. It is a reflection of the lack of any convergence between social and academic worlds.[1]

Further, the undergraduate may differ from the academic in ways other than just the getting of information. We can consider what the information *means* to either group, or, in terms of Harper (this volume), how to *place* it. The information world of an undergraduate is often devoid of, for example, any understanding of the *rhetoric* of a particular paper or perspective. Advancing in any field may be a lot to do with going from seeing just a bunch of alien names, research groups, etc., to seeing trajectories of argument and rhetorical frameworks; for example, McClosky (1985) investigates and discusses the rhetoric of economics, and Latour discusses the rhetorical structure of scientific papers. See also Gilbert and Mulkay (1984) and Woolgar (1988).

We can also see this in the informational world of the desk officer at the International Monetary Fund (Harper, this volume). Not only is the information content important, but so too is the political and organisa-tional meaning of this content. In the case of the desk officer's placing of information from the economics institute of Arcadia, perfectly "good" informational resources are not utilised by the desk officer, because he or she knows that the hierarchy of the particular country does not use them either. What is far more informing is the biased "official" press, if one can see what might be behind what it says.

7.2.1 Casual Navigation: of Hanging out, Gossip and Bricolage

Searching or navigation varies from very directed to very casual. In the most directed sense we go to a web resource and search on keywords or we contact someone we know to be an expert. Casual searching presents a broad range of interesting scenarios. The academics in the scenario above "navigate" information through the colleagues they have and the positions they occupy.

We argue, in line with this, that sitting at our desks in an office can be a form of navigation. We put ourselves in the middle of a dynamic mix of information and people and we interact with both these entities as part of our working day, not to mention the "corpuses of information" (cf. Harper, this volume) we find on our desk, signifying our current projects. In some flexible working trials it has been noticed that people will come in to their desks when they want to catch the mood of the "office". Sometimes we also move through the space and find information or people serendipitously.

This type of "navigation" is very useful when what we need to know is not clearly defined. In an office we are among a resource that can help us with information in a general area even if we do not know what the

---

[1] However, we must be careful to remember that the difficulty here lies in the non-confluence of academic informational resources and the social worlds of the undergraduate. Their social worlds may be rich in informational resources where the academic's are not; finding cheap places to drink, parties after the pubs have shut. Not all academics, sadly, will have this kind of information "to hand".

question is exactly, nor exactly when it will arise. Further, we argue that searching for what we cannot define could be addressed in a more "social" way. We need to know more about CSCW so we go to a conference as well as go to a library. In fact with the speed of change nowadays it is often felt that if it is in a book it is too outdated (though often publishing lends information "authority"). We therefore gravitate towards a "place" where we can search by *being there*, by experiencing a rich flow of information and conversation. We find what we are looking for quicker, more effectively and more usefully for us. This is coming on information through being who we are talking to some one who may just be the right person. It is, through this social interaction that information may come to us through them becoming part of our social network.

But this is not all. There is an interesting thing about social navigation, of knowing "who" rather than often knowing "what" (or to be a little more realistic, of knowing "kind of what but are not sure" but knowing "who may know this kind of thing, perhaps"), which seems a profound advantage over other types of information browsing or search. It is often the case that what is needed is not written down anywhere but is "*in someone's head*", at least to an extent. It may be that in talking to others, that conversation and the whole business of asking the question may actually provide part of the answer. It may be that the current set of concerns of the other means that a *creative bricolage* is created by which an "answer" is seen which grows out of the interaction. In fact, to go further, the idea of "questions" and "answers" rather breaks down, and might be seen as *post hoc* categories imposed on the interaction (cf. Silverman, 1998). It may for instance take a long time to see just what the "answer" actually is, and when we find it, it might help us phrase our question.

Thus, there is a whole complex of issues surrounding information gathering, which makes it a profoundly social process. Taking into account this kind of rubric, we start looking at quite different approaches to information "seeking" than traditional information retrieval models. We need to see others, what they are doing with information, so that we can "use" them for our own informational needs, and for them to use us whether by asking or by looking at what we do with it.

We have also hinted that there are a number of more "societal" concerns in terms of the efficacy and usefulness of this kind of system, in terms of what one gets out and what one puts in (cf. Dieberger, this volume). There has to be an equal spread of benefit to all users, otherwise such systems are likely to gather dust. Other "political" aspects of such a system should not be ignored either. An information sharing system that is seen to be a place where we are peered at by our hierarchy rather than a place to share with our peers may also fail. This failure will be directly attributable to the culture of the organisation in which it is trialled (cf. Grudin, 1989). We would argue that people have to be able to negotiate and control their usefulness to others as well as arguing that a system must balance the often conflicting concerns of the management and the managed.

7.3 From Applications to Agents: Ecologies in the Interface

We will now begin to look selectively at some new possibilities for looking at our information worlds, particularly tools which might help us manage information which occurs virtually.

New types of computer tools are beginning to encroach on the hegemony of the user driven application. These tools are characterised by the fact that the user only partially drives them, only occasionally is manipulation direct. These new computer tools are commonly referred to as agents. Whereas applications need to be driven or constantly controlled via an on-screen window, agents do things for you even when you are not directly in control of them. Agents such as BT's ProSearch and Jasper, or GMD's BSCW can be configured to send you information as and when it "happens". They make us aware of things others are doing and things that have happened "elsewhere". The kinds of information that these agents are beginning to deliver is also not straight "readable data" for instance web pages and documents. These agents are also starting to deliver information about user activity, newness, relevance, interest and awareness. The information delivered is often meta-information.

As they do things for you we argue that these agents will need a place to show us what they are up to. They need a place to be seen to be working, a place to deliver the "bricolage" of results. The typical place for this information to "happen" is the e-mail inbox. While this undoubtedly brings information to one's attention it can also clutter up one's inbox with *too much* information. Instead we argue that the place where some of one's information "happens" cannot demand one's full attention all the time, it has to use one's powers of peripheral awareness to help you manage your communication and information needs. In the way we use our peripheral awareness to manage the information being streamed to us in a real space, so we have to do the same with online information. In particular, the information that is not exact, which is more about change and flow rather than specific fact. For example, the fact that someone is looking at my document or that someone is looking for me, I might want to know, but do not need to know in a way that requires my full attention. This kind information has to be peripheralised as similarly oblique information is peripheralised in the real world. Of course, the real world is rife with the possibility of information overload, it has super-high fidelity resolution, infinitely variable views, chaos, people, sounds, seasons, objects, etc. Add to this the complexity we add ourselves through documentation and physical architecture and you could argue that we need protection from life. But on the whole, people manage with life and with copresent communication. "Copresence is 'thick' with information. Under any media condition words derive their meanings only from contexts; copresence delivers far more context than any other form of human exchange" (Boden and Molotch, 1994).

How are we able to survive this deluge of information in the real world? Well, some of it is down to this use of "peripheral awareness" (cf. Heath and Luff, 1992a; Heath et al., 1993). The only way to put the equivalent of those useful by-products of co-location into a shared space is to avoid cramming it all into the same channel. Otherwise there is a danger that information manifested in the real world through a multitude of audio, visual, temporal and spatial channels now gets diverted into a single, often inappropriate, channel; usually e-mail. We need a space where those channels of information can be "peripheralised".

It is important to realise that this type of peripheral information space should not be an application in which one does one's work. Rather, it is a space one inhabits. So the information space might, in fact, be space for "hanging out" in, a place to manageably meet our colleagues or people you "ought" to interact with if only you were co-located. It is also a place where your information resources, as generated by your agents, "happen" and can be interacted with in a manageable way. The peripheralising of some of the information may help to reduce the sense of information overload.

Tools for dealing with information overload are talismanic in today's business world. In the past, there was too little information delivered too slowly. Now, there is too much, arriving all too fast. There is also a realisation that a key issue is also not so much dealing with information as generating knowledge and understanding the appropriate information. Information is arriving so quickly and in such quantities that it can be helpful to view it as if it was organic in nature. We can combine a peripheral information space with that of a growing, changing, organic information metaphor to help users cope with the quantity of information, cope with their inability to ever master all of it, and cope with the tools for manipulating and "training" search strategies.

We will now go on to talk about an organic information space which has been developed at BT Labs. This information space make use of the various elements discussed above, albeit in a number of different ways. It is called the Knowledge Garden. It is a prototype taken to "proof of concept" stage and was conceived to be the type of interface we might be using in the next three to five years. In addition, the effort required to build a space that truly "grows" has meant that some of the navigation and design assumptions of the work had to be coded into the "growing" algorithms. We have a garden that grows but our thinking about interacting with that garden has moved on somewhat. The spaces cannot fully be "used" and so true user feedback has been difficult to get, however, any feedback has been generally favourable and has led to the development of new interfaces being prototyped as we go to print.

7.4 Organic Metaphors

> *Like Cybernetic space, the garden is an invented*
> *place, clearly and always a fiction, a contrivance.*
> (Hunt, 1997).

It could be said that the driving technologies of the age give rise to the figures of speech that we use to describe the world around us. From the advent of the mechanistic age the way we looked at the world became mechanistic. Ideas that worked for engineered devices were assumed to work for other areas of human endeavour like economic theory and the study of human behaviour. Now we see the rise to prominence of the bio-chemical technologies. As a result we notice the development of more organic ways of looking at the world. The recent UK Renault Laguna advert describes it as an organically developed automobile, the new 3 series BMW is described using imagery of DNA strands.[2]

Another, older, ecological metaphor that has a bearing on our chapter is the cultural image of the garden or the Arcadian landscape. The garden as a strong cultural image has a very long history and a strong cross-cultural identity. From the past we can look at the epic of Gilgamesh and see the Garden of the Gods. In Christian theology the earliest scenes are played out against the Garden of Eden and the key moments set around the Tree of Knowledge while in Muslim culture the afterlife is seen as a garden paradise.

In Japanese culture we are familiar with the Zen garden or the Shinto shrines and similarly the Celtic tradition is closely associated with nature. We have a strong Arcadian folk memory. The Knowledge Garden acknowledges this memory and takes advantage of our architectural and social preponderance to "get a view", to diminish the claustrophobia of our environment. The Windows desktop of today is, in truth, a claustro-phobic windowless environment. In the real world we don't tend to want to sit in a windowless room. With the Knowledge Garden users can look into the organic social world while the very "life" of the space encourages us to "stay connected to it" because like copresent interaction it "both engages and entraps us" (Boden and Molotch, 1994). We want to be con-nected to the life *in* the screen. Connected to the information and the people we find in there, in our shared garden. When the video-phone was first marketed in the UK in the early 1990s it was sold in pairs, because communication devices rely on a certain market momentum. It was vital

---

[2] http://www.bmw.co.uk/new3series/home.html

that people buying them had someone to phone! Similarly the design of the Knowledge Garden relies on people being present online, at least through an agent intermediary. The physical, financial and psychological cost of staying online all the time is too high. Thus, in the Knowledge Garden, agents give an indication of the gardens inhabitants degree of online presence. In the garden we might "see" someone who is not online at all but representation in a way to indicate this to others by the agent.

7.4.1 Tacit Properties of an Organic Metaphor

The name "Knowledge Garden" alone can elicit strong responses from people even without any graphical images to reinforce the concept. We have found that people's responses are about what they expect to be able to do or to find. They expect that the information will be growing with both wild and controlled qualities. Even when cultivated there is a perception that the garden is not (need not) controlled completely. People understand that gardens have to be tended (not controlled) to get the best out of them.

> Gradually, as my awareness grew, I realized the garden was not my problem. The yellow roses and the weeds were still there, always had been. My job was to cultivate the roses and get rid of the weeds, you know, keep the garden neat and orderly. Gradually I'm supposed to build a path through it, winding past a fountain and a stream, through mazes and by benches where I can rest and smell the roses; the possibilities are endless.[3]

We have found that people seem quite happy to consider information in an organic way. Viewed in an organic way they realise too much information is "not their problem" their job is to cultivate the information and get rid of the "weeds". They can imagine information growing, dying (in importance) and are happy to engage with the metaphor. In fact other systems using the "language" of organic metaphor already exist (Ackerman, 1996), although none until now have combined the language of metaphor with the visual imagery and tools to allow the user to fulfil the "purpose" of the garden.

The garden metaphor allows the user a place to "hang out in" that does not need to be driven. It can happily sit in the corner of their screen as it is a space not an application.

> A garden … is a place that offers a sense of separation from the outside world. That separation must be created by making

---

[3] http://www.hevanet.com/vanrees/god/stories/garden.html

threshold – whether real or implied. This threshold creates the
ability to leave one world and enter another. That is the
fundamental function of garden: to allow a person the
psychological space to dream, think, rest, or disengage from the
world … It is meant to describe another type of psychological
space, to help you touch real self (Schwartz, 1997).

We are using this ability of the garden to separate us a little from the
real world and allow us to enter into a shared online Arcadian space.

The organic world is mutable and chaotic, we know this and expect it.
In fact without a certain amount of chaos, of variance based on recognisable laws, the natural world does not seem natural at all. We know that
there is a largely unchanging part that varies only in small understandable details. We also know there is gradual change and there is a small
amount of radical change. The world generally remains the same but the
gradual change serves as a backdrop to our actions and allows us to talk
about the changes around us as a way of beginning conversation. The
chaotic events can be used to remember things or again to help us to
communicate. The organic and chaotic nature of such a metaphor can be
useful when searching for information by remembering exactly the
"incidentals" of a space, the things that we could never search on before
without recourse to asking another sentient being.

The mutability inherent in the organic metaphor can be used to meet
our identified requirements for a social navigation system. Now changes
in the real world happen, however, changes in a virtual world have to be
purposely built in. Because of the high overhead of content production
this means that in practice virtual worlds do not change once they have
been created. There are a number of ways to get affordable and useful
mutability into virtual worlds. These are detailed in the paper "Strategies
for mutability in virtual environments" (Anderson and McGrath, 1997).
The strategies range from letting users generate content through simple
chat or even geometry creation to worlds where the geometry and
animation (the "incidentals") of the space are part of an evolving environment generated by agents. In the Knowledge Garden the mutability
occurs by linking information to the "incidentals" of the space and therefore provides an information rich backdrop to human communication.
It is

… a composition of man made or man-modified space to serve as
infrastructure or background for our collective existence; and if
background seems inappropriately modest we should remember
that in our modern use of the word it means that which
underscores not only our identity and presence, but also our
history. (Jackson, 1984)

187

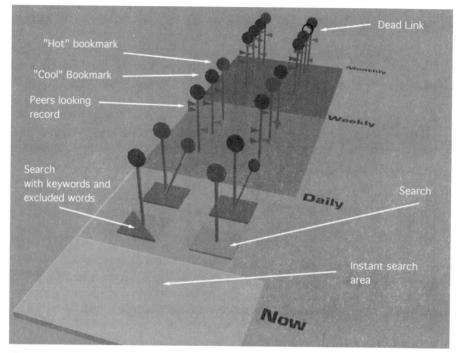

Figure 7.1 An early concept design of the Knowledge Garden showing what the geometric "plants" signify.

7.4.2 Arcadian Interfaces: Some Examples

The garden has always possessed the potential to offer its visitors the same sort of experience as is nowadays available in forms we call virtual reality.
(Hunt, 1997)

John Dixon Hunt argues that the garden was the first virtual reality environment and so it is no surprise to know that the concept we have developed takes visual cues and underlying structure from real gardens. There is no slavish copying of reality though, "the ordering devices of abstract art and minimal art are appropriated and applied to the landscape realm" (Schwartz, 1997). The metaphor is used to the point at which it stops becoming useful to aid the understanding of the space. There is no need to take the metaphor too far, there is no "Privileging internal coherence over empirical validity" (Cubbit, 1998). There are no worms, there are no fallen leaves, there are no picket fences. Our garden is an abstraction of elements of real gardens, and as with any abstraction, there is always a moot point over what is abstracted, what falls by the wayside. Like any process of abstraction, what we are leaving out could be in some ways a political decision (see Figure 7.1).

Many contemporary garden images are becoming idealised and increasingly geometric. We can take the example of the garden that the Teletubbies on BBC TV live in. Their environment is a cross between a garden and a geometric play space. The emerging use of this kind of garden imagery could be a reflection of our increasing ability to dominate nature through our biological knowledge. The garden becomes a place we can bend to our will. It has been product-ised. If we look also at the work of the Landscape artist Martha Schwartz we see this notion of geo-metricised nature again. Her Splice Garden combines the "natural" and the geometric. The Splice Garden, while looking like a fully natural (though very controlled) garden space, is in fact made of totally inor-ganic materials. The geometrically shaped bushes are in fact, all plastic, and the grass is Astroturf. Her stated intention was to "create a garden through abstraction, symbolism, and reference". The Splice Garden was created for the Whitehead Institute in Cambridge, Massachusetts, USA. The Whitehead Institute is a microbiology research centre and the gar-den is a "cautionary tale about the dangers inherent in gene splicing: the possibility of creating a monster" (Schwartz, 1997). If we look at Martha Schwartz's work in the Center for Innovative Technology we see that it includes a circular garden where visitors to the centre drive their vehicles to park when they arrive for a meeting. The cars then park on flagstone "welcome mats" before the visitors entering the building. This imagery and layout is very reminiscent of the imagery in the Knowledge Garden and the history of this architectural design is pertinent to our discussion. The clients for the work objected to some aspects of the design because "It was expected the building could convey an idea or exhibit a radical form, but the landscape was to be the non-intellectual, passive realm in which the building would stand in contrast" (Schwartz, 1997). Despite the changing way we are beginning to view nature there are still some who think that intellectual pursuit and technological excellence are to be sep-arated from natural imagery (see Figure 7.2).

7.3 The Knowledge Garden

We have discussed in some detail the kind of qualities we would want in our organic social navigation system. Now we want to turn our attention in more detail to the work in progress at BT Labs in Suffolk and how it is addressing some of these issues. The Knowledge Garden aims to provide a unified two- and three- dimensional shared, dynamic information interface and has been built from the following underlying building blocks:

- A shared space to peripheralise information and "hang out in".
- Jasper agent technology to provide the relevant information with which to populate the space.

Figure 7.2 The Splice Garden by Martha Schwartz. (© Martha Schwartz, Inc. Reproduced by permission.)

- ProSearch technology to seed the garden with proactively gathered information (Davies et al., 1997).
- ProSum technology to abridge the information automatically for quick reference (Davies et al., 1997).
- APIA availability software to provide users with information about who is around to talk on-line.
- Autogenerative landscape algorithms to create a mutable, navigable, meaningful space.

With these building blocks the Knowledge Garden provides the following features:

- An easy-to-use, engaging, unified information interface.
- Agent generated navigation tools.
- Collaborative, communal interaction and communication.
- Live, self-updating information.
- Agent-brokered information.
- Shared access to information places.
- Persistence.
- Communication (audio, whiteboards, etc.) for shared place.

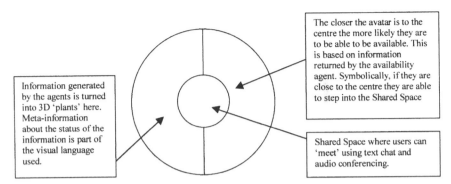

The closer the avatar is to the centre the more likely they are to be able to be available. This is based on information returned by the availability agent. Symbolically, if they are close to the centre they are able to step into the Shared Space

Information generated by the agents is turned into 3D 'plants' here. Meta-information about the status of the information is part of the visual language used.

Shared Space where users can 'meet' using text chat and audio conferencing.

Figure 7.3   A schematic view from above the Knowledge Garden.

The Knowledge Garden takes the form of a circle with an outer circle split into two. One half of the outer circle is where the APIA availability software returns its information while the other half is where the Jasper and ProSearch agents return their results. The centre is a shared space where users can meet online and swap information or discuss information (see Figure 7.3).

The closer the avatar is to the centre the more likely they are to be able to be available. This is based on information returned by the availability agent. Symbolically, if they are close to the centre they are able to step into the Shared Space

The Knowledge Garden concept is defined, first, by the capability to navigate a shared, self-generating hierarchical information structure from which the user can browse and view HTML-based documents. This provides a constantly updating and persistent information window on the desktop, utilising a unified two- and three-dimensional interface to their best advantage. In the Knowledge Garden the user can navigate directly to specific information resource in a shared three-dimensional "place" containing representations of context/activity driven and user-defined information. The information resources visible in the space are automatically generated from information supplied by the Jasper, ProSearch and ProSum information agents (Davies, et al., 1995).

The Knowledge Garden was built on previous BT projects such as the Portal[4] and the Mirror[5] and extended the learning done on these into a framework for the user interface. The Portal was an experimental VRML (virtual reality modelling language) Internet site acting as a "virtual visit" to the research projects at BT Labs. It was written in VRML version 1, but used PERL programming language to auto-generate geometry. The

---

[4] http://virtualbusiness.labs.bt.com/vrml/portal/home/index.html
[5] http://virtualbusiness.labs.bt.com/SharedSpaces/

191

Figure 7.4   Image of the portal.

geometry was designed to give a sense of which projects were being visited most and who had visited. It created a kind of asynchronous shared space by leaving a "ghost" avatar on a project area that could be clicked on to see what country the person visited from.

The "ghost" avatar faded out over a number of days. Thus online presence in a project area could be seen over time (see Figure 7.4).

The Mirror was a ground-breaking collaborative experiment in Inhabited television, created by BT, Sony, Illuminations and the BBC. Six on-line worlds were available to over 2000 viewers of the BBC2 series "The Net" in January and February 1997. Social chat and interaction were mixed with professional content and programming to create online communities. The worlds of the Mirror reflected the themes of the six broadcast television programmes in their overall settings and individual audio-visual elements. Moreover, they were also designed to experiment with specific aspects of Inhabited television content, to explore which would be most appealing to both new and experienced participants. The six virtual worlds were built around the following themes: space, power, play, identity, memory, and creation. Creation world, in particular, was interesting to this discussion. It featured ecological imagery and a changing cycle of day, dusk, night and dawn played out against a background of changing music. The space also featured an art show where users were invited to upload their own art and an opening night was held online which held the attention of the visitors for several hours (see Figure 7.5).

The lessons learned in Portal and in the Mirror, especially the generation of automatic content and the maintenance of a sense of community, form part of the design rational of the Knowledge Garden. Another key

Figure 7.5   Image of the Mirror.

driver for the design of the Knowledge Garden was the maturity and availability of the underlying information agents Jasper and ProSearch.

7.3.1 Jasper Shared Information Store

Given the immense amount of information available on the World Wide Web (WWW), when information of interest is found, it is preferable to avoid copying entire documents from the original location to a local server. In addition, it is important to help people manage the distribution of information among their colleagues, after all, one person's vital e-mail is another's junk mail. In the Jasper information agent (Davies et al., 1995) a defined set of users can "store" pages of interest. Jasper extracts the important details from these documents, including the summary and keywords, as well as the document title, its URL, and the date and time of access. This information is maintained locally and has several purposes. The summary gives a user an idea of the content of the document without the need to retrieve the remote pages. A quick link to the full remote information is also provided. Jasper locally indexes the pages that have been stored. Over time, a rich set of pages is built up by Jasper from different users' entries.

When a user stores a page in the Jasper system, that user's agent automatically informs other users with matching profiles, by e-mail. A reference is also added to every users "What's New?" page along with a predicted interest rating.Furthermore, if the document does not match

193

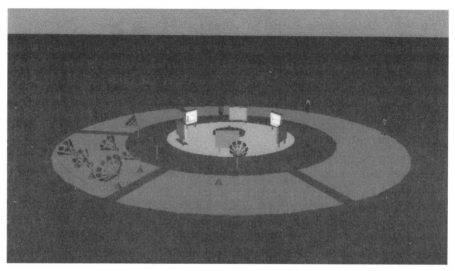

Figure 7.6 The Knowledge Garden.

the profile of the user who stored it, then Jasper prompts that user to update their profile accordingly and suggests suitable additional keywords. In this way Jasper learns more about the user's interests as the system is used.

Of course, systems such as this are prone to the "cold start" problem. That is, no one will use it as no one is willing to put the effort into starting it. This problem can be partially addressed by the addition of the ProSearch agent which proactively searches on the Internet or intranet for information as defined by your interests in your Jasper profile. The combination of the Jasper and ProSearch agents with the Knowledge Garden concept allow for changes in the output from the agents. More detail of what these changes are is described below.

7.3.2 Information Representation within the Garden

Within the shared environment of the Garden the ability to generate WWW- based information representations is key. Jasper and ProSearch, described above, are used to provide shared information resources and the ability to generate group- or personal-based searches and representations within the Garden add another opportunity for social navigation inside the shared three-dimensional spatial interface (see Figure 7.6).

The Knowledge Garden exploits the pages stored in the Jasper system by using it to furnish our "place to hang out in" with "incidental" information and in which users can navigate through in a logical, intuitive and accessible way. This arrangement of information is achieved by using the

Figure 7.7   Knowledge Garden document cluster.

meta-information in the Jasper store and results from an automatic clustering process which groups together URLs (WWW pages) containing related information. The resulting cluster structures of the Jasper store are thus used to create a front end onto the Jasper system, using VRML. This clustering work is described in more detail in Davies et al. (1996). It is not expected that this front end will replace the existing front end to Jasper, which is of a traditional, two-dimensional web page arrangement. Rather, the Knowledge Garden will augment the access to Jasper by providing people a more serendipitous method of accessing the stored information.

The Knowledge Garden is also divided into sectors, visible in Figure 7.7. Each sector represents a different information source. The user group who own the garden space define the sources that appear in their garden. That is, they decide on the resources that will supply their garden with information and dedicate a portion of the space to that resource. Current sources of information supported are the Jasper information agent, a news feed sector and a "Grow your own searches" area supported by the ProSearch agent. An algorithm takes the results generated by each agent and automatically turns it into a notional three-dimensional plant shape. The algorithm also generates a path through the information to help the user with navigation. This takes the form of a list of views from which the user can choose and which cause the viewpoint on to the garden to be moved to a good view of the information resources.

In Figure 7.7 we can see clustered groups of documents (Data Mining, Education, Electronic Commerce, and so on). Each document is represented by a stalk with a coloured square at its end. The colour coding of

195

the squares on the stalks represents the status of the particular document: red squares indicate that a document has been updated since it was stored in Jasper, black that the link is "dead" (that is, the URL associated with this document is no longer valid), while a blue square indicates that neither of these conditions apply. The smaller squares halfway up the document stalk represent a locally held summary of the information, as generated by Jasper. From the opening view of the Knowledge Garden these plants and their stalks can be seen and an overall "feel" for the status of your information can be gathered easily. The more red we have in our garden the more "new" information we might want to look at. If there is a lot of black in the garden then our information resources are both out of date and diminishing and should be pruned and updated. The idea is to keep the garden generally blue in colour indicating that we are up to date with our information resources. All this can be seen at a glance from the opening view on to the space.

As the user navigates towards a particular sector, more detail becomes visible. This feature makes use of the ability of the VRML specification to swap more detailed information into the space as the user gets closer to any particular place. As in the real (and analogue) world the closer we get to things the more detail we see. This feature in the garden has benefits for the user in that from a distance the most important information can be seen. As the user gets closer to the area of interest the computer displays more and more detail, showing less "important" or less headline information to the user without them specifically asking to see more. This has also been done to maintain a high frame rate on the users computer. As VRML uses real-time rendering we need to ensure that there is only enough information on the screen as is necessary for the user. If too much information is on screen then the world can slow down to an unusable speed. The plants are geometric in shape for the same reason, to keep the complexity of the space to an efficient level.

When a plant "bud" is selected, the associated URL is loaded into a separate two-dimensional browser window. The selected stem then starts to wave, analogous to touching stems on a real plant as one walks through a real garden. The wave period decreases over time. This visual representation allows, for instance, a "busy" or "hot" plant to be immediately visible to other users by virtue of the number of moving stems.

The two-dimensional browser is separated out from the garden because computer-based three dimensions is of little use for reading text in anything other than small quantities. At some point, once the users attention has been attracted in the three-dimensional world, it makes sense to go to a two-dimensional view of the information. Should the user click on the small "bud" half way up the stalk of the plant they will see the summary information rather than the original document. This is done because sometimes it can take a few minutes to download a document from a remote site and it may be quicker to look at a locally stored summary before deciding if the full document needs to be accessed and read.

To instigate a new and *persistent* search the user clicks on the ProSearch link in the garden and from there can create a new search based on keywords. So, for example, if the document was about Teleworking the query extracted might be:

{teleworking, cscw, mobility, flexible working}.

This query is then passed to a search engine that searches WWW for documents that match the query. After some post-search filtering, the ten most relevant documents are then represented as stalks on a plant that grows in the three-dimensional space. As the ProSearch agent starts to return documents over time the user can "cut" results which are irrelevant. Such unwanted results are a common occurrence in online searching scenarios. When the user cuts such an unwanted "bud" ProSearch automatically looks at the offending page for possible keywords which the user might not have wanted. This information is presented to the user where they can decide to add "exclude" keywords to the underlying search string. This is an interesting point to note. Typical users find it difficult to create refined search strings and yet in the garden the simple act of cutting and pruning helps the user to train their own searches. Taking the gardening metaphor further, users can also take "cuttings" from information plants and grow their own copy within their personal environment. Another feature of online searching scenarios is finding information we did not know we were interested in until we happen across it. In such a scenario the user typically wants to keep the search focused on the original search task. If the user takes a cutting of the interesting "bud" then the document represented by that "bud" is analysed and a query in the form of a set of key words is extracted from it. ProSearch identifies any keywords in the page *additional* to the original search and the user is invited to refine their search as another plant. The usefulness of the organic metaphor is clear. The users intuitively grasp the idea of training a plant and apply it to their "searching" problem to refine a persistent information search.

7.3.3 People Representation within the Garden

Territorial well-being requires a sense of shared as well as of private space, a feeling of community or neighbourhood in a space that is neither "mine" nor "yours" but "ours".

(Solomon, 1998)

In Figure 7.7 we can see representations of people at the far side of the space. Increasingly people are becoming familiar with the notion of the online embodiment, the "avatar". The avatar is driven by the user in that they move it around in three-dimensional space through the direct manipulation of their computer mouse. In the Knowledge Garden the representations of users are different from this notion of avatars. The Garden makes use of two types of avatar one is the typical avatar model, direct manipulation of a representation of your online presence. This is used in the centre of the Garden, in the shared meeting space. Another use of embodiment in the garden is based on the realisation that "In cyberspace we are where our attention is focused, but we have no presence until we are visible in public" (Waterworth, 1998). This second type of avatar is used to give other users of the space a sense of how present you are online. We acknowledge that presence online is not a simple "are you or aren't you" question but is more usefully thought of as *degrees* of presence online. If I know (through visual cues) that you are "80% present" in the space then maybe I can entice you into full presence through trying to contact you. Similarly, if I can see that you are only "10% present" I can sensibly leave a message for you instead. The rate of change of presence online can also be useful to us. We can *see* a person who is busy or a person who is active through the rate-of-change of their availability. The use of this type of avatar allows the user to "catch sight" of people online as they move between tasks, rather as they would in the office environment, in the corridor or the coffee area. In the real world "Proximity is negotiated as the need arises ... such discussion tends to happen particularly when matters appear to become sensitive, complex, or uncertain" (Boden and Molotch, 1994). In the Knowledge Garden proximity can be gauged and acted on simply and easily through the information afforded by the availability display.

This part of the garden displays the availability of people, it shows the likelihood of they being able to enter into a interaction with you or with others. How does it do this? As the user, at his or her terminal, interacts with applications an agent sends "availability" cues to the Knowledge Garden. This agent is called the *availability of people information agent* or APIA. The cues are based on a collection of information sources none of which on its own tells us much but taken together can give useful information. The APIA agent returns information on desktop interaction like mouse movement, opening and closing windows, it can access the diary of the user to see if we are in a meeting or look and see if we have many phone messages waiting. The information returned drives the position of the avatar in the space. The more available or "there" the agent thinks the person is the closer it puts the avatar to the centre of the Garden. Symbolically the avatar or person is therefore able to "step into" the centre where a synchronous meeting can be held. Of course online, just like in the real world, our availability can be misunderstood. I can think you look busy when you are not really too busy to talk to me, and likewise I can think you available to talk and be wrong. When there are mismatches in perceived availability we negotiate our communication between our desire to talk and the others desire not to be drawn into communication. In the APIA system we can always override the representation if we desire to be uninterrupted.

7.3.4 Information Sharing within the Garden

Once the users have "stepped" into the centre of the garden they are able to enter into a synchronous shared collaborative working space. By making the Knowledge Garden multi-user, users can not only access the rich variety of information resources within the Garden, but collaborate with other users across the Internet. The avatar representations of users are not just visual representations, but contain communications and profiling information about them. There is an interesting parallel with Paul Rankin's "Star Cursor" work at Philips Research (Rankin et al., 1998).

Thus, when avatars meet in the shared space in the centre of the garden, they can communicate via a rich variety of media. The communications channels are set up automatically within the Garden. These include:

- text
- speech (both Internet Telephone and PSTN telephone)
- audio
- white board
- application sharing.

Users endeavouring to research information on a particular topic not only have access to the wealth of links stored within Jasper and any other information sources represented in the garden, but can be automatically put in touch with (perhaps unknown) colleagues. Once these colleagues have been put in touch they can then go on to meet in the shared environment.

7.4 (By Way of Some) Conclusions

The Knowledge Garden is an example of using an ecological approach to social navigation. The work is experimental and without user analysis data it is hard to assess at present. However, we believe that such Arcadian information environments encourage a fresh approach to social navigation. At BT Labs elements of the ideas in the Knowledge Garden are continuing in new CSCW applications with very positive results beginning to appear. The Knowledge Garden concept, to an extent, relies on a type of computing power and a ubiquity of network access that will not be possible for some time yet. This however, means that there now is the time to explore and refine such ecological approaches to shared information spaces.

It is important to reiterate that we do not envisage an informational world devoid of other people. Rather, like our informational searches in the real world, we acknowledge that seeing other people interacting with information artefacts, meeting them in a place where we tend our informational resources, and being able to strike up casual conversations with people are not a side issue which may make the interface to an "informational tool" more friendly. Rather, they are a crucial and central aspect to searching for, understanding and using information. Our information worlds are social worlds.

These developments are in an early stage, so this chapter is necessarily a "work in progress". However, we feel that this "ecological" approach shows promise and may be heuristic further than the present domain. There are many issues with which it and systems like it will have to cope. For example, taking Harper's work in the International Monetary Fund (1999), how well will these more autonomous systems fit in with the work practices of an information professional like the desk officer? We cannot say truthfully ourselves that we have dealt with more than a small proportion of the issues that have been raised by social navigation and this book. The Knowledge Garden and its accompanying technology is but a start.

There will be many many challenges to such systems as they develop, especially if we think beyond the keyboard and screen technology used at present. Will these types of systems have new ways to deal with degradation of performance over low-bandwidth networks? How will we cope with scalability questions? Just what is an optimal size of "community" to work with when one is information seeking with others? How exactly will it work across the divide of virtual and "real" worlds; that is, from the Knowledge Garden to information artefacts and settings which we currently use and which we inhabit?

The authors wish to open the concept of Arcadian information spaces for discussion and debate to the wider community.

Acknowledgements

The authors gratefully acknowledge Chin Weah Chia, Martin Crossley, Rob Taylor-Hendry, Amanda Oldroyd, Matt Shipley, Phil Clarke, Andrew Hockley, Luis Collins, Chris Hand, Elaine Raybourn, Richard Harper, John Davies and Mirko Ross.

Social Navigation of Food Recipes: Designing Kalas

Martin Svensson and Kristina Höök

8.1 Introduction

How can we empower people to find, choose between and make use of
the multitude of computer-based, net-based and embedded services that
surround us?[1] How can we turn human–computer interaction into a
more social experience? How can we design for dynamic change of
system functionality based on how the systems are used? These issues
are fundamental to a newly emerging field named *Social Navigation*.
Researchers in the field are observing that much of the information seeking in everyday life is performed through watching, following and talking
to people. When navigating cities people tend to ask other people for
advice rather than study maps (Streeter et al., 1985); when trying to find
information about pharmaceuticals, medical doctors tend to ask other
doctors for advice (Timpka and Hallberg, 1996). Munro (1999) observed
how people followed crowds or simply sat around at a venue when deciding which shows and street events to attend at the Edinburgh Arts
Festival.

As shown by Harper (this volume), this even applies to what might be
considered a prototypical information retrieval scenario. He studied the
work done by "desk officers" at the International Monetary Fund (IMF)
who retrieve information concerning different countries and their
economies. He found that a piece of information might very well be valid
and important, and still completely uninteresting since the people with
power in the country are not reading and acting upon it. Thus, it is the
overall social texture of the information that determines its value. A
recent study by Soininen and Suikola (2000) shows that social aspects
come into almost every step of an information retrieval process, ranging
from the problem formulation to the evaluation of the retrieved items.

---

[1] This chapter is derived from Svensson et al. (2001). © ACM 2001.

Even when we are not explicitly looking for information we use a wide range of cues, both from features of the environment and from the behaviour of other people, to manage our activities. Unfortunately, in most computer applications, we cannot see others; there are no normative behaviours that we can watch and imitate. We walk around in spaces that, for all we know, have not been visited by anyone else before us. In an application we might be lost for hours with no guidance whatsoever. On the web, there is no one else around to tell us how to find what we are looking for, or even where the search engine is.

It should be pointed out that there is a difference between concluding that social navigation happens in the world no matter what we do, and deciding that it is a good idea to design system from this perspective. Social navigation is not a concept that can be unproblematically translated into ready-made algorithms and tools to be added on top of an existing space. What we can do is to *enable*, make the world *afford*, social interactions and accumulate social trails. Social navigation will often be a dynamic, changing, interaction between the *users* in the space, the *items* in the space (whether grocery items, books, or something else) and the *activities* in the space. All three are subject to change.

We have designed an on-line system that recommends food recipes using this social navigation design perspective. We describe our design approach, the system, and a first user study of the system. Based on the study a second system is then built and evaluated in a more realistic setting.

8.2 Social Navigation

Dourish and Chalmers introduced the concept of social navigation in 1994. They saw social navigation as *navigation towards a cluster of people* or *navigation because other people have looked at something*.

Dieberger (1997b) widened the scope of social navigation and also saw more direct recommendations of, for example, web sites and bookmark collections as a form of social navigation. Since then the concept of social navigation has broadened to include a large family of methods, artefacts and techniques that capture some aspect of navigation.

Through the book *Social Navigation of Information Space* (Munro et al., 1999) the field was established. The book brought together several different perspectives on social navigation – ranging from how it happens in the world today and how it can draw upon perspectives from urban planning, architecture, film studies and other design disciplines, to how it could be applied in designing information services and virtual worlds. A number of systems have been implemented that exhibit some of these properties. The most well-known commercial example being the Amazon site recommending books: "others who bought this book also bought …". Research laboratory work includes the Footprints system (Wexelblat and Maes, 1999) that visualises history-enriched information. It presents different visualisations of history information as maps, trails and annotations allowing users to see where within a page activity had taken place. Similar ideas are explored in IBM's WebPlaces (Maglio, this volume) . It observes peoples' paths through the web and looks for recurring paths. In the mobile context the GeoNotes system (Persson et al., this volume) lets people annotate the physical world with virtual post-it notes. GeoNotes uses a recommender system to help people find the interesting notes to read. Yet another is the history-enriched SWIKI-variant implemented by Dieberger (Dieberger, 2000). This system keeps a record on how often pages on a collaborative web server have been accessed and when they last got modified. It then annotates links to these pages with markers indicating the amount of recent traffic on that page, whether the page has not been accessed for a long time, or if that page was recently modified.

What is missing in many recommendations or history-enriched systems is feedback on whether the item bought, read or visited in the end met the user's needs and whether she enjoyed it. Reviews can provide some of this feedback, but can vary widely in quality. epinions.com tries to improve on this by having reviewers themselves rated so that it can be determined whether a review was written by an "expert reviewer" or not.

8.2.1 Defining Social Navigation

A slightly modified version of the definition of social navigation given by Dourish and Chalmers is: "Social navigation is navigation that is conceptually understood as driven by the actions from one or more advice providers." An advice provider can be a person or artificial agent providing navigational advice to somebody trying to navigate a space. Our definition also opens up for the possibility that the social layers are faked – thus only conceptually understood as if they have been induced by others, similar to how patina on furniture can be faked to make it look antique.

We differentiate between *direct* and *indirect* social navigation. The first is where there is a dialogue between the navigator and the advice provider(s), as in chat systems. In indirect social navigation we follow traces left by other users, either in real-time or as aggregated paths from previous usage.

In order to exclude items such as maps as social navigation tools, two additional properties are needed to describe the phenomena we aim to capture: *personalisation* and *dynamism*. Two examples illustrate their importance:

- Walking down a path in a forest is social navigation, but walking down a road in a city is not.
- Talking to a person at the airport help desk that explains how to find the baggage claim is social navigation, but reading a sign with (more or less) the exact same message is not.

Both methods in these examples seem to convey the same navigational advice; the difference lies in how advice is given to the navigator. In the first example, the navigator chooses to follow a path based on the fact that other people have walked it. Conversely, walking down a street is not driven by the fact that other people have walked the same street. The street is an intrinsic part of the space. One way to think about this is that social navigation traces are not pre-planned aspects of a space, but rather are "grown" – or created *dynamically* – in a more organic or bottom-up fashion. In this way, social navigation is a closer reflection of what people actually do than it is a result of what designers think people should be doing.

In the second example the navigator gets the impression that the navigational advice is *personalised* to her and the situation allows her to ask for additional information. Also, the advice ceases to exist when the communication between the navigator and advice provider ends. The person at the help desk may have to use different terms, or even speak a different language, to convey the same message to each particular customer. The help-desk worker can also recognise a repeat visitor, and modify the presentation of information based on knowledge that a past attempt has failed.

Another key distinction between social navigation and general navigation is how navigational advice is mediated. In social navigation there is a strong temporal and dynamic aspect. A person chooses to follow a particular path in the forest because she makes the assumption that people have walked it earlier. Forest paths are transient features in the environment; if they are not used they vanish. Their state (how well-worn they are) can indicate how frequently or recently they have been used, which is typically not possible with a road.

We see therefore that social navigation relies on the way that people occupy and transform spaces, leaving their marks upon them – turning a space into a place in the terminology of Harrison and Dourish (1996).

8.2.2 How Does it Help?

How might the presence of social navigation capabilities affect user behaviour? Since the field is new, very few user studies exists that attempt to address these issues, but the following effects are discussed (Dieberger et al., 2000):

- *Filtering.* A couple of user studies show that history-enriched environments and recommender systems might help filter out the most relevant information from a large information space (Wexelblat and Maes, this volume; Lönnqvist et al., 2000).

- *Quality.* Sometimes it is not enough that the information obtained is relevant, it must also possess qualities that can only be determined from how other users react to it (the social texture discussed in the introduction). Only when an expert verifies that a piece of information is valid, or when a piece of art is often referred to in the literature, will it be of high quality in the eyes of a navigator.

- *Social affordance.* Visible actions of other users can inform us what is appropriate behaviour, what can or cannot be done. At the same time, this awareness of others and their actions makes us feel that the space is alive and might make it more inviting. Here the focus is not on whether users navigate more efficiently, or find exactly what they need more quickly; instead, the intent is to make them stay longer in the space, feel more relaxed, and perhaps be inspired to try out new functionality, to pick up new products and new information items, or to try out new services that they would not have considered otherwise. Users can quickly pick up on the "norms" for how to behave when they see others' behaviour.

- *Usage reshapes functionality and structure.* Social navigation design may alter the organisation of the space. In amazon.com, the structure of the space experienced by visitors is changed; one can follow the recommendations instead of navigating by the search-for-terms structure. Social navigation thus could be a first step towards empowering users, in a natural, subtle way, to make the functionality and structure "drift" and make our information spaces more "fluid". To arrive at systems that enables these properties the design must convey the meaning of the social layering to users, as well as how their individual actions in turn will influence the system.

By necessity, in most cases users will have to accept that their actions are "visible" to other users. This may infringe on their privacy resulting in loss of trust in the system. Erickson and Kellogg (this volume) use the concept "social translucence" to capture that privacy is not the only issue here, but that users also need to understand what information they are disclosing and how it is used. Social translucence entails a balance of visibility, awareness of others and accountability.

The designer of a social navigation system must find pedagogical means of conveying how actions are aggregated and displayed to others, as well as protecting the privacy of users.

8.2.3 Modelling Social Navigation

In order to implement a social navigation system, some basic software functionality is needed. The Social Navigator (Svensson, 2000) is a toolkit that provides simple primitives by which user behaviour can be modelled. It centres around three concepts: *locations*, *people* and *movements*. Locations can be defined in various ways: it might be a web page, a geographical place, or a database entry. People are always attached to a location and movements between locations are automatically time-stamped and stored.

Flags can be attached to on-line users signalling, for example, their visibility or to what extent they can be trusted. Flags do not have a predefined semantics but can be used to signal various aspects depending on the domain.

The Social Navigator is implemented as a Java servlet and accessed through a web server, which allows for net-based communication between a variety of different clients, ranging from browsers to stand-alone applications.

8.3 On-line Food Shopping

We decided to apply our ideas for social navigation to the domain of food shopping over the Internet. In a typical on-line grocery store, there will be 10,000 different products to choose from. Navigating such a space is not only time-consuming but can also be boring and tedious. As shown by Sjölinder and colleagues (2000), some users will have more difficulties than others to efficiently make use of the existing on-line stores. In a study on an existing hypertext based on-line store, they show that elderly users spent on average twice as much time finding items on a shopping list than did younger users. In both age categories, users sometimes completely gave up when searching for certain items. On average, users spent 12 minutes to find 10 ingredients.

According to Chau et al. (1996) product presentation, customer navigation and search for products are major factors leading to acceptance or rejection of electronic shopping by consumers. A recent study by Frostling-Henningsson (2000) showed that on-line food shoppers do not gain any time from shopping for food on-line, instead they appreciate flexibility in time and space. Shoppers feel that they can avoid the tedious, boring food stores, but they lose the sensuous pleasures of seeing, touching and smelling the products. This is somewhat compensated by getting status among friends from being able to tell stories about how they shop for food on-line. In a study by Richmond (1996) on shopping in a virtual reality environment, it was found that users also want to be able to access the social aspects of a physical store, they want to socialise with other people.

Given the problems with navigation and the lack of social interaction and sensuous pleasures in the existing on-line grocery stores, the domain should be an excellent application example for social navigation techniques.

8.4 EFOL Design

It is difficult to recommend food based on other users' shopping, as the ingredients bought do not necessarily tell us what is going to be cooked. It is at the level of the meals that somebody cooks that we would expect to be able to model users' food preferences. Thus, we decided to recommend recipes to users. The recipes we cook from convey a lot about our personality, which culture we belong to and our habits.

EFOL (European Food On-Line) allows users to shop for food through selecting a set of recipes where the ingredients are added to their shopping lists. Recipe selection allows for accumulation of user behaviour so that we understand which groups of users are most likely to choose which recipes. Shopping from recipes also makes it easier for users to plan their meals ahead and shop for all the ingredients needed without having to search for each one of them. Through adding pictures of the courses the shopping also becomes more appealing to the eye.

Based on the user clusters, the recipes are in turn grouped into recipe collections. Instead of making each recipe a "place" where users can meet, the recipe collections can be natural meeting points.

As the intent was to try various different forms of social navigation, we also wanted to populate the space – providing some form of direct social navigation. The idea was to make users aware of other users, their choices of recipes, and also to enable chatting to discuss recipes.

The interface can be found in Figure 8.1. It shows a recipe in the bottom-right window, and next to it the ranked list of recipes in the current recipe collection. Above the recipe, a chat window for the recipe collection is opened. Finally, to the left, there is an overview map with all the recipe collections. In it, currently logged on users are visualised using simple avatars. Let us now discuss the design in more detail.

8.4.1 Indirect Social Navigation in EFOL

Recipes in the system are grouped into recipe collections. A collection is a set of recipes with a special theme, for example "vegetarian food". They are also places where customers can meet, socialise and get recommendations about recipes. Recipe collections are formed and given their names by their "editors".

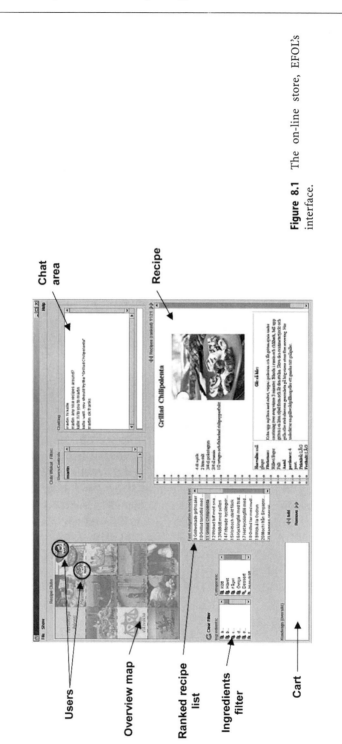

Figure 8.1 The on-line store, EFOL's interface.

Users can move around between collections to get different recommendations. Each collection contains a list of recipes that is ranked based on the usage pattern in that particular collection. In a way this can be viewed as the system giving personalised advice to users based on what others like.

While in traditional informational retrieval systems the search is based on the words in the existing documents, recommender systems instead base their search on user behaviours (Resnick and Varian, 1997) . One of the problems then becomes how to start, or bootstrap, such a system before any user behaviour has been collected. This affects both the problem of items that have not been rated by users, as well as how to classify new users in the system. One solution is to combine search based on the words in the recipes with collaborative filtering. Users can thus constrain the recommendations given by the system, for example, to find recipes that contain a particular ingredient. This gives users the desired control over the recommendations while it also gives the user a chance to find recipes that have not yet been rated by any user.

8.4.2 Dynamic Recipe Collections

A common problem with existing recommender systems such as MovieLens (Konstan et al., this volume) or Firefly (Shardanand and Maes, 1995), is that they give little or no feedback to a user on what user group she belongs to, or what user groups a recommendation is built upon. The only feedback a user gets from the system is the recommended items, which is a poor way of reflecting a user's interests back to her. One problem is the rather complex task of automating the "labelling" of user groups. For instance, it would be extremely difficult for the Firefly system to automatically label a cluster of users as "reggae lovers with a flavour of ska".

Labelling of user groups not only tells the user something about which recipe collection she is at right now, but also gives information about other existing clusters of recipes and users. This will allow a user not only to navigate the recommendations but also the user groups. In this way, a user can try out selecting recipes from different groups, thus getting access to a more diverse collection of recipes.

Our solution to the labelling problem is to put an editor back into the loop. There are two types of editors – the system editor and ordinary users. The system editor looks at log data collected from the recommender system and cluster users based on which recipes they have chosen and "names" them with fuzzy names that convey somewhat of their content: "vegetarians", "light food eaters", or "spice lovers". To enhance this process, the system is based on a filtering algorithm that uses an *explicit* representation of user preferences as recipe features (e.g., ingredients, fat level, time to cook) that change over time. It should thus be relatively easy for an editor to find similarities between users or recipes, and get an intuitive impression of why they are similar. Returning to the definition of social navigation, one could view the system editor as upholding the dynamicity of the system, that is, over time users preferences will change, and so will the various recipe collections.

The second type of editor is any user of the system who can at any time create a new recipe collection with a certain theme that she finds interesting, for instance, "Annika and her friends club". These collections, obviously, do not have to reflect actual clusters of users as those found by the system editor. However, if a group of users choose recipes from such a collection on a regular basis their user profiles will converge. Again, this allows users themselves to shape and model the space they inhabit.

Visual recipe collections might provide the users with more insight into the social trails of their own actions as well as other users' actions that have led to the recommendations they finally get. It also provides some insight into the inner workings of the recommender system. This could be a model of the system's functionality that users build after having used the system for a while.

Real-Time Indirect Social Navigation

In addition to the recommender functionality, users have a real-time presence in the store through icons (avatars) representing them in an overview map of the recipe collections. As the user moves from one collection to another, the avatar will move in the overview map (see Figure 8.1). Our intention is to provide awareness of other on-line users. Since the user can see which collections are currently visited by numerous logged in users, this will hopefully also influence their choice of recipe collection and recipes.

Direct Social Navigation in EFOL

The system also provides chat functionality tied to each recipe collection. Collections thus become "places" in the information space. We could have chosen to make each recipe a place for chatting, but since the database contains three thousand recipes, each recipe would not become sufficiently inhabited.

The implementation allowed users to be invisible, but in the user study we decided to disable this functionality, so that the effects of awareness and privacy issues could be studied.

Social Annotations

As discussed in the introduction, the social texture of a piece of information might be relevant. This is probably true for recipes: it is the style of the recipe, the author, the kind of life style conveyed by the recipe, and knowledge of cooking, that matters when we choose whether to cook from the recipe or not. Through adding the name of the authors and making it possible to click on them to get a description, users get a richer context for evaluating and choosing among the recipes. Each recipe also has a number denoting how many times it has been downloaded.

8.5 Evaluation

In a qualitative user study we tried to establish to what extent our social navigation design intentions succeeded. We wanted to know whether the recipe collections aided users in filtering out good recipes, whether they were influenced by other users' actions in the system (moving between recipe collections and chatting), and whether they understood that the system changes with its usage. We also wanted to check to what extent they felt that their privacy was violated.

Subjects

There were 12 subjects, 5 females and 7 males, between 23 and 30 years old (average 24.5 years). They were students from computer linguistics and computer science programme. The two groups did not know one another before the study. None of the subjects had any experience of on-line food shopping prior to the study.

Task and Procedure

The subjects used the system on two different occasions. They were asked to choose five recipes each time. Their actions were logged, and we provided them with a questionnaire on age, gender, education and a set of open-ended questions on the functionality of the system. They were given a food cheque of 300 SEK (£20) and encouraged to buy the food needed for the recipes.

8.5.1 Results

Overall, subjects made use of several of the social navigation indicators. They chatted (on average 6.5 statements per user during the second occasion), they also looked at which recipe collections other users visited, and followed them around. About half felt very influenced by what others did in the system.

Concerning the effects of adding pictures, we found that half of the subjects got hungrier from using the system than they were before starting and 75% of the subjects were in the same or a better mood after using the system (despite a set of technical breakdowns during the sessions).

Privacy Issues

After using the system subjects answered the question "Do you think that it adds anything to see what others do in this kind of system? What in such a case? If not, what bothers you?" One subject said: "It think it is positive. One can see what others are doing and the chat functionality makes it more social. One could get new ideas." Not everyone was as positive: "No! I cannot see the point of it, I have never been interested in chat-functions."

We looked closer at this difference and found that the subjects could be divided into two groups. One group, consisting of 10 subjects, who felt influenced by others, and one minority group, consisting of 2 subjects who claimed not to be. The logs from their sessions with the system also backed up this difference; the first group chatted and moved between collections without hesitation. In their comments, they also stated that visible activity in recipe collections influenced them; they were attracted to collections where there were other users and they became curious about what the other users were doing in those collections. When asked about other services they would like, they were positive towards functions such as sharing a recipe with a friend, more contact with the owner of the food store, and being able to comment on a recipe and see others comments.

The remaining two subjects were consistently negative towards social trails. They did not like to chat, they disliked being logged, they did not want more social functions added to the system, and they could not see an added value in being able to see other users in the system. Their claims were again backed up by log data: they did in fact not chat, and one subject did not even move between recipe collections.

The division into the two groups is also in line with whether they would like to use the system again. The ones who did not want to use it again were the ones who claimed not to be influenced by the actions of others. Interestingly enough, more or less all participants found the system fun to use – even the ones claiming they did not want to use it again.

When investigating subjects' answers to the open-ended questions, certain aspects of social trails in the interface do not seem intrusive at all, while others are more problematic to some users. The fact that the recipes show how many times they have been downloaded is not a problem – it is not even mentioned. Neither is the fact that choosing a recipe will affect the recommender system. When asked whether they were bothered about being logged, one subject answered: "It does not bother me at all. There are so many facts about me spread everywhere anyway, so what does it matter? Besides, one gets logged in order for the recipe recommendations to get more individualised and that should lead to saving time". This view keeps coming back; as long as there is a perceived benefit, and the name of the user can be faked, most users do not mind being logged.

The two users who disliked being logged answered: "Well, maybe. I do not like being logged" and "It does bother me somewhat that others can see what I do, for example I did not jump as much to the other recipes collections but stayed in the 'Personal Corner' [the default collection] because of this. But when it concerns something like a recipe I do not think that it matters that much whether I get logged or not. One is relatively anonymous anyway since one does not log in with email address or any other personal information." Thus, seeing the avatar moving between recipe collections is more intrusive than the fact that choosing a recipe affects the recommender system.

Otherwise, subjects did feel influenced by how the other users avatars moved between recipe collections: "If there are many stands in a collection one gets curious and wants to go there and check it out" or as another subject said: "I got somewhat distracted from seeing them jump around. It was a little bit exciting when someone else entered the same collection [as me]." A worry we had as designers of the system was that users would feel that they were not rewarded when following other users. Once a user has moved to a collection with many visitors, the only thing that changes is that she can chat with them. She cannot see which recipes they are looking at nor which ones they have chosen from this collection so far. The list of recipes in the collection are of course ordered by how popular they are, but this ordering is not only based on the actions of the concurrent users, but is also inferred from what other users, not currently logged into the system, have chosen in the past.

Finally, of course, the chatting is even more intrusive than the logging and avatar movements. As one user pointed out, he did not mind getting his choice of recipe logged, but if the contents of the chatting could be used and saved in the system, he would be bothered. But again, chatting was only intrusive to some. Most (9 subjects) saw it as a positive addition.

In general, being logged does not bother users – they know that this happens all the time anyway, and they do not mind sharing their preferences for food. It is when their actions are not anonymous and other users can "see them" that a minority of users react negatively.

Social Affordance

Through adding social trails to the interface we hoped that it would encourage users to explore the space, and perhaps guide them to a better understanding of the functionality, "the appropriate behaviour", in the space. One subject said: "Yes, I found it interesting to be able to see what the others were doing. The only thing that bothers [me] is if one sees them doing something and then one does not understand how to do the same thing. Right at the beginning I did not understand how to switch recipe collection and then it was frustrating to see the others change collection all the time." While this subject expresses frustration, she still captures our intention: to reveal system functionality through making other users' actions somewhat visible.

Social Experience

Adding social navigation to the design definitely made our subjects feel that it was a social experience: "The system became alive and more fun when one could see the other users." Another user said: "I think it is good to introduce social contact. In many systems on the net, several users may be logged in, but you cannot feel their presence." One user said that the best part of the system was "To have a chat function so that one that not feel all alone in one's struggle against the system."

Users also asked for other forms of social functionality, such as being able to share a recipe with a friend, being able to chat with the owners of the store, getting in touch with professional chefs, or publishing a week menu for others to be inspired by.

Understanding Recommender Functionality

Finally, despite the fact that these were students from a course on intelligent user interfaces, they did not have any clear picture of how the recommendations happened, or why there were recipe collections. They hypothesised that the order of the recipes was affected by their choices, but they did not have any clear theories of why or how this happened or how it related to the recipe collections. Even if our subjects did not fully understand the dynamicity of the recipe collections or the fact that they represented user groups, they got a better insight into the workings of the system than would have been possible if there had been no recipe collections at all. One user said: "Yes, maybe a recipe that often gets chosen is more representative of the recipe collection and can be recommended to others."

8.5.2 From EFOL to Kalas

While EFOL was a small-scale study that needs to be redone in a more realistic setting with a larger number of users, it still points at some strengths and weaknesses in social navigation that need to be further investigated. Strengths of the EFOL solution were that we did indeed create a social, pleasurable and entertaining system. We also succeeded in turning the space of recipes and ingredients into a *place*. The Kalas[2] system is our attempt to tackle some of the shortcomings found in EFOL. Weaknesses that need to be carefully considered when designing for social navigation includes first of all ensuring for a stronger privacy protection for those users who wish to be anonymous. This can easily be achieved with the Social Navigator toolkit (Svensson, 2000) through adding a flag to each user signalling their visibility status.

Secondly, users should be able to comment on individual recipes, and also to come back and vote positively or negatively on a recipe that they have previously cooked from. These votes should affect the recommender system, preventing the snowball effect. An interesting extension to comments is to use "anchored conversations" (Churchill et al., this volume). A "sticky chat" started anywhere in a recipe, would then be stored with it. These chats allow for both synchronous and asynchronous conversations which could convey a richer, social picture of the recipes and how to cook from them.

Through creating different visualisations of users, friends, chefs and store-owners, users can choose whom to follow, rather than just blindly follow an anonymous crowd. Users can then make a more informed choice, thereby reducing the snowball effects.

Concerning the third problem on how to convey the recommender system functionality, a possible solution would be to show the contents of a user profile to the user. Another approach is to avoid explaining the contents of a user profile altogether and instead provide information on those users who influenced a recommendation.

8.6 Kalas

As can be seen from Figure 8.2 (see also colour plate 13) and Figure 8.1, Kalas and EFOL have completely different interfaces. More or less everything in the interface has changed, although the basic elements are still there: there are recipes, people can chat, they can see others who are logged on, and they get recommendations of recipes in recipes collections.

Overview Map

In both EFOL and Kalas people move by navigating the overview map. In the first version the various collections were grouped in 4 rows and 3 columns. At first this seems like a perfectly reasonable idea. The problem

---

[2] Kalas in Swedish means party.

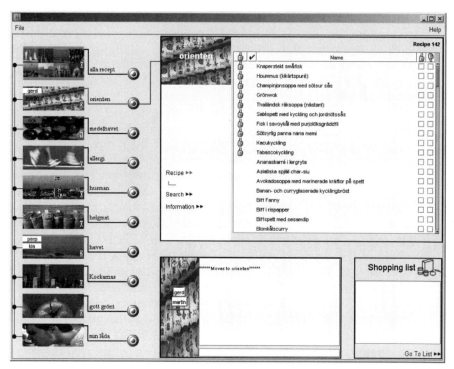

Figure 8.2 Kalas ranked recipe list (*see also* colour plate 13).

is that people have difficulties finding the boundaries between collections, and that ordering a "space" this way could enhance the notion of belonging to certain collections.

In Kalas the map changed to be more "flat like", just the available collections listed from top to bottom. Collections were clearly separated to minimise the confusion of where users are. The way people navigate was also changed to clicking a button to the right of the collection rather than clicking the collection itself, mainly due to difficulties clicking heavily crowed collections.

In a system like Kalas there should not be a limit to the number of collections available. As was pointed out earlier, new collections could be created by editors or users, or even generated automatically. The new overview map also supports scrolling of collections. If there are more than 10 collections (the maximum number that can be visible) the left-hand side of the map allows for scrolling up and down collections.

Individual Recipes

Individual recipes have undergone several changes (see Figure 8.3). Recipes are now placed in the top-right corner instead of the bottom-

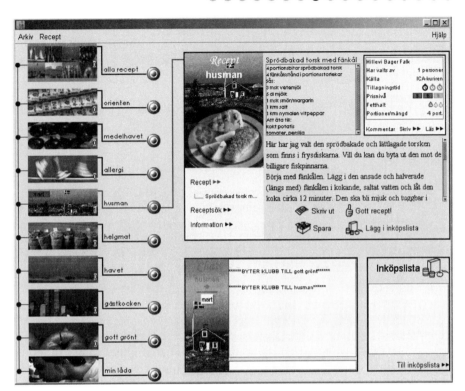

Figure 8.3 Recipe.

right corner, giving them a more central place in the interface. Based on the design ideas brought forth in the EFOL study, recipes can now be annotated with user comments. The social information (times downloaded, recipe author) and comments are placed in the top of a recipe, making them more visible.

Another notable difference is that the ranked recipe list is not shown when looking at a recipe (cf. the list on the left in EFOL). Instead a user has to click the recipe button to the left to bring back the list of recipes, thus compacting the amount of information at one time in the interface.

Implicit and Explicit Ratings

In EFOL there was only one way of giving feedback (ratings) to the recommender system: by putting recipes into the shopping cart.

In Kalas we (1) added a special collection ("my collection") that was used to store user-selected recipes, (2) made it possible to get printouts of recipes and shopping lists. As was indicated in the EFOL study users wanted a way to explicitly state their opinions about recipes. Thus, (3) explicit positive ("thumbs up") and negative ("thumbs down") votes were

217

added. In a system that depends on user feedback it is vital that feedback is easy to give. Therefore explicit votes are accessible from within recipes, recipe lists, when writing comments, and in the "my collection" collection.

Thus, in Kalas, there are four different implicit ways of saying that a recipe is interesting: adding it to the shopping list, adding it to "my collection", printing it, and one explicit "thumbs up".

Ranked Recipe List

EFOL used an extremely simple recipe list with recommendations displayed in ascending order. There was no other way to sort the list. It was pointed out earlier that people did not understand how or where this ordering came from. As a solution, we discussed, for instance, various ways of explaining explanations. An easier solution, that gives some explanation, is not to sort the whole list by recommendation, but only to show the top 10 recommended recipes with the rest sorted by title. The "thumbs up" symbol was used to indicate a recommendation (see Figure 8.2). Although it is not an explanation as such, the recommendations should be more visible to users.

In EFOL we focus on social navigational techniques to aid people in the right direction. In a real system one cannot, however, only allow people to navigate in one direction (as was done in EFOL's ranked lists). Kalas allows for sorting recipe lists in either of three ways: (1) by recommendation, which is the default mode, (2) by recipes already seen, or (3) by recipe title.

My Box

For the first study it was perfectly all right to "pretend" that EFOL was connected to an on-line food store; our subjects were a small group of students that received some money for doing it. Putting a system out to "real" users without the back-end store is another story. The benefit of using it will simply not be that great as it stands. The implicit feedback we want to get for the recommender system will be far too haphazard. The solution is obvious, there has to be another reason for using the system.

My Box (Figure 8.4) is the special collection where users can store recipes, change their profiles, go invisible and mark others as friends. All actions that trigger the recommender (recommend, print, save, etc.) are visible in here. Instead of having a recipe list with a special theme, the My Box recipe list contains all recipes a user has chosen and how she chose them. For example, in Figure 8.4 we see that Ugnsbakad torsk was saved on 1 May. Thus, it is both a recipe history and a place to manage your profile.

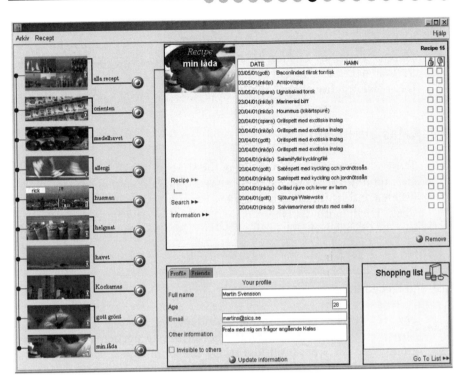

Figure 8.4 My Box.

When a user enters the system she automatically starts in My Box. She immediately sees what she did in her last visit, and more importantly, gets a chance to react to those recipes (clicking "thumbs up" and "thumbs down") without much effort. My Box not only acts as a history, it is also a tool to help people give feedback to the system. And again, the difficulty with explicit feedback is to get people to go about and rate information.

A Note about Invisibility

Privacy issues are important in these kinds of systems, which the EFOL study showed. In Kalas people can be invisible at the price of loosing some of the "social functionality". They still can see where other (visible) users are in the overview map, but lose the ability to see or participate in chatting. The reasons for this are:

- To participate in a discussion when no one knows you are there is not fair to those who believe that there are only certain people listening.
- Since social navigation builds upon the fact that people expose themselves, some features should be lost if a person chooses not to be exposed. In a sense, a user can only gain as much as she contributes.

In Kalas there are only three visibility modes, friend, visible and invisible. The control of invisibility could be more fine grained than that, for example, people could be "not up for chatting" or "busy at the moment". Various degrees of invisibility would then give access to more or less of the social functionality in the system.

8.7 Kalas Evaluation

The evaluation is a continuation of the study of EFOL. We again concentrate on how the social features in the system aid and affect people. The difference this time is that we move away from the controlled environment. The hypothesis is that people act and react differently in the real world, especially when it comes to social phenomena. In here we will only present a sample of preliminary results.

Task and Procedure

The study took place over a period of six months (June through November 2001), and it was open for anyone to participate. The target group were users of an on-line recipe site hemma.net.[3] During the first month of the study we advertised for the study both by sending e-mail to hemma.net's users and by providing links on hemma.net's homepage. People who chose to participate were totally free to use the system whenever they wanted and also to stop using it at anytime. The study was divided into four parts: pre questionnaire, post questionnaire, gathering of log data, and a small number of in-depth interviews.

Subjects

A total of 598 subjects completed the first questionnaire (530 females and 68 males), varying between 19 and 79 years of age. Most people (309), were between the age of 30 and 50. They were also frequent Internet users: 445 accessed it every day and 129 accessed it 2 to 4 times a week. 225 subjects had education in computers and 89 of the subjects where skilled in cooking.

Of the 598 subjects who answered the first questionnaire, 279 subjects used Kalas. This could be explained both by problems starting Kalas and from the fact that we launched it during the holiday season. Finally, 76 subjects completed the final questionnaire.

---

[3] A Swedish recipe site with over 10,000 unique visitors per week.

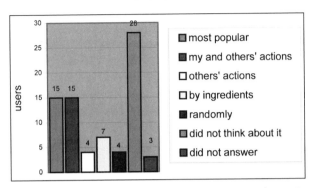

Figure 8.5 How do you think Kalas choose recipes for you?

8.7.1 Results

The results presented will in general be based on the final questionnaire. For the questionnaire we used a Likert scale ranging from 1 to 7.

Overall, people found Kalas easy to use (only 6 people found it more difficult than average). The same result holds for using the system. Subjects understood the major social features of the system: 64% recognised the symbol for an on-line user, 88% were aware of the chatting facility, 92% knew that it was possible to comment on recipes and 83% understood how to vote on recipes. In general people did not chat or communicate by other means. With only 279 users (which we thought would be enough) there is a high probability that you log in to the system when no one else is there. This could explain the slightly less recognition (64%) of users' on-line representation.

Recommender Functionality

Did our subjects understand how Kalas recommended recipes and did they like what was recommended to them? We asked the question: "How do you think Kalas chooses recipes for you?". In Figure 8.5 we see that 28 subjects did not give it a thought, which in a way sounds reasonable. Surprisingly, 34 people believed that it had something to do with what others did – a result totally different from the one we got in the first study. The "thumbs up" symbol is probably a very strong indication that something is interesting to others.

People understood the recommendations, but did they like them? Most people (29) gave the recommendations a rating of 4 on our 7-point scale. Twenty subjects gave recommendations a 5 rating and 18 rated them 6. In effect, people were neutral or positive to recommendations. One should point out that subjects tend to be "nice" in these types of questionnaires, and that the pre-selected recipe collections could be good to start with.

221

Finally, let us examine the log-data to see if people acted on recommendations (i.e. voted positively on recommended recipes). Out of the total number of 1271 implicit and explicit votes, people gave 364 positive votes on recipes from the 10 top-most recipes in the recipe lists. Out of those, 277 were recommended. We also calculated the number of negative votes cast on the top-most recipes. Out of 12 negative votes, 10 were from lists sorted by date. The other ways of sorting recipes (apart from searching) only accounted for a few of the votes. In conclusion, people tended to give positive feedback to recommended recipes and negative feedback to recipes that were not recommended.

Explicit Voting

EFOL was built around implicit voting to *minimise* the burden on users. There are several problems with that approach; users do not have the ability to give explicit feedback to the system, to name one. In Kalas users can give explicit feedback, both positive and negative. There were 59 users giving a total of 246 explicit votes (the total number of votes being 1271). Of these, 7% were negative and 93% positive votes.

It was argued earlier that the My Box collection was a place for users to give explicit feedback. If we look at where people cast their votes we see that 17% of the votes where given from within the My Box collection (remember that all recipes found here are recipes previously chosen). Thus, people give feedback on things they have previously chosen. It also tells us of the importance to allow people to vote on recipes that they have not necessarily chosen in the past.

8.8 Summary

Through first defining and then applying a combination of social navigation design ideas and our tool, the Social Navigator, we have turned an on-line grocery store into a social place (EFOL) where shopping is done through picking recipes. We have showed how an initial qualitative study can inform us in designing a second system (Kalas). In our second study with 279 users we see, for instance, that the way recommendations are presented is crucial in understanding them. We believe that both implementations and studies can stand as design examples for how social navigation can enhance on-line shopping in various different domains.

Acknowledgements

This PERSONA project is funded by the i[3] EC-scheme and by SITI (Swedish IT Institute). The authors wish to thank the PERSONA project members, and the anonymous subjects who took part in the study for valuable input and discussion.

9

Results from the Footprints Project

Alan Wexelblat

9.1 Footprints

The Footprints project was a multi-version, multi-year investigation into the application of social navigation principles to the problems of assisting web navigation. Inspired by Hill and Hollan's original work on Readware (1993), we developed a theory of interaction history and built tools to apply this theory to navigation in a complex information space. The guiding principle was collecting, filtering, organising and redisplaying interaction history. We built a series of tools – map, paths, annotations and signposts – based on a physical-world navigation metaphor. This chapter[1] presents results from the use of three versions of the system by a voluntary user group over two years and a controlled study with paid participants. Our user study showed that users who had the aid of Footprints were able to get the same amount of work done with significantly less effort in a given period of time.

Digital information has no history. It comes to us devoid of the patina that forms on physical objects as they are used. In the physical world we make extensive use of these traces to guide our actions, to make choices, and to find things of importance or interest. We call these traces *interaction history*; that is, the records of the interactions of people and objects. Interaction history is necessary to enable social navigation for people distributed in time; if I cannot directly observe what others are doing I must have available to me some kind of record of that activity.

Physical objects may be described as *history-rich* if they have associated with them historical traces that can be used by people in the current time. For example, if you are driving your car down an unfamiliar highway and approach a curve, you may notice that the guardrail has a number of black streaks on it. Realising that these streaks have been formed from the "interaction" of the guardrail and the bumpers of other cars, you

---

[1] This chapter is derived from Wexelblat and Maes (1999). © ACM 1999.

slow down. You are able to negotiate the curve safely because you can take advantage of the interaction history.

Interaction history is the difference between buying and borrowing a book. Traditional information retrieval theory would say they were the same object, given the same words, same pictures, same organisation, etc. However, the borrowed book usually comes with additional information. This may be a direct record, such as notes in the margins, or it may be annotative markings such as highlights and underlines; it may also be modifications to the object, such as dog-eared pages. Even the physical object reflects its history: a book opens more easily to certain places once it has been used.

The phrase "interaction history" encompasses three kinds of representational forms:

1. *Sequences of actions, relationships of elements on which people have acted, and the resulting structures.* Sequences are time-related actions which form a purposeful variation. For example, assembly instructions, or the directions in a cookbook recipe.

2. *Temporal collage.* Multiple states are shown directly, as in the ubiquitous "before and after" pictures used to show dramatic changes. The situations depicted in the before and the after pictures existed separated by some amount of time, but they are shown simultaneously, as if they had existed together. In this form of representation, time becomes part of the content.

3. *Recurrent opposed states.* History can be inferred from the contrast of the present state both with remembered past state(s) and with expected future state. For example, when I edit a source-code controlled file in Emacs, it displays the legend "CVS:1.6" as part of the edit mode line. This bit of history reminds me that the source file is "checked out" from the version control system, and raises the expectation that I will check it back in at some point.

In Gibson's terms (1987) – later brought to bear on digital artifacts by Norman (1988) – the history-rich object acquires new *affordances* and we can use these affordances to interact with the object in new ways. We make use of interaction history in the "real" world every day in dozens of different ways without conscious reflection. We think it is natural to do so, and most of our use goes unremarked. In fact it is not natural: car bumpers and guardrails are man-made artefacts that we have come to understand and "read" as a part of becoming adults in our society. The fact that we undergo such extensive learning strongly suggests that interaction history is highly valuable. Our project was called "Footprints" by analogy with the footprints we leave in the world, one of the earliest and still important forms of interaction history.

Footprints was a platform for experimentation in an attempt to understand what is valuable about interaction history in the physical world, and to find ways to capture history for use with digital information. The lack of interaction history information in modern digital systems represents a significant loss. People use digital systems purposefully, whether that purpose is problem-solving, entertainment-oriented, educational, or whatever. To achieve these purposes they must do some form of interaction, which then represents an investment of time, energy and attention. Work done by users to achieve their purposes in information systems should leave traces. These traces should be accessible to future users who could take advantage of the effort expended in the past to make their own goal-seeking easier.

For example, early in the course of the Footprints project, my adviser spent a fair amount of time shopping for a new car on the web. She visited a number of car manufacturer and car dealer sites, read reviews on-line, and looked at various independent reports and tests of a number of different vehicles. At the end of this process, she had not picked a particular car to buy – in fact, her list of possible choices was longer than when she began. But all the work done in this process was lost when she finished. If others wanted to take advantage of her work, they might ask her (if they happened to know she has done this task) and she might remember some of what she had done and learned. But anyone who did not know she had done this work cannot recover any of the things she found, nor to avoid any of the mistakes she made.

In the digital realm, problem solvers must often approach situations as though they were the first and only people ever to make use of the information. Maes' digital footprints are unavailable, so we all must become novel information foragers – in the sense of Pirolli and Card (1995) – over and over again. The Footprints system alleviated some of this kind of problem by allowing users to leave traces in the virtual environment of the World Wide Web, creating history-rich digital objects. These objects were then presented in relevant contexts to later foragers, giving them additional information and guidance.[2]

The term "history-rich object" and its association with records of the interaction of people and digital information derives from work by Will Hill and Jim Hollan (1993). We took their initial insight and expanded upon it. The original work did not present a theoretical basis for interaction history or guidelines for future developers. As part of the Footprints project I developed a first-generation theoretical framework, stated in the form of properties. These properties are present in all interaction history in the physical world, and should be considered by designers of history-rich social navigation systems.

Because Footprints' tools were directed towards web navigation, we also found ourselves gaining some insights into the ways people navigate

---

[2] For reasons of time and personal preference Footprints never explored the problems and opportunities associated with making recommendations.

in this kind of virtual space. It is still an open question as to what degree these navigation patterns of behaviour apply in other realms, but they form primitive units that can be constructed or anticipated by designs of future navigation-rich systems. These are observations, and still need statistical verification.

The next section of this chapter gives a basic introduction to the theoretical framework. Following that, I describe the Footprints tools. Finally, I present results from an experiment in having people use Footprints in a controlled task.

9.2 Interaction History Framework

We have developed a framework for talking about interaction history. This framework presents six properties that characterise interaction history systems. The goal of the framework is to bound a space of all possible interaction history systems, and to give designers of such systems guidance as to what things are important in building history-rich interfaces. We use six properties to describe this space.

Property 1: Proxemic versus Distemic

Urban planning and social anthropology use the words *proxemic* and *distemic* to describe the closeness relationship of people and spaces. Specifically, how physically close people are for certain actions, and the degree to which those actions are governed by formal externalised rules versus informal socio-cultural understandings. Proximity is a function of both physical distance and the cognitive distance between the person and the space. A proxemic space is one that is felt by users to be transparent, in that the signs and structures can be easily understood by virtue of the cultural upbringing and social background of the participants. People feel close to, or part of, the space. Conversely, distemic spaces are opaque to users. Signals go unseen, usually because the people in the space lack the required background or knowledge to translate or comprehend what they experience. We feel "close" to our bedroom even when far away from it and experience a certain "distance" when we sleep in someone else's guest bedroom.

Interaction history systems may be more or less proxemic based on how well they relate to their users and how well they take advantage of users' past experiences and knowledge. For example, the personal computer desktop interface pioneered with the Xerox Star was intended to be proxemic in that it attempted to recreate a space with which the user would be familiar. The Emacs mode-line history noted above (CVS 1.6) would be completely distemic to anyone who did not know that cvs is a concurrent version-control system that uses numerical markers to distinguish successive versions of a source file. Netscape Navigator's bookmarks may also constitute a proxemic system because users can arrange, group, subdivide and categorise as they please. A proxemic group space is something like a collaborative workbench, where the tools are arranged so as to be easy to reach for all the people who use the bench.

Footprints attempted to make its tools as proxemic as possible, supporting the users' preferred means of web navigation while offering enriched alternatives. Other social navigation systems might wish to be more distemic, in order to ensure that widely dispersed or varied users can all comfortably perform navigation activities.

Property 2: Active versus Passive

Most interaction history is passive; it is recorded and made available without conscious effort, usually as a by-product of everyday use of objects. Conversely, when we stop to think about leaving a record, we are creating an active history element. The active/passive distinction is concerned with the user's mental state and relationship to history-rich objects. For example, if you stop to carve a warning sign along a trail you are creating active history. Although the sign itself remains static, you have stepped outside the conventional function of travel in order to leave a marker; this conscious change of levels is what constitutes "active-ness" in interaction history.

The most common example of this distinction is in web browser software, for example Netscape Navigator. The "history" or "go to" list is passive history because it is recorded for the user as she browses; the "bookmarks" or "favourites" list is active history because the user must stop to think that she may want to return to this location in the future. The challenge for history-rich computer systems is to find ways to allow interaction history to be passively collected when necessary so that users are not constantly thrown out of the cognitive state necessary to getting their tasks done.

Property 3: Rate/Form of Change

History moves forward, building as more interactions take place. This "accretion" process is how history builds up. However, interaction history in the physical world does not only accrete, it also fades out. One of the challenges for history-rich interfaces is deciding how to deal with this simultaneous accretion and fade. Just as a complete video playback of a meeting is usually not as useful as a summary, the total accumulation of history must be summarised so that it can be observed and used quickly.

A good real-world example of this are patient charts in hospitals. These charts are annotated and added to by many different personnel under different situations over time, yet a physician must be able to come into the room, pick up the chart, and understand essential facts of the patient's current state at a glance.

In the digital realm, Hill and Hollan's "Editwear" tool (1993) used a modified scrollbar to show areas within a source file which had been more or less heavily modified. Dozens or hundreds of accesses were summarised by an unobtrusive thickening of the "thumb" component of the scrollbar.

The fade function – the process by which history is removed – has three components, each of which can act independently: obscuring, losing and disconnecting. Taken together, the three components make up what we call "forgetting." We separate them here because each of the components is amenable to different approaches.

Obscuring is the process by which new history blocks the perception of old. A new coat of paint obscures the wear on the previous layer. History is often layered and while this layering gives a richness to historical objects, it also covers up things which may be valuable. In the digital realm, layers are easily seen in versioning systems such as Microsoft Word's "track changes" functionality or source-code control systems.

Losing is the process by which interaction history is removed. Old objects may be replaced by new parts or, more seriously for organisational memory, people move on taking experience and knowledge with them. History-rich objects may also be outright discarded. This may be out of necessity, as when the object has worn out and can no longer be used for its intended purpose, or out of neglect, as when an object is found to have no present value and its historical value is not yet recognised. Modern computer systems, particularly desktop systems, encourage frequent "upgrading" – replacement of old software with new versions. However, such upgrades may result in lost history, both in terms of saved information (past conversations lost when instant messaging software is upgraded) and accumulated knowledge (changes to keyboard shortcuts).

Disconnecting describes the situation in which the interaction history is still available, but the connection between the history and its present interpretation has been lost. Engeström et al. (1990) document this in Scandinavian hospital situations, where doctors' evaluation of patients' conditions did not match up with the notes written in the relevant charts. The evidence (history) was still there, but its connection to the present had been lost. Doctors complained that the charts "did not make sense" in that they were logical but did not correlate with the doctors' understanding of the current situation.

Combining these three components, fading can be thought of as a decay function, much as we talk about decay functions for signals. In such a function the strength of the signal/history trace lessens over time in a way that can be regularly described.

In interaction history, there are two elements which make up the "signal strength". The first element is the durability of the object. A diamond will be mined once, cut once or twice, and worn by a few people over many years. Conversely, a drinking glass will be cut once, used for a few years by a number of people, perhaps chipped or cracked, then discarded. The second element is the durability of the trace. A fingerprint will not last long – usually only until the next cleaning or the next smudge overlays it. A carving will likely last much longer.

The two strengths may not be additive. The fingerprint is no more likely to last on the diamond than it is on the glass. In some cases they may add: a carving in stone will likely last longer than one in wood. The durability of a trace is usually directly proportional to the degree to which it changes the object, or our perceptions of it.

Accretion and fade functions will vary in any history-rich interface. A key benefit of modelling interaction history explicitly in digital systems will be to help users distinguish obscuring from loss, and to help prevent disconnection.

Property 4: Degree of Permeation

Permeation is the degree to which interaction history is a part of the history-rich objects. History may be inseparable from the object, as in a flight of worn stairs, or it may be completely separate, as in records of stolen art. In a history-rich interface, we must decide how closely to link the objects of interaction and the history information. Digital data will only retain that history information that we choose to keep; therefore, any record of this information must be captured and displayed by tools that we create explicitly for that purpose, or by display systems built into existing tools; for example, the mode-line modification to Emacs described above. The tools we have built to display interaction history information are described in the next section of this chapter.

In the physical world, interaction history both highly permeates history-rich objects, and yet is peripheral to most uses of the object. We may enjoy the feel of a well-worn grip on the handle of a favourite tool, but it does not get in the way of our using the tool. As we consider integrating digital interaction history with the tools available to computer users, one design goal may be to achieve a similar close integration between the data and the history; however, by making history closely permeate digital data, we risk destroying the very thing we are trying to enhance, because digital affordances are much less related to peoples' physical skills and require a greater share of cognitive and attentive skills.

In most cases, therefore, the history information must be kept peripheral, as it should be an enhancement to the user's task environment. If interacting with the history information becomes a central focus, we have probably changed the task too much. Bear in mind that we cannot remove the history information too far from the user's environment: separate data risks becoming just another distraction on an already-cluttered display.

An appropriate analogy for what we are trying to accomplish here is to a painting: the painting may be appreciated for what it is alone, or it may be framed. A good frame will enhance our interaction with the picture; it complements our looking. Interaction history is like the frame; the picture is the information to which the history relates.

Property 5: Personal versus Social

History can be intimate to a person: what have I done? Or it can be social: what has been done here? Many tools focus on personal histories; for example, bookmarks in web browsers that allow users to revisit sites they have noted. Group histories, such as knowledge repositories and shared digital libraries are more rare but may be more valuable because most problem-solving tasks are collaborative in nature. One of the primary benefits of interaction history is to give newcomers the benefit of work done in the past. In fact, the slogan for the Footprints project was:

We all benefit from experience, … preferably someone else's

The other value of social history is that it promotes organisational learning. While it is true that organisations cannot learn unless individuals within the organisation learn, it is also true that if the learning is confined to individuals then it cannot benefit the group as a whole.

Radley (1990) notes that the artefacts with which we interact on a regular basis are constructive of forms of social practices. That is, we build and continue to use precisely the kinds of objects that enhance the social rituals essential to our maintenance of home and workplaces. It is not coincidence that the writing desk and the social practice of writing personal letters disappeared at about the same time. The world of material artefacts governs our relationships with the past in socially-significant ways. History-rich objects must be understood not as mnemonics – in which case any one object could substitute for any similar object – nor simply as triggers for memory – in which case a reminder of the object would be as effective as the object. Instead, history-rich objects much be seen as the basis from which we remember. The object is an active participant in the social construction of the past.

This is not to say that personal interaction histories are insignificant. On the contrary, an ability to see and review a record of what we have personally done in the past (and perhaps why we did it) can be invaluable. Anyone who has had to go back and review or enhance his own source code after months or years of not working on it can attest to this fact. The key here is to balance the personal with the social uses of interaction history information.

Property 6: Kind of Information

We can capture many kinds of interaction history information. What kinds are important to capture are, to a large degree, dependent on the task that the observer is trying to accomplish. Since we cannot possibly characterise all the kinds of information available, we focus on the uses to which interaction history might be put. We categorise the kind of information available loosely into *what, who, why,* and *how*. Each category offers a particular kind of value and is appropriate to particular kinds of tasks.

- Knowing *what* was done can be useful if users are *searching for value*, particularly among clutter, or if they are in need of reassurance. This is particularly helpful for novices who lack the kind of practice that helps them know what is reasonable to do with a given computer system. Knowing what was done can also *give guidance*; that is, the process of directing someone in a task or journey.
- Knowing *who* has done something is important for reasons of *companionability* (doing things with friends), *sociability* (doing things with people who are similar to me), and for establishing *authority* and possibly *authenticity*.
- Knowing *why* something was done can be important for reasons of *similarity of purpose*. I may care a great deal about something that was done by people with a goal similar to mine. A related reason is *goal discovery*, the process of starting off on one task and realising that it relates to, or can be co-accomplished with, another task. Knowing *why* something happened is also crucial for *explanation and learning*. Software engineers often find themselves concerned with design rationale as they attempt to maintain software systems. Having the code, the comments and the documentation is often not enough since some questions can only be answered by knowing why a particular approach was chosen, and why other alternatives were rejected, if they were even considered at all.
- Knowing *how* some bit of interaction history was done can be important for issues of *naturalness*. For example, Microsoft Office's assistant has a "show me" mode in which it will show the user how to select the correct options from menus, how to fill in dialog boxes, and so forth.

In the physical world we adapt our artefacts to work together: streets are built to be wide enough for the cars of the day; bridges are raised to accommodate higher trucks and buses which must pass under them, etc. These adaptations and uses provide natural ways for wear to be recorded. We see how things have been done in the past because they leave their traces. Software which was built to show this kind of use information might be termed "wearware".

9.3 Application to the Web

Concurrent with the development of the theoretical framework, we built a series of tools applying interaction history to the problem of navigation in a complex information space. Successive versions of these tools have been described in Wexelblat (1998a, 1999) and Wexelblat and Maes (1997, 1999)[3]. The Footprints tools assumed that people knew what they wanted but needed help finding their way to the information and perhaps help understanding what they had found. Therefore, we did not use history to make recommendations; instead, we provided tools that used history information to contextualise web pages. This is information foraging: exploration combined with exploitation.

Our architecture was based on a proxy server (front end) and a database (back end). Both parts were written in Java and worked on any OS platform with standard web browsers. The front end controlled the user interface tools, and recorded logs that were sent to the back end once per user session and incorporated into the database overnight. Interaction history information seen by users changed as they moved from web page to web page, but the database itself changed only slowly. The one exception to this was user comments, as noted below.

Our tools were based on a metaphor of navigation – maps, paths and signposts – familiar from the physical world, that we implemented in the digital realm. There are, of course, many other tools that could have been implemented, but these both fitted our metaphor and allowed us to explore interesting points in the space of possible interaction history systems described by the theoretical framework above.

Each tool visualised interaction history information in a different way, but all the tools were active aids to navigation rather than static visualisations. The tools worked in coordination with each other and with user actions. When a person selected a document in one tool, it highlighted everywhere, assisting users in understanding how the various views were related. View focus was also coordinated, so that refocussing one view caused all the other views to refocus appropriately. Tools also had control

---

[3] The data collected in Footprints tools was taken with the understanding that it was to be used for personal research only; thus, when the project terminated the data were destroyed. This required that the Footprints system be shut down. An interesting social tension remains to be explored in the need to retain history data for unspecified times and unknown purposes.

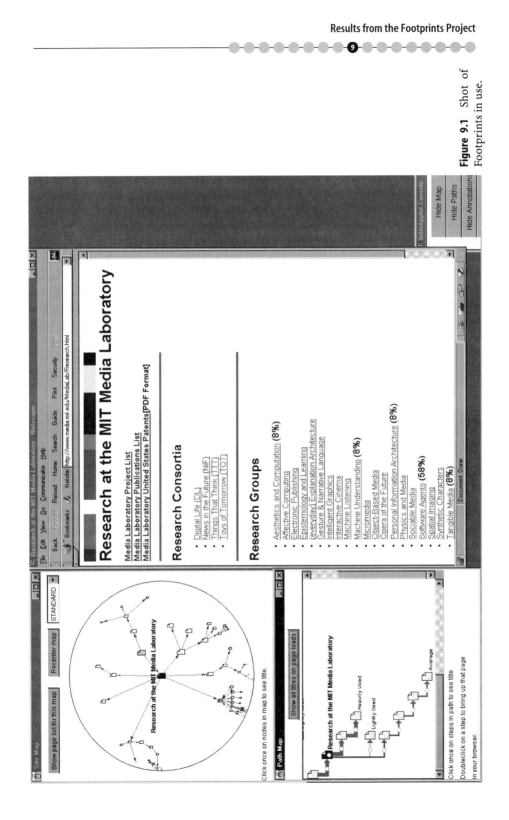

Figure 9.1 Shot of Footprints in use.

buttons for manipulating document titles and for helping users who got lost; these are explained below.

On start-up Footprints provided a control panel window (not pictured) that allowed the user to show or hide each of the tools separately. Users could also shut down Footprints from the control panel, if they decided they did not want their data logged at any particular time. The Map and Path tools appear in separate windows alongside the web browser. The annotation tool affects the display of the current web page itself in the browser. Figure 9.1 shows a screen shot of a user visiting the Media Lab Research web page with all three tools turned on.

Over the course of the project, we designed, implemented and tested several versions of these tools. Our goals were always to test our theories and to make systems that people would actually use. During our development time the volunteer user community waxed and waned. Some versions of tools were seen by only a handful of friends; others were used by several dozen regular people. As a result, our designs changed significantly over time, though our basic metaphor stayed the same. All our tools used web navigation transitions (going from one URL to another) as their basic information – the "what kind" of information from our framework. Footprints validated each night, when the database was updated, that the pages it displayed were accessible; therefore, the rate of change of all Footprints history information was the rate of change of the web itself. Footprints did not have a direct notion of user identity; all user data was anonymised and merged with the data of other users.

This had the advantage of protecting users' privacy – no one could tell what web sites any particular user had visited – but it had the disadvantage of not allowing users to see each others' paths. This was a deliberately chosen trade-off; other equally valid trade-offs could be made but the focus of our research was on the interaction history itself and not on mechanisms for personal privacy.[4]

The first tool is the map, detailed in Figure 9.2. This map shows the traffic through a Web site. Nodes in the graph are documents and links are transitions between them. Note that this is not all the documents and transitions available at the site; Footprints displayed only the ones that people actually visited or used. This is, typically, only a small fraction of the actual site content. Additionally, the tools tracked all transitions made by the user, whether they came from selecting a link on the page, typing in a URL, selecting a bookmark, etc. The result of this was that links shown on the map tool often did not correspond directly to links embedded in the web pages of the site.

---

[4] One of the most frequent questions I get is, "Did users visit pornographic sites?" To my knowledge they did not do so, at least with the tools turned on. Footprints did not record when the user turned the tools on or off, again for privacy reasons.

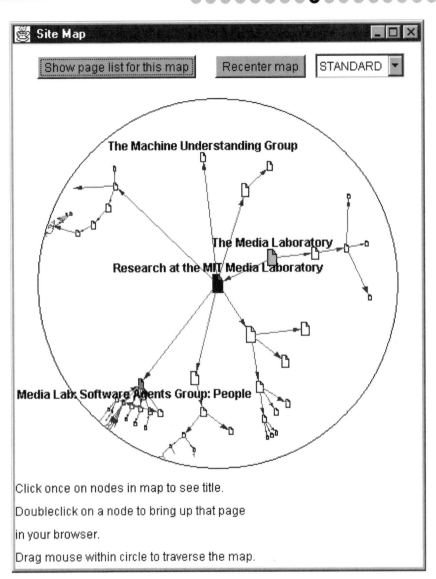

Figure 9.2 Footprints site map.

In Footprints these user-created transitions were considered to be as important as the transitions (i.e. links) provided by web page designers. In some sense they are more important, since they reveal users' models of how information *should* be connected. As we described in earlier publications (Wexelblat, 1998b; Wexelblat and Maes, 1997) we theorised that the patterns shown in the maps and paths were an externalisation of users' mental models of how the information was related. This model might correspond better or worse to the designer's model for any given user at any given web site. This theory is reinforced by our experiment with Footprints, described below.

The map visualisation we used was derived from the hyperbolic graph viewer of Lamping, Rao and Pirolli (1995). That is, the circle shown was a 2D representation of a sphere on which the nodes and arcs were first laid out, then projected down to a flat plane. The result was a high degree of magnification and view detail in the central focus area, and a corresponding reduction in size and detail as the graph reached towards the edges.

Users could drag the display in any direction to bring nodes from the edge towards the centre. Individual nodes could be single-clicked to show their titles, or double-clicked to bring that document up in the web browser. Titles might overlap, given the small size of the view and the length of many web page titles, so we added the ability to rotate the map, as one spins a record platter.

Popularity of documents in the map view was shown by shades of red – the hottest documents were in red, then shades of pink down to white were used (shown in these images as shades of grey). The document currently displayed in the browser was shown highlighted in black. Although this obscured the colour shading information, we found that the solid black node helped users keep their location in the graph with just a glance, reducing confusion and orientation time when using the map.

Because users could get lost ("Where am I relative to the layout of the map as a whole?") while viewing the map, we provided a *Recentre Map* button that redrew the map centred around the node in which the user had expressed the most recent interest, either by single-clicking or double-clicking. We found that recentreing the map around the user's current location was usually not what was wanted, because users would navigate via the map view. Thus their focus of attention was not "What page am I on?" as shown in the current browser window, but "Where does this page, in which I am interested, fit?"

The titles of all nodes in the map could be viewed by clicking on the *Show Page List for this Map* button. Since showing that many titles at one time cluttered the display, the list of titles were shown in a separate window. This window presented the titles alphabetised, with the current document highlighted. Clicking on any title showed the title in the map view; double-clicking on a title brought up the document in the web browser.

In the terms of our theoretical framework, the map view is social, combining data from all users. It is passive in that the data are added without requiring user intervention. It is distemic in that it requires users to learn new rules for interaction, and unpermeated in that the data are kept and displayed separately from the web documents to which they refer.

The second tool was the path view, shown in Figure 9.3. If we think of the map as the "high-level" overview of a whole site, the path view was

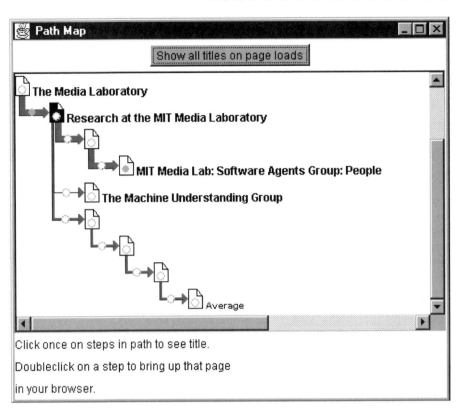

Figure 9.3   Footprint paths.

"lower" level in that it showed what individual paths have been followed by other people.

Paths are coherent sequences of nodes followed (pages visited) by an individual. The map is much like a real-world map, with each document appearing once just as a city would appear once. The path view is like a list of bus routes that go through these cities. A city appears at least once on each highway; likewise, a document in the path view appears at least once on each path.

The number of paths formed this way was very large, of course, so we only showed the paths that were relevant to (included) the current document. Notice that paths with common starting points were merged, so users could see branching – forks in the road – more easily. For example, imagine that the following sets of paths are in the database.

$$A \rightarrow B \rightarrow C \rightarrow D$$
$$A \rightarrow B \rightarrow C \rightarrow D$$

237

$$A \to B \to C \to D$$

Then if the user was looking at page B, the representation would be:

```
A
 L B
    |- C
    |   |- E
    |   L D
    L D
       L F
```

The two representations of "D" are not collapsed since they represent different paths through the space – third in one traversal, fourth in another. The multiple representations of A and B are collapsed, however, since their positions in the path space are identical – first and second, respectively, in all traversals. If the user then selected page C, the representation would change to:

The ABDF path is removed from the display because it is no longer relevant – it does not contain the current page. Other paths containing page C (that do not also contain page B) would be shown if they were in the database. If the user backtracks, the previous path is redisplayed.

Paths also responded to single clicks – by showing titles – and double-clicks, by taking the user to the selected document. There was also a button that allowed users to see or hide all titles at once. Since the path view was arranged in a stair-step fashion, titles could be shown in the same window without overlap problems. Paths were also coded for degree of use. The thickness of the line representing the path increased as the path got more heavily used; we also use a text string – *Lightly Used*, *Heavily Used*, *Rarely Used* – to give an approximate level of use. Paths are social, passive and unpermeated in the same way as maps; however, they are intermediate between distemic and proxemic because they take advantage of users' familiarity with tools such as outline listings and hierarchical file browsers.

The next tool was annotations, seen in the text of the web page in Figure 9.1. These were our only inactive aids. Annotations were marks –

in our case numbers – inserted in the web page that showed what percentage of users had followed each link on the page. Footprints parsed the HTML of the page in order to insert the annotations; therefore, we could not annotate links that were "inside" image maps, applets, etc. We also spent some time trying to find a method of annotation that would not interfere with the user's reading of the web page. Unfortunately, most of the tools that we would have liked to use, such as display font, size, and colour are all under the control of the web page designer. Any attempt to manipulate these invariably looked good on some pages and horrible on others. In the end, we settled for simple numbers in whatever the adjacent font/size/colour happened to be.

Annotations were social and passive as with maps and paths. However, they were proxemic and permeated as they represent the "wear" directly in the page.

The final tool used by Footprints was signposts, or comments. These are the means by which users can enter feedback on the interaction history they have seen. Figure 9.3 shows a path view both with comments (filled circle, upper left) and without comments (open circles). Unlike other systems that only allowed comments on pages, Footprints allowed users to comment on both pages and paths. This was useful, for example, in marking forks in the road. One of our beta test users provided an annotation that said "Go this way for software agents; go that way for artificial life" just as if he had been writing a signpost for a physical path's branching.

Users could click on the circles to bring up a simple text window. If comments already existed for that path, they were shown and the user had the option to add a comment. Clicking on an "Add Comment" button took the user to a text input widget. Comments were social, active, proxemic and permeated.

Unlike the passive history information, comments were entered into the database immediately. Once the user clicks "OK" on the Add Comment window, the path view updates so that the circle is filled if it was not before. This turned out to be important feedback for users, who could not otherwise determine that their input had been accepted by the system.

Clicking on the filled circle brought up the comments, including the new one, sorted so that the most recent comment was at the top. Older comments appeared below. We did not delete comments; this allowed users to read the entire history and converse or exchange ideas by adding comments that referred back to earlier annotation. Since the fade function for Footprints as a whole was based on the viability of pages, we had a natural lifespan for comments as well.

With our small user population this lax policy worked; there were simply never enough comments in the database to be overwhelming clutter. If a similar system was used by a larger audience it might prove necessary to have a quicker fade function, or perhaps some kind of rating/

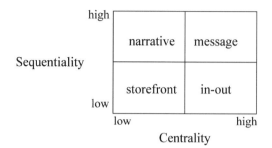

Figure 9.4 Navigational experience types.

filtering for comments, such as done on noisy conversation boards like Slashdot.

9.4 Patterns in Navigation

One of the serendipitous insights that arose from observation of the large body of navigation data generated and visualised in Footprints was that there are patterns in the way people move around web sites.

We distinguish four basic navigational units, which are characterised metaphorically by the kind of experience they represent: *narrative, storefront, in–out,* and *central message.* We organise them along the orthogonal dimensions of *sequentiality* and *centrality,* as shown in Figure 9.4.

Sequentiality refers to the order in which nodes are experienced. An arrangement with high sequentiality is likely to have a low branching factor and is likely to be longer. Centrality refers to the tendency to lead towards a node or group of nodes which function as the centre of the experience. Centres are returned to often and contain items of high importance. Sequentiality leads to structures like Lynch's (1972) edges and paths. Paths represent courses or routes which are customarily followed. Lynch refers to them as channels, in acknowledgment of their effect in organising and directing flow. We follow paths not because we are required to do so, but because the path provides arrangement and relationship among elements that would otherwise be incoherent or disconnected. Edges are the dual of paths: linear sequences of features or sites, but rather than encouraging following, edges serve to bound areas and often to block paths that would penetrate them.

Conversely, centrality is important for nodes and districts, though landmarks may also function as centres. Districts are sections of the terrain which cause people to experience an inside of/outside of dichotomy. Ethnic districts, such as a "Chinatown", are one common example of this. We also see it in heterogeneous spaces like the web where identities transcend web server locations. For example, the MIT Media Lab "web site" is

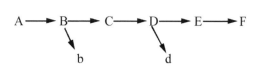

Figure 9.5   Narrative experience example.

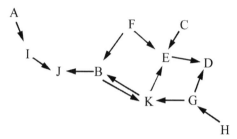

Figure 9.6   Storefront experience example.

in fact served from more than half a dozen machines, each of which serves a different set of pages. Nevertheless, the Lab pages as a whole can be seen as a "district" in web space. Nodes are strategic spots or focus points. They serve as junctions between points on paths, as entry points into districts, and so on. In the physical world, a node is often a meeting place such as a street corner hangout or cafe. In information spaces, nodes are places to which users return for valuable information or to help orient themselves.

A *narrative experience* is something like being told a story. A typical narrative experience is show in Figure 9.5.

It depicts a linear sequence of nodes – tell me something, tell me something more – with minor branches off the main "story line" to get more detail or explanation. In web spaces, these diversions are usually pictures or diagrams too large to be included in the main flow of text. A narrative experience is highly sequential, like most storytelling. It is also not very central; the story may have a central point or narrative climax but from the outside this part of the trail is unlikely to look any different.

A *storefront experience* is something like walking into a grocery store – shelves of merchandise with vague categorisation and no obvious ordering among the items (see Figure 9.6). This lack of order precludes any hope of sequence. There may be a storefront (or portal, in current popular web jargon) but this entry point is rarely returned to by users once they have passed it. The information may be structured – as a catalogue, as an archive, etc. – but models of how the structure can be navigated are

---

[5] The designer of the space may have had a model of navigation in mind, but that model did not translate to the users. If it did, then either centrality or sequentiality would be higher. Remember we are describing end-user experience here, not intended design.

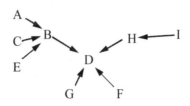

Figure 9.7   Central message experience example.

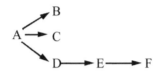

Figure 9.8   In-and-out experience example.

lacking, so the users must supply them.[5]

A *message experience* is one which has both high sequence and high centrality (see Figure 9.7). Usually there is a central node or cluster of nodes around which the experience is focused. Message experiences may be pedagogical – there may be a central theme or lesson which the teacher repeats several times to help students remember it. Or it may be a commercial message where the external elements are product presentations and the central message is "give us your credit card number". Sequence is important in a message experience because the message – the lesson, the pitch, etc. – will not be heard or understood properly if it is delivered out of context.

Finally the *in-and-out experience*, shown in Figure 9.8, is all too common on the web. Here the message pattern is reversed and instead of coming to a central node, browsers begin at such a node. From this node, they make a number of forays, usually in an attempt to find something which satisfies their immediate need. This is usually caused by pages which have – or are nothing but – a set of links to other pages. These links may be more or less well described; unfortunately, they are often just a few words. Therefore, users must click on the link and visit the target web page in order to determine if it satisfies their need.

The in-and-out experience is highly central because the page containing the list of links serves as a centre point. However, the sequentiality of the experience is low because there is usually no obvious order to the links. There is, of course, the order in which they appear on the page, and some enhancements may be offered on the page to emphasise this ranking. For example, a search engine may rank its results in terms of presumed relevance to the user's query and put the ranking numbers next to the links. However, there is nothing to prevent the user from selecting the second suggestion, then the fifth, then the third and so on.

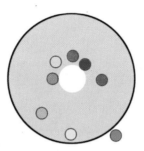

Plate 1 The Babble Cookie.

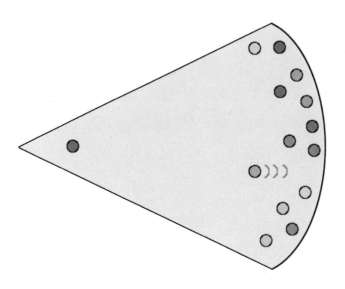

Plate 2 The lecture proxy.

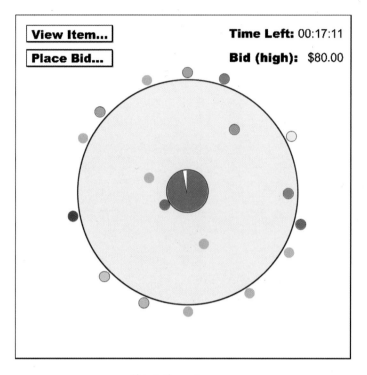

Plate 3 The auction proxy.

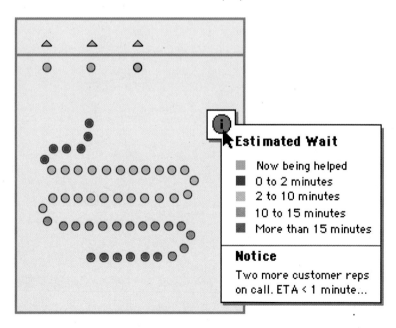

Plate 4 The queue proxy.

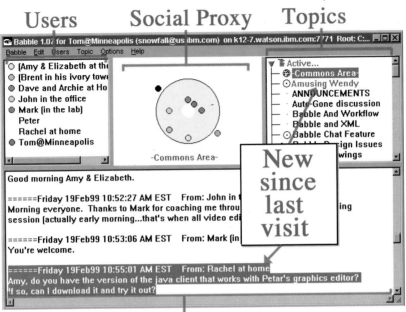

Plate 5 The Babble user interface.

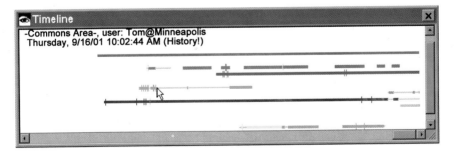

Plate 6 The Babble timeline proxy.

Plate 7 The Day World.

Plate 8 The fly-through design.

Plate 9 Authoring interface: place label, message field, and the signature pop-up menu. User name is displayed at the top of the window.

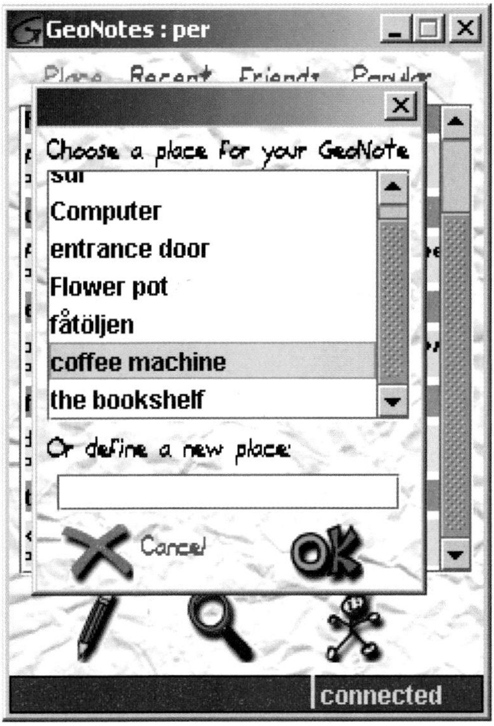

Plate 10 Choosing a place label.

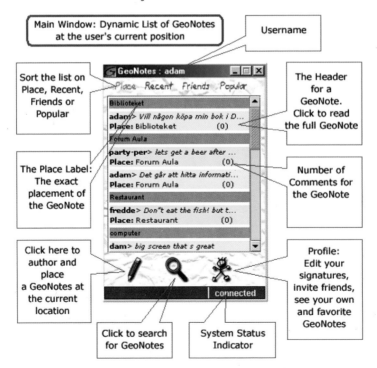

Plate 11 GeoNotes reading interface. This GeoNote has received no comments.

Plate 12 GeoNotes main window.

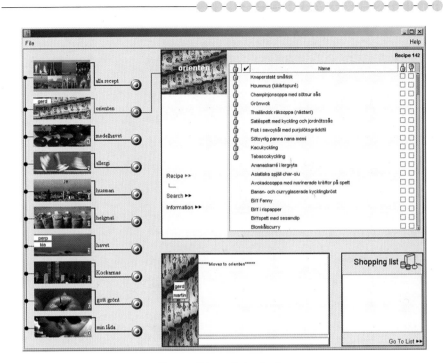

Plate 13 Kalas ranked recipe list.

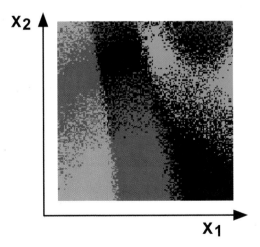

Plate 14 A prosection showing the success (green) or otherwise of a design defined by values of X_1 and X_2.

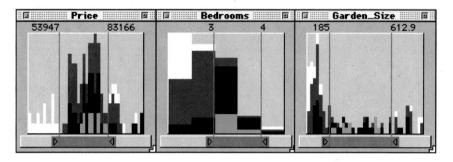

Plate 15 The colour coding of individual houses in the Attribute Explorer histograms provides sensitivity information. Black houses lying outside a limit will turn green if that limit is extended to encompass them.

Number of Bedrooms

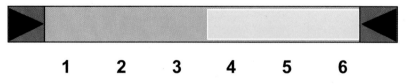

| 1 | 2 | 3 | 4 | 5 | 6 |

Plate 16 The colour coding indicates that object selection will be unaffected while the lower limit stays within the grey region. When a limit moves into the yellow region selection will be affected.

These four basic experience elements can be combined in many ways. For example, a web site designer might create a narrative-style experience that leads into a storefront. This way a naive or new user can get a gentle (albeit constrained) introduction to the material while an experienced user can simply jump in, trusting her skills and past experiences to help her navigate. Multiple narratives can also lead to a central message; this is a common pedagogical tool.

Value judgements should not be associated with these experience types. Knowing whether any given experience is good or bad requires knowing both something about the content of the pages and the intention of the designer.

9.5 Experimental Results

In addition to the qualitative results described above, we wanted to get some quantitative data from the Footprints tools. We therefore performed a controlled experiment to evaluate both the subjective and objective usefulness of the tools. That is, we wanted to know both whether the tools were perceived as helpful and whether they could be shown to have a measurable impact on task performance.

Subjects performed a timed (20-minute) browsing task, one group unaided and one group with the Footprints tools. They were told that they had approximately £x to spend on a car and were to find cars that might be interesting to them. They were encouraged to use their normal web browsing patterns and tools, including any foreknowledge of automobile web sites, search engines, etc. The work done by the first (unaided) group was captured and used to create a special, limited Footprints database. The second group had available all the interaction history generated by the first group. We did not record the interaction history data from the second group, though, so each subject had available the same set of history data.

Subjects in the second group received a 5-minute instruction on how to use the Footprints tools, prior to starting the task. We based the instruction on a data set we created around the Media Lab web site.

We had a hard time finding useful measures to evaluate a system designed to help people with an imprecise task such as browsing. After some initial pretesting, we settled on two objective and two subjective measures. Objective measures were the number of alternatives generated – that is, how many car makes/models subjects found – and the number of pages visited to generate those alternatives. The goal of having these dual metrics was to gauge the ability of subjects to exploit the information and their efficiency in doing so. The underlying assumption is that there are likely to be a number of intervening pages and a large number of false starts built into the space of web pages that subjects might visit.

Our intuition was that the history structures and visualisations provided by Footprints would allow people to avoid these false starts and cut down on the number of intervening pages. Thus, we hoped to see the number of alternatives generated increase and the number of pages visited decrease.

Subjective measures were the users' sense of satisfaction and judgement of how easy the task was. Our subjective measures aimed to answer three basic questions: how well did the exploration go? how easy was it to do the task? and how good or bad was the organisation? Each question was asked in two different ways, to separate possible different effects. For the first question, we wanted to measure how well subjects felt they had covered the space of possibilities. We asked subjects to tell us how satisfied they were with the car choices they had written down. We also asked them how satisfied they were with the experience of browsing they had during the experiment. Our goal in splitting out these two questions was to see if there was an effect of Footprints on either the perceived quality of the results or the quality of the experience.

Twenty subjects participated in each of the two conditions. Subjects were volunteers given a token reward (a coupon for ice cream) for participation. All subjects were required to be familiar with Netscape Navigator before the experiment. Full details of the experimental conditions and evaluation can be found in Wexelblat (1999a).

The experiment partially supported our first hypothesis and gave a surprising result on our second. The number of alternatives generated by the two subject groups was not significantly different; however, the mean number of pages required to generate that same number of alternatives was significantly less with Footprints. It took 24.8 pages for the unaided group versus 18.75 pages for the Footprints group ($p < 0.05$).

In measuring the subjective responses, no significant differences were observed, with one exception. This may simply be subjects telling us that five minutes of instruction followed by twenty minutes of use is not enough to form an opinion of something as novel as an interaction history toolset.

There was a significant interaction effect across conditions for those subjects who had, prior to the experiment, looked for car information on the web. This is shown in the ANOVA table (Table 9.1), which tests the interaction of user's previous activity (*looked* means that they had looked

Table 9.1 Interaction of previous experience with satisfaction

Variation source	Sum of squares	DF	Mean square	F	Sig of F
Main effects	1.607	2	0.803	1.5	0.237
Expmt#	0.207	1	0.207	0.385	0.539
Looked 2-way interacts	1.079	1	1.079	2.014	0.164
Expmt# / Looked	4.872	1	4.872	9.093	0.005

for car information on the web before this experiment) with their response to a question about their satisfaction with the experience. Satisfaction was measured on a scale of 1–5, with 1 representing "Totally Satisfied" and 5 representing "Totally Dissatisfied". Table 9.1 shows that while there is no significant effect for either effect considered separately, the two-way interaction of experimental condition (unaided vs. Footprints) and previous experience (looked vs. has not looked) was significant ($p < 0.01$).

This was surprising as we had been assuming that interaction history models would help naive users; instead we found a situation in which experienced users were more satisfied than less experienced users.

Our post-hoc explanation for this phenomenon is that we have inadvertently demonstrated an effect which we had previously noted. I believe that interaction history visualisations such as those provided by Footprints give users access to the cognitive models of information organisation created by past users. Simply put, the way people interact with an information space should be shaped by how they *expect* the information to be organised. This may or may not match up with how the information is actually organised.

In fact, on the web it rarely matches up. If it did, users would have much less trouble navigating than they do. However, when we allow people to see patterns, it is possible that such patterns can be recognised. This is, I believe, what is happening here. Subjects who have experience with car information on the web have formed models of how the space is organised. With Footprints, they can see others' models and recognise similarities between their own models and what they see. This leads to them feeling more satisfied because they are less lost and less bewildered. Our post-test conversations with subjects lent credence to this interpretation. Several subjects mentioned that they "recognised things" in the Footprints displays and homed in on what was familiar to them. It was our impression that these subjects seemed the most pleased when we talked to them afterward.

This relates to our notion of proxemic/distemic: those who had a pre-existing mental model found the Footprints representations much more proxemic and were able to make much better use of them. This conclusion was reinforced by other subject-reported experiences. In particular, subjects who rated their level of web expertise lower reported having a harder time finding information that was relevant to their problem and less satisfaction with the solutions they found.

In reviewing the logs of tool use during the experiments, we saw three patterns. Some subjects simply took off in directions we had not seen before and so received little or no help from Footprints. This suggests that our test data set could have been improved. Other subjects started off using Footprints information then went off in new directions since their tastes in vehicles differed from those of our first group of subjects. These subjects usually started with a popular site such as Yahoo! or Edmund's for which we had lots of history data from the first group. This variety of use patterns was expected; we cannot possibly cover all the possible car makes and models in which subjects might be interested.

The third group of subjects did not start out using the Footprints information. They had different search strategies. However, they ended up using Footprints information once their searches brought them near to popular car-related sites. At this point, the map proved particularly useful; as one subject put it: "As soon as I got there, the map had a bunch of alternatives and I used those." This is not too surprising since subjects across both conditions overwhelmingly preferred to have a map when navigating in the physical world, as opposed to any other form of navigational aid.

9.6 Related Work

Our theoretical work derives from two major influences. The first is ethnographic studies of how people work in teams in real situations, primarily research from Hutchins (1995), Orr (1996) and Suchman (1987). The second is urban studies, particularly the work of Lynch (1972) and Brand (1994). From these we have developed our theory of how interaction history information can be used by people involved in their normal problem-solving tasks.

Hill and Hollan's original work (1993) involved a series of tools, called "editware", "readware", and so on that were oriented toward helping people on a software development project keep track of which portions of the code and documentation were being the most heavily modified, most heavily read, etc.

Chalmers and his collaborators (1998) have also been applying history (or activity-centrism as they call it) to tracing users' paths through the web. Their tools are oriented towards providing recommendations for possible web pages to visit, based on differences between the current user's paths and paths recorded in the system's history database.

The notion of paths through digital information and their use is at least as old as Bush's famous MEMEX essay (1945):

> The owner of the memex ... runs through an encyclopedia, finds an interesting but sketchy article, leaves it projected. Next, in a history, he finds another pertinent item, and ties the two together. Thus he goes, building a trail of many items. [H]is trails do not fade.

Hypertext systems have used map and path mechanisms for many years. However, these are typically top–down created artefacts put in the system by the designer for guidance or pedagogical purposes. Zellweger's "Scripted Documents" (Zellweger and Polle, 1989) are an excellent example of this. This notion is also being carried into the web domain by projects such as CMU's *WebWatcher* (Joachim et al., 1997), a tour-guide agent for the web, and *Walden's Paths* (Furuta et al., 1997), a K-12 educational application of scripted paths.

Some related work falls into the category of assisting social navigation. Dieberger (1997b) describes an enhanced MOO system, which keeps track of how many people use passages between rooms in the MOO and augments textual descriptions with information on how heavily used the passages appear. Dahlbäck, Höök and others in the PERSONA project (Dahlbäck, 1998) have been exploring a number of different aspects of social and personal navigation, including the uses of artefacts in these processes and individual differences in the navigation process.

Other related work has been done in the area of community-created information sources. Hill and Terveen, particularly in their PHOAKS project (Hill et al., 1995, 1996), have been active in creating new techniques for mining existing information – on the web and in Usenet newsgroups – for traces that can be collected and made available to future users. PHOAKS collects URLs that have been positively mentioned from postings and Frequently Asked Questions documents. These URLs are then provided as recommendations on a central server to people interested in the topic of the newsgroup from which they were extracted.

9.7 Conclusions

We built a set of tools to support undirected web browsing in application of a theoretical framework for how history-rich systems can be constructed. The tools were based around the concepts of applying interaction history to a social navigation problem, relying on the fundamental underlying assertion that work done by past users can be important to helping current users solve problems such as navigation in a complex information space. Our tools were in use and available on the web for anyone to download for over two years. E-mail discussions with members of the user community showed that the Footprints tools were particularly popular with web information users and web site designers.

The experiment reported here showed that our tools are successful in two respects:

- they enable users to get the same work done with significantly less effort, and
- experienced users were able to recognise the information models left behind by other users and reported a significantly higher sense of satisfaction when working with the aid of these models.

247

Finally, we set out to take something pervasive in the physical world, characterise it, and extract use from it for the digital realm. We have begun to show success in this endeavour; we have given history to digital information.

Acknowledgements

Work on Footprints was done as part of my doctoral dissertation under the direction and supervision of Dr. Pattie Maes. Code for the Footprints tools was written by Felix Klock, Alex Lian and James Matysczak. Jennifer Smith provided statistical help in analysing the results of our experiments.

10

WebPlaces: Using Intermediaries to Add People to the Web

Paul P. Maglio, Rob Barrett and Stephen Farrell

10.1 Introduction

The web is a social phenomenon, with businesses and individuals finding myriad reasons to both publish and access information. However, though millions of people are using it at any given moment, the web is a lonely place – much more like a catalogue than a bustling downtown. Users have individualised experiences that hide the presence of others. People think of the web as a kind of physical space in which they move to obtain information (Maglio and Barrett, 1997b; Maglio and Matlock, 1999), but they do not think of it as a kind of *place* that affords social interaction (Dieberger, 1999). Erickson (1993) defines "place" as "space plus meaning", and Harrison and Dourish (1996) define it "as space which is invested with an understanding of behavioral appropriateness, [and] cultural expectations" (p. 69). Put simply, a sense of place derives from a shared understanding about a space, and interpersonal interactions are required to create shared understanding (see also Munro, Höök and Benyon, 1999). To transform the web from a simple *space* into a *social place* requires the structure of an interactive culture.

Establishing an interactive culture on the web might take many different forms. What model should be used for integrating awareness with the web? A web place could be defined as a web page, and people in that same place could interact in the context offered by that web page, as a shopping mall or other public space where people looking into the same store window have an opportunity to interact simply because they share neighbouring physical space. As with physical places, the range and form of people's interactions may be limited by accepted social norms. Total strangers may ignore each other unless there is a particular question or important comment. Even close friends in such a setting would likely obey cultural norms, for instance, avoiding intimate conversation that might be overheard by others.

There are other ways of conceiving of place on the web. Consider that co-workers, who share nearby physical locations (or maybe nearby logical locations), are usually isolated from each other in that each has an independent view of the web and is oblivious to the activities of the others. A notion of place on the web could be established for such a closed group so that each is made aware of the web activities of the others in the group, and affordances provided for interaction around those web activities. This view could be seen as an enhancement of instant messaging applications, where friends or co-workers are aware of each other's web presence. By integrating the web with instant messaging, the place is a virtual gathering of people with an external relationship (such as a group of co-workers) and web travels create additional attributes of the place.

Isolated and idiosyncratic social places already exist at specific web sites, and there are various means for adding awareness and interaction to specific sites and pages (e.g. Cohen et al., 2000; Svensson et al., 2001). This approach, however, provides only individual focal points for social interaction rather than providing social interaction pervasively across the entire web. In these cases, the site designer chooses to add awareness and interaction into a particular page. Social affordances are not built into the plumbing of the web. By contrast, our interest is in integrating the whole of web browsing into a notion of place so that social interaction transcends the limited web sites that are specifically designed for awareness (cf. related discussion in Dieberger et al., 2000). For us, the key is to make interpersonal awareness and interaction an integral part of web activity rather than being relegated to cul-de-sacs on the information superhighway.

Transforming the World Wide Web into a social place that affords user-awareness and user-interaction is a complex task. Working towards this goal, here we describe how intermediaries can enable the integration of awareness and interaction with the web. In developing an intermediary-based system for awareness and interaction in this context, we have uncovered a number of difficult issues for turning the web into a place that has some social importance for users. In this chapter, we first describe a framework for thinking about what it means to integrate awareness with the web (see also Maglio and Barrett, 1998). Next, we detail the Web Intermediaries (WBI) toolkit and the WebPlaces system we implemented on top of it for awareness and interaction on the web. Finally, we discuss open issues and possible paths forward from this starting point.

10.2 The Design of WebPlaces

We define *web places* to be locations in web space that are bound together by usage patterns, user interests and web connectivity. In designing our

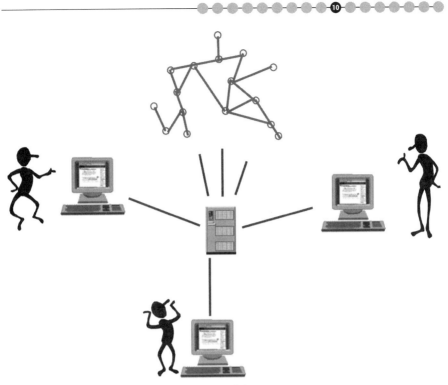

Figure 10.1 Users of the same proxy.

WebPlaces system to incorporate social awareness and interaction on the web, we are faced with two main questions: (1) *which users* should be made aware of which other users? and (2) *how* should these users be made aware of and be able to interact with one another? We discuss each of these in turn.

10.2.1 How to Define Place on the Web

Let us begin by considering how to decide who should be made aware of whom on the web. The question of which users form the current group amounts to asking what defines the place. How should we determine which users are in the same place? A web user's sense of place might be centred on usage patterns, interests or web connectivity. Some places might be defined by the structure of the web itself, and others by the way in which users access the web. In the trivial case, users might form a group when they are part of the same organisation and thus use the same proxy server to access the web (see Figure 10.1). In this case, the users are likely to have similar interests or share similar views precisely because they are part of the same organisation. This is like forming a community

251

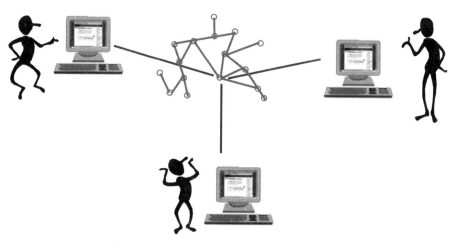

Figure 10.2 Users at same page, site, or domain.

from people who routinely wait at the same bus stop but travel to different destinations.

In a slightly more interesting approach, place might be defined by specific pages or sites (see Figure 10.2). Users are considered to be in the same place when they are currently viewing the same web page, or pages on the same web site, or pages hosted in the same domain. This is a little like forming a community from the people getting off the same bus at the same bus stop.

A third method for associating users browsing the web is to find those who are exploring the same region, that is, who are visiting pages that are within a few links of each other (see Figure 10.3). This definition of place associates place with the topology of the web. For instance, one user who is looking for information on a particular disease might happen to be visiting pages that lie within two or three links of pages others who are researching the same disease happen to be visiting. By taking advantage of the topology, well-defined communities or places can be found (Gibson et al., 1998). This is like bringing together people who take different bus routes to the same destination.

Communities can be tied to topics or categories of current interest. Traditional chat systems, such as Internet Relay Chat (IRC), are organised around content areas, such as Perl programming or soap operas. However, the web opens up new possibilities for connecting users who have similar interests, as determined by the topic areas they are currently browsing (see Figure 10.4). For instance, users searching for the same thing at different search engines might be considered to be in the same place. This might be like grouping together people who take different buses but wind up at similar kinds of destinations, such as museums or cafés.

252

Figure 10.3   Users exploring the same region.

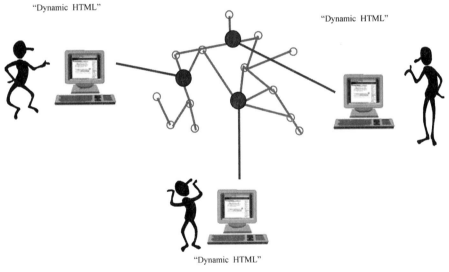

Figure 10.4   Users exploring similar content.

There are yet other ways to build user groups or communities. For instance, communities might grow from the repeated use of predefined paths that groups routinely follow using the WebPath Browser (Gruen and Moody, 1998) or they might be cultivated from groups of sites where web users naturally congregate (Chalmers et al., 1998?). In the most general case, communities might be formed from web users with similar browsing histories (see Figure 10.5). This is like creating a community from people who routinely take the same buses.

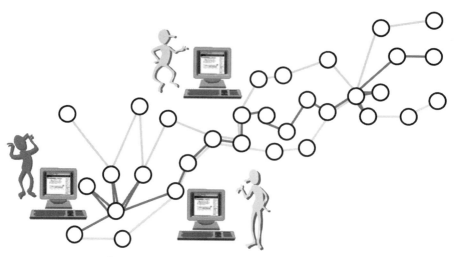

Figure 10.5   Users with similar browsing histories.

10.2.2 WebPlaces' Notion of Place

Given this general framework of possibilities, we designed the WebPlaces system using a simple definition for social group. We started with the idea that the social group is defined by an external affinity that has already established the group members (e.g. as shown in Figure 10.1). For example, group membership might be defined by a workgroup, analogous to a list of friends in an ordinary instant messaging application. This definition of group makes the membership configurable, yet mostly static, which eliminates many possible problems, such as members popping in and out of groups without warning, locating people who are not members of one's group, and managing the size of the group to be large enough to be interesting yet small enough to be workable. We imagined a WebPlaces would have about five active members in it at a time.

10.2.3 How should Users be Made Aware of One Another on the Web?

The possibilities for awareness and interaction range from simple lists of names with textual chat to three-dimensional immersive environments, and the kind of interaction afforded can vary by media type (e.g. chat, voice, or video) and by timeliness (e.g. real-time interaction vs. asynchronous interaction). In any event, the first issue is where to display place information. One approach is to provide a tight connection between the web page and its associated place. This could be accomplished by

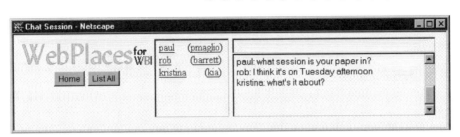

Figure 10.6   Textual representation of place.

embedding the awareness and interaction within the web page itself by annotating the page with additional place information, either statically (e.g. modifying the page's markup) or dynamically (e.g. using an applet). Place information might include lists of people present, real-time interaction such as chat, and page annotations (e.g. Cadiz et al., 2000; Dieberger, 2000; Wexelblat and Maes, 1999). With this approach, the users clearly see that the place is associated with a web page, but it has the drawback of being ephemeral. People consider places to be substantive and lasting, so having the place disappear and reappear when loading every page might be disorienting and loses the persistence that is expected of a place.

Another approach is to put place information in a window separate from the web page itself, providing a stable orientation point for the place, though it does put some distance between that point and the page itself. This has the advantage of providing the opportunity for an identical view for each person in the place. If multiple web pages are considered to be part of the same place (e.g. if all pages describing the art of building telescopes are a single place), then embedding the place information in the pages themselves can be misleading to users because it implies that they are viewing the exact same information. Separating the place from the actual web page weakens the link between the particular page and the place.

We decided to follow the second approach, displaying place information in a separate window. The next question concerns the type of information to display about a place. Our first version only had a textual display of users and an associated text chat area (see Figure 10.6). In using this version, however, we found that it did not effectively provide relevant information. For one thing, we found ourselves constantly glancing at the conversation or chat window to see whether anyone had said anything recently. For another, we discovered that knowing what a user is doing on the web is important; it lets others know, for instance, that the user is still at his or her computer and can be contacted. Both these observations concern how to display what is happening within a group of users. We had provided no visualisation of the space, nor any indication

255

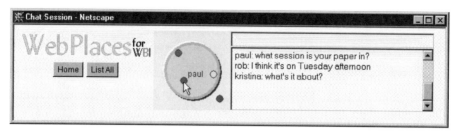

Figure 10.7 Babble-derived representation of place.

of user activity within the space. Thus, we shifted to a graphical display based on Babble (Erickson and Kellogg, this volume), a computer-mediated communication system meant to facilitate long-term, ongoing conversations. One design goal of Babble was to enable those involved in a conversation to be made aware of many social cues, such as users' presence and actions with respect to the particular conversation. The Babble group struck on a very clever and very simple graphical representation called the *social proxy*, which displays a conversation as large circle, individuals as small coloured dots within the circle, and conversational actions (e.g. chatting) as motion of the dots toward the centre of the circle. In addition, a user's dot drifts outwards in a line towards the edge of the circle if the user is inactive for a while. We have adapted this display for our purposes (see Figure 10.7).

In the WebPlaces' social proxy, the circle represents the place (defined by the community of users), and each small coloured dot represents an individual user. Motion of a dot towards the centre of the circle represents a group interaction (e.g. chat), motion of a dot towards another dot represents a user–user action (e.g. whisper), and motion of a dot around the circle represents an individual user action (e.g. browsing). In addition, if a user takes no action for a while the user's dot drifts away from the other users' dots. Thus, we have modified Erickson and Kellogg's social proxy to maintain social awareness in a user community rather than in a specific conversation. To do this, we have included actions that are not specifically related to the ongoing conversation, but that are nonetheless relevant to the users who are gathered together. By coding various types of actions into these iconic motions, we indicate both the state and activity of the people in a place. A casual look at the social proxy indicates the busy-ness of the place, the participating users, the kinds of activity, and so on. In practice, this seems to be effective.

10.2.4 How should Users Interact with One Another on the Web?

Our WebPlaces system provides capabilities for both indirect and direct interaction between people in a place. One kind of indirect interaction is

Figure 10.8 Context menu for interacting with another user.

conveyed by the movement of the user proxies in the Babble-like display: letting users know who is logged on, who is active, and so on. Another kind of indirect interaction is "following" others to web pages they had viewed recently, requiring explicit action on the part of one user to follow another (see Figure 10.8). In the interest of awareness, even this indirect action has consequences for the Babble-like display: when one user follows another, their social proxies move closer together. Of course, a user can choose to hide his or her state from others, but in this case, the user cannot see the state of others: lurking is not permitted. Beyond these indirect interactions, users can also interact directly, either through public chat or private whispers (see Figure 10.8). Because the WebPlaces display is separate from the web browser, it can be covered by other windows, so users can also ring others with either audio or visual alerts to draw their attention back to the display.

In summary, our WebPlaces approach starts from the observation that to give web users a sense of place – a social context, ways of being aware of and interacting with others – we must group web users, make them aware of one another, and enable them to communicate and interact with one another. There are many possible approaches to grouping users, and we have chosen to rely on existing real-world workgroups as a first step. Awareness can also be established in many ways, and we have chosen to adapt the social proxy idea, as it can convey much information about user state and user interaction at a glance. Finally, we have chosen to implement several simple methods of interaction – namely chat, alert and follow – for users to communicate with others.

10.3 Intermediaries

The main goal in building WebPlaces is to enable awareness and interaction on the web pervasively, that is, across all web sites and all web users. Though it is unlikely we could actually achieve such an enormous goal, our design choices will influence how close we can get. Although adding awareness to individual web pages and web sites may seem like a first step, we believe this is the wrong approach for enabling awareness on a

257

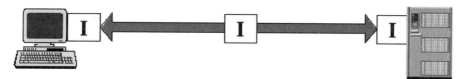

Figure 10.9 Intermediaries can be placed in the information flow at the client, server, or in between.

large scale. How can new functions, such as awareness and interaction, be added across the entire web without modifying all web servers and all web browsers? Our answer is to use intermediaries, computational entities that can be positioned anywhere along an information stream and can be programmed to tailor, customise, personalise, or otherwise enhance data as they flow along the stream (Barrett and Maglio, 1999; Maglio and Barrett, 2000). The intermediary-based approach has the nice property of being pluggable at many points along the information stream (see Figure 10.9), so it can add function without disrupting the existing infrastructure.

In particular, we implemented WebPlaces on top of the Web Intermediaries (WBI) toolkit.[1] Because intermediaries provide a useful place to monitor user activity, affect what users see and coordinate activities among users, they can play an important role in the design and implementation of places, whether on the web or elsewhere. Specifically, WBI was used to monitor user web activity, modify web pages to launch and update the WebPlaces window, and produce special pages of information for log-on, viewing user profiles, and so forth. In this section, we first describe the general web intermediaries framework, then the specific WBI toolkit, and finally the implementation of WebPlaces.

10.3.1 Web Intermediaries

Web intermediaries can be used in a variety of ways to enhance a user's web experience by tracking history of web browsing and then *personalising* web pages based on past history (Barrett et al., 1997; Maglio and Barrett, 2000), or *annotating* pages with information that the original authors did not anticipate (Maglio and Farrell, 2000). Web intermediaries can also be used for *transcoding* web content on-the-fly to tailor it for the user's particular browsing device, such as a cellular phone or personal digital assistant (Ihde et al., 2001). In addition to personalising, annotating and transcoding, we had previously identified three more broad

---

[1] For details and download information on WBI, see http://www.almaden.ibm.com/cs/wbi/.

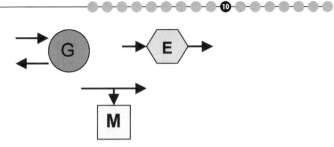

Figure 10.10 Intermediaries can be implemented with three basic operations. Generation produces raw information. Editing modifies raw information. Monitoring observes information flow.

categories of intermediary function: *filtering* or removing information, *aggregating* or combining information from several sources, and *caching* or storing information for reuse later (see Maglio and Barrett, 2000). Now we can add another function: *awareness and collaboration*.

Web intermediaries can operate on information flow in three basic ways: (1) monitoring the flow, for instance, to observe and model user behaviour, analyse the browsed information, or develop histories of usage; (2) editing the information, for example, by adapting it for the particular user or situation, or by enriching the requests with additional information about the user, browsing device or situation; and (3) becoming the information source itself (an extreme form of editing), generating responses to information requests from their own resources. Moreover, intermediaries can operate at various points along the information flow: (1) residing on a user's workstation, operating on all transactions from that one user across all servers that the user accesses; (2) residing (logically, if not physically) on the information server, operating on transactions from all users who access that server; and (3) residing at an intermediate point, such as at a proxy or firewall position, seeing all transactions for a logical group of users, such as all of the users at a particular site or enterprise. A uniform intermediary framework, such as WBI, provides standardised programming interfaces for adding intermediary computation at each of these points along the information flow (see Figure 10.9).

10.3.2 The WBI Toolkit

Our web intermediary toolkit, WBI, is a programmable proxy server that was designed for easy development and deployment of intermediary applications (Barrett and Maglio, 1998, 1999; Maglio and Barrett, 2000). With WBI, intermediary applications or *plugins* are constructed by composing three basic operations: *monitors*, *editors* and *generators* (known collectively as MEGs; see Figure 10.10). Plugins are made up of multiple

259

MEGs that work together. Multiple plugins can be installed in WBI to combine applications, such as transcoding and caching. WBI dynamically routes web transactions through MEGs by matching the information about transactions against rules that are associated with the MEGs. For instance, the rule associated with a monitor that records the text that users see might be keyed on a document's "content-type", such as "text/html". Plugins are defined by their MEGs and the rules that control when the MEGs are involved in a transaction. For instance, a caching proxy is easy to implement as a WBI plugin that monitors transactions to store documents and then generates documents from the local store when they are available. WBI handles all the plumbing, allowing the application writer to concentrate on application details rather than on details of the hypertext transfer protocol (HTTP).

More precisely, for any given HTTP transaction (a request-response pair), WBI can modify the HTTP request (a Request Editor) or the HTTP response (a Document Editor), transform a request into a response (a Generator), and watch data flowing along the stream without affecting it (a Monitor). Each individual MEG is associated with a boolean combination of rule conditions that are matched against the HTTP header of the request or response to determine whether it should be applied to the transaction. In addition, each MEG is associated with a priority number that is used to order the MEGs in the event that more than one applies. When WBI receives a request, it follows these steps:

1. The original request is compared with the rules for all Request Editors. The Request Editors whose rule conditions are satisfied by the request are allowed to edit the request in priority order.
2. The request that results from this Request Editor chain is compared with the rules for all Generators. The request is sent to the highest priority Generator whose rule is satisfied. If that Generator rejects the request, subsequent valid Generators are called in priority order until one produces a document.
3. The request and document are used to determine which Document Editors and Monitors should see the document on its way back to the original requester. The document is modified by each Document Editor whose rule conditions are satisfied, in priority order. Monitors are also configured to monitor the document either (a) as it is produced by the generator, (b) as it is delivered from the intermediary, or (c) after a particular Document Editor.
4. Finally, the document is delivered to the requester, which may be the browser or any other sort of client.

For example, we have developed many WBI plugins that personalise and customise information for individual users or groups of users (Barrett et al., 1997). The *Personal History* plugin uses a monitor to

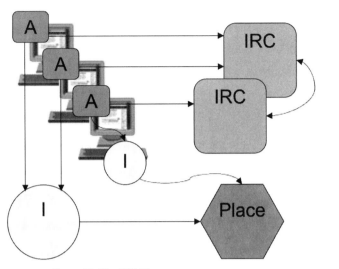

Figure 10.11 WebPlaces system components.

record the sequence of pages visited by a user along with the content of each page. Keyword queries retrieve a list of pages the user has viewed sometime in the past that contain the given keywords. Path browsing allows a user to view paths he or she has taken through a particular page. If the user knows only that some relevant page was seen shortly after going through the IBM home page, then by browsing only the paths taken through the IBM home page, he or she is likely to quickly find the sought-after page. Using the pages monitored and stored by the Personal History plugin, WBI can customise web pages by adding links to pages frequently visited by a certain user. Because web users rely on routines and standard behaviours to access information (Maglio and Barrett, 1997a), WBI's *Short Cuts* plugin adds links to pages that a user routinely visits shortly after visiting the current page. This plugin uses a document editor to add links when there are pages in the database that the user habitually visits within several links of the current page.

We have also developed many plugins that annotate web pages with information that the pages' authors did not anticipate. For instance, the *Dictionary* plugin turns ordinary words on web pages into hyperlinks that point to their definitions (Maglio and Farrell, 2000). In this case, a document editor analyses the text of web pages for words or phrases whose definitions are contained in some web-based dictionary. If a word or phrase that has a definition is found, it is transformed from ordinary text to a hyperlink that points to the definition. In this way, pages containing highly technical medical or legal information can be made accessible to non-specialists.

10.3.3 WebPlaces Implementation

The WebPlaces system consists of four parts (see Figure 10.11): (1) client applet, which provides the user interface for awareness and chat; (2) place server, which maps from URL to place; (3) client proxy, which ensures the applet is loaded and queries the place server for the current place; and (4) chat server, a two-channel system that sends talk and action events to all applets in the same place. The client applet, loaded into its own window when the user begins browsing, is the main user interface to WebPlaces. The applet keeps the user aware of activity in or near the user's current place, implements the user side of real-time chat, and provides access to other WebPlaces functions and web pages through buttons and menus. The place server provides a function that maps from URL to place. Depending upon the environment, this function can be implemented in different ways. For example, it might map people who are browsing URLs that share the same hostname into the same place, or it might map people who are browsing web sites on the same topic into the same place. The WebPlaces client proxy monitors web-browsing activity. Run either on the user's workstation or on a network server, the proxy authenticates the user, monitors the user's web browsing activities, and produces WebPlaces web pages that deliver information to the user. Each time a new page is loaded through the proxy, a callback alerts the applet of its current place. The chat server provides a medium for talk and action events to be propagated to all of the applets. The chat server in our implementation is a standard IRC server (Oikarinen and Reed, 1993). The place is created when the first person enters, and it is destroyed when the last person leaves.

The system was designed to minimise the shared state between the different components so that any of them can be restarted independently. The client applet is, in essence, an IRC client. If it loses its connection to the server, it will attempt to reconnect until successful. When it reconnects, it gets an updated listing of people in that place. It holds two channels open to the server. The first channel is for standard text messaging. The second channel is to communicate actions such as browsing, ringing another user, and so on. The information conveyed on the second channel is used to animate the social proxies. The place server performs the simple function of mapping URLs to places. For example, http://www.ibm.com and http://www.almaden.ibm.com might get mapped to a place called "IBM". In the case of the specific prototype we have been using, all URLs are mapped to the same place, as all users are part of the same workgroup. Though the place server might use any algorithm to answer queries posed to it, it does not rely on any other part of the system. The client proxy is the hook into the web browser that ensures that the applet window is open and that the applet is notified of the current place by the place server. It too is stateless. With each page visited, it queries the place server and inserts the appropriate markup into the resulting document. It also provides functions to view, through the web browser, the available places, users in each place, and other statistics. The chat server, based on IRC, is a standard system that makes no assumptions for WebPlaces in particular. If it is restarted, the various clients will reconnect and the various places will be reconstructed dynamically.

All four components can run on a single system, or can be distributed across different systems. The clients' applets, of course, run on the personal computers of the various users. The place server needs to answer a single HTTP request for every web page a user on the system views, so its load is likely to be relatively light. Nevertheless, the place server can be distributed to many machines provided that each implements the same function. The client proxy can run on a users personal machine, can be shared by some users, or can be shared by all users. The chat server, can run on a single server or a cluster of servers. As a whole, the scalability of the system is limited to the capabilities of IRC clustering technology, which routinely runs tens of thousands of users.

We now describe each of the WebPlaces components in more detail.

WebPlaces Applet

The WebPlaces applet is loaded by JavaScript code that is added to each page by the client proxy. The applet is loaded into its own browser window. The client proxy also inserts applet parameters that tell the applet the user ID of the user and the location of the chat server. When the applet is first loaded, it opens a chat session with the IRC chat server through a persistent socket connection. It registers itself in two channels. The first channel is for text chat events, the second is for action events. For example, if one person says "hello" in a place, then that message is sent through the text channel. If that person then moves from one web page to another in the same place, then a message indicating this movement is sent to the action channel. The applet uses this information to construct a visual representation of the place, in this case, the Babble-like display discussed previously. As the user browses around, each new place that is loaded causes a JavaScript callback to be invoked telling the applet what place the user currently is in. Should that place switch, the applet leaves the two channels of the place it is currently in, and joins the two channels for the new place. So the user navigates with a browser, the browser notifies the proxy of the current URL, the proxy asks the place server to map that URL to a place, and then, when the new page is loaded, the proxy inserts code to tell the applet of the current place.

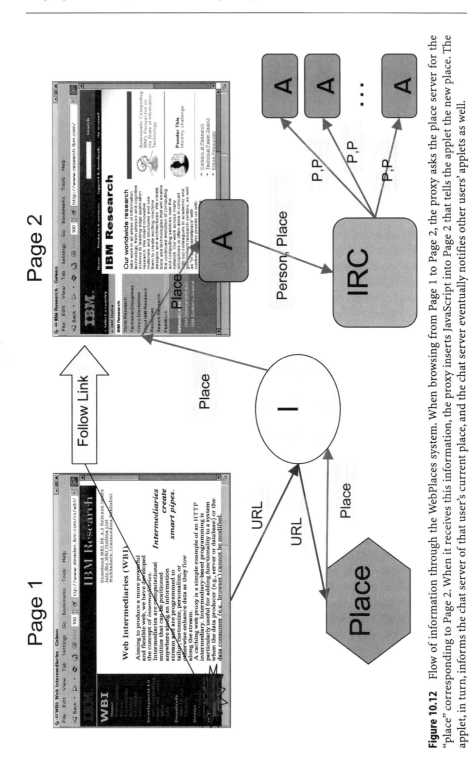

Figure 10.12 Flow of information through the WebPlaces system. When browsing from Page 1 to Page 2, the proxy asks the place server for the "place" corresponding to Page 2. When it receives this information, the proxy inserts JavaScript into Page 2 that tells the applet the new place. The applet, in turn, informs the chat server of that user's current place, and the chat server eventually notifies other users' applets as well.

Place Server

The place server is responsible for mapping a URL to a place. It is implemented as a simple web service that responds to a HTTP request. For example, a request might look like "http://place.almaden.ibm.com/?url=ibm.com/foo.html" and it might return "domain-1:IBM: The IBM web presence". This result is parsed into three parts. The first is a domain that allows many places systems to operate in parallel in their own name space. The second is a brief name for a place used by the chat server to distinguish channels. The final part is the full text title for the place shown the user interface for the applet.

The place server can implement different algorithms to determine the current place. For example, one system we developed mapped topics on a popular discussion web site into different places. On that web site, each topic had a distinct ID that was embedded in the URL. Custom code was written to derive that ID, to map from that ID to the full topic text and to create a specialised place server for that web site. Other functions might depend on the organisation from which the user is connecting, or might use clustering of URL's based on a public web directory, or might simply use the domain for the URL.

WebPlaces Proxy

The client proxy performs four functions: authenticate the user, monitor user web browsing activity, customise the pages the user sees, and produce new personalised web pages for the user. These functions are all implemented as a WBI plugin, which is built out of components that monitor HTTP traffic, edit HTTP requests and responses, and generate HTTP responses to specific requests. Figure 10.12 illustrates part of this process. More precisely,

1. The client proxy authenticates the user. It uses the "Proxy Authenticate" mechanism of HTTP/1.1 (Fielding et al., 1999). Whenever the user accesses a page, the proxy checks for a valid proxy-authenticate field in the HTTP request header. If it is not present, the proxy returns an authentication challenge, which causes the browser to prompt the user for a user ID and password. When the proxy receives a valid authentication, it uses that information to uniquely identify the user among the pool of registered users. When communicating with the other components of the system, the client proxy produces a unique identifier for each user by concatenating the user ID and the IP address of the client proxy. This identifier is unique across all users of all client proxies.

2. The client proxy monitors the user's web browsing activities. Whenever the user accesses a new web page, the request is passed

265

through the client proxy, which parses the request to extract the requested URL. The proxy then passes the request to the appropriate web server to retrieve the requested document for the user. It then checks the response code received from the web server to ensure that the page has been successfully retrieved. If so, the client proxy sends a message to the place server to determine the place for the current URL.

3. The client proxy manipulates the web pages that the user sees. Currently, the proxy's modifications are transparent to the user. JavaScript is added to each web page to instruct the browser to create a new window (if it does not already exist) and to load the WebPlaces applet into it. This mechanism ensures that a WebPlaces window is always present on the user's workstation. The user can minimise it if desired, but if it is deleted, the client proxy's script will re-create it the next time the user loads a URL. The proxy also inserts into the resulting web page a JavaScript callback which alerts the applet to the current place. The client proxy's ability to manipulate web pages can be used for purposes other than the creation of an applet window. For instance, the client proxy might also provide person- and place-dependent annotation on web pages, including additional links to web pages of interest to others in the current group, personal annotations that the user or other users have made on particular web pages, or even artefacts that other users have left in the place.

4. The client proxy produces new web pages that present the user with personalised WebPlaces information. Because the proxy intercepts all web page requests, linking to special URLs, such as "http://_web-places/showuser" can produce special information displays and forms. URLs such as these are used to display the user's state, information about other users, to send and receive messages, and so forth. Links to these pages are produced by the WebPlaces applet or from WebPlaces pages.

Chat Server

The chat server is responsible for maintaining communication channels shared by all of the applets. Our system used a standard open-source IRC server. Our server was configured to operate independently of the global IRC networks. It was also configured to allow special clients to connect with advanced privileges so that they could send data rapidly without triggering the IRC "flood-protection" code. One such special client was the history server.

The chat server did not need to maintain information about the different places because IRC servers create and destroy channels on demand as users enter or leave them. Channels on the chat system correspond to *occupied* places. If there is anyone in a place, then the corresponding channel will exist. There is not necessarily a channel for every *possible* place. As a result, the chat system can reliably maintain the places and communicate messages between the various clients in each place without having any specialised knowledge of what the places are, or which ones exist. To the IRC chat system, a place is just a label.

In order to discriminate communication between applets about actions and chat, each place would correspond to two channels on the chat system. The auxiliary channel was distinguished with a preceding special character (an underscore "_") in order to avoid name space collisions with other places.

Auxiliary Servers

Some features were implemented through auxiliary servers. These auxiliary servers are implemented as IRC "bots", automated programs that connect to IRC channels and provide special functions. One such bot is the history server. Its role is to recall the last 10 things spoken in each place and recite them to each person who enters that place. Another bot is the transcript server. Its role is to keep a running log of all of the communication that occurs in each place. Yet another server sets the IRC topic for each channel to the full text title of the place. For example, if a channel is created called "IBM" the title server will contact the place server, find out the title of the place "IBM" is "The IBM web presence", and will set the IRC topic accordingly.

10.4 Where to Go From Here?

Our WebPlaces system was a first step toward incorporating real-time social interaction into the web. How big a step did we take? The first key question was who should be included in a user's social group. The model we chose, an explicit and fixed set of friends, is acceptable and functional – yet far from ideal. The success of instant messaging systems has demonstrated that people wish to interact with such groups of friends. Adding the web to the instant messaging paradigm enriches the experience, but it falls short of the overall goal because it has such a limited notion of social interaction: it eliminates chance encounters that widen the social network. Simplicity and small size are gained at the cost of inflexibility and closed social circles. The social function of WebPlaces would be enhanced by the incorporation of features that would allow "bumping into" new people while browsing the web.

At the outset, we distinguished five basic ways to define the social group: Users who are (a) pre-defined as a group, (b) visiting the same page at the same time, (c) exploring pages that are closely linked together, (d) exploring pages with the same content, and (e) following similar trails through the information space of the web. Our current implementation relies on the first of these: group formation based on existing relationships. In this case, the users are likely to have similar interests or share similar views precisely because they already form a social group.

One important attribute of intermediaries as a development and deployment platform is that different place structures can be implemented easily. For instance, consider a server-side deployment of WebPlaces. In this arrangement, we would choose a particular server and deploy the intermediary at that site, running right in front of the actual web server. The intermediary modifies the web pages appropriately to create a set of places for the users of that server. By choosing a popular and well-structured server, such as a corporate intranet directory, the different notions of place and definitions of groups of users can be implemented and tested.

The second key question is what affordances should be provided to create a social place in the context of the web. Our design functions well within its notion of place. Awareness of presence and activity is presented in an intuitive way, and both direct communication and indirect communication are facilitated. However, its limitations become more apparent as we envision the next step. For example, our implementation has only a single place – the group of friends – which is assumed to be consistent across the entire group. It might be confusing if users A and B are part of the same group, but user B also includes user C as a friend and user A does not. The analogy with a real place would break down because their conversation might reveal that they have different views of who is in the "same" place. Maintaining symmetry is important.

Our affordances are greatly simplified by the existence of only a single place for a given user. If places become more tied to browsing activity (e.g. users might move from the place having to do with current events to the place having to do with computer programming), then thought must be given to how the transition between these places is handled, how easy it is to return to the previous place, and the whole idea of mapping these virtual places into a visual representation space. Such issues might be more easily handled within a well-organised set of web pages (e.g. within the Yahoo directory classification system) than with a less obvious virtual arrangement.

Our current implementation affords direct social interaction through chat and ringing, and indirect interaction through presence and activity displays, viewing of profiles, and following others on the web. There are obvious possible extensions to these affordances, including such things as voice chat and personal video, exchanging files, viewing summaries of previous browsing activity, and seeing activity cues about things other than web browsing activity (e.g. keyboard and mouse activity, current application in use, and so on). However, some aspects of affordances are less clear and will require more exploratory work. For example, should users have ways to interact with the place itself and not only the people in the place? Users may want to alter the place through notations or footprints, leave artifacts relevant to the place that others may want to see, view the history of the place (who has been here before? what were they doing?), or explore why this place exists at all (what range of things define this place?).

Another exploratory area is the best visualisation of the place and the meaning of space within the place. Our Babble-like visualisation maps space within the place into activity and level of social engagement. The space could just as well correspond to other things, such as for a topic-based place it could represent the user's distance from the "centre" of the topic. Continuity and symmetry are also important properties of places. Continuity has two aspects: continuity in time and in space. In time it implies that yesterday's place still exists today, though maybe with small changes. The places must have enough inertia in their dynamics that the users can develop an understanding for how the place is organised. Likewise, places are usually continuous in space so that small amounts of movement result in small changes in place. This leads to the concept of symmetry where reversals produce the expected results. Moving to the right and then moving back to the left should return to the same place. Symmetry also has a social meaning: when users look at one another, they should see corresponding pictures. Symmetry can be difficult to maintain if different users are given the possibility of choosing different visualisation modes of the same space.

10.5 Conclusion

The WebPlaces system was our first approach toward transforming the World Wide Web into a social place that affords user-awareness and user-interaction. In implementing this system, we demonstrated how intermediaries could be used to integrate awareness and interaction with the web. Yet we have only just begun to explore this problem of social interaction. Many open issues remain. What is the right way to group people on the web? What is the right way to display groups? What are the right ways for people to interact? Far from being the last word, our implementation serves mainly to call attention to these.

Part II
Theories and Principles

11

Where the Footprints Lead: Tracking Down Other Roles for Social Navigation

Paul Dourish

11.1 Introduction

In the early 1980s, researchers working in the area of interactive systems became increasingly interested in the topic of cooperative work. Human beings are, after all, social animals, and most activities in which we engage are conditioned by and conducted in coordination with other individuals. We work collectively. However, until this point, the focus of interactive systems research had largely been on a single user sitting at a desk in front of a computer screen. The field of computer-supported cooperative work (CSCW) emerged in response to this focus. It drew attention to the range of concerns that lay outside this computer/human dyad but which fundamentally affected the nature of work at the computer, such as the social setting in which the activity took place, and the role that that the activity played in an individual's collaborative actions. In the years that have followed, CSCW has legitimised this concern and reoriented HCI to take into account the social context in which work is conducted. At the same time, it has also had an influence on the development of everyday technologies for computer-based work; as the Internet has become a more commonplace computational phenomenon, so technologies such as workflow and groupware have moved out of the research laboratory and into everyday computational practice.

The topic of social navigation offers an opportunity to take this even further. Social navigation is one of the most direct expressions of the fundamental principle that the action of a user at a computer is driven not simply by a set of internal goals and cognitive processes, but by the social setting in which they find themselves, by the action of others, individually and collectively, and by the social nature of the work being conducted and the goals sought. In other words, social navigation provides an opportunity to take those aspects of computer-based interaction and information seeking which might still be regarded as primarily single-user activities, and to invest them with a sense of the social. In systems supporting social navigation, the social and collaborative aspects of work are not limited to the overtly cooperative activities such as meeting support, communication and shared workspace manipulation, but to activities that would seem, still, to be grounded in the model of a single user sitting at a computer. Reading on-line documents, navigating file systems, searching a database, finding a book to read and sorting electronic mail might all seem like fundamentally individual activities; private and encapsulated in one person's head. However, the use of social navigation techniques allows us to be able to capitalise upon the social nature of the everyday world, and so to enrich the interface with collaborative support for individual tasks.

This volume presents a wide variety of current research into the role and function of social navigation. This chapter is concerned with potential new opportunities for the application of the social navigation concept in interactive systems in general, and will argue that social navigation is a more general phenomenon than current practice would suggest. As a result, the focus here will be less on current research on social navigation and more on those other areas to which it might be applied. The body of the chapter will discuss how we might apply understandings of social navigation to address wider problems in the design, development and analysis of interactive and collaborative systems. A consideration of new opportunities in research on social navigation, however, should begin by looking at the origins and scope of the term, and so that will be the first topic.

11.1.1 Perspectives on Social Navigation

How should we consider social navigation? What range of phenomena and systems does the term name, and how do we come to consider them as aspects of a single concept?

Although there had been investigations of collaborative systems as far back as the NLS/Augment work of Engelbart and his colleagues in the 1960s (Englebart and English, 1968) and which persisted throughout subsequent developments in data communication networks, it was only in the early 1980s that the term "computer-supported cooperative work" was coined and the field began to develop a more uniform identity and a shared base of understandings from which to build. At this point, a variety of systematic investigations began into the role of mutual cooperative behaviour through computer systems, the role of computational technologies to support coordination and collaboration, and the use of data-sharing to support concerted action.

The Tapestry system (Goldberg et al., 1992; Terry, 1993), developed at Xerox PARC, introduced the idea of "collaborative filtering", which became one of the key ideas that has driven subsequent work on social navigation. Collaborative filtering systems provide a user with recommendations of their likely interest in data items on the basis of "interest matches" derived from previous ratings from a set of users. Tapestry operated over a database of electronic mail messages and allowed users to exploit "votes" that previous users had entered concerning the value or interest of the message. By selecting an appropriate group of users based on overlaps in interest, Tapestry could allow an individual user to exploit collective experience.

Recommender systems, as these sort of applications have become known, have become one of the most visible forms of social navigation in everyday systems. The work of Pattie Maes' group at the MIT Media Lab (Shardanand and Maes, 1995), Will Hill and his colleagues at Bellcore (Hill et al., 1995) and others has explored the use of collaborative recommendation of books, films and music, and these technologies have been incorporated into deployed technologies such as electronic commerce systems. Recommendation systems vary along a number of different dimensions, but the basic insight is similar to that of the collaborative filtering system in that they provide users with a means to use information that others have left behind as a cue to exploring an information space. In particular, recommendation systems typically use information about individual interests (e.g. which books they like and which they dislike) to build a profile which can be matched with the profiles of other individuals. If the system can determine that two people have similar tastes in books (because there is enough overlap in their stated likes and dislikes to imply a correspondence), then it can suggest that books that one likes but the other hasn't seen are probably good ones to recommend. In electronic commerce settings (such as an on-line store), profiles can be developed on the basis of shopping habits, reducing the overhead in generating the profiles in the first place.

Spatial, Semantic and Social Navigation

In a short paper presented at HCI' 94, Dourish and Chalmers (1994) introduced the term "social navigation", which included systems of this sort. However, the focus of that brief exploration was broader, and the term "social navigation" was coined to describe a particular phenomenon, in which a user's navigation through an information space was primarily guided and structured by the activities of others within that space.

"Social" navigation was contrasted with "spatial" and "semantic" navigation. Spatial navigation relies on the structure of the space itself, often a two- or three-dimensional metaphor of some spatially-organised real-

275

world phenomenon (such as an office, street or landscape). Virtual reality systems, for example, place considerable reliance on spatial navigation, offering users a spatial organisation by which to explore an environment. "Semantic" navigation, in contrast, relies on the semantic structure of the space. A hypertext system, for example, provides "links" between semantically-related items and offers a means to move from one item to another according to these semantic relationships.

Dourish and Chalmers were attempting to clarify the distinctions between the three forms to support better evaluation of the important features of navigational systems. This concern arose from the emergence of collaborative virtual reality systems or "collaborative virtual environments" (CVEs), with their strong appeal to spatial models. CVEs use a 3D visualisation metaphor to organise data and interaction, and so are firmly grounded on a spatial model; by exploiting our familiarity with the spatial structure of the everyday world, they can provide smooth and intuitive interaction with large information spaces. In CVEs such as DIVE (Carlsson and Hagsand, 1993) and MASSIVE (Greenhalgh and Benford, 1995a), a user may have visual access not only to data items or objects in the space but also to other individuals and to their interactions. This gives them the opportunity not only to interact with data items, but also to be able to see (and hence be influenced by) other people's interactions in the space; and researchers studying CVEs have developed a range of mechanisms for providing participants with a control over views of each other's actions (Benford et al., 1995).[1] However, the arguments that apply to the familiarity of interaction with objects in a three-dimensional space to do not apply unproblematically to interactions between individuals. Is inter-personal interaction in the three-dimensional space driven primarily by the structure of that space? Is spatial structure enabling social action, or is social action happening within a spatial structure?

This confusion arises because semantic and social navigation may well take place in spatially-organised settings. Semantic and social navigation do not name types of systems; rather, they name *phenomena of interaction*. They may all occur in the same sort of "space". For instance, imagine browsing in a bookstore. If I pick up a new book because it is sitting on the shelf next to one I've just been examining, then I'm navigating spatially. If I pick up another book because it was referred to in a citation in the first book, then I'm navigating semantically; and if I pick up yet another because it was recommended to me by someone whose opinion I trust, then I am navigating socially. The conceptual separation between "spatial", "semantic" and "social" styles of information navigation was

---

[1] However, the restricted field of view and cumbersome mechanisms of navigation and exploration afforded by current CVEs can introduce problems for mutual orientation and reference (Hindmarsh et al., 1998).

intended to provide terms in which these different forms of behaviour could be discussed.

This is the basic principle from which the investigations to be presented here proceed: that social navigation is an *interactive phenomenon* rather than a class of technology. In this chapter, I will take the term "navigation" as an adequate term for all information-seeking activities. The space to be navigated is the notional space of potential information items, be those book recommendations, web pages, interesting data items, other people, or whatever. Navigation does not, in itself, imply "movement" in any typical, spatial sense. What will be of concern is how the information-seeking activities can be framed socially and how this framing can assist an individual in the course of their information-seeking activity.

New Opportunities for Social Navigation

In light of these considerations, we can take a number of different perspectives on social navigation. One would be to think of social navigation as an explicit activity, in which a user calls upon others to request advice or pointers, either directly or via an intermediate (perhaps an artefact like a FAQ list). Another, more commonly accepted amongst researchers in the field, is to think of social navigation as essentially an intrinsic element of individual interaction, one which respects that individual action is carried out within a complex of social relationships and provides a means to exploit this connectivity to other individuals to help people organise information.

In this chapter, some alternative conceptions of social navigation will be presented and explored. In the first, social navigation will be considered as an aspect of collaborative work, in which information can be shared within a group to help each group member work effectively, exploiting overlap in concerns and activities for mutual coordination. In the second, it will be presented as a way of moving through an information space and exploiting the activities and orientations of others in that space as a way of managing one's own spatial activity.

These last two perspectives will be the main topics for the rest of this chapter. The following section considers the notion of social navigation in the context of collaborative systems, and particularly with relation to the idea of "awareness" in collaborative workspaces. The subsequent section will consider the relationship between social navigation and the conceptions of "space" prevalent in collaborative and interactive systems. By taking these two particular perspectives, I hope to be able, first, to cast some light on the fundamental nature of social navigation broadly construed and, second, to open up new avenues for the use and design of social navigation facilities in interactive tools.

11.2 Social Navigation and Collaborative Awareness

The idea of social navigation is firmly based on the fact that information about others and about others' activities can be beneficial to an individual in the conduct of their activity. In collaborative systems, this idea is clearly strongly related to the topic of the mutual "awareness" between collaborators of each other's activity. In this section, I will pursue this relationship in more detail and use the perspective of social navigation to highlight opportunities for a broader conception of collaborative awareness.

11.2.1 Awareness in Collaboration

The topic of "awareness" has become a significant focus of research activity in the CSCW domain. The principal idea behind this notion is that the activity of others within a group setting can be a critical resource for the individual in managing their own work (Dourish and Bellotti, 1992). The term "awareness" has come to refer to the ways in which systems can present this information and so provide to participants in a collaborative activity an "awareness" of the action and activity of others.

This feature of collaborative activity is clearly not restricted to electronically mediated settings. Excellent examples can be found, for instance, in the work of Heath and his colleagues studying a variety of collaborative settings such as transit system control rooms (Heath and Luff, 1992a) and dealing rooms (Heath et al., 1994). In these settings, a common observation is that the detail of coordination between individuals is tied to a "peripheral monitoring" by which they maintain an understanding of the state of each other's activities, so as to be able to organise their own behaviour in correspondence. At the same time, individuals also choose to organise their work so that it can be successfully monitored; that is, they display the state of their own activity.

Consider an example. In their study of a London Underground control room, Heath and Luff (1992a) present a detailed analysis of an interaction between two individuals in the control room. One, the Line Controller (Controller), has responsibility for the movement of trains on the line, while the other, the Divisional Information Assistant (DIA), has responsibility for information provided to passengers about the service. Health and Luff observe that the DIA's actions can be seen to be tied to the precise detail of what the Controller is doing, to the extent that, on overhearing the Controller discussing a problem with a driver over the in-cab intercom, the DIA can tell that this problem is going to result in a service disruption and is *already beginning* to announce to passengers the consequences of this disruption *before* the Controller has informed him of the nature of the problem. This sort of very tightly coupled interaction depends upon a detailed understanding, on the part of the DIA, of the Controller's activity and the consequences it might hold. Conversely, when "reworking" the schedule (to accommodate changes in the service resulting from local disruptions), the Controller will talk through the changes he is introducing in such a way that he can be overheard by the DIA precisely to enable this sort of interaction.

In other words, what we find in studies of naturalistic collaborative work is that the twin mechanisms of peripheral monitoring and explicit "display" provide collaborators with the means by which to couple their work. These observations have motivated the development of technological approaches that provide for the framing of individual activity within the context of the group.

11.2.2 Designing for Awareness

The developers of CSCW systems have drawn from these observations the importance of awareness information for coordinating collaborative activity and so they have developed a range of mechanisms for providing awareness information in collaborative technologies, with considerable success in a variety of domains (e.g. Tang et al., 1994; Donath, 1995; Fuchs et al., 1995; Palfreyman and Rodden, 1996). However, the emphasis in these technical developments has largely been on the first of the two mechanisms found in real-world settings, that is, on the peripheral monitoring. Systems have provided a variety of means for what Dourish and Bellotti (1992) referred to as "shared feedback", by which collaborators can see the results of each others' actions. For instance, the SASSE system (Baecker et al., 1993) provided a variety of ways by which users could see each other's work, including "radar views" and distortion effects on the display of the textual workspace. Gutwin et al. (1996) provide an overview of a variety of techniques for visualising the activity of others.

These systems have provided for ways to see the work of others, and so have supported the "peripheral monitoring" aspect of the awareness-based coordination of activities that Heath and Luff have so vividly demonstrated in their studies. Relatively little work, however, has gone into the area of the explicit production of activity information for coordination purposes. In fact, in general, this question of how information is to be produced for awareness purposes – corresponding, for example, with Heath and Luff's observations of the mumbling Line Controller – has remained relatively unexplored so far.

Certainly, it raises some hard problems. It immediately leads to a set of concerns about what kinds of uses people expect the information to be put to, not to mention the sorts of privacy and protection issues raised, in the context of ubiquitous computing environments, by Bellotti and Sellen

279

(1993). However, some potential solutions to these problems lie in the ways in which similar issues have been tackled in research into social navigation.

11.2.3 Taking the Social Navigation Perspective

The fundamental relationship between social navigation and collaborative awareness technologies is simple, and lies in their mutual concern with the means by which an individual can exploit the information of others. What is interesting is that so many social navigation systems, and particularly the recommendation systems that have become so popular, are based not simply on the information of others, but information about the activity of others, which is fundamental to collaborative awareness. So I can capitalise upon information about what books other people have bought, what web pages they have visited, what newsgroup articles they have read, and so forth. The reason this tends to be the case is that activity information is easy to capture at low overhead to the user; it is much more convenient for my system to record which books you have bought from an on-line store than it is to present you with a list of 300 books and ask you to rate them each on a scale from 1 to 10. However, despite this pragmatic explanation, the relationship between the two concerns is still suggestive.

It is particularly suggestive because it opens up opportunities for further cross-fertilisation. In particular, there are a number of features from social navigation systems that could be fruitfully applied in systems providing collaborative awareness.

Aggregation

One interesting feature of social navigation systems in comparison to traditional collaborative awareness technologies is that of aggregation. By this, I mean that social navigation systems might bring together information from a number of individuals at the same moment, presenting either information about a plurality of users or about a fictional composite user.

Consider the case of the book recommendation system again. The sorts of observations we might expect from such a system are ones like, "People who liked *The Thought Gang* also liked *Mr. Vertigo*, *My Idea of Fun* and *Towing Jehovah*". What is significant about this, from the perspective of collaborative awareness systems, it is that the information is not about a single individual, but rather, reports a trend which is based on observation from a variety of individuals. In all likelihood, there are some number of individuals who purchased all four books, but there may not be; what is presented is an aggregate observation based on data gathered from a number of individuals.

In collaborative awareness systems, however, the focus has normally been on presenting information from different individuals separately. Most displays tends to present me with the information about the current activity of Joe, Katie and Brian independently, presenting a fairly direct and faithful rendition of their current activity. Awareness systems generally do not provide any sort of interpolation or generalisation of information. And yet, at the same time, this introduces serious problems about scalability. Since there is no generalisation, and only individual reports, problems arise over the number of individual reports that can be accommodated, and how they can be presented together. The social navigation approach offers an alternative that could be of considerable benefit in trying to address this problem.

Presentation

A related issue concerns the terms in which information is delivered and presented. Partially, perhaps, as a result of the potential aggregation of information from different sources, social navigation systems have had to consider the possibility that the terms in which information about the activity of others is presented to a user might not be the same terms in which it was gathered.

In the case of inherently aggregated information, such as votes, this is inevitable; the gathering of information is in terms of positive or negative votes about some item, whereas the presentation of the information is in terms of the mass of votes for or against; a quantitative measure, and so of quite a different sort. However, there are other ways in which the form of the information is altered for presentation – web pages rather than links, books rather than purchases, or whatever. In other words, the designers of social navigation systems, since they are focused primarily on the notion of helping the end-user rather than simply presenting the information, are open to the fact that the form in which the information is most usefully presented might not be the same as that in which it was gathered; while the designers of collaborative awareness systems have often been concerned with verisimilitude as a primary design criterion, showing the movement of mouse cursors and text edit points as accurately as possible, or giving direct views of the activity of others, as in video-based systems such as Portholes (Dourish and Bly, 1992). Exploiting, again, the clear foundational relationship between social navigation and collaborative awareness opens this up to some question, and points the way towards new approaches to awareness that consider more how the information is to be exploited, and hence how it might best be transformed and presented.

281

Decoupling

One final feature of social navigation systems relevant here is that they are both synchronous and asynchronous. Most awareness systems, on the other hand, tend to be synchronous only, displaying the user information about other collaborating individuals in real-time, but giving them less information about what the others may have done in the past when the user was disconnected or engaged in another task. Although there has been some work on asynchronous means for conveying awareness information, such as Hill et al.'s "edit wear" and "read wear" (Hill et al., 1992), collaborative awareness systems have largely focussed on synchronous solutions. The value of social navigation systems as an asynchronous mechanism for sharing activity information and for capitalising upon such shared information is, surely, ample indication of the value to be derived from asynchronous collaborative awareness.

The problem here is one of coupling. In the typical, synchronous, collaborative case, the presentation of information about a user's activity is directly coupled to the activity itself. As surely as one user's keystrokes result in characters being entered into a text buffer, they also result in indications of typing activity on another user's screen, and so on. There are not, typically, mechanisms for decoupling the awareness information – although some awareness "widgets" are a start in that direction (Ackerman and Starr, 1995). In the same way that technologies for social navigation aggregate and re-represent information about individual actions for presentation as indicates of group trends, they also introduce a decoupling that extends the usefulness of this information beyond the synchronous case.

11.2.4 Summary

What this exploration suggests, then, is that the concerns of collaboration awareness and the phenomenon of social navigation are closely related. They both rely on being able to present information about the activity of individuals in a way that allows other individuals to capitalise on it for the management of their own activities. What is more, by looking at collaborative awareness through the lens of social navigation, we have been able to identify a number of aspects of system design – aggregation, presentation and decoupling – that could help address current problems in the development of awareness technologies when we think of awareness as being a form of social navigation and information management.

The phenomenon of social navigation can also be applied to other areas of concern in collaborative systems. In particular, we will now go on to explore it in another context. Taking the term "navigation" more seriously, we can consider social navigation in relation to recent trends investigating the notions of "space" and "place" in CSCW systems.

11.3 Social Navigation and Models of Space

The very term "social *navigation*" invokes a spatially-organised world, a world of paths, proximity and wayfaring. Spatial metaphors are one of the most widespread conventions in interactive system design, and are also carried across to the design of collaborative systems. However, in a collaborative setting, we are more directly faced with a need to pay attention to the social phenomena of space, and the social construction of meaning in spatial settings. The distinction at work here is that between "space" and "place", and the relationship between the two. Collaborative systems design has traditionally paid little attention to this relationship, although it has begun to receive some more attention lately.

In this section, we shall consider this relationship, starting from the position, again, that social navigation is a phenomenon of interaction. This section will briefly recap on its consequences for the design of collaborative systems, and then consider how social navigation fits into the picture when the notion of space has been reformulated.

11.3.1 On "Space" and "Place"

Collaborative systems are frequently organised around computational spaces of some form. We encounter systems employing media spaces (Bly et al., 1993), shared workspaces (Ishii, 1990), argumentation spaces (Streitz et al., 1989), etc. The idea of "space" is widespread because it is so fundamental to our everyday experience. Our conception of the world is fundamentally spatial; our own three-dimensional embodiments in the world are the most fundamental part of our everyday experience. The use of space as an organising metaphor for interaction – and, indeed, for many other things besides (Lakoff and Johnson, 1980) – is a natural one.

On the other hand, and just as we found earlier in considering navigation in shared virtual reality systems, the idea of "space" is one that deserves some consideration. Spatial settings are conveniently familiar and all-encompassing, but just what role is spatiality playing when it is adopted as an interactional metaphor? Further, what role does it play when the interaction is collaborative or social in nature?

Interface developers have only been in the space business for a couple of decades; perhaps it's not surprising that our view is relatively unsophisticated. So, in trying to look at these questions, one place to turn is to the Built Environment (architecture, urban design, etc.), where issues of space, of interaction and of design have been combined for thousands of years. Drawing on architectural and social theorising, I have argued, elsewhere, for a reconsideration of the notion of "space", and in particular, a reassessment of the relationship of "space" to "place" (Harrison and Dourish, 1996). The argument presented in that paper was rooted in the philosophy behind the design of "media space" technologies. We observed, in particular, that media spaces had been designed around an understanding of the relationship between the structure of the environment and emergent understandings of the action that takes place there. It is no coincidence that the original developers of media space technologies had backgrounds in architecture. The technology was dubbed media "space" precisely because its design took an emergent view of the relationship between space and place.

What is this relationship? At its most primitive, it is the relationship between structural and social aspects of the designed environment. *Space* refers to the three-dimensional structure of the world, and the configurations of light, air and material that create lots, buildings, rooms, conference centres, churches, theatres, casinos, shopping malls, offices, nooks, parks, and the various other familiar configurations of spatial setting with which we are familiar in the everyday works. Alongside this world of spatial settings is a world of places. While spaces take their sense from configurations of brick, mortar, wood and glass, places take their sense from configurations of social actions. Places provide what we call *appropriate behavioural framing*; on the basis of patterns of social action and accountability, places engender a set of patterned social responses. Spaces provide physical constraints and affordances, based on things like the fact that it is easier to go downhill than up, that humans cannot walk through walls, and that light passes through glass. In parallel, places provide social constraints and affordances, based on things like the fact that western society frowns on public nudity, courts and churches are places for more dignified affairs than nightclubs, and that joyful exuberance is an acceptable response to sporting events but not to conference presentations.

Until recently, this relationship has, largely, gone unexamined in the CSCW literature. On the other hand, the emergence of collaborative virtual reality systems and observations of the natural and compelling nature of interaction in spatial settings has become more prevalent. This has resulted in a variety of recent explorations of collaborative and interaction systems from the perspective of architectural and urban design, including the work of Erickson (1993), Fitzpatrick et al. (1996), and Benyon and Höök (1997), as well as the contributions of Chalmers and Dieberger in this volume.

Space and place are fundamentally intertwined, of course; they each influence and condition the other. However, they are distinguishable. The design of the built environment is precisely about the artful manipulation of the relationship between space and place, between physical structure and social action (and, of course, about the history of the relationship between the two).

In his book *City: Rediscovering the Centre* (Whyte, 1988a), William Whyte presents a detailed study of the everyday elements of urban life.

His concern is with the functioning of urban spaces, in particular the densely populated daytime downtown areas. On the basis of photographic and statistical studies, he builds up an image of spaces that "work" and spaces that "don't"; ones which succeed or fail at creating a sense of place. He documents where people like to stop and have conversations, or eat their lunch; which spots attract crowds and which are deserted. Throughout his discussion of patterns of activity on streets, at plazas and in parks, he emphasises the idea that "what attracts people is people". The role of space is to frame human action.

Space and Place in Collaboration

What can we learn from this? What would such a reconsideration say about collaborative systems?

The functioning of virtual spaces and physical spaces are clearly very different (it is all too easy to forget that the relationship is metaphorical), but we can find evidence for similar relationships between space and place in a virtual setting. Harrison and Dourish present a number of examples from the research literature of virtual spaces working or not working. For instance, experiments in the use of video technology to link public spaces for the purposes of informal communication have had very mixed results. While some, such as the PARC/Portland link reported on by Bly et al. (1993) have been extremely successful and popular with participants, others such as the Virtual Window discussed by Fish et al. (1990) have languished largely unused.

We can speculate about the reasons, and the potential consequences for design; clearly, the set of issues surrounding the deployment of these sorts of technologies are extremely complex. On the other hand, one clear indication is that the immediate social context is important. The issue is how the virtual space that the technology creates comes to be peopled and inhabited, how people come to have an understanding of what it does for them and how they should act. Harrison and Dourish point particularly towards a notion of *appropriation* – the extent to which the technology lends itself to be taken over by the participants and turned to their own uses, so that they can structure the space around their own needs and activities and make the technology their own. In other words, what we find to be important is not the technology itself, not the "space" that it creates, but the creative peopling of that space to turn it into a place, where people do things.

The other significant consequence for the development of collaborative systems echoes an earlier observation. It was noted earlier in contrasting social navigation with spatial and semantic forms that social navigation can take place both in and out of spatial settings. It may be that social navigation is effected in a spatially organised environment,

285

but it may also happen in non-spatial settings. Analogously, at a conceptual level we may find "places" that are non-spatial at heart (or, at least, ones whose spatial nature has nothing to do with their functioning as places). One simple example is an electronic discussion group such as a mailing list, web forum or Usenet News group. These have many features that we associate with "place"; they have a set of behavioural norms and expectations that frame the activity of individuals and against which activity can be considered. However, they do not offer what we would think of as "spatial" features; there is no up and down, no near and far, none of the "technology" of the everyday world. They are space-less places. Space might be a convenient, compelling and familiar metaphor for the development of collaborative systems, but it is not fundamental, nor necessary to their social functioning.

This reflects the fact that what places (rather than spaces) offer is what we called appropriate behavioural framing. Dieberger (this volume) presents interesting evidence for the ways in which people have mutually held understandings of what he calls the "social connotations" of places; social connotations are the consequences of behavioural framing, and they operate in both real-world and virtual environments. Discussions of appropriate postings to newsgroups or other forms of discussion forum reflect the same concerns in non-spatial settings.

So these two concerns – appropriation and appropriate behavioural framing – help to set up an initial framework for considering how the ideas of space and place apply to collaborative technologies in general. The next question to ask is how they help explain a relationship between space, place and social navigation.

Social Navigation from the Perspective of Spatial Settings

When we think about it from the perspective of spatial settings, we immediately encounter some interesting features of the term "social navigation" itself. Indeed, we are immediately confronted with two diametrically opposed positions, from which "social navigation" is either an oxymoron or a tautology.

Social Navigation as an Oxymoron

The first position is that "social navigation" is an oxymoron. After all, navigation is a phenomenon fundamentally rooted in the physical world, an arrangement of, and orientation to, the elements of the physical world. From this perspective, navigation is a purely physical phenomenon, and not a social one.

There would seem to be at least two responses to this. The first is that, although navigation in the everyday world might be a purely physical phenomenon, there is no physical instantiation of the virtual information spaces we are concerned with when applying "social navigation" in electronic settings, and so the support of social features is a more pressing requirement in virtual environments. The second is that the purely physical construal of everyday navigation is a flawed one, and that, in everyday settings and the physical world, our navigation and wayfaring are actually highly socially-conditioned phenomena. This response leads us to the second position.

Social Navigation as a Tautology

The second position is that "social navigation" is a tautology. From this position, all navigation behaviour is social action and fundamentally conditioned by social forces. We can follow up this observation in a number of different ways.

One example is to take "navigation" itself, as a practical matter. Hutchins has developed this position in considerable depth in a number of investigations (Hutchins, 1990, 1995). His particular concern has been the practice of navigation on board large ships. He has produced a detailed analysis of the practice of ship-board navigation, from the perspective of distributed cognition, observing how the measurements and calculations which comprise navigation on ships are distributed over a group of individuals working together. Navigation is not so much performed as achieved through a complex of interlocking individual activities.

The tools of navigation are, themselves, socially constructed. Maps, for example, which might seem to be objective representations, faithfully detailing the structure of the environment, are rife with social and political concerns. Who draws the maps? What ends do they serve? Who decides what constitutes a "permanent feature", what is or not named, what is or is not mapped and recorded? What is the reality of the straight black lines that delimit one region from another? Wood (1992) presents a wide-ranging analysis of the power of maps, arguing that maps construct the world rather than represent it.

The other tool of navigation, of course, is the world itself, but even that is not straightforward. Lynch (1960), for example, discusses the "imageability" of cities. Not all places are equally navigable, and the actual practice of navigation depends on specific features of the environment. Chalmers et al. (1996) has explored how imageability features could be incorporated into virtual information spaces. However, what those features might be, what constitutes navigability and how navigation takes place – none of these are human constants. A number of social scientists, including Suchman (1987) and Hutchins (1983) have explored the metaphor of the differences between western and Polynesian navigational practices, which have allowed Polynesian sailors to navigate, without instruments, long voyages inconceivable to western observers.

287

11.3.2 Place for Social Navigation

The distinction between "place" and "space" provides a frame for analysing the structure of, and action within, computational environment for collaboration. How does this frame relate to social navigation? There are at least two ways we can see a relationship between these ideas. The first is the question of how a space becomes populated; and the second is how social activity might transform it.

If it is sense of "appropriate behavioural framing" that distinguishes, conceptually, between space and place, then the most important factor is the presence and activity of people. In other words, the fundamental benefit we gain from social navigation is that it is a way of populating the information space. Social navigation, after all, hinges on two fundamental features; first, the presence of multiple individuals within some space, and second, the communication of aspects of their activity to each other (which we called "awareness" in the earlier discussion).

By seeing something of the activity of others, I can gain an understanding of the behaviour of individuals in a space, and so gain a sense of the style of appropriate action. When the space is populated, it becomes invested with a sense of appropriateness. That sense of appropriateness is, of course, a phenomenon which emerges from the activity of the individuals themselves; it is subject to change over time, and continually evolves around the contents of the space, the proclivities of the people there, the affordances it offers, and so on. It becomes a place, with a set of understood behaviours, norms and expected practices.

The power of social navigation, or the foundations upon which social navigation is built, is to give the space meaning. That meaning comes from the collective sense of the action that takes place within the space, which itself is captured, made manifest and communicated by social navigation technologies. Since a user can see something of what has happened in the space before, then they can gain a sense of the history of the space and hence gain a sense of a set of spatially oriented practices. The book recommendation system at an on-line bookstore gives someone a sense of what other texts are read by people who are interested in a topic that they are investigating, which in turns gives them a sense of which authors are prominent and respected in the area (and by extension which ones are not), which books are regarded as definitive, and even, perhaps, of what other people find this topic interesting, other things they like, and so forth. The space of books has become populated by other people, and an individual's activities within the space are guided by a sense of how that space is currently configured and inhabited. Recently, others such as Benford et al. (1997b) have begun to investigate the opportunities for considering the World Wide Web as a space to be populated, so that the space itself begins to reflect something of the actions that take place within it.

The other side of the coin is the impact of the user's action on the space. In other words, if a place is a setting for action, how is the setting influenced or changed by the action that takes place there? One form of this impact is, again, the domain of workspace awareness technologies described earlier; for example, the "edit wear" approach is a way of leaving a mark in the space as a sort of "computational erosion".

One particularly interesting place to look at the way in which a place can not only frame action but also serve to represent and communicate it is in MUDs, persistent text-based virtual reality environments (Dourish, 1998). Most modern MUDs are programmable, allowing users to create new objects and behaviours that can be left in the space, cloned, copied, given to other users, used generally, and so forth. One facet of this is that a common way of learning the programming language that supports the development of new MUD objects is to examine and change other objects. In this way, programmed objects become units of exchange in what MacLean et al. (1990), in a different context, have called a "tailoring culture". The MUD provides the mechanisms that support the development of this culture by allowing customisations to be made explicit and shared. What is particularly interesting about this setting, however, is that the MUD is also a place of social interaction and behaviour. This has two effects of the development of programmable artefacts in MUDs. The first is that the "objects" that are created are not simply artefacts, but can also be new modes of behaviour (new capabilities for players achieved through the creation of new "verbs" in the available lexicon) and new responsive places for interaction to happen (new "rooms" with special abilities). The second is that the patterns of social interaction in the environment set a context against which the development of these new programmable artefacts is set. For example, Cherny (1995) presents an analysis of conversational behaviour in a MUD and documents the emergence of specific conversational patterns that are part of the established culture of that specific environment. One interesting feature is the way that, although these patterns of conversational behaviour emerge independently, they consequently became embodied in the user-configurable *technology* of the environment, and, hence, became available and inspectable to the participants in that environment. In other words, the place itself changed to reflect the commonly occurring patterns of activity within that space, and in such a way that aspects of those behaviours could be "read off" the space.

This ability to reflect patterns of activity such that they can be "read off" the setting in which they occur is, clearly, a generalised form of the approach taken by social navigation systems. The perspective of "space" and "place" gives us a means to understand the role that the setting, and in particular, the setting as a populated site of social interaction, plays in making these connections.

11.4 Conclusions: New Opportunities for Social Navigation

The concept of "social navigation" has come of age. Since early observations about the role that could be played in information systems by information about the activities of others, and how, through that channel, individual use of information systems could be enriched more directly with social practice, these forms of systems have become familiar, accepted and even commonplace. In particular, with the rapid spread of the Internet and networked information systems, the use of social navigation, principally but not exclusively in the form of recommendation systems, has become integral to how we consider asynchronous interpersonal interaction and the management of socially-organised behaviour in virtual information environments.

It is time, then, to step back and consider just what social navigation *is*, how it works, and what it means. It is important to recognise that social navigation is not a sort of technology, but rather is a phenonemon of interaction. In particular, it is fruitful to consider how it relates to other perspectives on collaborative computational practice. In this chapter, I have been concerned, firstly, with these sorts of reflections and, secondly, with what we can learn from them for the design of new technologies.

This chapter has focused, in particular, on two current perspectives in collaborative systems. One is the perspective of collaborative awareness. The notion of collaborative awareness as a fundamental concern in the development of (especially synchronous) CSCW tools has a longer history than social navigation, but shares a great deal in common with it. What is particularly interesting is how the two areas of research have taken different perspectives on the same fundamental issue of providing a means for individuals to discover and exploit information about others. The techniques which have been developed in social navigation systems, in addition, hold promise for tackling some of the problems with current approaches to awareness. We might hope, in the end, to see collaborative awareness and social navigation seen as aspects of the same phenomenon, and a unified design approach emerge.

The second perspective that has been explored here is that of the conceptual roles played by notions of "space" and "place" in collaborative settings, and how each of these influences the behaviour of individuals and groups in collaborative settings. One interesting feature here is that social navigation is built upon the same foundations that motivate a "place"-centric perspective on collaborative systems, one oriented around "peopled" spaces and a sense of "appropriate behavioural framing" that emerges from the visibility of social conduct within a space. As such, then, the lessons learned from investigations of social navigation have an important role to play in explorations and further development of this place-centric view.

Along the way, various underlying concepts have emerged as features of the landscape. Social navigation systems support *aggregation, transformation* and *decoupling* of information, allowing them to present awareness information in terms of trends rather than specific actions. Populated social places offer *appropriation* and *appropriate behavioural framing*, distinguishing them from simple spaces, which are characterised in terms of their dimensionality.

What emerges from this is a picture of a reflexively populated information space. By "populated", I mean that it contains not just information, but also people who are acting on that information, and who can see the effects of each others' actions and exploit that information in managing their own activities. By "reflexively" populated, I mean that not only does the structure of the space have an impact on the action of the users, but that the action of the users can also have an impact on the space. The space is malleable, adjustable to reflect patterns of action and the needs of the users who inhabit it. It supports the forms of appropriation encountered in the discussions of media space design and similar environments. The lesson of those experiences is that simply populating a space is not sufficient, but that appropriation and malleability are equally important. Similarly, the lesson of social navigation is that the social element of information seeking are critical resources in the development of collaborative systems, whether those are based on physical real-world metaphors or chart new virtual spaces. The explorations in this chapter have suggested that these lessons have some bearing on each other, and that social navigation has a role to play in the broader design of interactive and collaborative systems. At the same time, considering the role that social navigation can play in other sorts of collaborative settings has prompted reflections on underlying principles that may, in the future, help to frame a theoretical account of the mechanisms supporting socially-supported information seeking.

Acknowledgements

Consideration of these issues over the years has been hugely enriched by stimulating discussions with a variety of colleagues, particularly Victoria Bellotti, Matthew Chalmers, Tom Erickson, Bill Gaver, Steve Harrison, Christian Heath and Kia Höök.

12

Social Connotations of Space in the Design for Virtual Communities and Social Navigation

Andreas Dieberger

Future information systems will be populated information spaces. Users of these systems will be aware of the activities of others, and what information they find useful or not. They will be able to point out and share information easily and even guide each other. These systems therefore will be social spaces. People associate social connotations with various types of spaces. These social connotations raise expectations about appropriate behaviour, privacy, trust, and private or public space in these virtual communities. This chapter discusses the relationship between social navigation and spatial metaphors and how social connotations of spatial metaphors can influence social activities in virtual space. We discuss a number of open issues in virtual communities in general and social navigation in particular, that are related to social connotations. We also present a pilot study that indicates that social connotations are perceived differently in real and virtual spaces.

12.1 Introduction

Although many people may access an information system at the same time, most systems maintain the illusion of a dedicated resource and the only indication of a large number of users simultaneously accessing a system might be an unusually slow response time. Humans are social animals, but our social skills are mostly unused in today's information systems. Admittedly there are virtual communities and chat systems, but these are only small pockets of social activity in a sea of antisocial information spaces.

Navigation is a social and frequently a collaborative process (Hutchins, 1995). A goal of social navigation is to utilise information about other people's behaviour for our own navigational decisions. Future information systems will be populated spaces where there is awareness of other people's activities, where people rate and annotate information, and give guidance either directly or through intermediaries.

The success of chat rooms and web bulletin boards shows that people feel a need to interact and to share thoughts and information. Social navigation processes are very common in everyday life. The number of cars parked in front of a restaurant is an indication for its popularity as is the length of a waiting line before a theatre. We frequently base the choice of a movie or restaurant on friends' recommendations or on articles written by well-known critics. Few people would choose a dentist based solely on the listings in a doctor's directory if they can get a personal recommendation from somebody they know. The same is true for buying cars, selecting books and sometimes even meeting people. All of these processes are variants of what we call social navigation.

Social navigation is not identical with recommender systems. As Dourish (this volume) points out, social navigation is a much broader concept. Dieberger describes several simple forms of social navigation that evolved on the Internet by themselves, even without tools that supported them (Dieberger, 1997b). It is time that we realise the need for well-supported social interaction in information spaces and move beyond these simple tools.

Social activity typically is rooted in a space. A spatial metaphor can provide a framework to structure an information space and give a spatial basis to social interaction, even if the metaphor is only hinted at. People associate "social connotations" with spaces. These social connotations trigger expectations of appropriate behaviour and the social content of a space. A space with social meaning can become a place and serve as a social metaphor for interactions in it.

The main reason for studying social connotations is that we need to better understand what expectations and social rules people infer from particular types of spaces and places. Many current computer-mediated communication (CMC) and computer-supported collaborative work (CSCW) systems employ very generic spatial metaphors, like "room" or "conference". By choosing such a nondescript metaphor the system misses the opportunity to convey information on appropriate behaviour, social norms, and on what to expect in the system. The space we choose for a system communicates a message on privacy, trust, the use of private and public spaces and so on to the user. In current CMC systems these issues are often dealt with using technical features like encryption or passwords. In physical spaces such issues can often be solved through a shared understanding of what is appropriate behaviour and what is not (Catedra, 1991). We advocate that a thoughtful design of CMC and CSCW systems can create a similar shared understanding of what is appropriate in virtual interaction spaces without imposing hard restrictions on users.

In this chapter, social navigation is first introduced in a more detailed form, it is then contrasted with recommender systems, and examples of social navigation tools on the web are given. We discuss the relationship between spatial metaphors and social connotations and how social metaphors can shape "places".

We then focus on open issues for social navigation systems, such as how to address concerns about privacy, trust and how to find expertise in a community. We will describe how social connotations can set expectations for a shared space. In the last section a pilot study on how social connotations are perceived in real and virtual spaces is presented.

12.2 Social Navigation

Social navigation encompasses all activities where two or more users collaborate directly or indirectly in a navigational task. We use the term "navigation" in a very general sense. It may encompass finding information, deciding on the usefulness of information based on other people's recommendations, or deciding whether to join a group of people for a chat. Dourish and Chalmers introduced the term "social navigation" in their discussion on spatial, semantic and social navigation (Dourish and Chalmers, 1994).

Early forms of social navigation evolved out of the web's lack of perceivable structure. People began creating structure in the form of pointer pages or favourite link pages (Dieberger, 1995b). These web pages represented personalised information spaces that were shared freely on the Internet. Web sites with useful pointer lists, frequently asked questions, and other helpful information evolved into navigation landmarks and simple social navigation tools (Dieberger, 1997b). Other early examples were e-mail or news group messages with pointers to web pages. Dieberger has described several such early examples of social navigation (Dieberger, 1997b). Since then our tools have improved tremendously and we can post all kinds of documents on the web, embed links to them in e-mails and word-processing documents. It is even a well-established process (albeit not an easy one) to point out web pages in spoken conversations, television and radio commercials. Systems like Tribal Voice's Powwow (http://www.powwow.com/) even allow users to give guided tours through web space and thus support "direct social navigation". Despite these advances we consider these tools rudimentary, because they are far from making social navigation as natural a way to interact as it is in the physical world.

Over the past few years there is growing interest in systems that support choices based on the experiences of other people. These "recommender systems" are also instances of social navigation. For many people the terms "social navigation" and "recommender systems" are even seen as synonymous. However, we agree with Dourish that social navigation can be a fundamental model of collaboration in information seeking, which is a broader concept than making choices based on other people's preferences and recommendations.

A good overview of recommender systems can be found in a special issue of *Communications of the ACM* (Resnick and Varian, 1997). Among the systems discussed is Phoaks (People Helping One Another Know Stuff), a system that generates recommendations by mining newsnet messages for recommendations through a "frequency of mention" (Terveen et al., 1997). The Referral Web (Kautz et al., 1997) uses a representation of a social network to find expertise in an organisation. Recommender systems typically base their recommendations on interest profiles of other people. An exception is content- based recommendation like in the Fab system (Balbanovic and Shoham, 1997). It points out items that are similar to documents that a user liked in the past.

While recommender systems often base their recommendations on the profiles of single users, indirect social navigation systems combine information of a large number of users and thus can avoid many scaling and privacy issues (see below and also Dourish, this volume). Social navigation can also serve as a mechanism to provide awareness about the aggregated activities of a user community. Many CSCW systems strive to achieve a feeling of mutual awareness among their users, because this is generally regarded an important ingredient to collaborative work (Hudson and Smith, 1996; Gutwin and Greenberg, 1998a, 1998b; Karsenty, 1997).

12.2.1 Direct Social Navigation

Direct social navigation typically is a synchronous process and involves direct communication between two or more individuals. An example of direct social navigation is asking for directions in a virtual environment or guiding each other. Such a direct exchange may be instantaneous, like in a chat or MUD system when both participants are present at the same time.[1] Using e-mail lists or newsgroups such an exchange can be asynchronous and the reply to a question might be seen by more than one person. Design issues in supporting direct social navigation are how to realise turn taking, how to find somebody who can give directions, how to approach somebody for help, etc. We will address several of these issues in more detail below.

---

[1] MUD stands for multi-user dungeon or dimension; they are text-based virtual environments often used for adventure-type games.

12.2.2 Indirect Social Navigation

Indirect social navigation is asynchronous and often provides information metaphorically. A typical example for indirect social navigation is a bulletin board system that points out the most active discussions and topics by placing the image of a hot pepper next to it. What sets indirect social navigation apart from direct social navigation is that it is a by-product of our activities – we do not have to actively create indirect social navigation information.

This author is working on a modified collaborative web server that places a footprint symbol next to links leading to recently accessed pages.[2] Depending on the number of accesses within the last 24 hours these footprints are shown in different colours and thus give an indication on the amount of activity. Other markers point out pages that have not been accessed for a very long time. The system also visualises the age of pages using various markers and maintains lists of recently accessed and modified pages. The markers create an accurate feeling for what areas are visited frequently and where there are active discussions. The markers not only guide users to active discussions, but also increase the awareness of other people's activities in the information space.

The footprint symbol is an application of the "read wear" concept introduced by Hill et al. (1992). Read wear enriches information environments by visualising which parts of it have been used most frequently. An example for such a history-enriched object is a reference book in a library that falls open at a frequently needed chapter. It also might show dog ears, highlighter marks and annotations, all of which tell us a story about the usage history of this information object (Marshall, 1998). Other examples for the application of the read wear principle are the Juggler and the Vortex system described in (Dieberger, 1997b) or bulletin board systems indicating especially active discussions.

Wexelblat and Maes' Footprints system goes a step further by visualising the usage history of an information space as commonly used paths (Wexelblat, 1998a; see also Wexelblat, this volume). This is useful both for social navigation as well as for identifying clusters of pages in a site and areas that are difficult to reach.

The classification into direct and indirect social navigation is not always sufficient. Social filtering is an indirect (asynchronous) form of communication that can help in navigation (see for example Konstan et al., 1997). Social filtering often requires a conscious effort, and therefore an act of information sharing. This act involves issues of trust, a feeling of ownership and a resulting desire to contribute to a community.

---

[2] This collaborative web server is a modified version of a Swiki "Pluggable web server" written in the Squeak dialect of Smalltalk by Mark Guzdial of Georgia Tech. For more information see: http://www.cc.gatech.edu/fac/mark.guzdial/squeak/pws/.

An important aspect of social navigation is its close relationship to a spatial framework. People associate social meaning with various types of spaces. The simple fact that an information space is presented as a meeting room, rather than a café, can influence social behaviour and therefore change navigation behaviour in this space.

12.2.3 Why Spatial Metaphors?

Humans are social animals operating in space. Rooting activities in a spatial reference frame makes people feel more comfortable, even if this reference frame is only hinted at. People often refer to spatial imagery to describe activities in information spaces. Good examples are the trajectory metaphors observed by Maglio and Matlock (this volume). Web navigation obviously is conceived in terms of a cognitive map similar to a cognitive map of a physical space, in terms of landmarks and routes.

Many information systems feature metaphorical spaces. Harrison and Dourish distinguish between spatial, semantic and social navigation (Dourish and Chalmers, 1994; Harrison and Dourish, 1996; and Dourish, this volume). Spatial navigation relies on the structure of space itself and typically is based on two- or three-dimensional metaphors of space. Semantic navigation instead relies on a semantic space, very much like one would see in hypertext. Social navigation on the other hand is primarily guided by the activities of others and thus is navigation based on a social space. Semantic and social navigation are not systems per se, but rather "phenomena of interaction" and can take place in the context of a spatial setting (see Dourish, this volume).

We argue that social navigation benefits from a spatial framework, even if this framework is weak. A common example is a web chat room: all users in the chat room are seen as having the same distance from each other. Although some systems allow users' avatars to change position, this position does not influence how people can communicate. Talking to a person at the other side of the room is as easy as chatting with a person you are touching. In a chat room all users are talking at the same time in the same loud voice, whereas in a real world situation a person's voice is less perceivable the farther one moves away from the person. Similarly, private communication (whispering) works independently of location in a chat room, which clearly is a stretch of the metaphor.[3]

---

[3] Features that stretch a metaphor beyond its breaking point are "magic features" (Dieberger, 1995a), because if they occurred in a physical space we probably would speak of magic. Magic features are sometimes used to deliberately break a metaphor to provide shortcuts and special functionality that does not fit into the overall user interface metaphor.

Despite these gross inconsistencies a chat room is a functional social space and carries meaning for the user. People even react sensitively to other people's perceived positions and move their avatar away if somebody else suggests a movement that would bring them too close. This behaviour is similar to what would occur in an encounter in physical space (see Jeffrey and Mark, 1998, and this volume).

12.2.4 Space vs Place

Harrison and Dourish (1996) point out that we should not focus on spatial metaphors, but rather talk about "places". Places are "spaces invested with understandings of behavioural appropriateness, cultural expectations, and so forth". We do live in space, but we act in place.

People perceive spatiality in information systems even from a simple description and infer assumptions about social processes in this space or place. These expectations are shaped from previous experiences in the real world or virtual spaces. In that respect these expectations could be called "social perceived affordances". Perceived affordances can signal a user that certain activities are supported by an object on a display. For example a displayed button can be perceived as affording to be clicked (Norman, 1988, 1999). We believe that these expectations go beyond being simply conventions, because users can infer expectations about spaces without having learnt conventions about them. Social perceived affordances tell users whether a space affords loud or silent conversations, giving a party, asking questions, etc. Social perceived affordances can tell users whether a space affords loud or silent conversations, giving a party, asking questions, etc.

Instead of the term "social perceived affordances" we will use the term "social connotations". Social connotations stem from a shared understanding of a space, based on experiences with similar real world spaces. Social connotations can change over time (see below). The social connotations of the place can be changed temporarily if, for example, a library is used for a reception after hours, where the main goal of people is to communicate with each other, and not to read.

In a spatial metaphor, the limits of the metaphor are quite strict. Given a space that functions like physical space, a user cannot walk through a wall (without hurting herself). Social connotations impose weaker restrictions on behaviour than spatial constraints. It may be considered rude to yell at somebody in a library, but it is impossible to reliably prevent people from doing so. Social connotations are thus weak "rules or guidelines of behaviour". There might be no immediate penalty for not following them, but one might be expelled from a community for repeated violations of a shared "code of conduct".

12.3 Open Issues in Social Navigation

In this section we will discuss a number of open issues in social navigation. Several of them are relevant mainly for direct social navigation systems, other issues concern only indirect social navigation. Social connotations are of relevance for any type of virtual community and therefore both for direct and indirect social navigation. For most of these issues there are no clear-cut solutions but every system and community has to find a reasonable way to handle them. How well the community succeeds in this task can well decide whether users accept a system or not.

12.3.1 Why Should People Help Each Other?

Direct social navigation sounds almost too good to be true: we live in an information space where everybody has plenty of time to help each other out. Everybody is friendly and helpful. In reality this will be seldom the case. In competitive or time-pressed situations users probably won't bother to point out information or give a guided tour. One could therefore assume that direct social navigation is rare.

Experience shows that people are more than happy to provide help and guidance, but that it is not possible to rely on (immediate) assistance. In the real world a limited amount of information is often given for free (asking somebody for the way in a foreign city), but a larger amount of information has to be paid for (a guidebook or guided tour through town, for instance).

Kollock and Smith (1996) have stated that "… in many situations behaviour that is reasonable and justifiable for the individual leads to a poorer outcome for all. Such situations are termed social dilemmas". A famous example of such a social dilemma is the "tragedy of the commons" (Hardin, 1977). Hardin describes a group of herders having open access to a common parcel of land on which they can let their cows graze. It is in each herder's interest to put as many cows on the land as possible, but this might damage the commons such that the overall benefit for the group of herders would be eliminated.

Another common social dilemma is the "free-rider problem". Ostrom describes this problem such that "Whenever one person cannot be excluded from the benefits that other people provide, each person is motivated not to contribute to the joint effort, but to free-ride on the efforts of others. If all participants choose to free-ride the collective benefit will not be produced" (Ostrom, 1991). Ostrom describes a variety of communities to determine what features of each contributed to the success or failure in managing collective goods.

In virtual communities we can observe both of these social dilemmas. A common good that has to be managed reasonably is bandwidth, or attention span. If one participant uses all the bandwidth in a community by spamming or posting a lot of biased information the overall community goal cannot be achieved. Such behaviour can even permanently damage a community if there are no regulatory mechanisms in place to cope with such a disturbance (Kollock and Smith, 1996). An example is the alt.hypertext newsgroup, that was a popular place for hypertext researchers in the past but has been practically abandoned because of excessive spamming and unsolicited advertising posted by newcomers and outsiders.

Likewise, a virtual community consisting only of consumers will not be successful either. Virtual communities tend to find a balance between consuming and contributing such that the overall common goal is achieved. People tend to understand that even a small contribution can make a difference. Terveen and Hill (1998a) found that the majority of participants in newsgroups post only one or two messages over half a year and that only a few participants post a large number of messages.

Besides self-regulatory processes virtual communities can also be based on economical processes such that people trade information that is especially valuable. An example for such an economy is implemented in the Java developers' connection web site (http://developer.javasoft.com/). DukeDollars are a virtual currency that is used only inside the Java developers' connection. New members get an initial amount of 10 units. They can earn DukeDollars by visiting the site every week, which encourages people to visit regularly. They can also earn DukeDollars by answering other people's questions in the bulletin boards. The amount they receive depends on how useful the receiver rates their information. DukeDollars are spent when asking questions: the more DukeDollars somebody is willing to spend, the more likely he or she is to find somebody who provides a detailed solution very quickly. We mentioned above that one cannot rely on getting an immediate free answer to a question in a virtual community. The DukeDollar concept tries to tackle this issue, by allowing users to signal urgency through the amount of virtual money they are willing to spend.

An interesting aspect of indirect social navigation systems is that nobody is only a consumer. Social navigation information is collected automatically by the system when it is used. As there is no effort involved, people tend not to notice that they are contributing in very small increments to a shared resource that all community members benefit from. Indirect social navigation processes ideally occur permanently and are never disabled. Of course this permanent monitoring of a community's activities raises issues of privacy.

12.3.2 Privacy

Providing recommendations and read wear are forms of annotation. People sometimes are very picky about who can access their annotations. At other times people don't seem to care at all if anybody can access even sensitive information they have added to a document. In a study on how students annotated textbooks, Marshall (1998) reports she even found social security numbers and bank statements in books that were sold back to a university bookstore. Annotations are typically created for private use, but are rarely removed from a (paper) document before this document is circulated among colleagues or sold back to the bookstore.

It appears that users of the World Wide Web do not really care too much about privacy – they feel safe because of the sheer number of people on the Internet and because they think "nobody cares about my data anyway". On the other hand we do know that as computers get more powerful it is easily possible to scan large amounts of e-mail or newsgroup messages for key phrases and potentially harmful information. The Internet is not a safe haven for sensitive information.

Systems collecting information on our activities put us in a similar situation as in a media space where a camera is constantly pointed at us. After a certain time most people forget about the camera and live blissfully unaware of the fact that they are broadcasting live. An example is the "Jennicam" (http://www.jennicam.org/index.html) which is a web camera installed in a student's room. Jenny reports on her page that she lives a normal life completely ignoring the camera and the potentially thousands of people watching her day and night, even while she is intimate with her boyfriend.

People tend to forget if somebody can see them, when they cannot see the other person. Bellotti (1997) reports that people forgot they were still broadcasting live if a conversation partner switched off their cameras. In indirect social navigation systems we have a similar situation, because there is no apparent observer. The system collects data about our activities, no matter what we do and makes this information available to all users in an aggregated form. Because of this fact there is a certain risk that people underestimate the privacy issues of social navigation systems.

Care must be taken that a system cannot reveal private information about a user. A possible solution is to show read wear only after a sufficient amount of data from a larger number of users has been collected. This guarantees both privacy and unbiased information. If a user consciously wants to give recommendations or openly talk about his or her interests using direct social navigation that is fine, but the system cannot make the decision what to publish and what to keep secret. Privacy issues as well as issues of when awareness of other users becomes an intrusion are discussed by Hudson and Smith (1996).

12.3.3 Finding Expertise

An important goal of recommender systems is locating expertise to solve a problem. Examples are Answer Garden (Ackerman, 1994) or Answer Garden 2 (Ackerman and McDonald, 1996) that are designed to facilitate informal flow and capture of information on expertise and thus build an organisational memory. Referral Web (Kautz et al., 1997) helps finding an expert by assuming topical expertise among a number of co-authors and identifies experts by their participation in co-author relationships. Phoaks (People Helping One Another Know Stuff) (Terveen et al., 1997) is a collaborative filtering system that allows identifying who contributed information. Identifying contributors is an important feature, because it allows the user to make judgements about a contributor's expertise.

Less ambitious than these systems, a few virtual communities on the web allow users to identify favourite community members. For example, on the Motley Fool (http://www.fool.com/) a community to exchange investment information, people can identify other users as "favourite fools" such that all postings of these "experts" are highlighted. It is even possible to get a summary of all postings by a "favourite fool" over a period of time, no matter what board they were posted to. It is also possible to ignore people whose contributions were considered useless in the past. While ignoring spammers and obnoxious community members is a common feature in virtual communities, highlighting contributions of people who are considered experts is relatively rare.

A problem most of these systems do not address is that finding expertise involves more complex issues than just tracking down an expert. McDonald and Ackerman (1998) report that people often choose not to ask an expert for assistance for political reasons. For example it might be considered embarrassing if a work group cannot solve a problem internally. Sometimes, when experts are perceived as having a "bad attitude" asking them is reserved for the most critical problems.

People who are most approachable or who give most recommendations are not necessarily the ones who are the most appropriate people to ask. The number of recommendations by a user does not determine the usefulness of these recommendations. Whittaker et al. (1998) report that 3% of the users of a newsgroup account for over 25% of the messages. Similar ratios are likely to occur in direct social navigation. The number of postings does not necessarily indicate the quality of these contributions.

Identifying a user as expert is especially important in direct social navigation situations. In indirect social navigation information is averaged over a larger number of people and it is impossible to track down the contributors anyway. An interesting aspect of indirect social navigation is whether information (for example, read wear) caused by expert users should have a different weight than that of ordinary users.

A special case of social navigation occurs when the provider and consumer of social navigation information are one and the same. This type of (social?) navigation can occur in information spaces used by only one person. Read wear of this kind leaves a track record on past activities and can be useful to ease access to commonly used documents. An example for such a use of read wear occurred in the Vortex system (Dieberger, 1997b). Frequently used information items migrated to the top of a list of resources and were shown in a more prominent font. A snapshot of this list of resources provides information not only on the resources, but also on their frequency of use by the owner of the information space. The advantage of this situation is that the receiver of the social information can have complete trust in the information (see below). This type of social navigation information could be also used in an educational setting: imagine an information space containing resources, with the instructor's read wear on that space. It would provide information on the resources relative usefulness and frequency of access based on the activities of the instructor. Trust is not an issue in this case, because students typically can trust the instructor's recommendations.

12.3.4 Trust

While a recommendation from an expert might be more valuable, because one can be sure the information is correct, it may be harder to get that recommendation. People might therefore look for alternative sources of recommendations. But how can one know whose recommendations to trust, and whether indirect social navigation information is relevant for the task at hand?

A possible solution for issues of trust is to have people vote on the usefulness of other people's contributions. MessageWorld (Rose et al., 1995) was an early system that forced people to rate every message they saw. Experiences in this system showed that any additional effort required to provide a rating is prohibitive. The Java developers' connection also requires rating of messages, but the rationale there is to determine what amount of DukeDollars the author of the message is to receive. As these messages are in direct response to a question the reader has sent out, the motivation for providing the rating is very different.

Many of these issues are eliminated, when the social navigation system supports a closely-knit group of users with similar interests – for example a work group in a company. If a person knows all the people in the system she knows approximately what the expertise of each colleague is, and whose recommendations to trust. For this reason we think that social navigation can be especially useful in well-defined communities of users with related interests.

If all users in the community have common goals, it is safe to assume that no recommendation will be deliberately misleading. Similarly, information from special sources can be considered trustworthy and correct. An example would be a "knowledge concierge" for a work group or a company. Knowledge concierges have the additional advantage that the social cost of asking is very low, as it is their job to answer questions.

Nielsen reports that the number of outbound hypertext links on a web site increases the credibility on a web page (see Nielsen's Alertbox of 1 October 1997 at http://www.useit.com/alertbox/9710a.html). Terveen and Hill (1998a) describe a study where links between web sites indicate emerging collaboration between web authors. These studies indicate that the amount of references to outside material is an important factor in the perception of material and that referring to other people in a recommendation can also raise the level of trust in the material.

12.3.5 "Yesterday's News" – Ageing of Social Navigation Information

All meta information has a time component. A recommendation from last week may indeed be last week's news and therefore irrelevant for today's work. Different types of information age differently. While the population statistics for a country are useful for a long time, information about a sudden rise in the stock market may be useless after only half an hour.

When we receive a recommendation in a direct, live conversation, the age of the recommendation is known and we can check on the age of any underlying information. Indirect social navigation tools, however, aggregate information over time. How to decide over what time periods to aggregate information? Wexelblat (1998a) defines six dimensions of history, one of them being the rate of change: "the rate of accretion and the rate of decay will vary in any history-right interface". This rate of ageing became a very bothersome problem in the Juggler system: read wear cues sometimes pointed newcomers to information items that were outdated. By accessing these items users increased the read wear again and further extended the life span of the outdated information or even caused newer, more relevant information not to be seen (Dieberger, 1996, 1997b).

We partly solved this issue by defining a decay function on the read wear. A similar problem in the modified Swiki server mentioned above was avoided by pointing out only read wear within the past 24 hours, which is a reasonably short amount of time. Information ages at different rates. Some areas on the Swiki server get visited frequently, whereas others are often empty for days. Each of these areas requires a different rate of ageing on read wear, footprints and recommendations – whatever social navigation cues might be used.

Related to the issue of age of recommendations is a change of interests. Users' interest profiles not only change over time, but they change between projects and contexts. When browsing the web at home I might be interested in seeing information on the stock market or cheap airfares to the Caribbean. While working I would like to see information related to my current project, or maybe a project I'm supposed to work on next week. A possibility to cope with such different contexts could be virtual workspaces like they were used in the Rooms project (Henderson and Card, 1986). While in a context (Room) that contains the tools and documents for a project, I will see recommendations and read wear according to these interests. When changing to a different work context, the weights in my interest profile change as do recommendations and social navigation information.

12.3.6 Change in Virtual Communities

Social connotations may give a good initial indication of what social interactions are appropriate in a space, but it is a "shared understanding of a space's meaning" that distinguishes space from place and this shared understanding can change over time.

A virtual or real community is a living organism and appropriate behaviour changes with what people are present, and with the context of their activities. This effect is very visible in chat rooms or MUD systems over the course of a day. People tend to log into these systems early in the morning and in the evening. Depending on the time people from all over the world come online and offline the behaviour and style of conversations in the community changes. It is a remarkable experience to stay online in a familiar virtual community for over 24 hours and experience this constant change. The change is perceived as especially intense in a system based on a strong spatial metaphor, for example, a MUDcommunity. MUD environments typically feature elaborate spatial environments with villages, buildings, a pub, monsters and treasures to hunt for etc. (Erickson, 1993; Schiano and White, 1998). Such a familiar environment can change in an almost frightening way when there is not a single person around that you know. To make things worse, these people behave as if they had always lived in this space, they express ownership, but they talk differently, maybe have different rituals and behaviours and a different common history.

A radical change in the social connotations of a space can also occur when a space is used for a different activity than usual. An example is the space of a classroom that is used for a student party. In such a situation all assumptions about communication patterns and appropriate behaviour are completely upturned. This shows that social connotations are influenced not only by space, but also by the people and activities of the space.

The degree to which participants are able to influence the character of a virtual community might be one of the key ingredients to a successful one. Harrison and Dourish (1996) write:

> It is only over time, and with active participation and appropriation, that a sense of place begins to permeate these systems. The users must forge the sense of place; it cannot be inherent in the system itself. Space is the opportunity, and place is the understood reality.

Change in the social connotations thus is a key ingredient to make a space into a place.

12.3.7 Social Connotations and Communications Patterns

Social connotations may influence dominant communication patterns in a space. In a lecture hall, one can assume a very specific communication pattern between one teacher and a group of students. Communication occurs mainly from the teacher to the student and is discouraged between students. The communication pattern changes entirely when the class engages in a group discussion.

A meeting room shows a different pattern. There often is a focus person, but turn taking and discussion among the other participants occurs frequently. The chairperson might intervene if a discussion moves off track, but – depending on the meeting style – the communication pattern is likely to be a network.

In a café the pattern resembles islands of communication with little communication in between, whereas at a party similar islands form, but with constant movement between the islands. In a sports bar people cluster along a bar to watch a game on a big-screen television. In this space we encounter yet another communication pattern: attention is focused on the television, and communication is open along a line perpendicular to the television. However communication is easiest with the people close to you because of the general noise level. Communicating with a person further down the bar might involve changing one's position.

This short list of places shows what a wide variety of communications patterns might evolve if virtual communities managed to move beyond the concept of a plain chat room with its lack of any communication pattern.

12.3.8 Perceiving Social Connotations from the Outside

In our discussion we generally assumed a user being inside a virtual community. One of the most promising uses of social connotations might be for users outside virtual communities. In the physical world it is typically possible to assess the character of a place already from the outside. Amy Bruckman (personal communication) describes the example of a fancy restaurant or a biker bar. In both cases it is possible to see even from the other side of the street what type of environment to expect. Similar visibility of social connotations for virtual communities is much harder to achieve, maybe because many virtual communities do not define what comprises appropriate and inappropriate behaviour as clearly as real world spaces do.

Instead virtual communities rely on a code of conduct sheet that often becomes available only after you have joined a community. Communities sometimes refer to rating codes and short descriptions. Communities change though, sometimes even for short times and it is unlikely that a community's description correctly mirrors the character of a community. We consider it one of the biggest challenges for virtual communities to become visible from the outside.

12.4 Social Connotations in Real and Virtual Spaces

Architects tend to know how to design physical spaces to convey certain social connotations although, according to Whyte (1988a), it is surprising how often architects manage to do it wrong. Metaphors map behaviour from a known source domain to a target domain. We know that certain spatial properties of spatial metaphors map well from physical space to the virtual space. However, we do not really know how well social connotations carry over to the virtual domain. To use more specific spatial metaphors in groupware systems we need to achieve a better understanding of how social connotations differ in real and virtual spaces. Only with this understanding can spatial metaphors help us convey a desired social metaphor to the user.

In information systems we generally talk about metaphorical spaces, whereas most of our knowledge about social spaces is based on physical spaces and places. Metaphors provide a mapping from a known source domain into an unknown target domain (Carroll et al., 1988). These mappings are not necessarily perfect mappings. Erickson describes an example of problems caused by an imperfect metaphorical mapping: the message of a voice mail system conveyed the impression that a co-worker was taking a message, creating the assumption that the message would be delivered the moment the receiver walks into his office. The reality is that the owner of a voice mailbox has to initiate action to retrieve messages, which can cause significant delays in the delivery of the message (Erickson, 1990). Social connotations of spaces and social metaphors also rely on a mapping from a source domain into a target domain. Virtual space can be perceived quite differently than real, physical space, especially in information spaces that are purely metaphorical as in chat rooms or MUD systems.

We describe a pilot study that tries to shed light on how social connotations are perceived in real and virtual spaces. We used textual descriptions of spaces because many virtual communities are textual. The study focused on questions that compared participants' expectations on appropriate behaviour for asking for help, on the number of people in a space, on privacy issues and so on. The study was conducted using two web questionnaires in February and October 1998.

The study consisted of 10 situations (hotel lobby, mall, café, cubicle maze, conference reception, etc.). The situations were set up such that participants would need to ask other people for help. We asked participants about appropriate and inappropriate behaviour, if they perceived a space as private or public, if they expected to know people and so on. We further studied people's assumptions on the presence of surveillance cameras in a space. This question aimed at expectations on logging of conversations and privacy issues.

The first run of the questionnaire used situations that were described as real space scenarios. The participants came from Internet discussion forums for human factors professionals who – we assumed – would host a wide variety of people, not only technically oriented (group A). In a second run the study setup was slightly modified to put the situations in the context of a virtual space. That second questionnaire was sent to experienced MUD users (group B). MUD users spend a lot of time in text based virtual environments and tend to be more technology oriented. For information on MUDs and textual virtual environments see references (Erickson, 1993; Bruckman and Resnick, 1995). It is a safe assumption that group B's results are representative for many designers of (textual) virtual communities.

Our first hypothesis was that group B would perceive social connotations differently than group A. Our second hypothesis was that these differences depended on the type of space.

One hundred and one participants participated in the first run, 73 of which completed all 10 situations. In the second run we had 50 participants, 26 of which completed all situations. In our analysis we looked at the percentage of participants perceiving a particular social connotation, and then subtracted the results of group B from those of group A. Negative values thus indicate that group B perceived a social connotation stronger than group A. We considered only differences above 30% in individual situations to be significant.

Results of web questionnaires must be taken with a grain of salt, because the participants are self-selected. Yet, we believe that the results of this pilot study are useful to point the direction to further research.

Hypothesis 1

Reported perceptions of certain social connotations were virtually identical in both groups, for example the perception of a space as *public*, *informal*, or if there were *rules of behaviour*. Other connotations showed significant differences, for example real spaces were consistently perceived as *safer* than virtual spaces (mean=0.2, standard deviation (SD)=0.16).

Most group B participants assumed the presence of *surveillance cameras*. We interpret this as expectation that conversations are logged. The average over all situations was not significant (mean=0.1, SD=0.224), but in some situations the difference was very strong: *reception, café* and *discussion* (0.4) and *bus station* (0.3).

A less surprising result was that group B assumed virtual spaces to be less populated than real spaces. We used categories of 1, 2, 3–5, 6–9, 10–30, 31–100, 100+ people in a space. Virtual spaces were at least one class below the real spaces, for example 10–30 people instead of 31–100, with library stacks and an apartment building as the only exceptions, which were in the same class.

Hypothesis 2

In several cases the perception of social connotations differed strongly depending on the situation. *Anonymity* was stronger in the real space in: *mall, café, bus station* and *concert or sports event* (0.3), however it was perceived much stronger in a *conference reception* in virtual space (–0.4).

Group A assumed to know some people in a *discussion* (0.5) and the *cubicle maze* (0.3), however group B perceived this stronger in a *concert* or *sports event* (–0.3).

12.4.1 Discussion

The results indicate that social connotations are not always identical in real spaces and spatial metaphors and that the differences may indeed depend on the type of spatial metaphor. Of particular interest is the difference in the perception of anonymity. A virtual conference reception, virtual parties and similar events are frequent uses for virtual communities. According to our pilot study people perceive such an event to be especially anonymous, which is exactly the opposite of the desired effect. We were also quite surprised to see that real spaces were perceived as safer than virtual spaces. People often justify visiting virtual communities because of their anonymity and safety relative to meeting strangers for real.

The more or less consistent difference in the number of people in real and virtual spaces is explainable from the simple fact that virtual communities do not support crowds well. In a large room a party of 30–40 people is nothing unusual. Thirty people in a chat room, all talking at the same time, tends to be a disaster. As we discussed above the reason for this problem is that the perceived distance between people does not have any influence on their communication in many virtual communities. In a chat room, participants either whisper into somebody else's ear or they yell at the top of their lungs. Therefore, most chat rooms either limit the number of people in a room or the majority of users ignores the public talk and resorts to "private communication" with one or two people using whispering or personal messages.

The results of our pilot study indicate that there is a clear need for more research into the differences of social connotations in real and virtual spaces. The influence social connotations can have especially on early phases of virtual communities make this a very important field of future research.

12.5 Summary

We motivated the study of social connotations through their connections with spatial metaphors in information spaces. Future information systems will be social spaces where people are aware of each other's activities and where it will be much easier to share and recommend useful information, or to even guide each other. These systems will be social spaces.

We described the concept of social navigation and argued that social navigation is not identical with recommender systems. Social navigation rather is a fundamental model of collaboration in information seeking. We distinguish direct and indirect social navigation processes: direct social navigation involves direct communication between two or more participants, indirect social navigation information is a by-product of people's activities in an information space. This distinction seems almost too simple to capture the wide variety of social navigation observable. However, it provides a useful distinction between processes that actively involve a limited number of participants, and processes that generate information on the activities of entire communities, which happen as invisible processes that users often are unaware of.

The concept of space, even if only hinted at, is an important foundation for social activities. People associate meaning with spaces and develop a shared understanding of appropriate behaviour, about private and public space, how to ask questions and so forth. We called these assumptions social connotations. Social connotations and user's activities in a space can turn it into a space invested with meaning – a place.

311

We argue that spatial metaphors in CMC and CSCW systems can be used as social metaphors that encourage and discourage certain behaviour in virtual communities. What is presently achieved using technical protocols, like password protection and other forms of access control might be achievable through shared understanding of social appropriate behaviour – as is the case in many communities in the physical world.

An important use for social connotations is to indicate the character of a place already from the outside. Most current virtual communities are unsuccessful at giving people a clear idea of their character before they get actually immersed in the community. This obviously is an important issue with communities featuring adult content. While this specific case can be solved using rating systems, there are many cases where the situation is not that clear-cut and where people entering a community are left unaware of what to expect.

In the section on open issues of social navigation we discuss how the social dilemmas of the "tragedy of the commons" and the "free-rider problem" affect virtual communities and especially direct social navigation. An advantage of indirect social navigation is that these dilemmas do not apply.

We identified and discussed a number of other open issues in direct and indirect social navigation systems, like changing social connotations, the rate of ageing of social navigation information, how to find expertise and so forth. Most of these issues are directly related to the perception of social connotations. This supports our claim that groupware systems need to consider the use of more elaborate spatial metaphors than "room" or "conference" to communicate social connotations and social metaphors.

What makes this choice more difficult is that social connotations can be perceived differently in physical and virtual spaces. We report on a pilot study that indicates that social connotations sometimes are perceived very differently in the physical space and in spatial metaphors and that these differences can depend on the type of space used. While only a pilot study these results clearly indicate that additional research into social connotations is needed.

Acknowledgements

I'd like to thank Andrew Frank for making me aware of social connotations of space, especially of their implications for communication patterns in a place. I'm also indebted to Elisabeth Churchill, Paul Dourish, Thomas Erickson, Andrew Frank, Kristina Höök, Werner Kuhn, and Teenie Matlock for valuable discussions on social connotations and their input on the web study. Furthermore, I'd like to thank David Benyon, Phillip Jeffrey, Teenie Matlock, and Alan Munro for their comments on drafts of this chapter. Last but not least I'd like to express thanks to Alan Cattier. Without his ongoing support of my research activities neither the web study nor this chapter would exist.

Informatics, Architecture and Language

13

Matthew Chalmers

Two complementary schools of thought exist with regard to the basic underlying assumptions and philosophies that guide our research in information navigation and access. As with all of HCI, and indeed most of informatics, we can place theories and design practices based in objectivity and mathematics at one end of a spectrum, and those emphasising subjectivity and language at the other. The first school of thought sees itself as part of traditional computer science, rooted in models that encompass the individual variations of users and that are often derived from experimentation and observation in controlled conditions. Mainstream information retrieval, cognitive psychology and task analysis exemplify such a philosophy. Complementary views are held by those who hold the sociological and the semiological as primary, and consider that objective categorical models are insufficient to model the complexity of human activity. Collaborative filtering, ecological psychology and ethnography are examples here. The techniques and systems presented in this book do not all lie towards one end of this spectrum, but instead show a variety of choices and emphases. This chapter, however, focuses on theory firmly towards the subjective and linguistic end of the spectrum: tools to let us place, compare and design techniques and systems. Such theory is noticeable by its near–absence in the literature of this burgeoning research area. Here we try to redress the balance, aiming to build a more abstract and general view of our work.

At the most applied level, this chapter deals with one approach to the design of social navigation systems – paths (Chalmers et al., 1998) – and describes its origin in an analogy with a theory of urban form, space syntax (Hillier, 1996). More generally, we relate the use of and movement through information to use and movement in urban space. While architecture has already affected informatics in a number of areas, for example in the pattern languages of Alexander, here we use architecture as a stepping stone between linguistics and informatics. Through these links we wish to reinforce the view that all three are instances or subfields of semiology. In so doing, we aim to make more visible the range of assumptions and models that underlie all interactive information systems. We are often unaware of the models of knowledge and information that we build on, and the possible alternatives. Here we aim to make clearer some of those buried layers – the "archaeology of knowledge" (Foucault, 1972) that determines many of the strengths and weaknesses of any system for information navigation.

13.1 What Underlies HCI?

The opposing schools of thought mentioned above were exemplified in a recent exchange in the pages of SIGCHI Bulletin, discussing appropriate metaphors for navigation and organisation of files on the desktop. At the time of writing, the most recent contribution was Nardi and Barreau (1997). At issue was the importance of location-based searching over logical retrieval. Fertig, Freeman and Gelernter put forward what might be considered a traditional computer science viewpoint, suggesting that continuing research, gradually adapting and extending the analysis approaches rooted in 1960s "document retrieval", would eventually succeed. It would create better automatic tools for indexing the content of large databases and collections, made up of varied data types such as textual documents, images, sound files and so forth. It would, therefore, allow users to gain a full return on their investment in storing large amounts of information. This despite the fact that textual document retrieval has, even by its own measures of performance, not dramatically improved since its inception, and retrieval of image, video and audio content is still rudimentary. Nardi and Barreau suggested that such improvements would be valuable but would not address what they consider to be the paramount information management problem, the volume and heterogeneity of ephemeral information that comes and goes in everyday work. They see the traditional computer science approach as giving insufficient attention to the intricate details of how information on an individual's desktop is interwoven with the rest of that person's working environment of people, institutions and cultures. Such concerns are largely absent from the practice and theory of data retrieval.

At the core of Nardi and Barreau's objections is a concern that

> the alternatives offered by many developers of personal information management systems seem to view documents in the work space as a collection that can be easily characterized, ordered and retrieved based upon common characteristics, or based upon full text retrieval. These approaches ignore the complexity and variety of information in personal electronic environments. [...]

Schemes that automatically characterize information may not provide enough flexibility to consider the richness of these environments, and schemes that allow characterization for visual retrieval may not easily accommodate all of the desired dimensions.

The same issues arise in the World Wide Web, where complexity and heterogeneity of representation are increasingly problematic. The mix of data types restricts the coverage of traditional indexing techniques and limits the consequent power of search engines. As Tim Berners-Lee (1997) pointed out with regard to search engines for web data: "they are notorious in their ineffectiveness. […] A web indexer has to read a page of hypertext and try to deduce the sorts of questions for which the page might provide the answer." Images, numerical data, audio, programs and applets: the variety of information is increasing along with the volume. Attempts are being made by various researchers to solve these problems, usually by adding some form of metadata. Metadata is data that represents the meaning or content of other data. It is often expressed in a formal vocabulary, and intended to allow programs to uniformly compare data originally from a variety of authors and sources.

Indexers and search engines may handle metadata automatically and objectively, but metadata is often created manually. If metadata is manually created, it is open to be written, read and interpreted as each person sees fit. For example, web page authors or site managers may enter informally structured textual data such as captions or tags into a formally manipulated metadata scheme. For example, the PICS format proposed as a standard for web metadata (Resnick and Miller, 1996) involves "labels" that describe a web page or site, for example, suitability for children, whether it is commercial or not, and even "coolness". They also suggest that there might be many rating services, each of which could choose its own rating vocabulary. This opens the door to completely subjective metadata, however. For example, how objectively and uniformly with regard to its competitors will a large corporation describe its own web pages and products? How "cool" will each home page be according to its author?

Also, even if the metadata describing a site is, to give an optimistic figure, one thousandth the size of its referent, the vast size of the web would lead to gigabytes of metadata overall. Ironically, we would then need "metametadata" tools to find good rating services. We have not solved the problem, but deferred or even exacerbated it by adding to the indirection and complexity involved in acquiring utile information.

In other words, we only delay the problem of matching available information to users' interests and activities by stepping up to a metalevel. Since metadata open to individuals' use slips down to be just more data, we are back where we started.

Nardi and Barreau are amongst those involved in contemporary HCI theory, which is critical of modelling the mind (and hence the user) as an algorithmic processor – an approach that was until recently considered the firmest foundation upon which to build interactive information systems. Typical research involved short-term controlled experiments in a laboratory-like setting, with experimental subjects introduced to new tools and techniques to be used in isolation from the other tools familiar from their everyday work, and away from their colleagues and workplace. Modern HCI theory criticises this as excessively reductionist, unrealistically examining use of tools that would normally be interleaved with other tools, as part of long-term work within a community of use. Consequently they fail to take account of the complexity and situational dependence of interaction, and this approach has not offered the hoped for practical benefit to designers. Work such as Activity Theory (Nardi, 1996) takes a more realistic view of the subjectivity, dynamics and social context of individual action. It broadens consideration from just the actor and the tool being designed to the other tools used, the intended outcome (at various levels of abstraction), and the community within which activity takes place. Activity theory has, however, been better for analysis and criticism than for driving system design, which we suggest is related to its greater concentration on activities than on artefacts, that is on work's goals and actions rather than on the information and tools that represent and mediate work. Here we shift the balance the opposite way, focusing on representation, categorisation and interpretation, and so becoming more directly linked to system design.

The claim that algorithms, themselves founded in mathematical logic and formal languages, form the ultimate foundation of informatics has also been denied by formal informatics itself. Wegner recently published a proof that interactive computing is an inherently more powerful computational paradigm than purely algorithmic computing (Wegner, 1997). He shows that the complexity and unpredictability of human interaction offers greater expressiveness and analytic power than formal algorithms. Interaction involves more than algorithms can express, that is interaction is not reducible to algorithms, and interaction-based approaches to system design are more powerful than purely algorithmic ones. Computer science's traditional demand that one should be able to use formal languages to ground the behaviour of programs is therefore seen as inhibiting the expressiveness and power of the programs it builds. Wegner uses formal informatics to show its own limits, echoing the history of mathematics (and indeed physics) where the dream of reducing the world to a pure, clean and objective mathematical model has been shown to be an illusion.

We suggest that a belief or assumption that mathematical logic and objectivity form the ultimate basis of informatics is a naïve, reductionist stance. All too common even amongst computer science professionals,

318

this is not based on the mathematician's view of mathematics but on "folk mathematics", that is a common-sense framework for understanding mathematics, widespread amongst the wider population. This is analogous to "folk physics" that has a rough notion of inertia and Newtonian mechanics, and only a vague grasp of relativistic physics and its successors, and "folk psychology" the pre-scientific framework commonly used in comprehension and discussion of human behaviour (Churchland, 1998).

In the next section, we attempt to look beyond "folk informatics" and see what we can learn from mathematics' reconsideration of its foundations this century. In effect we ask the question: even if informatics is based on mathematics, mathematics is not firmly grounded in objective logic, so what is mathematics based on?

13.1.1 From Mathematics to Language

Some programs represent models and theories which are not intended to relate to the physical universe or our lives in it, for example in some branches of abstract mathematical theory. More often, however, computational representations model aspects of our lives. We reduce and select from the infinite complexity of the world in order to gain the ability to store, index, manipulate and retrieve. This involves finite models, expressed in mathematically based formal languages, that represent properties and relations between real-world objects. It has long been recognised in mathematics that such languages comprise three types of structure: algebraic structures such as sets, structures of order such as lists, and topological structures such as graphs.

Since we use such mathematical schemes as foundations for building representations, we should be aware of how solid and objective they are. This has of course been a concern within mathematics itself, for example in Cantor's demonstration of a paradox in set theory. The set of all sets is shown to be indeterminable because the "metaset" of all sets is itself a set, and therefore should be a member of itself along with many other sets, but this is inconsistent with our definition of what a set is. The metaset slips down from metadata to data. Similarly we are familiar with the paradox in sentences such as "This sentence is false".

To those determined to find objective foundations for mathematics, the persistent lack of a non-perceptual basis for such an apparently simple and familiar mathematical framework as Euclidean geometry was a particular concern (Everitt and Fisher, 1995). This framework consists of five axioms, but no one had been able to show that the axiom of parallels was founded in more than (human) claims of apparent self-evidence. This, to use Everitt and Fisher's phrasing of it, postulates that given a straight line and a point not on that line, it is possible to draw one and only one parallel line that goes through the point. Also, Euclidean geometry is not in accord with modern physics' observations. On a cosmological scale, parallel lines do eventually meet. Even logic was under pressure, as quantum physics began to cast doubt on the law of the excluded middle whereby, given a logical statement p, only one of p and *not p* can be true. Hilbert led the formalist or foundationalist approach, trying to render mathematics genuinely consistent and independent of perception. As cited in (Karatani, 1995), this meant that "the solid foundation of mathematics is in the consistency of its formal system: mathematics does not have to be 'true' as long as it is 'consistent', and as long as this is the case, there is no need for further foundation".

Abandoning the claim to truth was not sufficient, however. The major blows to Hilbert's approach came from two directions. One was from within, in the form of Gödel's incompleteness theorem. This, in a self-referential manner related to that of Cantor, set up a paradox like "This sentence is false", wherein meta-mathematics, understood as a class, slips down into the formal system as a member of itself. Gödel proved that for any system of mathematics of significant expressive power, it was always possible to set up such a paradox or inconsistency. As later echoed by Wegner's proof, he therefore showed that the consistency of a formal language was only obtainable at the price of limited expressiveness. Gödel thus helped release mathematics from the illusion that it could consistently represent the world.

The other blow was from without, from Wittgenstein, who reinforced the view that mathematics was part of human history, and not an abstract ideal independent of it. Wittgenstein, the former doyen of axiomatic bases for language and knowledge, rejected the notion that mathematics' formal system can be solidly deduced from axioms. Proof is just another "language game" (Wittgenstein, 1958), involving our invention of rules, systems and notations whose truth, as with all our natural language, is determined by our own social use rather than from axiomatic deduction.

Gödel demonstrated the problem of inconsistency in the mathematical structures we use in computer science for representation, while Wittgenstein replaced the axiomatic basis of their truth and meaning with a social, linguistic basis. Together they were instrumental in discrediting positivism, the previously dominant paradigm whereby a symbol was a "positive term", that is, an objective absolute, based purely on a logical process of naming a thing in the real world. This concept of naming and reference, that connected mathematical symbols with things in the world, had been the core of positivists' concept of "truth". This concept was understood as being no longer justifiable. As a result, mathematics no longer claims to offer a means to consistently, truthfully and absolutely represent the world. We can choose to use it as a tool, pragmatically accepting its limitations and historical biases, but even then we should be aware that mathematics has a history of paradigm shifts and scientific revolutions, and we have no reason to believe that this historical process has ended.

Underneath mathematics, we find language: systems of symbols, with subjectivity tempered by socially constructed practices of proof and experiment. The contemporary view of language is that we cannot dig further: there is "no exit from language", partly because all our consideration and modelling of the world is ultimately understood and used by means of perception and language. If natural language is formalised or abstractly represented, then when we interact with that representation, use it in the world, in our human interpretation and activity, we necessarily involve subjective perception. We may try to step up to a metalevel by means of formalism and abstraction, as with the web metadata example earlier in this paper, but with human activity we slip back down to language. Within a controlled environment such as the computer we can manipulate such a "meta-representation" as part of a more formal, finitely defined system. In interaction, however, the informal, subjective and infinite reassert themselves.

What, then, can we take from contemporary linguistics and semiology, that will help in our theory-building? Only a few decades before Gödel and Wittgenstein revolutionised mathematics' core, a similar paradigm shift had taken place within linguistics. Wittgenstein's language games have often been identified with linguistics' new paradigm: structuralism. Structuralism (de Saussure, 1959) combined linguistics and semiology, and displaced positivism in those fields.

Saussure's view was that, unlike positivism, naming is a relative or differential process, in that the elements of a language at any given time form a structure where any element only has meaning because of its relations and differences with other elements. Again we see a contrast with a positivist view of a one-to-one relationship of naming a unique, absolute, ideal thing in the world. If naming and language was based on such absolutes, then observed temporal variations of meaning could not happen, for example, "cattle" refers to bovine animals in this century but meant "all kinds of personal property" in the Middle Ages. Also, how could one language use only one word where another language uses two or more, for example, we use "river" to cover both "rivière" and "fleuve" in French. (A "fleuve" is a large river, which may flow into the sea but the word does not refer to just an estuary or firth.) Japanese has several words for the number "one", used to suit the type of thing being enumerated. While we may use a word to signify a thing in the world, it does not refer to one absolute and abstract thing that each other language also has exactly one word for. Our meaning is derived from our use of the word's similarities and differences to the other words of our language. A word means what we use it to mean, or, to quote Wittgenstein, "the meaning of a word is its use in the language".

321

In de Saussure's theory of natural language, the medium can be any physical phenomenon that we can control and perceive. This includes speech, written text, sign language, dance, architecture and so forth. We can choose to use anything and any combination of media to communicate. It is this interpretative choice or reaction that creates significance, and so any action in any medium can be taken as significant, and hence as a symbol.

13.1.2 Representation in HCI and Information Access

Now we can see a fundamental limitation in the information navigation and access approaches that rely solely on the content of each information object in isolation, such as the words inside a document, and ignore objects' use in human activity and objects' interrelatedness. To assume that the words contained inside a document faithfully and fully describe the meaning of a document, irrespective of its use in language, is a naively positivist approach. Traditional content-based approaches can be seen as emphasising and operating on symbols and attributes which are contextually independent, for example, no matter who has a document and what activity they are involved in, the same set of words are contained inside the document. Of course, this specificity affords highly useful techniques such as indexing of contained words to allow quick searching, but we rely on the assumption that the context of use and the person involved are not important. This is true when one wishes to find all documents that contain a given word, but false if one wishes to find all documents that one's colleagues find useful, or that conform to one's interpretation of a given topic. The assumption in itself is neither good nor bad; it is lack of awareness of it and its consequences that causes us problems. We should realise what assumptions our representations are built on, and hence what they afford and what they inhibit.

That perception of a structure or representation is bound up with the perception of use that became familiar to many within HCI via the ecological theory of perception of J.J. Gibson (1986), later popularised by authors such as Don Norman. Gibson stresses the complementarity of perceiver and environment. The values and meanings of things in the environment arise from the perception of what those things provide or offer as potential actions or uses to the perceiver – in Gibson's terms, their affordances – and not by universally naming and categorising absolute or objective properties. He emphasises the way that a theory of meaning must avoid

> the philosophical muddle of assuming fixed classes of objects, each defined by its common features and then given a name. As Ludwig Wittgenstein knew, you cannot specify the necessary and sufficient features of the class of things to which a name is given. [...] You do

not have to classify and label things in order to perceive what they afford.

While many in HCI and information access have read Gibson or Norman, our field has not taken full account of the way that representation schemes have affordances: they are also objects with characteristic strengths and weaknesses to choose in accordance with our uses, interests and abilities. Revealing the underlying models of knowledge and interpretation gives a common framework and vocabulary for comparing and analysing such schemes, as presented in (Chalmers, 1999).

Within HCI, Suchman (1987) has been instrumental in establishing the importance of situated action: how particular concrete circumstances have a strong influence on behaviour, and how strict plans are often merely resources for more flexible, dynamic, contingent action, that is, more like maps than scripts (Schmidt, 1997). Like Gibson, Suchman generalises over objects in interfaces and objects in the physical world, treating them as elements of sign systems, as linguistic expressions:

> The significance of a linguistic expression on some actual occasion
> [...] lies in its relationship to circumstances that are presupposed or
> indicated by, but not actually captured in, the expression itself.
> Language takes its significance from the embedding world, even
> while it transforms the world into something that can be thought
> of and talked about.

Again we see the need to look beyond the content of the expression or object, towards the co-dependence and co-evolution of human behaviour and information structure, and the influence of context and situation of use not usually represented in our information systems.

13.2 Space Syntax

Having put forward the argument that information use is semiological, we can draw upon other fields or disciplines that have been accepted as semiological for some time. We focus on architecture here, amongst many semiological fields, because the path model of information access, discussed in a later section, was based by analogy with what we characterise as a structuralist theory of urban structure, the "space syntax" theory of Hillier (1996). The path model treats information objects like spatial forms, histories of information use like individuals' paths though the city, and language as the city. The notion of "language as city" was also at the centre of Wittgenstein's language games (1958, p. 8).

Around the start of the twentieth century, around the same time as linguistics' and mathematics' revolutions, architecture took its most decisive steps on from the notion that buildings and cities are purely functional objects, exempt from significance to and influence from cultural and symbolic concerns (Colomina, 1996). The shaping and use of architectural form was then understood as being equally as semiological as the shaping and use of letter, word and document form in written texts. Word and written symbol usage corresponds to the motion and occupation of rooms and spaces in being a temporally ordered sequence of significant action.

In this section we outline space syntax, prior to a section using it to briefly characterise several traditional information access approaches and a section which lays out the path model in detail. Space syntax offers a view of city structure and development based on aggregates or averages of individuals' movement. Moving through the city may be due to a variety of motives – plans, contingencies and so on – but Hillier and his colleagues have found that aggregate patterns of use and meaning for people are correlated with statistical consistencies in peoples' paths. Such consistencies are correlated not so much with the nature of individual building forms and functions, but instead with the patterns of connectivity and visibility that make up the urban configuration.

13.2.1 Non-discursivity

As with other forms of language, and as activity theory and situated action emphasise, we often do not know how to talk about why we act as we do – why we read the city in the ways we do, or why we collectively tend to favour certain paths and routes and not others, or why the city configuration works or fails. This non-discursivity of everyday activity is a key issue in the work of Hillier, Gibson, Suchman and Wittgenstein, and all reiterate points made in the 1920s by Heidegger (1962). Just as we are able to speak understandably and to understand what we hear without being able to express – to make discursive – why our language is as it is, movement in the configuration of the city is generally non-discursive. Space syntax is an attempt to find consistencies of use that we can talk about as theorists and designers, that is, to bring non-discursive aspects of architecture into the discursive.

Space provides the potential for paths of movement and view, infinite in the case of void, empty space but increasingly constrained as we introduce forms such as buildings. The city is at once a record of the functional processes that historically created it, and at the same time the strongest constraint on future development. Specific activities such as finding a particular building and assessing the most profitable location to place a specialist shop relate to the spatial form of the city through "general functionality": the ways that we as individuals find a system of spaces intelligible, and the ways we move around in it.

324

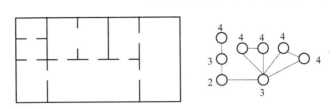

Figure 13.1 A floor plan with its connectivity graph. Each node in the graph represents one "room" and each arc between nodes represents a door connecting two rooms. Each node is labelled with its integration, showing the maximum path length to other nodes. The node of lowest integration may not be as good a movement node as the well-connected central node that bridges two rings. The top left "dead end" node is a good occupation node.

13.2.2 Integration

The "integration" of a configuration is a metric based on connectivity of spaces, and is a fundamental part of the vocabulary of the analytic side of the theory as a whole. We represent an urban configuration, such as the rooms of a building or the streets of a city, by a graph – an abstract representation of the configuration that simplifies but affords some useful analysis. Each node represents a separate subspace such as a room. The links between the graph nodes correspond to the connectivity of these spaces. Figure 13.1 shows an example. The integration of a node is the maximum of the lengths of the most direct paths one could take to each other node, that is, the maximum shortest path length to any other node. We can combine the effects of the nodes that make up a graph by summing these integrations. There is an extra normalisation factor to take account of the size of the graph, but essentially we obtain a figure that describes the graph, and hence the urban configuration. This figure, the integration of the graph, shows (amongst other possible interpretations) how well connected the space is, that is the degree to which moving around the space requires long routes that often connect you to only a small proportion of the nodes.

13.2.3 Visibility and Intelligibility

Visibility also plays its part. Although connectivity may make paths feasible, if the consequences of movement are not apparent – one cannot see where or to what a path may lead – then we diminish the confidence with which we make choices of movement. Hillier assumes uniform perception among the sighted majority of people – which makes it rather hard for him to explain how blind people can make sense of the city, for example – but his working notion is that, when a person looks from any point, he or she is aware of how lines of visibility extend outwards and connect to spaces he or she could move into. An "intelligible" configuration is one in which what a person sees from the nodes of the system is a good guide to the global pattern of depth. Rather over-formally, Hillier treated intelligibility as the correlation between integration and the connectivity of lines of visibility.

He suggests that minimising graph depth and integration supports intelligibility, and this is itself best supported by combinations of occupation and movement spaces. Occupation means the use of space for activities that are at least partly and often largely static, such as conversing, reading, sleeping, cooking, and working at a laboratory bench. "Dead end" spaces with a single link are essentially occupation-only spaces, links that collectively form rings tend to help the integration of spaces, and spaces with more than two links and connect at least two rings are the best movement spaces. Different types of space afford different patterns of occupation and movement according to their patterns of branches and rings. Occupation spaces afford detailed, localised activity, while movement spaces maximise the flexibility and efficiency of motion.

Movement through the city means that we encounter buildings and people along the way. No matter how planned such activity is, we gain a by-product in the encounters along our way. Configuration affects how well we can find our goals as well as come across the situations where unforeseen actions may take place, for example, in going to one shop in the city centre, we might pass another that prompts us to take a detour. Hillier suggests that maximised integration is the best way to gain the usefulness of this by-product, and leads to positive feedback between movement and development – the "multiplier effects which are the root source of the life of cities". To use Gibson's term, maximising affordances for encounter is what makes cities good.

Architectural space limits the patterns of co-presence amongst the individuals living in and passing through an area, and therefore co-awareness and affordances for interaction. In this way the spatial becomes involved with the social. As a social fact and a social resource, spatial configuration defines the "virtual community" of an area: the pattern of natural co-presence brought about through the influence of spatial design on movement and other related aspects of space use.

Configuration does not always incrementally co-evolve with the varied movements of everyday life and work in a "natural" or "passive" way. Cities also show structures that are the result of active planning and shaping on a large scale. This may be for economic reasons, for example, a city constructing a train line to encourage public access to its centre, or it may be for political or ritualistic reasons: "to make a statement". Examples are the dominant central axis of Brasilia, and the streets and spaces that focus attention on the centres of US government in Washington. Grand axes are extreme cases of how, at all scales, we can use paths and configurations as symbols and instruments.

Throughout space syntax, the function, categorisation, or content of the buildings involved are deliberately de-emphasised, and indeed it is Hillier's thesis that intelligibility and movement dominate them because all other aspects of function pass through them, and influence the urban form through them. These are strong claims, and yet Hillier presents many predictive analyses, backed up by a good match with observed behaviour in existing urban forms, without recourse to content analysis. He does not need content analysis for his theory to work, and even apparently intangible phenomena such as house prices, burglary rates and locations of teenage and drunkard "hangout" are quite accurately predicted by this very powerful theory which is now beginning to have wider application (Major, 1997).

13.3 Information Structures Seen as Architectural Plans

Part of the strength of Hillier's presentation of his theory was the analysis of example configurations of streets in cities such as London, and his involvement in urban regeneration projects such as King's Cross. We now use space syntax to look at simple prototypical cases of traditional information access techniques, as represented by simple connectivity graphs.

We employ several criteria in discussing each technique. Integration is usually first along with perceptibility. We must use the words "perceptible" and "visible" more loosely here, as we have no analogue of the objectively measurable lines of sight. Intelligibility, describing their informal correlation, is then mentioned. Another issue related to intelligibility is scale. This is not considered at length by Hillier, perhaps due to the size and flatness of cities generally restricting the variation in the number of perceptible buildings to within a few orders of magnitude. We discuss scale here, because in information environments the number of objects varies from a handful to billions. We also look for good occupation and movement objects, and a tendency towards the minimisation of graph depth.

13.3.1 Hypermedia

Let us reuse the architectural floor plan from above, and consider the graph of connectivity to represent bi-directional links in a simple hypermedia structure, as in Figure 13.2. We do not include the object that provides access to the hypermedia structure, for example the desktop or command line, in this or the following figures.

In simple or "pure" hypertext, connectivity is the sole associative medium and the only perceptible nodes on a page are those which are linked to it. The scale of a hypermedia object is usually relatively small,

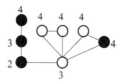

Figure 13.2 A simple hypermedia graph. Textual nodes are marked in black, while nodes of other types are in white. Arcs are bi-directional links. Integration values are unchanged from the architectural floor plan of Figure 13.1.

being kept under the control of a small number of authors – often one. Integration is dependent on the author of the links, and will worsen in larger graphs unless connectivity is kept high. This not generally being the case, there is a tendency towards deep tangled networks of connections. Perceptibility tends to be poor and intelligibility tends to be low – it is easy to become "lost in hyperspace". This also contributes to the poor general functionality of hypermedia; the authoring process does not tend to produce shallow graphs, or a mixture of objects serving as good general purpose circulation spaces and others as local "occupation" spaces.

One of the reasons connectivity stays low is to take advantage of one of hypermedia's strengths, namely that the explicit association expressed by links is directly under the subjective control of the author. The author need not rely on indirect association by, for example, using rules for categorisation or metrics of similarity to classify or measure objects' association with others. He or she doesn't have to say *why* two objects are associated, just that they are associated.

13.3.2 The Web – Indexed Hypermedia

If the web was purely a large hypermedia structure then it would suffer badly from the scale-associated problems described above. Unlike "normal" hypermedia its authors are huge in number and there is no sense of collaborative authoring of one large design or configuration. These problems of scale have been attacked primarily by indexing, which boosts connectivity. Considering our hypermedia example above as a web site, we can see the effects of adding a search engine in Figure 13.3.

Indexing has helped the integration of the non-textual objects and some of the textual objects, but the central non-textual nodes are still distant from the textual nodes to the left. In an architectural analogy, the search engine is like a narrow corridor that connects all objects but does not help with perceptibility. Improving connectivity with indexing tends to improve integration, especially for structures of large scale. This is dependent on the data types of objects, however: if many objects cannot be indexed then integration becomes skewed. Site authors can allow nodes to be indexed by adding captions or other metadata but then face

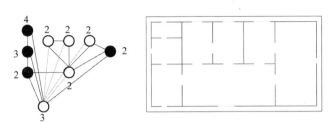

Figure 13.3 A text-based search engine, accessible from any object, has been added to the structure of Figure 13.2. Bi-directional links connect the engine to textural objects while uni-directional links (light grey lines) show the linkage from non-textural objects. Integration values confirm that indexed objects are still distant from non-textual objects. On the right is a "floor plan" with the search engine as a narrow corridor accessible from all rooms but with "one-way" doors (in grey) blocking access into non-textual rooms.

the difficult task of guessing what indices to offer (as in the Berners-Lee quote above). Perceptibility is not improved and, since highly connected areas still tend to have low perceptibility, intelligibility is also not improved. Search engines are good circulation spaces, as we tend to pass through them for varied reasons and in varied directions. They tend to reduce overall graph depth and make other nodes more like occupation spaces. In this way they aid the general functionality of the overall con-figuration, and would be good places to introduce features that afforded awareness of other people if the web was to directly support the social aspects of use.

Another asymmetry arises with search engines: the most used indices are in search engines and catalogues which cover many sites, and yet site authors and administrators have direct control only over their own site. They have a tendency to ignore these "external" links and work primarily with their own "internal" links. From the user's point of view this distinc-tion is not so important, and they need not give greater authority to con-nections defined by site authors when they can use the links from external search engines.

13.3.3 Indexed/Categorised Databases

If we now do not consider inter-object links, and focus on indexing alone, we rely on search engines completely (Figure 13.4). Generally we cate-gorise some pre-existing corpus of data and use category-specific indices as our associative medium. We thus partition information in ways that may not be in accord with use.

An index and search engine generally aid integration on a large scale but do little to support perceptibility between objects of a type. They tend to offer neither between objects of different types. More formally, in a heterogeneous set of objects integration values are very high as one

329

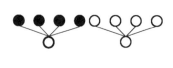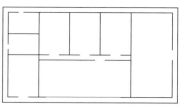

Figure 13.4 On the left we see two sets of four objects. Each set contains homogeneous objects. Shown below each set is an index for that type. On the right is a corresponding floor plan, with two groups of rooms inaccessible from each other. Connectivity among each set is afforded by its index, represented as a narrow corridor that offers little perceptibility.

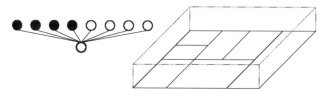

Figure 13.5 Objects of arbitrary types can be connected by placement in a visualised space. This space plays a configurational role similar to that of an index and offers the potential for maximal perceptibility. It is represented here as a space above the rooms, cf. the narrow corridor of Figure 13.3, as it offers access to and visibility of all rooms.

must move via different engines. Intelligibility is therefore extremely poor. As with the web, indexing aids general functionality. Direct association such as authored, tailored hypermedia linkage is de-emphasised in order to take advantage of indexing's handling of scale. Access to manageably sized subsets and more specific association depends on subclassification schemes (classifications of objects' components) and metrics such as Boolean matching, treatment as a high-dimensional vector space, and probabilistic models. These are indirect associative media, and problems of handling non-discursivity and overly objective formalisms tend to occur.

13.3.4 Visualisation

In visualisation, the primary medium for association is the low-dimensional space that objects are positioned in. Configurationally, this is similar to an index (Figure 13.5). Visualisation offers a means to connect heterogeneous objects and allows us to make perceptible complex interrelationships.

Integration is generally very good, and the potential for perceptibility is high due to the great deal of information that can be handled when presentation and interaction are in accord with our perceptual skills.

Realising the potential for perceptibility is not a trivial matter, however. Position, colour and other graphical dimensions must convey association, and their perceptual subtleties and interrelationships – bound up with our culture and language – make this a difficult design problem. Scale is another significant problem. Features such as screen resolution, legibility of symbols, occlusion and clutter all inhibit perceptibility of object sets of the scale handled routinely by large database systems. Many visualisation systems add in a search engine in order to help with such problems. While intelligibility can be very high for smaller sets of objects, this tends to decline for larger sets.

The embedding space of visualisation aids general functionality, just as search engines do. The space is even more clearly a "circulation space", and positioned objects are dead-end occupation spaces in a low-depth configuration that supports a variety of paths of movement.

13.4 The Path Model: An Information Access Approach Based on Activity

Given the common semiological features of architecture and informatics, and the independence of categorisation of spaces and predictive power of Hillier's architectural theory, it appears useful to work towards an analogous informational theory. This might involve some of the over-abstraction of space syntax, but would be based on movement through and visibility of computer-based information. Association and similarity of information would be interwoven via consistent patterns of use. The configuration would record the functional processes that created it, and in this way constrain and guide future development of structure. The path model is a step in this direction.

What should we take as the fundamental basis, or model, of information access? We suggest that it should be the use of symbols over time in the course of an individual's activity. Traditionally, informatics has focused on the form of the datum, with functions involving use and activity being built around the categorisation and formalisation of data representations. As Gödel showed, this approach leads to formal inconsistency – the metaclass slips into the class. Wittgenstein showed that separation between the structure and use of a language of representation ignores the social origins of meaning. We need to shift away from a view centred on formal categorisations that are separated from use, with activity peripheral.

The analytic and predictive power of Hillier's theory comes from activity being at the centre of the model. Movement and visibility between spaces, rather than the individual space, is at the centre of his theory. Presence at a spatial position and visual perception were each quite easily – perhaps too easily – defined in the case of the city. With information, we are forced to conflate perception of an object and presence in an object, since we have no strict equivalent of the reader being at a precise position within one and only one object. So, while movement through information space is an analogous basis for representation, movement should be construed as the change in perception of information as one reads, writes, hears, scrolls, changes 3D viewpoint and so forth. We move among information in many ways and, whether explicitly or implicitly, in this way we build a path of associations.

In the case of a simple web browser we might construct paths by logging which pages are successively loaded, approximating the order in which they are presented to the user. Use of web tools is usually interwoven with that of others such as mail tools and editors. Also, there is little, if any, fundamental difference between objects on and off the web. Therefore to understand web use we should also log use of documents and tools on the desktop. Ideally we would look at all media that form the environment of the user, for example, where that person is, the papers and books on the desk, what music they can hear, who else is in the room, what the weather is. The list appears endless and, somewhat inconveniently, it is. We should of course concentrate our efforts first on the most obvious and amenable targets for logging. Nevertheless, we as system builders (or information authors), should be aware of our assumptions about which categories of information and tools – computer-based or not – will be important to our systems' users (readers).

As with the city, our reasons for movement may be myriad. The association between items of information may express pre-planned action or our behaviour may be more contingent upon the situation. Rather than attempt to model the meanings in users' minds, Hillier was able to take statistical consistencies in users' paths as the social expression of meaning, and in this way bring the non-discursive into the discursive. Similarly we do not attempt to directly represent or formalise the consciousness of each user, but instead look for meaning in statistical consistencies within the collection of users' paths through information objects.

In the architectural case, uniqueness or identity of spaces was relatively straightforward and familiar, because of the way that individual spaces were defined as partitioning the total space under consideration. Here we begin by assuming that each information object has a unique name or identifier. An object might be a document, a program, an image, a person, or even a path, but its identifier is not dependent on the type or form of the object. Internal changes do not change the identifier of an object, and a copy of an object has a different identifier to the original. The metric of object similarity should not be based on identifiers or naming, but on association, or linkage, in paths.

Let us consider that at any given time we model our perception of objects as a set of object identifiers. A path has an identifier such as *path12*, an author identifier such as *Matthew*, and a time-ordered sequence of sets of identifiers of objects, such as (*doc77, image3, Bill*). For example:

path12, Matthew, ((doc77, image3), ((doc77, image3, Bill), (image3, Bill))

Periodically, we record the set of objects most obviously perceptible to a user, and add this set to their path. Each such record might be made either after a chosen time interval (which might lead to contiguous object sets which are equal) or when some discrete move was considered to have been made (i.e. a change in the set of perceptible objects). Other schemes are also clearly feasible, for example time-stamping each set. (Current implementations rely on time-stamping.) More difficult to justify and to implement would be the association with each object of a probability describing relative strength of perceptibility. Perhaps some tools involved in information access will not be able to coordinate with others in order to define the set for a given moment in time. Instead, either concurrently or as part of a later analysis, another program combines individual logs. By means of time-stamps, for example, it weaves logs together to form the sets of contemporaneously accessed objects.

A null path has no objects in it. Two paths are equivalent if they have the same author and contain the same object sets in the same order. Time-stamps would offer even greater specificity. One can imagine a variety of metrics of path similarity, with each giving a maximum value for equivalent paths, and decreasing as authors, object sets and orders differ. Contiguous path segments, and paths defined by selectively filtering out particular objects from a larger path or inserting selected objects into a shorter one, could be compared similarly. This allows us to compare our recent behaviour with our own past (i.e. comparing a short segment of a path, with end "now", with the full path so as to find similar episodes in the past) and of course with the paths of others.

Two objects are similar if they consistently tend to be in similar paths. This is irrespective of the objects' heterogeneity or homogeneity of content or form, as it is their use that we focus on here. A path's start and end might be defined by the earliest and latest of all logged activity by the person involved. Alternatively we might delimit paths upon noticing prolonged periods of inactivity, or abrupt changes in the membership of the set of objects worked with. One danger here is that inactivity in the logged behaviour may be due to an inability to log significant activity, rather than a lack of activity that might be logged. We should also be aware that such partitioning based on inactivity, object set consistency, etc. is pre-categorisation or pre-judgement that may not suit later use.

We emphasise that we do not assume that following paths in this way is the only way to move through information, or that a tool based on path extension would be the only one in active use on a computer at any one time. Instead, here we look for a way to model the movement made via whatever ensemble of tools the user cares to use. This ensemble may or may not include a tool based on paths, but nevertheless we can consider the tool that initially offers information access, for example the desktop upon log-in, to be an object. Like most objects, it offers access to a number of subsequent objects, in this case mail tools, web browsers, path-based tools and so forth. In this way, our analysis can always involve a single configuration of objects.

13.4.1 Perceptibility and Intelligibility

When perception of an object A makes another object B perceptible then we say that A is connected to B. This does not mean that the ability to perceive the connection is necessarily easy or natural. As mentioned earlier, we diverge from Hillier here, whose "line of sight" visibility was simpler to measure, treated as if it was an objective, formal property. Here, it is more obvious that perceptibility may involve complex actions and interpretations understood only by the community of use (and not by we outsiders, the analysts), but nevertheless the space syntax analogy suggests we represent this by a practical, binary property: connectivity. If one could use perceptibility to define (unidirectional) connectivity, one could form graphs of connections between objects, and apply Hillier's integration to express how well connected individual objects and configurations are, and intelligibility as the correlation between visibility and integration. The degree of perceptibility for the community of users will hinder or help their everyday use, and will be affected by the degree to which their informal language of use is in accord with the formal language of analysis. As yet, we cannot go so far. Here we must rely on more intuitive notions of perceptibility. Note another aspect of movement and view that Hillier assumes, but that we cannot: people can always see each other within the same space, and often in connected spaces. This is a simpler assumption to accept for cities than for most information systems.

Perceptibility is a vital feature of movement, determining affordances for movement and our confidence in moving. An intelligible configuration is therefore one in which what is perceptible of the objects is a good guide to the global structure. One perceives where to go, as well as how objects fit together at the larger scale. When at a given object, it is often the case that some connected objects are more perceptible than others. An HTML page makes linked pages visible by colour, font, location on the page, a textual description and so forth. The changing background colour of the page, a position far down a very long page, or having an unhelpful description may make a link less perceptible. The page design may also reflect, or fail to reflect, where we might move in the larger-scale configuration, for example, a clear step up to the parent directory in a graphical file browser, or another confusing step in a maze of "See also" cross-references in manual pages.

An extreme case, showing maximal connectivity and minimal perceptibility, would be a tool akin to the "Go To" field in a web browser, but isolated and used only once. One could type in an arbitrary URL, and then jump to the page. All objects are connected to the tool, but none are perceptible. This is somewhat similar to the case of web search engines, which are connected to a very large number of pages but do not make those pages easily visible or perceptible.

When we look at objects and how we move around them, we can again focus on occupation and movement. Occupation means the use of objects for activities that are at least partly and often largely "static": reading a long piece of text on page, interacting with an embedded Java application. Making a strong analogy with Hillier would suggest that "dead end" spaces may be best for occupation and that such "focused" texts or applications should be kept distinct from highly-connected objects. Connecting objects, such as well-connected ring-bridging objects, complement occupation objects. They offer flexibility and efficiency of movement and support more dynamic activities. Together with designing so as to minimise depth, implementing such distinctions should enhance the general functionality of the configuration, increasing the affordances of encounter with objects and, assuming some kind of mechanism for perceiving people in nearby information spaces, of encounter with people.

13.4.2 Adaptation and Social Effects

Some information access techniques require a start-up or training period, whereas others operate immediately. In either case, the pace of creation and evolution can be much faster than that of urban environments. Cities generally present the same visible configuration to all and, like the basic access techniques discussed above, do not adapt differently and specifically to each individual user. Given the dynamics of computers, however, one must ask how quickly information access can be tailored to individual habits and needs.

In the path model, we define a new path as we move through information, ostensively expressing our interests or activities. The path will be continually logged, adding to the configuration of paths shared by our community of users and adapting the relative path similarities. Given our current position at the end of our path we may find corresponding periods in other similar paths, and objects that consistently arise slightly further along from those periods. These can be presented to the user, that is, made perceptible, affording future movement and triggering-off adaptation in the form of further logging, reconfiguration, and presentation.

Now we see what "retrieval" can mean here. Having created or accessed an information object in the course of our work, we can be presented with other "relevant" objects without dependence on their homogeneity. Furthermore, relevance is derived from the context of similar human activity, and not raw data content or "expert opinion".

It is feasible that mere presentation of possible paths for information movement might be logged, trigger reconfiguration, and spark new presentation. Setting such a "hair trigger" which did not wait for (or give weight to) user choice among possible paths of movement might offer an interesting "guided tour" if the pace were calm. If too fast, however, the tool might bolt off wildly into the informational horizon. This sprint towards infinity, a surfeit of adaptation, would be at least as bad as having no adaptation at all. Between these two extremes, controlled adaptation would move at the pace of the user, taking account of evolving activities and choices, and continually offering appropriate awareness of objects and affordances for action.

Since paths are associated with people we make manifest the community's use of information. Association and meaning are thus socially determined. The patterns of co-perceptibility in the city are strongly linked to co-awareness and the social, and similarities in the way people act in information potentially can make those people perceptible to others. Paths offer a means to find out about people's past activities and, as paths grow and adapt, people's ongoing activity. This may be useful when, for example, this enhances interpersonal communication and community. The act of writing a proposal for a research topic could trigger presentation of relevant references and authors, and also local people with experience in the topic. Note, however, that we do not have inherent symmetry as is normal in physical visibility on a street, or audibility in conversation. Like all information that identifies people and may be accessible to others, either at the time of action or at some later date, paths raise issues of privacy and invasiveness (Bellotti and Sellen, 1993).

13.4.3 Implementations

In 1999, application of the path model had been in two areas: a URL and file recommender tool and 2D visualisation of URLs and files. This work was carried out while the author was at UBS Ubilab, in Zürich, Switzerland. An earlier system, for URLs only, was described in Chalmers et al. (1998), and so we offer only a brief description of the more technical details. Web usage was a convenient area for early experimentation because the URL naming system offered unambiguous references to heterogeneous objects; we use the web regularly, and browser activity is easy to log. We extended the Muffin web proxy (muffin.doit.org) to log URLs in a relational database. We now also log the use of local files inside the *xemacs* editor, with logging triggered by switches between editor buffers. Since we only recorded loading of URLs and switching of buffers, and not visibility on screen, a path involves not object sets (as discussed above) but a sequence of individual time-stamped URLs. Each user can turn path logging on and off at will. By default, each path is potentially visible to all those who contribute paths, that is, the set of paths is treated as a shared resource. We are also experimenting with adding the content of web pages and files to the path.

We treat the person's most recent path entries as an implicit request for recommendations. Every few minutes, the system takes the most recent path entries, that is, the end of the path, and searches for past occurrences of each URL (or, more generally speaking, each symbol). Currently, this search can either cover one's own path or all paths within the shared path set. In the interface, a slider is used to set how long this "recent" period is, and one can select which paths (or owners) to draw from, thus allowing people to use knowledge of their colleagues to steer the recommendation process.

The system then collects the context of each past occurrence of each of the most recently used symbols – the path entries following soon after each past occurrence. Another slider sets this period's length. The system then collates these symbols, removes any which are among the set of recently used symbols (since we don't need to recommend symbols the user just used), and then presents the top ten from this ranking as a recommendation list. The system thus recommends to the user symbols that were frequently used in similar contexts but that it has not observed recently in the user's path. The people whose paths contributed to recommendations are not identified in this list. An example recommendation list is shown in Figure 13.6 and four snapshots of a visualisation of the same example are shown in Figure 13.7.

This example is intended to demonstrate how recommendations, such as ski information given weather pages, might not be the most obvious thing for a system to do until one considers the context of use and history behind it. The recommendations suited the author extremely well, as they were useful in his particular situation. If the winter weather was good, then a ski trip could go ahead. In this case, he got the Klosters information from his own path, and the Arosa information from another person's path. Never having been to Arosa, or to the Arosa web site, the recommendation was therefore both novel and relevant. The example also offers a contrast with tools based on content. The likely recommendation would simply have been for yet more weather pages. Lastly, the recommendations include heterogeneous data: JPEG images as well as pages of HTML. This demonstrates the ability to mix media that are usually indexed and searched by disjoint systems. Since paths involve identifiers, and similarity involves patterns of use of identifiers, it doesn't matter what the content "inside" an identifier is.

http://www.arosabergbahnen.ch/	18.0
http://www.arosabergbahnen.ch/Grafiken/collage.jpg	15.0
http://www.klosters.ch/images/tn_gotschna.jpg	9.0
http://www.klosters.ch/gotschna.html	9.0
http://194.158.230.224:9090/telenet/CH/180/2.g-html	9.0
http://www.arosa.ch/main.html	9.0
http://www.arosa.ch/skiauswahl.html	9.0
http://ad.adsmart.net/src/goski/mountains^1?adtype=ac&bgcolor=F...	9.0
http://www.arosabergbahnen.ch/home.html	9.0
http://www.arosa.ch/	9.0

Figure 13.6 A snapshot of a URL recommendation list from our system. Starting to choose a day for a ski trip, the author accessed web pages with detailed weather reports for the mountains of Switzerland, including the *telenet* service of a local university. Recommendations were drawn from six sequences of past activity in three people's paths, and were mostly for web sites of ski resorts near Zürich, such as Arosa and Klosters. The numbers in the right-hand column are the tally values used in ranking relevant URLs.

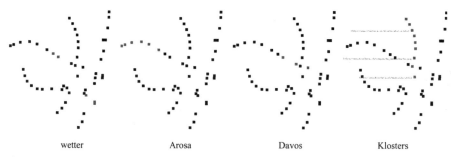

wetter   Arosa   Davos   Klosters

Figure 13.7 Four snapshots of an interactive "map" of URLs based on the path model, scaled down from actual screen size, and with the frame and controls of the surrounding visualisation tool cropped. Following access of web pages with detailed weather (*wetter* in German) reports for the mountains of Switzerland, recommendations involved URLs for wed sites of ski resorts near Zürich, such as Arosa, Davos, and Klosters, as well as URLs for other weather pages. Each snapshot shows the same positions, based on co-occurrence of URLs, but shows in a lighter colour those URLs that match the given search string, e.g. *arosa* in *www.arosa.ch*. The *Klosters* snapshot also shows three URLs which have been "popped up" by the tool to show textual detail.

As with Chalmers et al. (1998), co-occurrence statistics were used to define a similarity metric in the layout algorithm of Chalmers (1996), and the resultant layouts were displayed in the visualisation tool of Brodbeck et al. (1997). Sections of paths cross at multiply-accessed symbols. Symbols adjacent to these recurrences are brought near to each other, building associations between different periods of time. Layouts now involve a relatively small number of symbols, which tend to form "strands", each of which is a sequence of symbols collected prior to symbol tallying, that is, one of the similar periods of past activity used in the recommendation process. Our previous visualisations involved layouts of complete paths, involving thousands of URLs. In both recommendations and in visualisations, we then used statistics of co-occurrence over entire paths. This diluted the specificity of recommendations and also involved a co-occurrence matrix of size $O(N^2)$, where N is the number of symbols in paths. We now avoid this quadratic data structure, taking advantage of database indexing facilities to generate required statistics on the fly.

Recommendations are made periodically – another slider in the interface sets how often – and take a few seconds to make. Most of the work takes place on a server machine devoted to the database. We can make a matching visualisation in under one minute on a Silicon Graphics O2.

Statistics for recommendation and visualisation thus form categorisations or abstractions over path entries that are not fixed *a priori*. Instead, recurrence statistics are made anew for each person at the time of, and using the context of, each recommendation operation. Each new entry in a path changes the pattern of symbol co-occurrences throughout the shared configuration of paths. Even if you have not accessed new information recently, your recommendations may still vary as other people's activities change their paths.

Ongoing work focuses on adding the symbols contained in web documents (such as words and URLs) to paths, in extending the interface to allow more active steering of the recommendation process, and in more specialised tools for logging and recommending Java software components. In adding content, the goal is to treat words, filenames and URLs equally within the same model. In active steering, the user could choose to add symbols to (and remove others from) the "recent" symbol set. At one end of a spectrum would be the removal of all automatically collected symbols, and the explicit specification of a query-like set of terms. At the other end would be the current implicit or passive specification.

13.5 Conclusion

In the path model and related systems, representation has human activity at its centre. Categorisation, in the form of statistical consistencies in similar past activity, is built around this shared, adaptive, relative system of symbols. In our recommendations and visualisations, we aim to show and support user activity, and to take account of the interdependence and interweaving of information tools such as web browsers, editors and so forth. We have described how the path model was built by analogy with a theory of architecture, which was itself built by analogy with structuralist linguistics. More generally, we tried to make clearer some similarities between fields that can profitably be used in both system design and theory. These similarities exist even while there are substantial differences. For example, mutability: bits are easier to move around than bricks. This difference is diminishing, however, as some information structures, such as home pages of large corporations and the search engines we so rely on, are made persistent, reliably available facilities. In architecture, banks, galleries and museums increasingly have their supporting structure on the outside, so that internal partitions and passageways can be easily reorganised. Buildings are made more adaptable to their current users while URLs become more corporate and fixed.

We suggest that it is the common semiological basis of informatics and architecture that makes for these similarities. Human activity involving information in computers is not so special. It is little different from activity involving other media of communication and representation. We thus gain an understanding of how the choices for future significant action of each individual, in and through symbols of all types, are influenced by the past and current activity of others. This gives rise to the "hermeneutic circle" of representation, interpretation and action. We have tried to make clearer how these foundations lie deep – almost hidden – beneath the theory and practice of informatics, and to show how we can build upon them in new ways when we better comprehend their origins, strengths and weaknesses.

Antoni Gaudi, an architect best known for his work in Barcelona, said that "originality is going back to origins". In this paper we have looked back through informatics to mathematics, in order to make more "ready to hand" our materials and tools for building new approaches to computational representation. Contemporary mathematics and philosophy show us that activity, language and the social are at the centre and origin of informatics, rather than on the periphery of a core of objectivity and positivism. This view does not make us discard positivist approaches for those based on structuralist, or even post-structuralist ones. As was pointed out by Ricoeur (1981), positivist approaches allow access to open systems while structuralist approaches, such as the path model, involve a closed, relative system of symbols. Structuralism needs positivist approaches to weave each new symbol into a pattern of use, and so begin another turn of the hermeneutic circle: taking a new symbol, interpreting it in terms of how to use it, and creating new patterns of co-occurrence of symbols. Thus, while path-based systems and related collaborative filtering systems may be able to represent and support more of the complexity and subjectivity of information than positivist information access approaches, the former are dependent on the latter.

We believe that the understanding gained from re-examining the origins of informatics opens up new space for originality in informatics theory and systems design. This shift towards what Wegner called the interactive paradigm will let us handle information that seemed intractable, combine tools that seemed unrelated and interweave theories that seemed incommensurable. This can be done if we face up to informatics' limitations and historical biases, and see what Paul Churchland calls the "deeper unity" of modern intellectual discourse, all the way from neurophysiology to philosophy of science. Informatics can then move forward to take its place with contemporary mathematics, philosophy and semiology.

Acknowledgements

The author wishes to thank the editors for discussion and comment related to this chapter, and also Dominique Brodbeck, Ruth Conroy, Nick Dalton, Paul Dourish, Luc Girardin, Christian Heath, Aran Lunzer, Marissa Mayer, Kerry Rodden, Lisa Tweedie, and those who directed the laboratories where the bulk of this work was done: Hans-Peter Frei of UBS Ubilab, and Yuzuru Tanaka of the Meme Media Laboratory, Hokkaido University. And Jeff Mills (Liquid Room), and Mogwai (Young Team).

14

Information that Counts: A Sociological View of Information Navigation

R. H. R. Harper

This chapter presents two empirical examples of information navigation work in organisational contexts. They show that information gains its relevance to any individual organisational actor in proportion to how actors in other organisations use that information. In this respect, it will argue that information is socially organised. The chapter will then discuss what implications this has for providing new sources of information and new information retrieval techniques with the World Wide Web.

14.1 Introduction

In this chapter I will analyse the structure that supports and is embedded in the information navigation work of individuals who are called "desk officers". These individuals are economists who work for the International Monetary Fund in Washington, DC. Their task is to be the conduit between the private information space of the Fund (as it is known) and the public information space of the world outside. Specifically, I will offer a sociological analysis of two topics: first, the institutional motivations that drive the navigational activity of these desk officers; and second, the parameters of relevance that guide their work, parameters that are institutionally set and yet endlessly renegotiated. I will argue and assume that these motivations and parameters are constituted and made observable by the methodical ways that desk officers operate. Following the sociologists Garfinkel and Sacks, I will take it that desk officers structure their behaviour to achieve, accomplish and display the rationally motivated, institutionally relevant nature of the information work (Garfinkel and Sacks, 1970). Description and examination of those methods can be used to make recommendations for the design and use of computer-based information navigation systems (Button and Dourish, 1996; Button and Harper, 1996).

The chapter will be structured in the following way. First, I will say something about the setting studied and report the fieldwork pro- gramme used in its study. I then present empirical examples related to the two areas of interest. I conclude by considering what implications these have for the role and design of web-based information systems.

14.2 The Fieldwork and the Setting

The Fund may be thought of as a financial "club" whose members consist of most of the countries of the world. Member countries contribute to a pool of resources that can then be used to provide low interest, multi- currency loans should a member find itself facing balance of payments problems. The Fund has some 3000 staff, of which 900 are professional economists. These economists analyse economic policies and develop- ments – especially in the macroeconomic arena. They have particular interest in the circumstances surrounding the emergence of financial imbalances (including those that lead to a balance of payments crisis), the policies to overcome such imbalances, and the corrective policy crite- ria for making loans. Key to this work is undertaking "missions" to the country in question. A mission normally involves four or five economists, supported by administrative and secretarial staff, gathering and dis- cussing macroeconomic data with key officials in the authorities of the member country. This leads to the creation of a picture or view of that situation which in turn is used in policy discussions between the mission and the authorities. Member authorities are obliged to agree to Fund pol- icy recommendations if Fund resources are to made available to them. Missions normally last about two weeks. A mission team's view of a member country, the outcome of policy dicussions and any recommen- dations for the disbursement of funds (or otherwise) are documented in "staff reports" prepared by the mission teams once they return to Washington. These reports are used by the organisation's executive board for its decision making.

Desk officers are a subset of the Fund's economists. Each desk officer works on a "desk". A desk is a label for a number of individuals whose responsibility is to gather, analyse and represent information about particular member countries. But for the sake of simplicity, I will treat these individuals and their roles as more or less one under the title of desk officer.

The work of these individuals was studied ethnographically. Ethnography is a much used term by sociologists and anthropologists – something of a catch-all word for a range of methods and approaches, just as long as they involve direct observation of one kind or another (Harper, 1999). In this case, the ethnography involved six months' field- work.

344

The structure of the fieldwork involved focusing on the *career* of staff reports, from the first draft of what is called the "briefing paper" prepared before a mission commences, through the mission process itself, to the post-mission review, and then to translation, printing, and circulation processes of the final staff report.

This was accomplished in two ways. First, I followed a hypothetical staff report around the organisation and interviewed parties that would be involved in its career. In all, 138 personnel, including 90 economists were interviewed. Second, I observed a Fund "mission" and its allied document production practices. I observed meetings between the mission team before the mission commenced, between the member authorities and the team during the mission, and observed post-mission meetings. Once this process was completed, a full ethnographic text was prepared and published (Harper, 1998). Some of the materials presented here have been analysed within that text, although I have attempted to bring a different slant on them here.

14.3 The Empirical Examples

14.3.1 Motivation

The first example relates to what motivates desk officers. Here I am not concerned with what motivates them personally (i.e. whether they want to become managing director of the Fund or have any other similar ambition). What concerns me is what motivates them by dint of their organisational role. Moreover, and following Garfinkel and Sacks, I am concerned with the methodical things that desk officers do which makes these motivations demonstrable.

As remarked, desk officers are meant to be at the juncture between the outside world and the private world of the Fund. Their role as "experts" means that they will necessarily receive a great deal of information related to their membercountry that they will have to sort through, manage and share with the Fund as whole at certain times during the year (and most especially when financial crises show themselves).

There are a number of ways of looking at this work and what motivates it, some of which are more appropriate than others for design. This can be illustrated by outlining what would appear to be a useful way but which in practice is misleading. This will enable me to more effectively convey what I mean by motivations and thus more accurately describe what role technology might have in supporting it.

One approach, the wrong one I believe, would be to simply describe and catalogue the information desk officers collect and then to assess its comprehensiveness and its timeliness. This could then be measured against some metric for information as a whole that one might devise, i.e. against some notion of what would be a full or comprehensive data set.

With this approach, one would probably start off with a list. This list would include the following sorts of facts: that desk officers routinely collect and receive newspaper editorials in the *Financial Times* and articles in the *Economist* as well as analyses of similar organisations to the Fund, such as the Organisation for Economic Cooperation and Development (OECD) and the World Bank. In addition, they receive *government bills* for financial or economic legislation, ministry of finance *budgetary statements*, and *financial statements* from commercial banks, all from the member country in question. Most desk officers also receive quarterly statements of *foreign currency holdings* from central banks, and *estimates of government fiscal revenues* are sent to them.

One could easily add to this list. The point is that an analyst is then able to make a comparison between what desk officers have and what may be thought of as what they would want/need in ideal circumstances. That is to say, the analyst may then ask such questions as "Is the information they have enough?"; "Is it the right sort of information?", and so on. If not, a system could be designed that would deliver it. For example, a system could automatically search for and deliver all newspaper articles referring to the member country. It could automatically notify desk officers of any new academic articles, or it could even automatically update spreadsheets when budget statements and balance sheets are released. In other words, the designer would want to expand the kinds of information desk officers can have access to and would want also, perhaps, to help expedite or ease the difficulty desk officers may have in sifting through that information. One might suggest that such design considerations reflect or are typical of the orthodox metaphor in human–computer interaction. (As it happens this is pretty much the way the economic profession examines work of the Fund. One result of these analyses is the claim that the Fund needs to broaden the scope of the materials its desk officers receive. For a review see Bird (1996).) This view takes for granted and assumes that the goal of any and all desk officers is to increase their informational resources.

Now, in contrast, the view I think much more appropriate puts those sorts of questions aside. That is to say, instead of asking whether desk officers have *enough* information, the approach I think appropriate involves asking what motivations lie behind the way desk officers organise themselves to deal with the information they have at hand. According to this view, it is not the extent, scope, or speed with which information is processed that is at issue, it is how someone like a desk officer *treats* it. And if one does this one will see that the nature of their task is more complex and subtle than it might at first appear. (For some more examples of this see Button and Harper, 1996.)

An example will illustrate this. The desk officer for a country I will call for the sake of confidentiality, Arcadia, received most of the materials I have just listed (and hence was like any other desk officer). This included newspapers. In particular, he received (via the embassy in Washington) copies of two "dailies" from Arcadia. But, as he explained to me, the utility of the information that these newspapers conveyed was quite limited:

Desk officer: "You've got to understand, Richard, that in Arcadia there is no real opposition. This paper [he pointed to one] is the official party paper. That tells the official party line. This one [he pointed to another] is meant to be the opposition paper but it isn't really."

Interviewer: "So what do you do with them?"

Desk officer: "Oh, I still read them. You get some feeling for events in Arcadia. Also you can get a feel for the views of the authorities. That can be useful in policy discussions. You can't trust the figures in them though."

Of course, in relation to the kinds of materials one finds in newspapers – official party ones or otherwise – it may be remarked that they do not convey the kind of "stuff" the Fund would be primarily interested in: namely macroeconomic data. As a result, it would hardly be surprising that a desk officer would not be too interested in what they find. The contents of newspapers may just be too inconsequential – though useful for getting a "feel" for a country. But here, I think, is precisely the thing that is of salience: the ability to distinguish between information that provides "a feel for something" and information that does something else. Let me explain.

To begin with, what one can learn from this is that the desk officer was able to "use" information because he already knew something about it. In particular, he knew a great deal about the institutional provenance of the information he received in those newspapers. There was then a reflexive relationship between the information searched for and what was already known. Reflexive in the sense that in knowing something about the information, a desk officer could see why that information might be useful. But the interesting thing here is not so much this general observation; instead what is interesting is how the desk officer in question used the particular set of information thereby identified.

For the desk officer had a methodical way of dealing with this information. Not in the sense that the desk officer received the papers arrive every day or so, it was rather that he *methodically allocated* the information he received into a broader context. He recognised that the information in the newspapers was far from factual and instead treated it as a resource for getting a "feel" for "better understanding" the authorities.

Thus, the relationship the desk officer had to information was not one similar to, let us say, the relationship a fisherman has to his nets – hoping simply to expand the methods by which he captures what he is after. Rather, the desk officer had a relationship with information wherein his task was to know where to place or allocate the information. This is what motivated the desk officer; he was concerned to put things in the right place, to allocate information into a broader context, a "field of relevance" if you like (or as the ethnomethodologists put it, into an "occasional corpus of knowledge" or a "topical contexture of meaning").

As it happens there was an incredibly rich field into which things could be placed. In this case, the desk officer's methodical activity involved a sort of taxonomising which depended on multiple criteria. For example, it involved an ability to place information within what one might call a moral order and all that that implies: not just facts and figures but also intentions, motivations, perspectives, hopes aspirations, and the denials of the Arcadian authorities. In this sense, the desk officer was seeking to understand the political situation in which the Arcadian authorities find themselves, not just their economic situation.

14.3.2 Institutional Relevance

Knowing where to put information – irrespective of the technological tools to support that task – is itself based on another set of concerns, related to institutional relevance. This is the second area of concern for me. Again, I will illustrate my interests with an empirical example but this time taken from the information work that desk officers undertake on a mission. The mission in question was to Arcadia.

During the mission, a meeting between the desk officer and one of the Arcadian officials led to a discussion of an economic analysis institute that had recently been set up. Thereafter, the desk officer and a colleague arranged a visit to the institute to find out what it had been doing. They discovered that it had undertaken a range of studies on recent macroeconomic developments in Arcadia. The desk office reported this in a meeting they had with the rest of the mission the following day. During this meeting, the desk officer made available two of the reports that the institute had given him which the team browsed through. The team discussed whether they could use the information in their own analytical work. Essentially, what they wanted to determine was where they could place it in the already mentioned field of relevance. In this case, however, the mission decided that it would be inappropriate to use the information despite the fact that it was "in one sense obviously relevant", as one put it. They decided not to do so because the institute's views were not taken on board by the Arcadian authorities themselves. What mattered was whether the information was "in sight" of the authorities, not whether it ought to be or was "naturally relevant". The outcome of the meeting was that it was decided that in the future the institute might get a higher profile in Arcadia and that therefore its work might well become more relevant. Accordingly, the desk officer decided to keep a note of what the institute did in the future and to track whether it started to have any influence with the authorities.

In practice, this meant that the desk officer did not so much ignore the institute's work as *put it aside* until such time that it became something the Arcadian authorities themselves started to use. Here, one might make a paradoxical contrast between the desk officers' use of newspapers and the decision of the mission to disregard the macroeconomics analyses of the institute. It is paradoxical because the important point is not what the information is in itself, but whether and where it can be placed in the field of relevance. In this case information that seemed a long way from macroeconomics (namely information in the newspapers) was viewed as "more relevant" than information that was quintessentially macroeconomic. This judgement was based on what the mission knew to be the concerns and perspectives of the authorities. Key to this was defining what was included in the authorities "sight" and what was out of their view. In this respect, the information-gathering work that the desk officer and the mission team undertook was built around the assumption that they had to understand the world-as-known-in-common by both the authorities and themselves rather than as might be understood by just one side. It was not enough that information is somewhere out there in the world and simply has to be gathered by some clever processes of human agency and technology. Rather, information was relevant when it was seen by all the parties concerned.

These two examples show then two aspects of information. On the one hand, the nature of information work involves the methodical allocation of information into a field of relevance. Connections between the items in this field can be complex and often orthogonal. The second example indicates that it is not simply the nature of the information itself that is crucial to its categorisation and allocation to a field of relevance, it is also whether other parties include that information or not in their field of relevance. Above all, both or rather all parties need to have a common field of relevance – they need to have more or less the same taxonomies of information with the same sets of information. Furthermore, exclusion or as in this case, the putting aside of information until the future, is one of those "natural" categories in the methodic taxonomising activities of these information workers.

14.4 Implications for Information Navigation on the Web

So, with these examples in mind, let us now start to think about a technology that might alter or impact on information work. The World Wide Web obviously comes to fore. One of the problems that is beginning to emerge with the web is that it is difficult for users to be sure of the exact provenance of the information they download. Bound up with this is the problem of how to appropriately interpret and use that information. As noted by Nunberg (1996), the web offers a kind of anarchic information world. Some commentators – web propagandists if you like – claim that it is precisely this that makes the web so exciting: those who access web sites are themselves defining what counts as good information and what is not, and furthermore anyone can set up a web site. But what authors like Nunberg are drawing attention to is how all information is bound up with broader systems of use that are not limited to the precise point of use at any moment in time.

So, for example, to understand what it "means" to use an article in an academic journal cannot be defined by what happens at the point of reading (i.e. the cognitive processes of understanding the contents of the article). Instead it is to understand that activity as one that occurs within broader institutional practice. That is to say, an academic journal article does not just convey information, its meaning is wrapped up in such things as what is known about the status of the journal; whether articles in that journal are reviewed; the status and expertise of those reviewers; and finally what the reader knows about the general impact of the article (i.e. whether it is viewed as an article that is expected to or has had a major impact in the relevant academic community). It is knowledge about these kinds of things that provides the context for "reading".

Now, with the web, similar "systems of interpretation" have not been developed yet, though of course with time they might evolve. At the moment the existence of informal ratings of web sites that are freely available on various bulletin boards is an indication of how web surfers are trying to create for themselves what one might call institutional processes that enable people to determine what is or is not of value. The fact that these ratings are informal is viewed as one of the things that makes the web so exciting: for here is an information world in which the participants are defining for themselves the institutional processes of use.

Nonetheless, it may be that the institutional processes of using the web will slowly become similar to already existing institutional patterns of information use. Thus it might be that the reading of a web site will become analogous to the reading of, say, an article in an academic journal. Readers will assume that the web site they have downloaded has been through processes of review, that the findings in question have been previously disseminated elsewhere, and so on. This seems unlikely, however. A more probable scenario is that the institutional practices that give meaning to and provide a context for the use of the web will be diverse, supporting a whole range of different systems of use and, furthermore, that these will be dependent on other, already existing, systems of interpretation and use.

And this leads us back to the examples of the information work of the Fund's desk officers. In the first example I noted that a desk officer knew enough about the institutional context of particular newspapers to know how to place the information they conveyed. Similarly, if the desk officer were to surf the web to get to sites purporting to present information about Arcadia, he would want to know who produced those sites. In particular, he would want to know things like whether the sites in question were "official party" sites or "genuine opposition" sites. Knowing these differences would enable the desk officer to determine what would be the appropriate use of the information he found or, as I have put it, how to place that information in the field of relevance. What would be key to the desk officer's information work wouldn't be simply the gathering of information, as if he (or she) was "surfing the web" to see what they could find; it would be being able to place that information somewhere. Information would be useful insofar as it could be allocated to some point in the field of relvance.

This leads on to the second example. This illustrated a somewhat different set of issues. It drew attention to the question of getting new information. With regard to the web, it would appear that a desk officer may be able to use the web to locate a great deal of "new" information that might look directly relevant to his or her concerns. But the problem the example highlighted is that a desk officer needs to distinguish between the information he can use in the "here and now" and that which he has to "put aside until the future". This in turn relates to such things as whether that information is viewed as "counting" by the authorities of the member countries themselves. As it happens, and to offer a little bit more emprical material, it may well be that in some cases member authorities disregard some information that a desk officer would prefer they took heed of. Here there are issues to do with the various pressures that a desk officer and the mission he or she is part of can bring to bear on the authorities and what resistance the authorities can offer to such pressure. In the case of Arcadia, the relationship between the authorities and the mission was in part a didactic one. Therefore the mission was in a position whereby it could direct the authorities to take account of information the mission thought appropriate. Even so, in this case and as I say, the mission decided to let the Arcadian authorities make the decision about the new economics institute for themselves.

What this is leading me to say is that what is interesting about new information resources like the World Wide Web is not how individuals like the Fund's desk officers will familiarise themselves with the "information tools" of the web – its various browsers, informal standards and so on – so much as how they will place the information they find thereby within a field of relevance. Partly they will be able to do so because they will already know, by dint of their knowledge of previous information delivery mechanisms, what position some information resource already has. So for example, many newspapers are beginning to release their articles on web sites. (This may be happening with the newspapers in Arcadia, I do not know.) But since the desk officers already know the provenance of that information (i.e. they know something about who owns the newspapers and so on), they will be able to allocate that information to the right place. The medium of its delivery will make no difference to their effective use of that information.

In contrast, they will have considerably more difficulty if they use the web to get new information resources, especially if they do not have sight of what those with whom they want to work have as part of their own (i.e. the other groups') field of relevance. In other words, there is need for the web-based searching activity of desk officers to be somehow linked to the similar processes of those individuals with whom they work within the governments they deal with so that when "new information" is found, it can come into view in a way that is acceptable and useful to all parties. Put another way, increasing access to information for desk officers via the web will be a wasted opportunity if that information is not presented in such a way as to be demonstrably identifiable as part of those relevances that all accept. The information runs the risk of being unusable if desk officers cannot tell how it is perceived and used by those they deal with on missions and elsewhere. There needs to be a way of integrating the navigation work of the Fund's desk officers with the ongoing establishment of a view by the member authorities themselves.

14.5 Conclusion

The main thesis of the chapter has been that the conception of which factors are important to the design of any new "information navigation" technology needs to include the institutional context in which the technology will find its place. What is meant by this context is both what motivates individual information workers by dint of their organisational role, and second, how these motivations are bound up with knowledge about institutional relevance. Key to both these issues is the methodical allocation of information into a field of relevance.

Although the emergence of technologies like the World Wide Web is suggesting to some that the methods for the electronic delivery of information are now so robust and comprehensive that that there will be a radical change in the nature of information gathering and use, I have been implying, then, that the social and institutional processes that have hitherto supported information gathering and use will continue to be fundamental. Furthermore, to the extent that this is so, then the conception of the ways in which "information-based" work practice is supported needs to be broadened. Instead of devising technologies that can support *individuated* information gathering and use, technologies will need to be developed that are supportive of collaboratively defined information in the following way:

- Technologically mediated information needs to indicate the socially organised provenance of that information. This will include indicating such things as which institution produced it; who owns that institution; what is the known perspective of that institution (political view, etc.), and so on.

- It means also devising technology which ensures that when information is used by any one individual, this can be indicated to other parties in the relevant institutional process. Information use needs to be tracked, logged and, ideally made concurrent with its use by others. Or if that concurrency of use will not occur (being rejected for whatever reasons) or if that information is "put on hold to another time", this too needs sharing somehow and made demonstrable.

To reiterate: the thesis has been that information work in organisations is socially organised. Individuals use information as part of their membership of work groups and organisations and indeed as part of society as a whole. Information tools need to be designed with this in mind. And doing so, I think, will shift the basis away from what has been the traditional metaphor underscoring human computer interaction – the individual and the machine – towards a view that asssumes that it is people in roles interacting with the machine; where it is organisations with particular concerns that converse with the machine; where it is, in a phrase, a conception where it is *society* interacting with the machine.

Navigation: Within and Beyond the Metaphor in Interface Design and Evaluation

Rod McCall and David Benyon

15.1 Introduction

Over the last few years we have been exploring an alternative conceptualisation of human–computer interaction (HCI) that sees HCI as the navigation of information spaces (Benyon and Höök, 1997). As a corollary cognitive engineers can be seen as the creators of information artefacts (Benyon, 1998b). The work is closely allied to some interesting developments in HCI, notably the concepts of "social navigation" presented in this volume and in (Munro, Höök and Benyon, 1999), but also to the ideas of distributed cognition (Hollan, Hutchins and Kirsh, 2002). Elsewhere in this volume (notably in the chapters by Spence and Chalmers) the concept of navigation itself is explored. In this chapter we report on our work concerned with exploring how well concepts that have been developed in disciplines such as architecture and urban planning transfer to information spaces.

"Navigation of Information Space" looks at people as inside, and navigating through, information spaces. Evaluating Navigation in Information Spaces, ENISpace, is a software system intended for use at both the design and evaluation stages of a software project that addresses several issues of usability from the "navigation of information space" perspective. ENISpace attempts to inform design and evaluation by providing a "lens" through which designers and evaluators can view a system. This lens focuses the designer's attention on navigational issues. ENISpace provides a rich set of guidelines related to aspects of navigation. The designer or evaluator considers to what extent these guidelines have been met in a particular information space. In this sense, ENISpace is a heuristic approach to evaluation, but the heuristics are focused on navigational issues.

ENISpace divides knowledge of navigation of information space into four sections. *People Within the Space* is concerned with putting people in contact with other people; with social navigation of information space (Munro, Höök and Benyon, 1999; Höök, Benyon and Munro, this volume). *Navigational Methods and Aids* is concerned with the design and deployment of maps or other features. *Conceptual and Physical Structure* focuses on how the physical structure of a space reveals (or not) the underlying conceptual structure. In terms of Dourish's distinction (Dourish, this volume) this corresponds to semantic and spatial navigation. A fourth section of ENISpace also deals with the relationship between these two. *Signs within the environment* provides advice and guidance on signage.

All sections and guidelines within ENISpace are examined against which aspects of navigation they effect. The mode of navigation is one aspect where we distinguish, "wayfinding" (Downs and Stea, 1977) characterised by the user having specific tasks or information needs, "exploration" where they have no explicit task and "object identification" where people are interested in the overall structure and configurations of objects in a space (Benyon and Höök, 1997). Another key aspect is the environmental knowledge gained by the user, which can be considered as landmark, route or survey knowledge (Siegel and White, 1975). Landmark knowledge is where the individual navigates by salient objects within an environment such as a church with a tall spire, route knowledge is when people can only navigate by following specific routes and survey knowledge where people have built up a "mental map" of the space.

ENISpace takes and structures knowledge from other domains that involve navigation and makes it available to designers and evaluators of information spaces. Currently the *Conceptual and Physical Structure* and *Signs within the environment* sections are implemented. In this chapter, we will discuss the experiences of 17 evaluators using ENISpace in the evaluation of the *Glasgow Directory*, an on-line guide to the city of Glasgow (Strathclyde University and The Lighthouse, 1999). Section 15.2 of the chapter provides the background knowledge on which the ENISpace guidelines are based. Section 15.3 describes the software system and how it presents the knowledge to designers. Section 15.4 provides the evaluation and the results. A brief conclusion is included in section 15.5.

15.2 Describing the Built Environment

Our view of cognitive ergonomics is to see people existing in and navigating within the information space as opposed to seeing the person as outside the space (Benyon, 1998a). This is an important change to mainstream thinking in HCI where the emphasis is traditionally on bridging the gulfs of execution and evaluation that are seen to exist between a person and a computer (Norman and Draper, 1986). Taking a view of seeing people as inside information spaces encourages us to look towards disciplines such as the built environment for principles and methods of design of spaces and to consider the conceptual overview that people build up of the environment. Others have considered navigation to be a metaphor for what people do in information spaces. We seek to go beyond navigation as metaphor (Benyon, 2001).

The foundation for navigating within information spaces examined in this chapter is a combination of several approaches to interacting, conceiving and perceiving spaces. These include the cognitive view of environmental mapping, symbolic interactionism (Rapoport, 1982) and social space patterns (Wheeler, 1971). There are, of course, many other disciplines concerned with space and navigation. Architectural design (Passini, 1996) has considered issues of navigation in relation to the construction of buildings, shopping malls and theatres. Chalmers (1999; this volume) looks at the idea of space syntax deriving from the work of Hillier (1989). Neisser (1976) deals with navigation in terms of cognitive maps; the mental representations which people have of their environment and Hutchins discussion of distributed cognition (Hutchins, 1995) and cultural differences have been explored with respect to navigation (Hutchins, 1983). The chapter by Buscher and Hughes in this volume also provides a review of the area. In this section we provide a background to the main issues of space, navigation and support for navigation in terms of signage.

15.2.1 Spaces and Places

Canter and Kenny (1975) suggest that interaction within the built environment is the result of a person's need for space and the desire to use it. They see four styles of interaction: a person interacting with artefacts, a person interacting with another person, groups interacting with artefacts, and groups interacting with other groups. Therefore, in addition to the physical characteristics of the environment, one needs to consider the range of meanings assigned by the people populating the space and the activities they undertake.

The cognitive view, as typified by Lynch (1960), is concerned with the use of internalised mental models during the navigational process and is based around the features of the environment, which aid in the development of environmental knowledge. However, a purely cognitive view ignores certain aspects such as how the meaning of the environment affects its usage and the subsequent mental models created. The problem with these views of navigation is that they are essentially individualistic, objectivist and cognitive. It is assumed that people just have to perceive some feature of the environment and can then develop some "cognitive map" of their environment which enables them to find their way to a specific location. Tversky (1993) has done much to look at cognitive maps of environments and Lynch (1960) has contributed much to the identified features of environments – edges, paths, nodes, districts and landmarks – that people are assumed to perceive.

Urban semioticians, however (e.g. Gottdiener and Lagopoulou, 1986) highlight the limitations of the Lynchian and cognitive perspective. The crucial thing missing from the traditional geographies and urban studies is the failure to appreciate how environments are conceived by people as opposed to simply perceived by people (Perziosi, 1979; Broadbent et al., 1980a; 1980b). As a result the interaction within the space is dependent upon the context in which that artefact and individual are placed as well as previous experiences. In essence, the environment is interpreted as a product of the people, artefacts, past experience, and activities. Norberg-Schultz (1971) describes "to be somewhere" in two dimensions, namely the spatial (cognitive aspects) and the affective aspects (emotional). This is similar to a model of spatial hypertext (Shum, 1990) which indicates that a hypertext object is both locational and attributional in nature. In essence, a spatial phenomenon is at a given location (in terms of distance and direction) and contains attributes which affect its interpretation and meaning.

Rapoport proposes the theory of symbolic interactionism which explains the effect an environment has on a person, as it is a combination of social and environmental aspects; similar to the idea of "being somewhere" (Norberg-Schultz, 1971). He argues that human beings act towards objects based on the meanings, meanings are derived through the social interaction process and finally that meanings are handled and modified through an ongoing interpretative process. This leads him to propose a dramaturgical model, which is similar to that of Laurel (1991) in relation to using theatrical metaphors in computer-based environments. This dramaturgical view sees the actor (navigator) as situated within a stage, which is populated by the setting, other actors and props. This in essence emphasises the view that all plans, actions and behaviours are carried out within a situated context.

The symbolic interactionist viewpoint (Rapoport, 1982) suggests that interaction within an environment is a product of an individuals plans and situated actions, a view also shared in relation to electronic environments by Suchman (1987). This view approaches behaviour from the perspective that it will be effected social, spatial and cultural aspects of an environment. In contrast, the social-space patterns view indicates that interactions are activities, which occur in relation to the nature of spaces, activity spaces and the behavioural fields of the individual and other participants (Wheeler, 1971).

One critical aspect of all these theories is the impact of the social and cultural dimensions on interaction and the subsequent behaviour within an environment. While it is beyond the scope of this paper to examine the social implications in any detail a brief examination will be provided in relation to the various types of spaces as well as environmental features.

15.2.2 Physical and Non-physical Attributes

At a high, abstract level Bacon (1974) suggests that any experience we have of space depends on a number of issues. These include *form and space* (the impact shape, colour, location and other properties have on environment), *defining space* (features which infuse character), *space and time* (each experience is based on partially those preceding it) and *involvement*. These all have an impact on navigation. For example if a person feels a screen is intimidating, lacks character or if the collective experience of the environment is unpleasant, they may be unwilling to continue exploring. Finally, excessive similarity between different areas of an environment can also cause confusion and thus problems with navigation (Abu-Ghazzeh, 1996).

In addition to the high-level aspects, the ability of an individual to perceive, conceive and interact within a space is dependent on a number of factors some of which are described by Lynch (1960, 1981). These factors include the ability to identify objects, structure the environment into stable schema and finally abstract a meaning from it.

A person should be able to recognise and recall an environment or objects, in essence be able to identify its elements. Recognition of artefacts permits an understanding of their use and meaning and may also include a perception of their reliability in any future tasks (Harper, this volume). As a result, the interaction or navigation within the environment the individual begins to develop various schema at different stages to aid in any future interaction or navigation within it.

In order for a person to be able to identify, structure and obtain meaning from an environment they become dependent upon a range of other aspects. These include the ability to correctly map the functional to the spatial aspects of the environment through a process known as congruence (Lynch, 1981). In addition to be able to map the spatial and non-spatial aspects of the environment the individual must become aware of the environmental features through the transparency of the objects and spaces. They also need to obtain a holistic view of the space and finally be able to progressively gain a knowledge of the space through it unfolding to them, rather than via direct presentation, which may cause information overload (Lynch, 1960).

People attach meanings to various aspects of the environment and also use them to describe the environment to others. Several studies have illustrated the importance of meaning. For example, Harrison and Howards (1980) found that meaning can be attached to an environment in various ways either from the perspective of physical functions or emotional/atmospheric responses. In addition, it was observed that people tended to describe an environment more in terms of meaning than physical function. Lynch (1960) also found that meanings were a substantial part of environmental descriptions used by individuals. From the physical viewpoint Rapoport (1982) found that people describe environments in a range of ways such as monotony, sterility, starkness, emphasis, isolation and a feeling of being boxed in.

Existential Space: Places, Paths, Areas and Domains

As a person navigates within a space, that person begins to create a schema of the environment. According to Norberg-Schultz this schema is a relatively stable image of the environment which arises as a result an individual's interaction with artefacts (Norberg-Schultz 1971). He defines this schema as a person's "existential space" and it is based on an interpretation of the environment through a range of perspectives and attributes drawn from perceptual psychology. This results in the environmental knowledge being stored in a cognitive or mental map. These basic attributes are that existential space is a combination of abstract topological information (e.g. proximity, distance, succession, closure and continuity) and concrete elements (the physical appearance of the environment, e.g. a façade on a building). He argues that it is the desire of people to express their existential space through architectural space and that this leads to the environmental properties uncovered by Lynch (i.e. nodes, landmarks, paths, districts, edges). He also argues these aspects are derived from an individual's need to perceive space in relation to centres or places, directions or paths and areas or domains. As a result of, the perception of these three aspects, a human will acquire place knowledge.

As part of the navigation process Norberg-Schultz argues that all individuals seek to subjectively centre themselves in a space, by attempting to reach a focus. As a result, the activity of attempting to find a centre results in the creation of places, which contain actions, activities and social interactions. These places are perceptually distinct relatively static (or invariant) structures within the space. Although the structures are relatively static, the final notion of place may either be expected (i.e. the interpretation perhaps depends upon prior experience) or result in the discovery of a new place.

As should be evident from the preceding discussion a person also needs to be able to move between different places and that places are not situated in isolation. As a result paths are either developed within the physical space or exist in the mental schema of the navigator. Paths within the built environment provide movement channels, in contrast existential space paths are the structures which support the concept of movement through space-time towards a known or unknown goal (Bacon, 1974). They constitute a journey towards the centre and may indicate a range of metaphors, for example, travelling forward to new experiences or back to the past. In contrast with places paths are defined by their linear succession whereas places are defined by their degree of closure.

Finally, spaces (in physical or in existential space) represent either past or future activities and this gives rise to the concepts areas and domains. These are similar to districts (Norberg-Schultz, 1971; Lynch, 1960) and places (Sorkin, 1993). They represent a means of dividing and filling out the existential space into a more coherent structure. In contrast to places, they represent areas to which the individual does not belong and hence provide potential places for activity. An example of a domain is a region within a town or city with which a person is aware of but has not yet undertaken any activity and therefore contains little meaning for them. The domain provides a means to map the environment and is heavily dependent upon the paths and places within the space as a result the perception of a domain is based upon physical, functional, social and cultural factors.

15.2.3 The Physical Environment

There are a number of properties of the built environment that effect the legibility, its meaning and the subsequent effect on environmental knowledge and behaviour.

Bentley and colleagues (1985) provide a series of guidelines and concepts on how to make an environment responsive to the needs of the people undertaking activities. These attempt to address a range of issues which effect the "choices people can make" (Bentley et al., 1985, p. 9) when designing an environment. These are:

- *Permeability*. How the design of the environment affects where people can and cannot go.
- *Variety*. The range of uses available to people.
- *Legibility*. The ability of people to understand the opportunities afforded by the environment.
- *Robustness*. The degree to which people can use a place for different purposes.
- *Visual appropriateness*. The detailed appearance of the environment and how this makes people aware of the available options.
- *Richness*. The choice of sensory experiences afforded to the users.

361

- *Personalisation*. The ability of the individual to customise the environment.

Permeability is critical to navigation and is essentially how the environment supports movement of individuals. The availability and use of routes (or path structures) and nodes are an aspect in the creation of environmental knowledge. Permeability exists on two levels, initially the physical existence of the routes and secondly the visual appearance given to the routes (Bentley et al., 1985).

Permeability is also dependent on a number of environmental factors and behaviours. One of the initial aspects is that of public and private space. Initially the paths must provide some form of cue as to what constitutes either of these types of space. In addition to providing this cue, it must also provide a link to the degree of privacy required by any particular route; this can be provided through the appearance of the route itself and can be enhanced through the use of entrances, which provide an interface between the wider environment and the private space.

Bentley et al. suggest that permeability depends on a number of factors, including the connectivity of routes and the nature of the environment itself. For example, segregated and hierarchical layout structures typically reduce permeability within an environment as they force the individual to take a certain path. In addition to segregation and hierarchical structures permeability is also reduced when neighbourhood block sizes are increased. Therefore in order obtain maximum permeability the environment should contain the smallest block size possible, connect as many of the smaller routes as possible to the main routes (roads), connect new routes to the local surroundings and finally be based around the usage patterns of its users.

15.2.4 Signs within the Environment

Signs are one of the main features of the built environment (Spencer and Reynolds, 1977; Bittner, 1992). They provide a range of cues to support navigation and other aspects of being. Signs have played a critical role in the environment within many cities as well as within university campuses, transit systems, banks, city halls and libraries (Spencer and Reynolds, 1977; Pollet and Haskell, 1979) and have been used for a variety of purposes by car drivers, as well as pedestrians (Finke, 1994). Typical examples of uses include directional cues to attract people to specific areas of a city. Signs have also been used in several cities and university campuses to enhance the vitality of the area. For example, the University of Maryland, Baltimore, attempted to infuse additional character into its campus by commissioning a themed range of graphically pleasing and perceptually stimulating designs. The value of signs and other aesthetic attributes was further highlighted by Ang and his colleagues (Ang et al., 1997). They indicate that aesthetic and spatial layout have some effect on the pleasure (favourable feelings) and arousal (level of excitement) experienced by users of banking facilities and may subsequently affect their approach-avoidance behaviour towards specific features within the environment (e.g. a cash point). As a result assuming an environment employs an appropriate signage strategy it should result in an increased usage of its features and subsequently aid in the process of deriving a meaning for aspects of the environment. Passini (1996) indicated that wayfinding is more accurate when signs are "readily and accurately perceived". Therefore, signs are not only a method of providing directional cues but are also aid in the identity of areas within cities, neighbourhoods or other complexes.

We identify three categories of sign: informational (providing information on objects, users and activities), directional (providing route or survey information) and warning and reassurance (providing information on the actual or potential actions within an environment). Within these categories exist a range of other sign types, for example, instructional, location, identity, advertising/public relations signs and building signs (Abu-Ghazzeh, 1997). Instructional signs provide "how-to" information to people, location signs can exist within directional or information sign types and provide location information. These are somewhat similar to identity signs which identify individual objects. In a study of signage in Amman, Jordan (Abu-Ghazzeh, 1997), it was also noted that, within the information signs category, two types existed which also provided information. These were advertising (e.g. a bill board advertising a specific product) or building signs placed on the exterior of a building and indicate its name or type of business. Advertising or building signs can exist alongside the basic types of sign and within a range of contexts – for example, within the external or internal built environment. A typical example would be signs outside a library providing directional information, then the placing of an informational/direction sign at the library entrance to indicate arrival and to reassure the users that they are at the right location.

Directional signs provide a range of cues to aid people when travelling a specific route, orientating themselves within the whole environment (Finke, 1994) or providing a direction (not via a specific route) to a particular destination. An example of the latter may be a sign that a cathedral in a town centre is one mile to the east, without actually specifying the exact directional instructions required. Sign hierarchies support the provision of specific route information; give indications of the destination (initial encounter), as well as other options, then provide clear information on when the decision has to be taken to take that specific route (transition) and, finally, a clear indication of arrival to reassure the navigator. (Such principles are advocated by Downs and Stea, 1977.) The sign

363

hierarchies contained within the Madison traffic system made use of a range of other cues to aid in the driver's orientation, e.g. each route made use of a distinct icon and colour. As a result, the driver is able to recognise the route without having to spend a significant amount of time reading the signs. Although sign hierarchies are useful for navigation care should be taken to ensure that the navigator remains oriented within the whole environment and not only that particular route. As well as supporting specific routes the signs also have to consider the types of routes or destinations to which they are alerting navigators. The signs should indicate whether the outcome is a major or minor destination, and this applies equally to internal (Selfridge, 1979; Pollet and Haskell, 1979) as well as external environments. The precise definition of major/minor will depend upon the nature of the environment and the important places or tasks to be conducted within it. Positioning also plays an important role in the effectiveness of directional signs with the key aspect being that the signs should be positioned at decision points. Selfridge provides a range of possible decision points including entrances, exits, intersections, stairs and elevators.

Informational signs provide additional complementary cues within the environment. There are a range of potential information signs including instructional, locational, identity, advertising/public relations (Marks, 1979) and building signs. The range of informational signs usually results in them containing combinations of different factors and complementing existing directional signs. Typical uses of information signs include the labelling of a building or type of business, provision of event information, labelling of an area inside a building (e.g. an issue desk in a library), to assist in navigation within a transportation system and to clearly identify areas of cities. As a result a range of techniques have been used to provide information to navigators. For example, in Cincinnati and Knoxville information points were erected in street areas; in the case of the latter they provide a stopping off point for people to relax in what was otherwise a busy environment (Finke, 1994). The City of Cincinnati's informational signs included wayfinding maps, building labels and general information. As an aid to orientation, various information points were placed around the city. These consisted of wayfinding maps as well as pictures of nearby buildings (or landmarks), allowing for easier recognition of the landmarks. There are, however, a range of important issues within any informational sign system. For example, Finke notes that there are problems with designing maps which are effective and care is required when deciding on the type to be used. Although signs may be used to provide specific information, they can also be used to aid in the environmental vitality and to provide orientation cues. As an example, in Renton, USA, sculptures were added as part of the sign system. They also had the effect of placing a landmark or anchor point within the environment thereby aiding in orientation. Finally, the implementation of informational signs requires careful consideration of a range of issues, including consistency, quality, and the number and importance of signs and the type of environment in which the sign is being used.

Warning and reassurance signs complement the informational signs by providing specific information. In the built environment these may include hazards, warning about impending crossing points or dynamic information indicating that a course of action may be fatal. Reassurance signs provide feedback to people to indicate that their actions have been successful.

Design and Placement Issues

The design and placement of signs is critical to their overall success, regardless of which group they fall under. Abu-Ghazzeh (1997) defines three high-level variables of environmental and sign design, which are essential for navigation; these are *identification* (enhances ability to identify space), *differentiation* (sign types are clearly differentiated in some way) and *distinctiveness* (the signs are distinct from the environment). He concludes that navigation can be aided by emphasising the perceptual variables within signs and this will improve environment learning. As a subset of these categories two further issues arise: *legibility* (the ability to differentiate the characters or symbols on the sign) and *readability* (the ability to correctly interpret the content of the sign). As signs are beneficial in allowing navigators to understand the *identity* and *structure* of the environment they should as far as possible complement the underlying design, layout (including decision points) and functional importance of the space. Typical methods of doing this involve using specific colours and icons to represent different objects or locations within the environment. In the latter case libraries have used colour-coded informational signs which corresponded to the colours used in different areas within the library (Downs, 1979; Selfridge, 1979); this provides a clear link between the environment and the signs therefore aids in identification and navigation.

The identification and readability of signs and spaces is also further enhanced by consistency of layout, size, wording and colour for similar sign types, while making use of inconsistency to aid in identification of different sign types. Also, in common with user interface design, external consistency with sign systems in other cities is also advocated. The readability of signs is further enhanced by a number of critical aspects including minimising the crowding of signs and also the use of clear, short and simple language. The third aspect, distinctiveness, implies that the sign system should be separable from the environment and visible from a range of angles while, at the same time, complementing exiting architectural styles. An example of these aspects of distinctiveness can be found in Philadelphia where the sign systems were designed and placed to not only complement the environment but also to be visible through the use of design and placement (Finke, 1994).

End Users

There is also a need to understand the effect signs have on various different types of user. In one study by Spencer and Reynolds (1977), it was found that an improved sign system within a library benefited people who were either familiar or unfamiliar with the environment. The study also found that people who were less familiar with the environment used signs less frequently than familiar users and experienced more navigational problems. As a result, it is perhaps possible to draw from this that inexperienced users of an environment do need to be encouraged to make use of signs and, as a by-product of this, improve their navigational performance. In addition to the types of users, the time available to people within an environment is also important when deciding on the location, positioning and content within signs. For example, car drivers have on average less time to read a sign than pedestrians, and as a result of this one city designed two separate sign systems.

Problems with Signs

Although signs may be a substantial part of any navigation system in the built environment they also suffer from some inherent problems. In certain stressful situations, perceptual narrowing occurs. Perceptual narrowing is where people reduce the amount of information they attend to and focus on what they deem to be the most relevant. In addition to this, road traffic accidents have been caused by a combination of stress and information overload on the driver as a result of too many signs. This may be a result of visual field of the driver decreasing during the stressful period as well as during the limits on short-term memory (Abu-Ghazzeh, 1997). Signs may also be seen to contradict some aspects of the strategies people adopt when structuring survey knowledge of an environment. For example, research has suggested that individuals seek to reduce the amount of information in their cognitive maps with the aim of reducing information overload (Downs, 1979), making order from a chaotic map (Rapoport, 1982) and placing an order on the structure. Therefore, as signs are an addition to the environment they may either be increasing the information overload on the user or may simply be ignored.

15.2.5 Conclusions

This review of design knowledge coming from the built environment points to a number of important features. Firstly, places demand some semantic, or affective, attributes. We might agree on certain significant features in the environment (such as nodes, edges, paths, etc.), or indeed we might not. But whether or not we agree, it is clear that people perceive types of space and associate certain feelings or meanings with them. Having a sense of place will aid navigation. There are good guidelines for defining physical aspects of spaces. In addition to those discussed here, Büscher and Hughes (this volume) discuss Alexandrine patters and Chalmers (this volume) discusses Hillier's work in more detail. The issue for us is not particularly which features best describe environments; it is that we can find and use such descriptions in the design and evaluation of information spaces.

We have also seen that sign systems represent one of the major tools for aiding navigation and, as part of this, appear also to aid in increasing the approach to (or use of) services. However as sign systems are integrated with the whole environment there is a need to understand the range of users (Passini, 2000), appropriate number of signs, environmental appearance as well as potential major and minor destinations (or locations) and objectives of the providers (i.e. aiming to increase usage of certain facilities). Finally, assuming that the sign system is well designed it should be easily recognisable and allow its users to follow it with confidence (Wechsler, 1979).

15.3 Overview of ENISpace

ENISpace takes this knowledge and experience from the built environment and packages it in a way that is suitable for evaluators of information spaces. Currently ENISpace is a prototype software system that provides access to guidelines derived from the above analysis. The guidelines are included as an Appendix. Evaluators are encouraged to consider whether a particular guideline is applicable within the environment being evaluated. ENISpace provides ways for the evaluators to rate the frequency and severity of any usability problems arising from applying a guideline. Evaluators are also able to supply comments in relation to each guideline. The system provides some basic reporting facilities which display information on the frequency and severity of usability problems. The reporting system provides a mechanism to view summary information which relates to problems in any one aspect of the navigation process, for example exploration or wayfinding. The system also provides an integrated browser which can be used to view further information and examples in relation to each guideline. This information can be accessed from within the data entry screen (Figure 15.1) as well as from within some of the reports which the software produces.

The software currently implements the sections related to *signs within the environment* and *conceptual and physical structure* within the space.

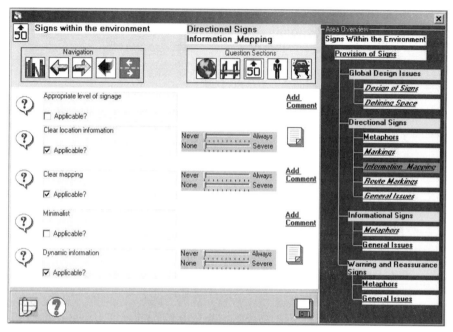

Figure 15.1 The ENISpace data entry screen containing (from left to right) online help, the guidelines and the applicability box, the frequency and severity indicators, the comment entry field and the overview map.

In addition to providing the basic guidelines the software allows the entering of data (Figure 15.1), loading and saving of data, use of on-line help via in integrated web browser (Figure 15.2), book marking of guidelines or on-line documentation as well as the creation of basic reports (Figure 15.3). Data entry consists of an initial profile of the environment, which is not currently used for any reporting purposes. In addition the evaluator can provide information on the frequency and severity of problems encountered; further to this they can also provide comments in relation to each guideline. The on-line documentation can either be accessed via the question mark next to a specific guideline (see Figure 15.3), via a bookmark or by opening up the help browser. Finally, the reporting features allow the creation of reports based on the guideline sections or types of navigation (e.g. wayfinding or exploration), and the evaluator can also set ranges within the reports which set minimum and maximum levels of frequency and severity.

The guidelines themselves are broken down into four main areas (see the right-hand side of Figure 15.1). Global design issues for all signs include aspects related to the design of signs, e.g. whether they are visible. The second group defining space provides two guidelines asking the user as to whether the signs aid in defining (e.g. its physical features) and

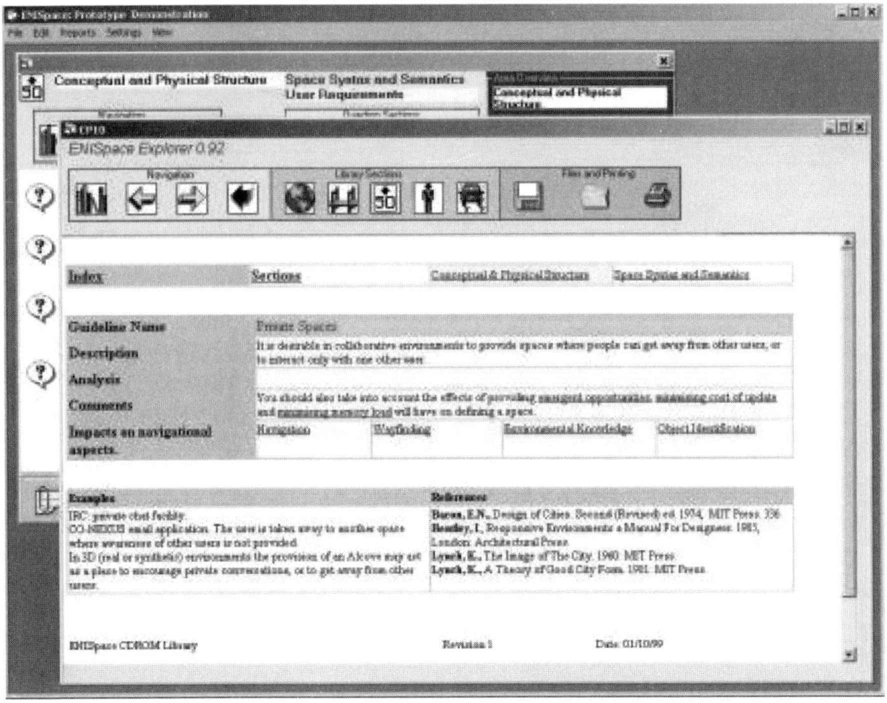

Figure 15.2 The ENISpace browser which contains supporting documentation for each guideline.

articulating (e.g. mood, ambience, etc.) the space. The remaining three sections cover issues specific to the individual sign types, included in each sign types is one part specifically covering metaphors.

The directional signs section covers a range of aspects from the markings on the signs in relation to alerting people to distance, time and various routes. In addition, it covers how the signs map to the environment, i.e. is there an appropriate number and do they map to the features within the environment. The route markings section covers information relating to making people aware of specific named routes and their journey along them; *initial encounter, approach, arrival*. In addition, it covers whether individual routes are clearly marked and transitions between different routes. Finally, the general issues section relates specifically to whether the directional signs aid in orientation within the whole space and not just individual routes, provide easy exit to the whole environment and whether they are appropriate for users tasks.

The information signs section is primarily concerned with providing information on other users, dynamic information and the markings of individual objects and locations and whether the informational signs integrate with other signs. Finally, warning and reassurance signs cover specifically information relating to the prevention of errors by users.

369

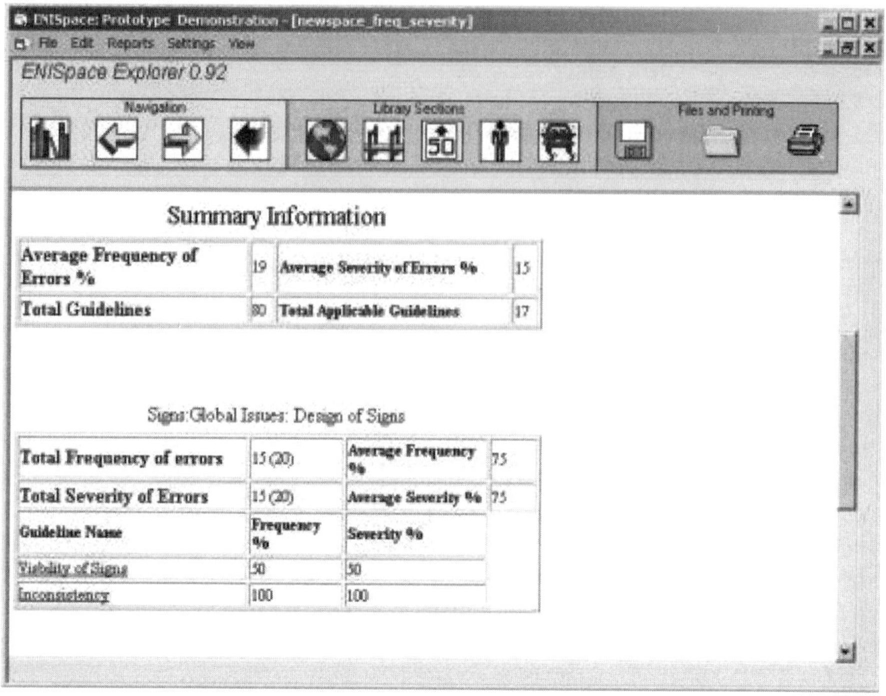

Figure 15.3 A sample ENISpace report containing an overview of the frequency and severity of problems in relation to each group and individual guidelines.

15.3.1 Conceptual and Physical Structure

The conceptual and physical structure guidelines (see Appendix) are based around the concepts highlighted and are broken down into a range of categories. Three high-level sections are provided: *Space syntax and semantics, Landmarks* and *Path/route structures*. The space syntax and semantics section contains three groups. Those covering *user experience* such as the need to minimise memory load and make customisation easy. The second subgroup, *definition and articulation*, relates to defining and articulating spaces, this includes aspects such as defining important spaces, defining related or different spaces and providing cues to aid in articulating the space. The final subgroup, *opportunities and activities*, covers a range of aspects relating to allowing opportunities to emerge through use and also whether the environment supports a range of tasks (variety). The landmarks section covers a range of issues ranging from the visual presentation of landmarks from the perspective of function and content to their support for users, orientation and route awareness. Finally, the path/route structures section examines the environmental (non-sign) markings of paths and routes within the environment, the

370

activities the path/route support and whether the markings support *initial encounter, approach* and *arrival*. Finally the awareness subgroup within paths and route structures covers aspects related to how the path/route structures are integrated with signs, other environmental features and whether the act of travelling along the path or route aids in awareness of features or other users within the environment.

15.3.2 ENISpace Software

The ENISpace interface is designed using its own guidelines in order to aid in navigation through the guidelines and by providing clear cues within the space. Informational and directional signs are provided in the form of an overview map at the right side of guidelines (see Figure 15.1). The interface additionally adopts an "information point" metaphor which contains an overview of the guidelines available within that section and also an indication as to which sections the evaluator has already viewed. The interface also adopts a browser style interface allowing for navigation both back and forward through the screens already visited within the system. The browser metaphor is further extended through the use of a bookmarking facility which can be used to provide shortcuts to any screen within either the software (e.g. guidelines) or the on-line help system. The bookmarking facility also permits the addition of icons to attach to each bookmarks. Consistency is used thoughout. For example, the signs section is consistently marked with a road traffic sign. In addition, colour backgrounds are used to provide districts within the interface to indicate their purpose and or final goal if an option is selected. For example, all navigation (browser style) options are placed on a light grey background, the on-line documentation options for each section (e.g. signs) are on an orange background whereas the same sections within the guidelines are provided on a light green background. In addition, colour is used to differentiate the information point (map area), and while the authors acknowledge that this may lead to the interface looking less professional than commercial applications, it does allow for quick identification of where the options are located within the interface. Finally, the conceptual and physical structure of the space are highlighted through the clear separation of the sets of guidelines and the provision of localised map (information point) for each section.

15.4 Evaluating ENISpace

In order to see the utility of the ideas embodied by ENISpace, we undertook an evaluation of the system. Recall that the concept behind ENISpace is to provide a "lens" through which designers and evaluators

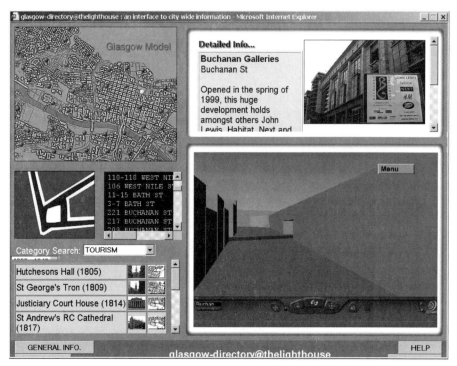

Figure 15.4   The main Glasgow Directory screen with various options available.

can look at software systems. We wanted to see the extent to which principles derived from accepted design principles from the built environment transfer to electronic information systems. We were aware of some flaws in the version of ENISpace that was to be evaluated; notably overlapping guidelines and an overly complex structure, but we wished to focus on the principles of transferring knowledge from the built environment, packaging it into a software system and making it available to evaluators.

Seventeen students on a final year HCI module used ENISpace to evaluate a software system called the Glasgow Directory. The Glasgow Directory is a multi-paned systems that provides the local population, tourists and other people with information about Glasgow It consists of six screen areas (see Figure 15.4) these are, clockwise from top left, (i) the interactive map, (ii) a building description complete with photograph, (iii) interactive 3D VRML world, (iv) the category search, (v) a street finder and, at the bottom of the screen, (vi) various user options. One of the principal aspects of the environment is to allow users to locate and search for a variety of attractions using various methods.

A description of each screen element in Figure 15.4 is as follows:

- *Clickable map.* The map contains a number of small dots, each representing a tourist attraction the user can click on. The VRML world and building description displays are updated to represent what the user has selected. If the user has already selected an attraction based on one of the other search options it is represented as a yellow dot, whereas those not selected are red.

- *Building details.* This option displays a small piece of information about the selected building, a still picture and, where available, a link is given. The link if selected by the user will open up a QuickTime VR model (QTVR) of an interior of a particular building. This QTVR model is displayed where the still picture was displayed and the user navigates the model via mouse and keyboard.

- *Interactive 3D VRML model.* This initially displays a 3D plan view of the region which contains the attraction selected by the user. From here, the user can "fly" into the region and walk around using keys or mouse. In addition, a small pop-up menu is provided which displays a list of landmarks within the 3D model; if the user selects one he is automatically transported to it. The region displayed is based on the options selected by the user from the clickable map, category or street search.

- *Category search.* Category search allows users to search for buildings by type (e.g. banks) and/or by date, which are selected from two pull-down menus. When the query has been run the results are displayed below the pull-down menus. The user can view the building in the context of the full 3D region and/or view the building details. Once the building has been selected the content of the interactive map, street finder, detailed building view and interactive 3D model are modified accordingly.

- *Street finder.* Street finder allows the user to search for a specific tourist attraction (not individual street names). Street finder displays information on a specific street, e.g. what tourist attractions it contains and, by the use of links, allows the user to update the views in other parts of the Glasgow Directory.

- *User options.* The main option provided by this panel is the database search option. The database search allows users to search for buildings, architects and streets within the city. The user can click on the displayed results and the street finder, interactive map and 3D model are updated. The database option also allows the user jump to certain attractions via the use of links, which are provided in a pull down menu. Some a other options are also provided, for example restart and general help.

Due to the restriction on screen real estate various panels within the browser change function depending on the options selected by the user.

373

Figure 15.5 The data guideline section (from left to right) the icon for the reference library, applicability check box, guideline, sliders and finally the comment icon. The comment icon indicates the user has stored a comment.

As typical examples: if the user selects the database option the QTVR window is replaced with a new panel which contains the various database options; if the user selects the QTVR movie link from the building details option, the panel is replaced with the QTVR movie; and if the user selects the general help option the interactive 3D model is replaced with another information display.

15.4.1 Method of Evaluation

The evaluators were asked to produce a report on the usability of the Glasgow Directory using ENISpace as the method of evaluation. The evaluators first familiarised themselves with the Glasgow Directory and then worked through a number of representative scenarios of use. For example, the data entry screen in Figure 15.1 shows an evaluator considering the aspects of information mapping within directional signs. They are asked to consider whether there is an appropriate number of signs, whether they map on well to the underlying environment, whether they were minimalist and finally whether they contained dynamic information. The box is checked if the guideline is applicable, a slider allows the evaluator to record a value for the guideline (see Figure 15.5), and a comment can be added. At the end of the evaluation, the details of each guideline recorded as applicable were printed out. Evaluators also produce a summary report when the evaluation was complete.

15.4.2 Results

The aim of the analysis was to see the extent to which knowledge from the built environment transfers to information spaces. A secondary aim was to look at ENISpace itself and to identify the types and frequency of problems being uncovered by the use of ENISpace. We were aware that there was overlap in the guidelines and that there was likely to be some ambiguity. Accordingly, both the summary reports and the detailed reports were examined. In Table 15.1, S refers to the number of summary reports and P refers to the number of instances the problem was recorded in the detailed guideline reports. So, for example, "Lack of

Table 15.1   Eight most common usability problems

Issue	S	P
1. Lack of signs/poor quality of signs/signs being obscured	15	53
2. No landmarks or little detail/no buildings of interest marked	10	28
3. Lack of details/buildings difficult to distinguish/buildings need texture	9	41
4. No back option	14	12
5. Several spaces are hidden (or change function)	11	15
6. No indication of direction/problems maintaining directional orientation	5	20
7. Approach and arrival not clear	2	17
8. Lots of functions stop short of what is expected (clear mapping)	1	14

signs" was mentioned in 15 out of the 17 summary reports and in 53 of the detailed guideline reports. Usability issues are ranked according to a combination of how often the issue appeared in these two forms.

The results demonstrated some variation, but also some consistency. A much more detailed analysis of the data has been undertaken than can be provided here, including a thorough keyword analysis of all the guideline reports and the summary reports. Here we will concentrate on the eight usability problems that were most highly ranked by our evaluators. They are shown in Table 15.1 and are discussed below.

Lack of Signs/Poor Quality of Signs/Signs being Obscured

"Some informational signs are not visible so the names of the information spaces do not show up at the start." (Evaluator 7, guideline: visibility of signs)

"There should be signs in the world that would support easier navigation." (Evaluator 14, summary report)

The most frequently identified problem related to the provision and quality of signs within the Glasgow Directory, in particular and as would be expected within the 3D VRML model. A number of evaluators agreed that the current system does not provide a sufficient level of directional signage within the environment. The problem was particularly relevant in relation to the 3D VRML model where it was noted that the environment only provided balloons to indicate where an object is located. In addition, these balloons do not make use of clear colour metaphors and, as the user approaches them, they become smaller, thereby providing a confusing directional cue. The evaluators indicated that the poor quality of signage and other problems relating to path and route structures resulted in the possibility for users to become disorientated.

375

No Landmarks or Little Detail/No Buildings of Interest Marked

"The landmarks in VRML are hard to distinguish from other buildings."
(Evaluator 5, guideline: landmarks and route awareness)

"Once within the VRML information space landmarks are not clearly
separable from other objects" (Evaluator 5, guideline: landmarks
clearly separate from other objects)

"When the model is loaded up there are no landmarks highlighted [...]
just a group of buildings which don't symbolise what type of streets
and landmarks." (Evaluator 7, summary report)

"In 3D the image structure is not always recognisible." (Evaluator 14,
guideline: clarity of function and content)

Problems with poor landmarking was indicated by 10 evaluators which
in turn commented on the problem on 28 occasions within the raw
reports, all related to the 3D VRML model. The evaluators commented
that it is important for landmarks to be visually separate from one
another, key ones were not enhanced, general made clear and that where
this was not the case users may have problems with navigation. Initially
users may experience problems with route awareness as they are unable
to map the positions of landmarks into any route model they may possess of the environment. In addition they may also experience problems
as the landmarks which are provided do not contain any cues as to their
function or use. Finally, in common with the concept of external consistency users may also experience problems because they expect a model
of a built environment to contain clear landmarks whereas the Glasgow
Directory provides no such cues.

In addition to the basic problems with landmarking several evaluators
also indicated the need to integrate any sign system, with landmarks and
the environment at large. They indicated that as the present environment
does not provide clear marking of objects via signs and that the level of
signage is inappropriate users may again suffer from problems.

Lack of Details/Buildings Difficult to Distinguish/Buildings Need Texture

"Building should be colour coded to distinguish them from Landmarks"
(Evaluator 7, summary report)

"All buildings in the VRML model are grey, it is impossible to know what
you are looking at." (Evaluator 8, summary report)

A number of evaluators highlighted problems with the VRML world
being too similar and not containing enough additional information.
Although some of the issues and comments mentioned are similar in

relation to landmarks the intention here is to discuss the environment as whole and not landmarks specifically. A total of 9 evaluators commented within the summary reports that the VRML world was too similar, the problem was also highlighted on 41 occasions within the raw reports. The evaluators highlighted particular problems such as the lack of colour and texture used within the environment which in turn made it difficult to identify buildings or areas within the VRML model. In addition, several evaluators indicated this lack of colour and texture also impacted on their ability to identify paths or routes within the VRML model, with several commenting that paths and routes were not clearly identifiable within the space as they were not marked in any sensible or unique way. The problem was emphasised further due to the lack of signs or poor quality of signs contained within the environment resulting in further problems with identifying building or locations. In common with the problems relating to landmarks, several evaluators indicated that the balloons used are too confusing to understand, or that the fact there is no key provided was causing problems.

No Back Option

"[In the information display space the user] cannot go back to previous information displayed." (Evaluator 9, summary report)

"[In the database search the user] cannot go back to the previous space." (Evaluator 9, summary report)

"There is no way of getting back [in] the 3D information space without navigating through the route I previously took." (Evaluator 15, summary report)

ENISpace provides a number of guidelines relating to the provision of paths and named routes within an environment. The princip being that where clearly marked paths and routes exist within an environment the navigational process will be clearer and therefore less confusing for the user. These concepts appear to have been addressed and agreed upon in this particular study as 14 evaluators indicated that the environment lacked or poorly implemented a back feature thereby causing usability problems. In addition, the problem was highlighted 12 times within the ENISpace guidelines. Within the overall ranking of usability issues addressed through ENISpace this particular issue was mentioned in second and fifth place in respect of the comments made in the summary reports and individual guidelines.

The lack of a back feature was highlighted in relation to a number of aspects of the interface including the QTVR model, VRML and the advanced database search. Initially the lack of such a feature causes problems with providing the most efficient route for a user to get to their desired destination and as a result, this combined with the poor path structure is likely to result in navigational problems. In addition, the problem also arose as a conventional browser would allow an easy to use back option, however the Glasgow Directory did not afford this function, thereby frustrating the user.

Several Spaces are Hidden (or Change Function)

"The space is regularly invaded with different information." (Evaluator 13, summary report)

"In some cases another information space is destroyed and placed by something new." (Evaluator 14, guideline: conceptual and physical structure → Clear approach)

"The designers have compromised screen space by hiding some information spaces and sharing screen areas." (Evaluator 17, summary report)

Eleven evaluators indicated problems with areas of the screen being hidden and only visible when selecting specific options or that screen areas appeared to unexpectedly change function. The evaluators indicated the problem under various guidelines related to the conceptual and physical structure of the space. The most frequently indicated problem concerned the database search tool, which is currently hidden by other options. The comments indicate that there is a problem with the definition of spaces in relation to other options, in particular how users may become confused when screen objects change. In addition, the comments would suggest there is a need to clearly articulate the space so that options can be discovered, even if they are not clearly visible at the outset. Thereby allowing users to correctly formulate a physical and conceptual view of the space and therefore navigate more effectively.

No Indication of Direction /Problems Maintaining Directional Orientation

"It is hard to tell which is North, South, East or West." (Evaluator 13, summary report)

"It should be noted that the North, South, East and West metaphors are missing." (Evaluator 17, summary report)

Five evaluators indicated there was a lack of directional signs within the VRML model. The problem was also highlighted 20 times ranking it fourth in terms of the number of times the issue was identified. Finally, the comments in relation to this problem were attributed to 11 individual guidelines.

ENISpace identified a number of usability problems within the environment. Initially evaluators indicated there were no generic directional signs (i.e. North, South, East and West) within the 3D environment. This resulted in a situation where the evaluators (and potential users) are likely to experience problems in estimating their current direction of movement, thereby causing difficulty with orientation. The evaluators also highlighted the need to integrate any directional signs with those providing information on the users current location within the environment.

Approach and Arrival are not Clear

"I felt that this was not achieved well." (Evaluator 14, guideline: conceptual and physical structure → clear approach)

ENISpace advocates the clear provision of paths and route structures within environment, in particular how these aid in route based navigation but also in gaining overall awareness of the information space. Although this particular issue was highlighted in only two summary reports, its importance is perhaps emphasised by the fact that it was identified 17 times. In addition a related issue, *building route knowledge is not possible*, was highlighted a similar number of times. Taking these two similar issues together it is clear there is a need for obvious path and route structures.

In common with other issues the majority of the problems highlighted were in relation to the VRML model. A number of evaluators indicated that the signs were either illegible, not provided or did not provide enough feedback therefore making it unclear when a user initially encounters a route and similarly on approach to a desired destination. In common with this, the conceptual and physical structure also appeared to contain problems, with problems being caused due to the lack of clarity of landmarks, which were common destinations. Further to this, users expressed problems in relation to lack of approach, arrival and within route marking cues. The problems were further complicated by responses indicating users may have difficulty in building up route knowledge. In respect of this six evaluators indicated that the VRML model did not provide clear path structures thereby making it difficult to get to the desired building or landmark. Thereby causing problems not only with the physical navigation but also landmark and route awareness issues. The lack of paths or routes was also highlighted in relation to a number of other guidelines in both the signs and conceptual and physical structure guidelines.

The type and number comments strongly indicate there is sufficient correlation between the ability to navigate within the environment and the provision of clear path and route structures. In addition there is some indication that evaluators understood the differences between the provision of paths and specific named routes.

Lots of Functions Stop Short of What is Expected

"Clicking on the picture you would expect the 3D model to update, it does not." (Evaluator 8, guideline: differentiation in paths)

A number of issues were raised in relation to functions within the Glasgow Directory not providing a clear mapping between what they expected and the actual outcome. The problem was highlighted 14 times, in 11 different guidelines however was only highlighted within one summary report.

The usability problems were primarily confined to the street finder tool and VRML world. The problems highlighted would suggest the need for clear signage in particular in relation to providing clear route information from the outset, for example clearly indicating what the final destination will be. The evaluators indicated a number of problems with the street finder tool when used in combination with the VRML model, typically that the sign systems did not clearly indicate that the users are not taken to their selected destination but a general area within the VRML model. In some cases this may lead to them having to manually navigate the world. This conflicts with the sign design concepts which state that routes should be clearly marked indicating the final destination. As a by-product of this, further issues in relation to the use of markings and metaphors were also highlighted. Finally, the evaluators also indicated problems with correctly conceptualising the space. In particular when users previous experiences are taken into account, which would indicate that user should be able to click on buildings to gain further information or that by clicking on a street that they should be able to directly go there.

15.5 Discussion

The results of this evaluation offer some evidence that the navigation of information space paradigm on which ENISpace is based is useful. Evaluators were able to look at usability from the perspective of ENISpace which has been designed to capture aspects of good practice taken from the built environment. In short, information spaces do share many of the features of geographical spaces and navigation in information spaces does share characteristics with navigation in geographical space (Spence, this volume). This is significant in that we see navigation in information space is not simply a metaphor for traditional HCI; it is a useful paradigm (Benyon, 2001). Elsewhere we have developed a dynamic site map for a web site based on Gordon Cullen's theory of landscape

(Wilmes and Benyon, unpublished) and used the ENISpace guidelines to design a 3D world (McCall and Benyon, 2000).

A natural question to ask is whether the problems identified would have been picked up by other evaluation methods. Of course much is down to the evaluator and the insight which he or she has, but we would hope that the method, or the orientation provided by ENISpace, did have some impact. Certainly in our experience a cognitive walkthrough (Polson et al., 1992) evaluation will identify potential problems which can be missed by a heuristic evaluation (Nielsen, 1999). We see little evidence, however, that Nielsen's heuristics would find the same issues as have been identified with ENISpace. The same is true for cognitive walkthrough Evaluation methods from 3D worlds such as VRUSE (Kawalsky, 1999), Kaur's method (Kaur, 1998) and COVEN (1997), do cover some aspects of navigation but not extensively. For example, navigation only accounts for two questions in VRUSE, asking if the user felt disorientated within the environment.

Although there are a range of methodologies that can be used for the design and evaluation of electronic environments, they all ignore important aspects of the navigational process. Finally, although they can all to a limited degree provide some guidance on navigation they do not provide specific information on design features which can aid in navigation such as signs or landmarks.

The study of the Glasgow Directory indicated that while evaluators did highlight relevant issues the current version of ENISpace does require improvement. These improvements relate to the wording of the guidelines (see Appendix) and supporting documentation. There is also a need to enhance the report generation system to provide a more diverse and practical range of reports. There is also a need to provide a better method of rating and assessing navigational problems in the systems being evaluated. However, it should be noted that by far the most useful evaluation information came from the comments rather than the scores assigned to the guidelines. Clearly, therefore, any enhancements in ENISpace should focus on being able to extract and report on this information more effectively.

The motivation of developing the navigation of information space view is not simply to have another view of HCI. In the past, poor usability was dealt with by gradually educating people in the interpretation of computer systems. Usability principles said "know the user" so that designs could be oriented to the sorts of interpretation that a relatively homogeneous group of people could be expected to possess. Twenty-first century HCI is not going to be like that. The typical view of how people interact with computers has been based, primarily, on a cognitive psychological analysis which sees the user as outside the computer. People have to translate their intentions into the language of the computer and have to interpret the computer's response in terms of how

381

Table 15.2 Conceptual and physical structure guidelines

Space Syntax and semantics	
User experience	*Minimise memory load*
	Emergent opportunities
	Minimise cost of update
	Relate to user experiences
Definition and articulation	*Define Important Spaces*
	Define spaces with different functions or requirements
	Clearly define spaces with related functions
	Articulate spaces with specific emotional intent
	Mutual exclusion
	Appropriate mapping of physical to conceptual stucture
Opportunities and activities	*Variety*
	Private spaces
	Robustness
	Clearly indicate size of space (X)
Landmarks	
Information provided	*Clearly visible*
	Clarity of function and content
	Clearly separable from other objects
	Emphasise key landmarks
Users	*Allow orientation*
	Appropriate number
	Functionally relevant (X)
	Relevant to users
	Landmarks and route awareness
	Gestalt
Paths	
Marking	*Clearly marked paths*
	Differentiation in paths
Activities and markings	*Clear within path markings*
	Activity based
	Clear inititial encounter
	Clear approach
Short distances in related areas	*Clear arrival*
	Short distances in related areas
	Integration with signs
	Integration with environment
	Path focal points (X)
	Awareness

382

successful they were in achieving their aims. With the ubiquity of "information appliances" (Norman, 1999) the single-person single-computer view of HCI becomes inadequate. We need to design for people surrounded by information artefacts and understand that interaction is not only about the individual but groups of individuals interacting with a combination of computers and media.

As computing devices become increasingly pervasive, adaptive, embedded in other systems and able to communicate autonomously we need see the human as interacting within the information space rather than being situated outside it. The design of information spaces has much to learn from architecture and how people read and interpret their environment.

Appendix

Tables 15.2 and 15.3 provide a list of all the guidelines of ENISpace at December 1999. In addition the ENISpace software provides a grouping structure and supporting documentation for the guidelines. Items marked with a (X) indicate that due to bugs they did not allow appropriate data entry within the system.

Table 15.3 Sign design guidelines

Provision of signs	*Directional signs*
	Informational signs
	Warning and resassurance signs
Global design issues	
Design of signs	*Visibility of signs*
	Visibility of environment
	Consistency
	Inconsistency
Defining space	*Definition of space*
	Articulation of space
Metaphors (all sign types)*	*Use of colour metaphors*
	Use of symbolic metaphors
	Use of language metaphors
	Use of auditory metaphors
Directional signs	
Markings	*Clear marking of distance/time to reach destination*
	Clear marking of direction
	Alternative routes
	Mark optimal routes

(cont'd)

Table 15.3 Sign design guidelines (*cont'd*)

Information mapping	*Appropriate level of signage*
	Clear location information
	Clear mapping
	Minimalist
	Dynamic information
Route markings	*Clear marking of route*
	Clear initial encounter
	Clear approach
	Clear arrival
	Clear transition
General issues	*Easy orientation within whole environment*
	Appropriate for users
	Easy exit
	Clear destination information (X)
Informational signs	
General issues	*Other user information*
	New options or information
	Uniquely mark objects
	Uniquely mark locations
	Sign integration
Warning and reassurance signs	
General issues	*Clear warning signs*
	Appropriate use
	Non-replacement
	Positive feedback

* Denotes that these guidelines appear several times in relation to each sign type within ENISpace but are listed only once here.

16

The Conceptual Structure
of Information Space

Paul P. Maglio and Teenie Matlock

In this chapter we examine how people think about the information space of the World Wide Web. We provide empirical evidence collected in interviews with beginning and experienced web users to show that much of people's conceptual experience of the web is metaphorical and understood through the process of conceptual integration. We argue that designers of tools for navigation and collaboration in information space should consider how people experience web space, including the natural tendency to metaphorically construe information space in terms of physical space.

16.1 Introduction

Navigation is a basic part of human experience. Walking across a parking lot, driving to work, and searching for an item in a store or library all involve navigation: moving from one point to another in physical space. Empirical research has shown that while navigating, people rely on different types of knowledge: landmark knowledge, route knowledge, and survey knowledge (Thorndyke and Hayes-Roth, 1982; Tversky, 1996). It has also been argued that people incorporate knowledge based on certain organisational principles (Lynch, 1960; Passini, 1984) and awareness of certain elements, such as paths, landmarks, districts, nodes, and edges. Navigation in electronic worlds has been compared to navigation in the physical world (e.g. Darken and Sibert, 1996a; Hirtle, 1997), but navigation in information spaces is not as well understood as navigation in physical space. Although recent research shows interesting results, much emphasis lies in how people perceive the environment, rather than how people conceive of the environment (Benyon, 1998a).

In this chapter, we argue that people rely on experience in physical space to structure experience in virtual information spaces such as the World Wide Web (WWW). Specifically, we are interested in people's *natural* conception of information spaces. We report the findings of a web-use study conducted in 1996 in which we analysed how people talk about the web to get at their natural conception of information space. We found that both experienced and inexperienced web users naturally talk about the web in consistent ways. For instance, people see themselves as metaphorically moving towards information, rather than information as moving towards them. We also found some differences between experienced and inexperienced web users in the way they talked about web activities. In the end, we argue that (a) the particular language people use is based on conceptual metaphor and is motivated by basic image schemata, which emerge from natural embodied experience (e.g. Johnson, 1987; Lakoff, 1987); and (b) web users' experience is structured by conceptual integration (Fauconnier, 1997; Fauconnier and Turner, 1994, 1996, 1998).

Before presenting our data and argument in detail, we first discuss some prior research concerning the way people think about the web, along with some background on metaphor and thought.

16.1.1 How People Remember the Web

Based on data collected from people asked to recall specific web searches, Maglio and Barrett (1997b) argued that web navigation is conceived in terms of a cognitive map similar to a cognitive map of physical space, that is, in terms of landmarks and routes (e.g. Anderson, 1980). In this study, experienced users searched the web for answers to specific questions. To identify key cognitive aspects of their activities, users were first asked about their plans, and their behaviour was tracked while they searched. Then a day later they were asked to recall the steps they had taken in each of their searches the previous day, and finally to retrace their steps. Participants were not warned on the first day that recall would be required on the second day. This method enabled Maglio and Barrett both to chart behaviour to uncover search tactics (using the behavioural traces) and to extract some of the structure of their internal representations (using the recall data).

The data showed that participants recalled only a few of the sites they visited. Specifically, they remembered key nodes that led to the target information. These nodes were called anchor points by analogy to the notion of anchor points in the cognitive map literature (Coulclelis et al., 1987). An anchor was defined as a node along a search path from which there is an unbroken sequence of links on successive pages that lead to the goal node (i.e. no URLs need to be typed in or explicitly recalled). Once traversed, anchor points are recognised as lying along the path to the goal – even if the same path is not followed to the goal in every case.

For the participants in the study, searching on the second day often meant finding anchors encountered on the first day, rather than finding paths found on the first day.

A second observation that emerged from the behavioural data is that individuals relied on personal routines when trying to find information. For instance, some participants routinely used a particular search engine, such as AltaVista, whereas others routinely used a particular hierarchical catalogue, such as Yahoo! It is not merely that these searchers preferred to use one approach over another, but that they conceptualised their search tasks in terms of their favourite routines. It often did not matter what was actually done on the first day, the searchers remembered searching as if their personal routines had been followed. On the analogy to cognitive maps of physical space, personal routines correspond to the familiar routes that an individual uses to get from one landmark (or anchor point) to another.

If people mentally structure web use in this way, tools for web navigation ought to present the web in this way. Because individuals tend to use the same search patterns over and over, and because they recall their searches in terms of their standard patterns – almost regardless of what they actually did – Maglio and Barrett (1997a) built a personal web agent to identify repeated search patterns and to suggest similar patterns for new searches. Because people focus on key nodes or anchor points when recalling their searches, and because these structure memory for the searches, Maglio and Barrett (1997a) also built a web agent to identify the key nodes in finding a piece of information, and to maintain personal trails in terms of these.

16.1.2 How People Talk About the Web

The key to designing information navigation tools lies in discovering how people naturally conceive of information spaces. Technically, the web is part of a network of geographically distributed machines connected via wires. The information accessible by users of this physical network is organised in a conceptual network of hyperlinks among documents. Despite this actual structure, people's conceptual structure of the web is rather different.

Matlock and Maglio (1996) found that web users often refer to the web as a multidimensional (most commonly two-dimensional) landscape. Obtaining information in this landscape is expressed as traversing interconnected paths towards locations that contain information objects, such as user homepages and commercial catalogue sites. Users say things such as, "I went to his homepage", and "I came back to where I saw that picture". Some of these information objects are talked about as two-dimensional and others, as three-dimensional; for instance, people say "in Yahoo!" which suggests a three-dimensional container, and "at AltaVista" which suggests a point on a two-dimensional plane.

In a follow-up study, Matlock and Maglio (1997) asked experienced and inexperienced web users to judge the sensibility of sentences containing metaphorical language (specifically regarding motion) about obtaining information on the web. Using a scale of one to seven, participants rated the sensibility of sentences containing verbs of motion. For instance, "John went to a new web site today"; "Do you want to climb up to the UCSC home page?"; and "I waited for the information to come to me". Sentences in which the web user was viewed as an agent, actively moving along a horizontal path, were rated as significantly more sensible than those in which the web user moved up or down, and as significantly more sensible than those in which the web user was passive. These results suggest that both experienced and inexperienced participants have clear and consistent ideas about how motion does and does not occur on the web.

Though there are many ways in which people might talk about the web (see Benyon and Höök, 1997), the fact that they naturally talk about it using particular metaphors is no accident. As Lakoff and Johnson (1980), Gibbs (1994) and others have argued, such language is motivated by metaphorical thought.

16.1.3 Metaphor and Thought

Prior to the seminal work of Lakoff and Johnson, metaphor was generally seen as nothing more than a literary device. Lakoff and Johnson (1980, p. 3) radically changed this misconception, offering compelling arguments to show that metaphor is an integral part of thought and action:

> Metaphor is typically viewed as a characteristic of language alone, a matter of words rather than thought or action ... that metaphor is pervasive in everyday life, not just in language, but in thought and action. Our ordinary conceptual system, in terms of which we both think and act, is fundamentally metaphorical in nature.

Subsequent work in cognitive linguistics and psychology has continued to offer theoretical and empirical evidence to show that metaphor is ubiquitous and serves many functions relative to conceptual experience (Lakoff, 1997; Sweetser, 1990; Turner, 1987). One of the functions of metaphor is that it helps people think about relatively abstract conceptual domains in terms of relatively concrete domains (Gibbs, 1994). For instance, spatial concepts are often helpful when reasoning about time (Gentner and Imai, 1992). On the standard view of metaphor, a relatively concrete source domain maps on to a relatively abstract target domain. Consider the often-cited metaphor THEORIES ARE BUILDINGS. In this metaphor, elements of the conceptual structure of BUILDINGS (source domain) map onto THEORIES (target domain). Linguistic evidence to support the existence of this metaphor includes statements such as: "You need empirical evidence to buttress your arguments", "The foundation of the theory is shaky", "His entire theory was toppled by the claim that Basque is a language isolate", or "Construct a different argument to support your theory". It makes sense that this mapping progresses from BUILDINGS to THEORIES because buildings are common in everyday experience. In western culture, buildings serve an important function: namely, people live and work in buildings. In addition, buildings offer protection from adverse effects of nature, and so on. Theories, by contrast, are important in the academic or philosophical world, but not commonplace to most people.

Another example of a metaphor is the MIND IS A CONTAINER. In this case, the concrete conceptual domain of CONTAINER maps on to the more abstract conceptual domain of the MIND. Hence, we understand the mind as a storehouse. Ideas can enter the storehouse, can be processed there, stored in a specific location, or even misplaced. Linguistic evidence for this metaphor includes expressions such as "The thought suddenly came into my head", "It's in the back of my mind", or "She lost her senses". This metaphor underlies many psychological theories (see Gibbs, 1994, for a discussion).

As pointed out by Coulson (1996b), the standard approach to metaphor arose in part to account for simple examples of analogical thinking, such as TIME IS SPACE. As such, the approach is parsimonious but cannot account for complex mappings requiring some degree of sensitivity (Turner and Fauconnier, 1995). Moreover, the standard approach falls short with respect to productivity: why do only certain elements of the source domain map onto the target domain? Consider THEORIES ARE BUILDINGS. As noted, foundation and support map onto the target domain, but doors and windows do not. Recent approaches have attempted to solve this problem by suggesting that there are a variety of types of metaphors, including primitive and compound (e.g. Grady et al., 1996).

Although more recent approaches to metaphor diverge from the standard model with respect to issues of mapping complexity, there is agreement that metaphor plays a central role in structuring how people think. But metaphor is only part of the story. Another part is image schemata, basic pre-conceptual structures that arise from embodied experience. Formed early in development (Mandler, 1992), image schemata structure both metaphorical and non-metaphorical thought (Johnson, 1987; Lakoff, 1987; Gibbs and Colston, 1995; Johnson, 1992).

389

Image Schemata

Daily life includes active physical motion toward objects or destinations (concrete or abstract): going to the door to let the cat out, walking or driving to work, and reaching out to grab a pencil or pick up the telephone. Life also includes abstract motion toward goals (abstract destinations): working to get a promotion, writing a dissertation to obtain a degree, and saving money for a trip. Each of these actions involves the image schema TRAJECTORY (also referred to as SOURCE–PATH–GOAL), comprised of a starting point, an end point, and a path between the two. Another image schema is CONTAINER, which arises out of bodily experience: swallowing things, entering and remaining in buildings, and so on. As we will see, these image schemata figure prominently in how people view obtaining information in the world and on the web.

In what follows, we explore the nature of people's metaphorical conception of the web. A specific goal of the study is to examine the presence and frequency of language reflecting underlying image schemata. We believe these elements structure much of users' conceptual structure of the web. Furthermore, as Lund and Waterworth (1998) have claimed, an important step in the design process is identifying image schemata to provide a more experientially based environment for the user (see also Waterworth, 1997). In the current study, we investigate how users with varying levels of expertise talk about the web. We first describe a study that elicited verbatim reports from both experienced and inexperienced web. We next discuss reasons people use the metaphors they do, and finally, some implications of our results for the design of tools for navigating and collaborating in information spaces.

16.2 Study: Users Describe Web Experience

The purpose of this study was to further explore how people think about the web in natural settings. We looked specifically at how people conceive of the actions taken while using the web; for instance, to what extent users see themselves actively moving through space and to what extent they focus on the physical environment. We also wanted to observe differences between beginning and experienced users.

We hypothesised that beginners would talk about their experiences using the web in terms of the physical actions they performed more than experienced users would because beginners are likely to have only a partial understanding of the web domain. Along the same lines, we hypothesised that experienced users would generate more metaphorically consistent utterances than beginners would.

We analysed the data both quantitatively and qualitatively. In the quantitative analysis, we counted utterances of various types to compare beginning and experienced web users. In our qualitative analysis, we followed a method similar to that of Raubal et al. (1997), who analysed the image schematic structure of talk about wayfinding in airports.

16.2.1 Method

Twenty-four undergraduates at the University of California at Santa Cruz took part, including 13 males and 11 females. All were native English speakers except five fluent bilinguals.

Participants first completed a questionnaire about their prior experience using computers and the web. They were asked about length of time using the web (e.g. one month or less) and hours per week used. Participants were then seated in front of a computer that was running the Netscape Navigator browser, which displayed the homepage for the University of California, Santa Cruz. They were then instructed to click on whatever icons or hyperlinks appeared interesting and to continue doing so for 5 minutes. The experimenter was extremely careful to avoid language that would bias the participant to think of the web metaphorically, such as, "Go to that page".

After each participant had spent sufficient time getting used to the task and experiencing the environment, he or she was instructed to look at a new domain: Yahoo!, a well-known catalogue in which information is organised hierarchically. The participant was again instructed to use the mouse to gain access to information that seemed interesting and to continue to do so for 5 minutes.

A tape-recorded interview followed the web session. To begin, the experimenter prompted the participant: "Tell me what you just did using as much detail as possible". If a response was not immediately forthcoming, the experimenter began, "Tell me what you did first", and so on.

16.2.2 Results

Participants were separated into two groups according to self-reported web experience: 12 beginners reported under 6 months of web use, and 12 experienced users reported over 6 months of web use.

Coding

In coding the data, we distinguished among seven kinds of verb phrases (verbs and conventional verb-preposition expressions) that correspond to seven kinds of web actions (see Table 16.1). For instance, the sorts of phrases coded included verbs such as "clicked" and verb–preposition combinations such as "went to". These were chosen based on discourse

Table 16.1 Verb coding scheme

Category	Examples
Outside	click, press, type, scroll
Inside	go, follow, have, look up
TRAJECTORY	go, come, bring, follow
User Agent	go, follow
Web Agent	bring, come up, bring, show
CONTAINER	have, contain
Information Action	look for, lookup, search
Miscellaneous	look, see

about the web that we had collected previously (Matlock and Maglio, 1996). Only utterances that referred to what the participant did while using the web were assigned to one or more of the categories shown in the table. For example, statements such as "I'm on a tight budget", or "Using the web is pretty fun" were not included in our analysis.

In analysing utterances, we wanted to be careful not to confuse language referring to the information space of the web with language referring to the user interface of the web. Thus, in looking at verb phrases, we distinguished among three general types of action: (a) *outside actions*, which reflect the user's experience with things external to the web (such as typing on the keyboard, using the mouse, and clicking on browser icons); (b) *inside actions*, which reflect the user's experience conceptually within the web (such as going to a web page, and following a link); and (c) *miscellaneous actions*, which cannot be definitely classified as either outside or inside. Expressions such as "I *typed* something", "I *clicked on* the grapes icon", or "I *pressed* buttons" were coded as outside actions.

Expressions referring to inside actions were split into three types: TRAJECTORY, CONTAINER, and information actions. Motion of the user along a path in web space highlights the TRAJECTORY schema, such as "I *went into* this thing called Yahoo", "I couldn't *get back to* where I was", or "It *brought me to* the anthropology page". Transfer of information along a path from computer to user also highlights the TRAJEC-TORY schema, as in "It told me" and "It said". Sometimes a web site is talked about in terms of a container, instantiating the CONTAINER schema, as in "Yahoo! *contained* some cool stuff", or "Yahoo! *had* what I wanted". At other times, the web is described as a general information resource similar to a library or a phone book, as suggested by expressions such as "I *looked up* Chewbacca".

The TRAJECTORY category was divided into utterances in which user is the agent and those in which web is the agent. Agency refers to who or what initiates and undertakes action. In some cases, the user is agent, as in "I *went* ...", whereas in others, the web is agent, as in "It *took me to* ...".

The miscellaneous category was used for verbs that could not be obviously classified into either of the other categories. This group mainly contained expressions beginning with "I *saw* ..." or "I *looked at* ..." because it is unclear whether these describe visual perception of the screen (an outside action) or visual perception of objects in web space (inside action).

Finally, note that we also could have examined use of prepositions to help code for TRAJECTORY and CONTAINER. For instance, *through* and *to* imply TRAJECTORY, and *in* suggests CONTAINER. For the present study, we looked specifically at verb phrases. A more thorough analysis would certainly include prepositions (for example, "I can't remember if I found information *in* Yahoo! or *inside* AltaVista") and nouns ("I took a direct *route* from the UCSC site to my homepage") as well (see Raubal et al., 1997).

Qualitative Results

We first conducted a qualitative analysis of the data. To get a feel for the data and our coding scheme, consider the following utterance, which is fairly typical of beginning web users (participant 4):

> ... I clicked on uh grapes ... and it brought me to um ... this place where they had choices and then I clicked on bookstore ...

Note the presence of two outside actions ("I *clicked* on ..."), an instance of TRAJECTORY in which the web is agent ("it *brought me to* ..."), and an instance of CONTAINER ("place where they *had* choices"). In this utterance, the user clicks on an icon on the screen, is taken to a new location, and then she clicks again.

Now consider an utterance produced by an experienced web user (participant 14):

> ... I went to net search because that seemed like a good wholesome opportunity for going somewhere else ... I probably typed something and it told me I couldn't do it, so I dunno, I just went and clicked around a whole bunch ...

Here we see three instances of outside actions ("typed", "clicked", and "do"), two instances of TRAJECTORY with the user as agent ("went", "going") and one instance of TRAJECTORY with web as agent ("told"). (The verb "seem" and the second instance of "went" were not coded because they do not refer to actions taken while using the web. The use of "went" simply means "proceeded to"). In this case, the user's report blends different types of actions: metaphorically going somewhere, typing something, receiving information, and clicking.

393

These sorts of responses are representative of what experienced and beginning web users do: they both mix outside actions with actions inside the web's information domain. Nonetheless, we observed some interesting differences. For the beginner, the web can function as a kind of conveyance that moves the user ("brought me to"), but for the expert, the web is a kind of roadway on which the user moves ("I went"). In addition, for the beginner, the web passively contains information ("had choices"), but for the expert, the web actively provides information ("it told me").

Consider the report of another beginner (participant 2):

> ... I went into the um Brian's tattoo something or other, but when I clicked into it, it said that like it was gonna show tattoos of his body and like front, side, whatever ... it had objects to click on, and I clicked on 'em and there was no pictures ...

In this report, we see one instance of TRAJECTORY in which the user is agent ("went into"), and two in which the web is agent ("it said", "was gonna show"). We also see two outside actions ("click"), and one CONTAINER ("had"). As in both previous cases, outside actions are mixed with inside actions. Like the first beginner, this one refers to a web site as a container. Unlike the first beginner, however, this one also refers to the web as a kind of roadway along which people can travel ("went") rather than as a kind of conveyance ("brought me to"). For this beginner, as for the expert, the web actively provides information ("it said").

The utterance from participant 2 illustrates something our coding scheme does not recognise: the novel use of "click" in the verb phrase "click into". Whereas the verb "click" refers to an outside action, the preposition "into" specifies an inside location. Usually the verb "click" is followed by the preposition "on", and the construction refers to an icon or hyperlink visible on the screen. In this case, however, "click into" refers both to something visible on the screen and also to something contained in the information space of the web. We will return to this point in the discussion of conceptual blends.

Finally, consider a second expert's response (participant 23):

> ... I couldn't get through. I returned to the first page I started on and selected travel.

In this case, we note two instances of TRAJECTORY in which the user is agent ("get through", "returned") and one outside action ("selected"). The path is blocked ("couldn't get through"), and previous steps were retraced ("returned").

In summarising our qualitative results, we can see that both beginners and experts use the same sort of language overall. In reporting on their

Table 16.2 Verb coding scheme

	Beginners (n = 12)	Experts (n = 12)
Outside	54	26
TRAJECTORY	56	87
User Agent	37	79
Web Agent	19	8
CONTAINER	22	11
Info Action	30	42
Miscellaneous	24	20
Total	186	186

experience using the web, most participants mixed language about actions they did outside web space with those they did inside web space, especially actions reflecting the schemata TRAJECTORY and CONTAINER. In talking about the web, people also described the web as moving the user, or described the user as moving on the web. Their verbatim reports also suggest that the web can simply contain information, or it can actively convey or provide users with information. In any event, people seem to prefer to talk about their experience in using the web in more familiar terms, such as physical motion, physical actions, and physical containers.

Quantitative Results

The total number of verbs in each category was computed for beginners and for experts, as shown in Table 16.2.

Because we collected frequency data, χ^2 was used to compare beginners and experts along each of the seven action categories. As shown in Table 16.3, significant differences were obtained for TRAJECTORY versus outside actions, for user agent versus web agent, and for CONTAINER versus all other verbs. Thus, experts used the TRAJECTORY verb phrases rather than outside action verbs more often than beginners. Within the TRAJECTORY category, experts reported themselves as agent (i.e. actively moving through information space) instead of web as agent (i.e. information moving through web to user) more often than beginners did. By contrast, verbs phrases of the CONTAINER type werereported more by beginners than experts.

Overall, all web users reported a similar experience while using the web. Both beginners and experts talked about their experiences as if they had been moving from place to place though in fact they had not gone anywhere. The data also revealed noticeable differences between experts and beginners. Beginners more often mixed in their experiences using

395

Table 16.3 Percentage of verbs in each category for each group. The χ^2 statistic compares the difference between groups

	Beginners	Experts	χ^2
TRAJECTORY vs outside	51%	77%	16.49**
User agent vs web agent	66%	91%	13.60**
CONTAINER vs all others	12%	6%	4.02*
Info actions vs all others	16%	23%	2.48
Miscellaneous vs all others	13%	11%	0.41

*p < 0.05; **p < 0.005.

the keyboard, mouse, and other elements of the physical (non-web) domain (e.g. "I clicked on ..." or "I typed in ..."), whereas experienced users did not. In addition, beginners were more likely to refer to the web as a container than were experienced web users.

16.3 Discussion

All web users in our study consistently used metaphorical language when talking about the WWW. In particular, they used verb phrases referring to physical motion to describe their experience using the web. However, there were differences between the language of beginning and experienced web users. In what follows, we discuss reasons why people use metaphorical language when talking about the web, and discuss implications for the design of tools for navigation and collaboration in information spaces.

16.3.1 Agency and Web Use

Our data suggest that web users – even those who had never used the web – view web activity as traversal along paths. In particular, participants most often see themselves as the agent, initiating and actively moving along these paths (even for beginners; see Table 16.3). According to the data, less often is the user viewed as the passive recipient of information or as a passenger being transported in some sort of web vehicle. This suggests that the semantic property of agency is primarily viewed as something inherent in the web user, rather than something inherent in the web.

One reason the user might view obtaining information on the web as actively moving through space toward objects is because of the ease of information access. The most common way of moving from one web page to another is by clicking on hyperlinks or using the browser's back button (Catledge and Pitkow, 1995; Tauscher and Greenberg, 1997). Much less often do web users type in full addresses to obtain information. Simply clicking on links and instantly seeing new information creates a sense of fluidity and hence, the illusion of motion. One way to test this hypothesis may be to systematically vary the delay between clicking on a link and the subsequent presentation of information. Results from such a test, especially if conducted with novice web users, will tell whether longer delays result in fewer utterances in which the user is the agent.

It seems natural to talk about information access metaphorically in physical terms. After all, obtaining information in a library, in a reference book, or by telephone involves directed action. Thus, the reason why users talk about the web in terms of physical space most likely lies in human embodied experience (Johnson, 1987, 1992; Lakoff and Johnson, 1998). The way people experience the web or other information spaces is shaped by human activities in the real world. A large part of human experience involves physical activities, such as standing up, walking toward a location, reaching out, and grasping what is desired. From these recurrent patterns of activity, people develop image schemata, as discussed previously. Thus, it is reasonable to assume that because directed motion toward goals is part of our embodied experience, it naturally structures how we think about and interact in information spaces, such as the web.

16.3.2 Conceptual Blends in Information Space

We now return to our finding that novice web users mixed talk about the outside domain with talk about the inside domain more than experienced users did (see Table 16.3). Recall the utterances of participants 2 and 4. These and all inexperienced web users often mixed inside and outside actions, seemingly unaware of the fact that they were switching between them. Sometimes this sort of blending happened at the sentence level, as in "I clicked on [outside] grapes … and it brought me to [inside] …". At other times, it occurred at the phrase level, as in "I clicked into it", in which the participant created a novel verb–particle construction. These results indicate that in using the web, people naturally integrate two or more domains to create something more than simply the combination of its parts.

Such conceptual integration (also known as "blending") is not unique to web activity or even to language use, as Gilles Fauconnier and others have demonstrated (Fauconnier, 1997; Fauconnier and Turner, 1994, 1996, 1998). In this framework, there are not just two domains, as in standard metaphor theory (Lakoff and Johnson, 1980), but multiple domains. Through a complex interplay of mapping, or projection, from one domain to another, an emergent structure arises. This structure is to some extent independent of the meanings afforded by the domains on their own. A blend emerges from two or more input spaces, a generic

397

space, and a blended space. The best way to show how the mapping works is through an example of how people create novel meaning by blending domains. The example comes from Coulson (1996a): two college students are up late at night studying for an exam. One student grabs a piece of paper, crumbles it up, and throws it towards a wastepaper basket. The other student grabs the crumpled piece of paper and also throws it towards the basket. The actions of the students develop into a game in which the paper is a "ball" and the trashcan is a "basket". The students' understanding of this activity as "trashcan basketball" arises through integrating knowledge about different domains. In this blend, trash disposal is one input space and the conventional game of basketball is the other input space. The blended space combines elements from both the input domains. Importantly, though it involves the incorporation of elements from both domains, the emergent structure in blended space differs in many respects from the two input domains.

An example closer to home may be seen in Fauconnier's (1997) discussion of the computer *desktop* metaphor. He argues that conceptual integration can account for the complexity of this familiar metaphor. According to Fauconnier, thedesktop metaphor is constructed on the basis of two separate conceptual inputs: (a) traditional computer commands, such as saving a file, and listing a directory; and (b) work in an office, including a desk, files, folders, and trashcan. To create the desktop metaphor, a cross-mapping occurs whereby computer files are mapped to paper files, directories are mapped to folders, and so on. General knowledge – such as image schematic notions of CONTAINER and TRAJECTORY – mediate the mapping. Structure is selectively projected from the inputs, yielding a coherent, well-integrated, emergent structure specific to the blend. What emerges from these mappings is a "world" in which a trashcan can sit on the desktop, in which double clicking opens files or applications, and in which objects are routinely dragged from one location to another. The integration is completely novel, but at the same time it is meaningful to the desktop interface user. Note that if the mapping from the office domain to the computer domain were simple (i.e. creating no new structure), the computer desktop could be no better than a real desktop: such an interface could only selectively mirror the world.

We believe conceptual integration provides a nice account of how web users think about the web. It provides a plausible explanation for how novice users can understand and use the web. For example, a person who has never seen the web can sit down at a computer, browse for awhile, have the feeling of shifting between inside actions and outside actions (e.g. "click into"). Conceptual integration also provides some insight into how experts talk about the web less in terms of outside actions than novice web users: Experts seem to rely on the input from the abstract web domain to a greater extent than they rely on input from the physical browser domain.

Conceptual blend theory also integrates web users' conceptual information much more effectively than would a standard metaphorical approach, which would be limited to a single source domain and a single target domain (e.g. Lakoff and Johnson, 1980). Of course, a traditional metaphorical account can explain the obvious metaphors: (a) WEB SPACE IS PHYSICAL SPACE, which reflects to how users view the web as a place; and (b) OBTAINING INFORMATION IS MOVING THROUGH SPACE, which reflects how users view themselves as moving along paths to information objects. However, it fails to say anything about how web users naturally blend inside and outside actions, or about how this tendency interacts with metaphorical thought.

Finally, as Rohrer (1997) argues, blending can also explain how people can understand and incorporate other, higher level metaphors of cyberspace, including the popular *information super highway*. There are two parts to understanding this metaphor. People understand it as highway upon which movement occurs, much in the same way the beginners and experts in our study understood the web, and as a road through time that allows travel into the future. Rohrer provides nice examples from headlines and news reports to show the dual, blended nature of this metaphor, for instance, "Prime Minister rides the info-highway", "Congress suffers wreck on info-highway", and "AT&T stalled on the info-highway". In each case, there is the notion of movement through physical space blended with the notion of "movement" into the future.

16.3.3 Designing Information Interfaces

If metaphorical language in fact reflects metaphorical thought, and people naturally think of the web as a kind of physical space in which they actively move along paths, what might be the consequences for the design of information navigation and collaboration tools?

Shum (1996) points out many potential uses for the concepts of physical space in the structuring and presentation of information, such as Euclidean distance in two or three dimensions, direction, orientation, and depth. Nevertheless, Shum also notes that the key to adapting spatial metaphors to information presentation lies in understanding user tasks. Thus, adding a notion of distance to the information interface solely because physical space has distance would probablynot be useful in all cases. For instance, distance in information space might reasonably be used to convey semantic relatedness (e.g. Chalmers and Chitson, 1992) or expected download delay (e.g. Barrett et al., 1997; Campbell and Maglio, 1999).

Our data show that even novice web users conceive of themselves as actively moving on the web under their own control. Thus, we believe that the power of spatial metaphors for information presentation is not merely the result of people's *ability to use spatial metaphors*. Rather, its

399

power lies in the fact that people *naturally use spatial metaphors* – that they cannot help but use them. It follows that interface designers should not construct virtual worlds that are merely consistent with ordinary experience and that merely use spatial attributes in task-relevant ways. Rather, the most useful information interfaces will target people's natural spatial understanding of information use and at the same time allow people flexibility to create an appropriate metaphorical understanding of the domain (see Kuhn, 1993).

Navigation in Information Spaces

Dieberger's (1997a) city metaphor for information navigation seems to be a good approach to information space design. In particular, Dieberger carefully balances spatially real interface elements with *magic features* that break the spatial metaphor. In a sense, magic features provide the user with known boundaries that can be used in guiding the conceptual blending process. For instance, because magic windows provide short-cuts between distal points in the information city, semantic-relatedness need not be determined solely by spatial proximity. Nevertheless, both sorts of connections can be understood spatially as TRAJECTORY, which provides a consistent basis for the mappings.

We also see much promise in Waterworth's (1997) experiential approach to information landscape design. This approach offers an alternative to the traditional human–computer interface (HCI) approach, which is based on an objectivist cognitivism (e.g. mental models). One advantage of the experiential approach is that users are offered a more meaningful interface, one that affords metaphorical thought and action. An excellent example of such a design may be seen in Lund and Waterworth's SchemaSpace (1998), which is grounded embodiment and which is structured – at least to some extent – in a way that reflects image schematic structure. For excellent discussion and compelling arguments against the traditional HCI approach and for details on the experiential approach, see the chapter by Waterworth and Colleagues in this volume.

The key point is that people should not have to adapt to information space; rather, they should play an active role in determining how the space is used through their activities and practice (Benyon, 1998a). As we have seen, people's conceptual experience of information space is largely structured metaphorically and based on embodied experience in physical space. We believe that web browsers or other tools for navigation in information space should be designed based on how people conceptualise and experience the environment.

Social Interaction in Information Spaces

Tools for collaboration in information space can likewise be informed by understanding how people conceptualise interaction in information spaces. Research on how people interact will likely reveal that people conceptualise virtual interactions with others much as they conceptualiase actual interactions. Nevertheless, differences between the two will undoubtedly arise, providing opportunities for creating interfaces that are both different from and possibly more effective than physical interaction.

For instance, consider Babble, a computer-mediated communication system meant to facilitate long-term, ongoing conversations (Erickson et al., 1999). One design goal of Babble was to enable those involved in a conversation to be made aware of many social cues, such as users' presence and actions with respect to a particular conversation. In addition to a text window that displays conversational content, Babble uses a very elegant graphical representation called a *social proxy*, which depicts a conversation as a large circle, individuals as small coloured dots within the circle, and chatting as movement of the dots towards the circle's centre. In this way, the Babble interface relies on a spatial metaphor in which an area of the screen represents a conversation, icons within the area represent individuals engaged in the conversation, and motion of the icons represents conversational action. This metaphor abstracts away many details of actual conversations, such as facial expressions and intonation, yet retains significant spatial relationships, such as proximity. In addition, unlike verbal conversations or other computer-mediated chat systems, Babble adds time-stamps to each conversational action and can store the text of conversations indefinitely. This enables Babble users to retrieve previous interactions and to reconstruct all previous conversational contexts. Thus, the Babble interface is in some ways similar to and in other ways more effective than actual conversation.

Though our empirical data do not specifically concern social interactions in information space, it is reasonable to expect similar results. From our perspective, then, using space to depict conversations follows the principle that people conceptualise information activities in physical terms. Moreover, movement of the dots in Babble follows the TRAJECTORY schema, just as a chat action follows a TRAJECTORY. Being inside the circle instantiates CONTAINER, just as being in a conversation suggests containment.

In any event, Babble provides an environment in which users can create and participate in conversations. This communication system was not set up as part of a larger information space. But why not? Consider that the web is a fundamentally social structure – it enables users to publish and to read what others have published. Although web users interact through published documents, these interactions are asynchronous and lack the richness of ordinary communication. The web misses the people behind the documents. Users are invisible to each other because social affordances are not built into the web.

401

The WebPlaces system was constructed to enable social interaction on the web (Maglio and Barrettt, 1998, 1999). The idea was to make interpersonal awareness and interaction an integral part of web activity by creating virtual places through which users can communicate. In this system, a *place* does not necessarily map to a location in web space, but might be automatically constructed based on the interests and activities of web users. To make users aware of one another, WebPlaces adapted Babble's social proxy: a circle represents the group or community of users, and small coloured dots represent individual users (see Maglio and Barrett, 1999). Motion of a dot toward the centre of the circle represents a group interaction (e.g. chat), motion of a dot toward another dot represents a user-user action (e.g. whisper), and motion of a dot around the circle represents an individual user action (e.g. browsing). In this way, Babble's social proxy was extended to maintain social awareness in a user community rather than in a conversation. Actions were included that are not specifically related to the ongoing conversation, but that are nonetheless relevant to the users who are gathered together. In coding various types of actions by these iconic motions, WebPlaces' proxy indicates both the state and activity of the users in a place. A glance at the social proxy tells a user how busy the place is, who is there, and what activity there is. Thus, by combining affordances of information space with affordances for interpersonal interaction, WebPlaces blends information activities with social activities, and in the process, WebPlaces creates a novel user interface that relies on TRAJECTORY and CONTAINER to structure user experience.

16.4 Conclusion

The way that people think about the WWW has implications for the way that they navigate it. The key to designing effective information navigation tools lies in discovering how people naturally conceive of information spaces, including the extent to which such spaces are thought of in terms of physical space. Likewise, to facilitate efficient collaboration in information space, it is critical that software be designed to reflect people's natural conceptualisation of the space. To discover how people think about the web, one type of information space, we studied how people talk about using it. In doing so, we found that people consistently refer to the experience in terms of user-directed motion through physical space toward information objects. That particular metaphorical language is used is no accident, even though there are many different ways to talk about the web. Such language is motivated by metaphorical thought, which is structured by the same basic image schemata that people rely on to mentally structure everyday life. Thus, the power of spatial metaphors for information presentation is not merely the result of people's ability to learn to use spatial metaphors. Rather, its power lies in people's tendency to naturally use spatial metaphors – they cannot help but use them. It follows that efficient interface design should go much deeper than constructing virtual worlds that merely include a few task-specific spatial attributes. The most useful information interfaces will target people's natural spatial understanding of information use, and at the same time allow people flexibility to create appropriate metaphorical and blended understanding of the domain. Because of the striking consistency in conceptualisation of information space across web users, collaboration would be well afforded by a user interface that makes explicit appropriate aspects of users' apparent common ground. The trick lies in discovering the conceptual differences between real space and information space, and then in using those differences to afford rich and effective interactions in information space.

Acknowledgements

Thanks to Rob Barrett, Seana Coulson, Gilles Fauconnier, Ray Gibbs, and Mark Turner for thoughtful discussions, to Chris Dryer for advice on statistical analyses, and to David Benyon, Alan Munro, Barbara Tversky, and John Waterworth for many helpful comments on a draft of this chapter.

17

Information Space Navigation: A Framework

Robert Spence

17.1 Introduction and Context

Navigation is a fundamental human activity which, in the physical world, has been carried out since time immemorial for purposes as wide ranging as adventure, conquest and foraging for food (Lewis, 1994). In electronic information spaces the aims are not wholly dissimilar. For example, in a menu system (Figure 17.1) a user is seeking a theatre to attend this evening: she may initially have no idea what's available, and is exploring to form a mental model of possibilities before making a decision: a trail (Field and Apperley, 1990) allows her to selectively retreat to a previously visited discrete category label. On the other hand (Figure 17.2 – see also colour plate 14) the information space may be multidimensional and continuous, and the engineering designer may be examining a two-dimensional prosection (Tweedie et al., 1996) associated with two parameters under his control and colour-coded to indicate the success (green) or otherwise (grey-scale) of any design defined by values of X1 and X2. A major consideration will be whether movement in that

Figure 17.1   One page of a hierarchically-structured menu system allowing selective retreat.

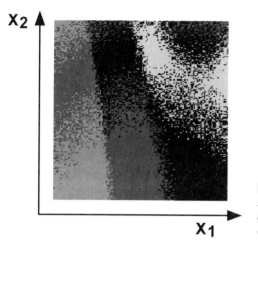

Figure 17.2 A prosection showing the success (green) or otherwise of a design defined by values of X_1 and X_2. (See also colour plate 14.)

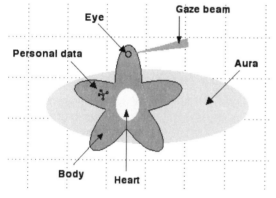

Figure 17.3a A StarCursor.

Figure 17.3b Auras of StarCursors.

space to examine other regions might be beneficial. A third example may be taken from a "collaborative virtual environment" inhabited by "StarCursors" (Figure 17.3a) each representing a human being (Rankin et al., 1998). The aura associated with the group of StarCursors shown in Figure 17.3b, coupled with their attractive body decoration, may encourage an approach with a view to social interaction. In each of these three examples earlier choices by one or more individuals may be displayed by some means, thereby supporting the potential for social navigation.

17.2 Aims of Navigation

The principal reason for undertaking navigation is that movement may be required to arrive at a desirable location or state in information space. Nevertheless, to summarise navigation merely as more or less direct movement towards a goal would be to ignore the exploration that is often carried out in order to discover *how* to move: all the three illustrations above will, for example, typically involve exploration prior to a movement towards an objective.

A word about terminology is appropriate here. In what follows we shall frequently speak of movement in information space whereas, in fact, little or no physical movement actually takes place. It would in fact be more appropriate to speak of *translation* in information space since any apparent movement in that space is usually illusory. Nevertheless, for reasons of familiarity we shall use the generally accepted term *movement*.

17.3 Three Essential Components

The literature on navigation in information space is extensive.[1] Variously, however, it has identified many aspects of navigation we consider to be essential. They include (a) movement in information space, (b) the typically iterative nature of that movement, (c) an internal (i.e. mental) model formed by the person navigating the space, (d) a data display, (e) the task being performed, (f) the user's domain knowledge, (g) strategy formulation and execution, and (h) perception, whether visual, aural, tactile or olfactory. In the framework to be proposed all these essential aspects are included.

---

[1] See, for example, Downs and Stea (1973), Wickens (1984), Dillon et al. (1990), Nielsen (1990), Waterworth and Chignell (1991), Darken and Sibert (1996), Darken (1997), Wittenburg (1997), Jul and Furnas (1997), and Spence (1997, 1999, 2001).

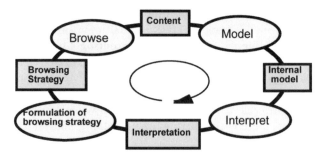

Figure 17.4   Navigation framework.

17.4 Nature of the Framework

Frameworks can take various forms and levels of detail. The one to be presented is of a granularity comparable with Norman's Seven Stages of Action (Norman, 1988, p. 45), a framework which is undoubtedly of considerable value to interaction designers during both the design and evaluation of interactive systems.

17.5 The Navigation Framework

The proposed framework[2] is shown in Figure 17.4. It comprises four perceptual/cognitive activities and the results of those activities. It assumes the presentation of some display of data to a user as well as some means of interaction, neither of which are shown explicitly.

In the following section we loosely describe each of the four activities prior to their more detailed consideration and definition in Sections 17.6 to 17.8. Section 17.9 then presents these activities in the integrated navigational framework. Sections 17.10 to 17.14 then focus upon interaction design to support each of the component activities of navigation.

17.5.1 Interpretation

A user will interpret displayed data in the context of their understanding of the task being performed as well as data stored internally (in Long-Term Memory) that is deemed to be relevant. The user will decide whether movement in information space can be beneficial. Thus, the

---

[2] The framework was actually suggested by our familiarity with the so-called 'DEAP (Design-Execute-Analyse-Predict) model (Box and Draper, 1987; Deming, 1986; Su et al., 1996) familiar to statistical modellers, which is an essential activity followed in engineering design such as the creation of products to exhibit high quality.

theatregoer viewing Figure 17.1 will form an opinion as to whether other opportunities for entertainment might be worth examination; the engineer viewing Figure 17.2 will probably decide to see if the green area enlarges as X1 increases; and the individual viewing Figure 17.3b may be attracted by the aura surrounding the group of StarCursors. In all cases they draw some conclusion about desirable movement in information space.

17.5.2 Formulation of a Browsing Strategy

As a result of the interpretation a user will decide what next to do in information space. In fact, this decision will have three components: (a) *location*: where to go in information space, (b) *scan*: how to view that space, and (c) *attention*: what selective attention is to be paid to the detail of that space. Thus, the theatregoer, on noticing that nothing of interest is showing in the West End may decide (a) to retreat to London (location), (b) carry out a rapid serial visual scan of items (scan), but (c) watch out for musicals (attention). Similar three-fold decisions will be made by the design engineer (Figure 17.2) and the individual in virtual space (Figure 17.3).

These decisions will be influenced by the user's understanding of what browsing is possible, usually gleaned first from the sight of available controls and then later from experience.

17.5.3 Browsing

Browsing is the execution of the formulated strategy. It is a perceptual activity in which the user "registers" what is seen in sensory storage. At this stage what is seen is not yet understood or interpreted.

17.5.4 Modelling

As browsing proceeds the user is able to construct an internal model (Norman, 1983) of significant aspects of the browsed data. Very little is known about the activity of modelling (Solso, 1998) though, as will be discussed below, the notion of Conceptual Short-Term Memory (Potter, 1993, 1999) is a useful aid to understanding the browsing-modelling process.

17.5.5 Navigation

It is suggested that, in most cases, the four activities of browsing, modelling, interpretation and the formulation of strategy will not only take

409

place in that order but be repeated cyclically many times in the course of a session (Figure 17.4). The engineering designer, for example, may sequentially examine many displays of the form shown in Figure 17.2 before finally deciding upon a location for the design (i.e. a choice of X1 and X2) that will then be put into mass production. That iterative activity is the *navigation* which is the subject of this chapter. The cycle time around the navigational loop may lie anywhere between about 200 milliseconds and many seconds depending upon the task and the navigational strategy adopted by the user. The next three sections consider the component activities in detail.

17.6 Browsing and Modelling

Browsing has been defined (Spence, 1999) as:

browsing: *the registration of content*

It is very similar to the act of perception (Solso, 1998) in which, for visual browsing, the result of perception is held – albeit momentarily – in sensory storage. The perception need not be visual: it may be aural, tactile or olfactory. Everyday examples include the scanning of a restaurant menu with the intention of seeing what's available, the riffling of a book's pages with the intention of gaining some idea of its content, and the activation of an "autoscan"[3] on a CD player to get a "flavour" of the music on a CD. Thus, the result of browsing is "content" (see Figure 17.4). As discussed earlier, browsing is characterised by three components, namely *location* (the material being viewed), *scan* (the manner in which it is scanned) and the *attention* which is paid, either consciously or unconsciously, to various features of the viewed material.

Almost immediately following perception (i.e. typically within about 100 milliseconds) the relevance of the content is established by reference to existing knowledge (residing in the user's Long-Term Memory) and the task being performed. If judged irrelevant the content is forgotten: if relevant it is remembered and placed in internal memory. A tentative model of this browsing and modelling process, strongly suggested by the work[4] of Potter (1993, 1999), is shown in Figure 17.5.

It should be stressed that, up to this point, the material being browsed has not yet been interpreted. It may be helpful, especially in the context of

---

[3] Autoscan is a facility, associated with a CD player, whose activation by a user leads to the playing of a sequence of short (a few seconds) excerpts, one from each track.

[4] Potter (1993, 1999) has proposed the notion of Conceptual Short-Term Memory (CSTM). To summarise, Potter points out that we are *continually* browsing – we look at our table, the waiter across the restaurant, the lighting fixture, the wall and so on – but that some internal mechanism rapidly determines whether what we see (or hear) should be forgotten or remembered. The "time constant" of the CSTM phenomenon would appear to be of the order of 100 milliseconds.

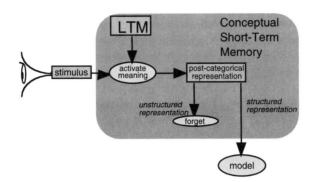

Figure 17.5 A model of the browsing and modelling activity of the navigation framework, as suggested by the work of Potter (1993, 1999).

opportunistic browsing[5] (see later), to expand our definition of browsing as:

browsing: *the registration of content prior to that content being forgotten or remembered, in the latter case being transferred to an internal model.*

This definition of browsing differs radically from a commonly-held view that browsing is essentially casual and unhurried in nature, and only undertaken with serendipitous intent.

17.7 Interpretation

Interpretation of a currently viewed display can take many forms. Sometimes there will be no need to move to a new region of information space: the user will continue to gain insight from inspection of an image such as Figure 17.1, 17.2 or 17.3. However, our concern in this chapter is with *navigation*, the essence of which is *movement* in information space, for whatever reason. In this context, where a user is endeavouring to move towards useful data (a common activity in data mining and on-line shopping, for example) a crucially important aspect of a currently viewed display is its ability to inform that user of the consequences of available movement and, if possible, a beneficial direction in which to move. Indeed, the latter would help the user to formulate a potentially beneficial browsing strategy.

---

[5] Browsing is not only associated with the *intentional* viewing of visual content in the context of a task. Thus, opportunistic browsing (de Bruijn and Spench, 2001), in which a user serendipitously notices some content and then decides it is of potential interest, is covered by the framework, the only difference being that the user is not consciously searching for information. Only the attention component of the browsing activity has been determined *a priori*, and that unconsciously.

411

Figure 17.2 affords a basis for illustration. The designer would observe that there appears to be an increase in the green area towards the higher values of X1. It might therefore be profitable to explore somewhat higher values of X1, since the green area might turn out to be quite large, offering valuable flexibility in the choice of X1 and X2. Similarly, with the potential for social navigation inherent in Figure 17.3, a user might be attracted by the musical aura emitted by the group and by their decorative clothing.

A definition of interpretation *in the context of navigation* helpful to both the interaction designer and the information space architect might be:

interpretation: *an estimation, from examination of a data display and supported by reference to a relevant internal model, of the consequence of moving in available directions in information space.*

To help a user both to form an internal model of information space and to move efficiently towards a goal, it behoves the interaction designer to provide, where possible, cues – typically in the form of icons and text – which indicate potentially beneficial movement in information space. That is not an easy task, however, for many reasons: for example, different users will be performing different tasks, they will have a variety of targets in information space, and the interactions needed to reach a target might be many as well as being dependent upon internal states of the system. In this context it is useful to define a property of information space called sensitivity:

sensitivity: *a specific movement in information space, a set of influential states and the sequence of actions required to achieve that movement.*

It is not difficult to design cues which encode sensitivity and which relate to *simple* movement in information space. One is already shown in Figure 17.2: immediately relevant to the engineering designer is the nature of the green area as well as the degree of crowding of the discernible grey-scale boundaries In Figure 17.3b relevant cues include the aural and visual aura, the clothing decoration and the wide gaze of the individuals.

The design of cues indicative of *distant* content is not so straightforward. A relatively simple example made possible by the structure of information space is provided by the familiar hierarchically-based menu system, in which category labels at any level are chosen to reflect the nature of the labels or content at subordinate levels. Where the space is not well-structured, as with the web, the design of local cues indicative of distant content is far from straightforward.

In view of current discussions about the concept of "scent" it is desirable to differentiate between sensitivity information and scent. The latter has been defined (Chi et al., 2001; Pirolli, 2002) as:

scent: *the imperfect, subjective, perception of the value, cost or access path of information sources obtained from proximal cues such as web links, or icons representing the content sources.*

Thus it is scent, triggered by the sight of cues encoding sensitivity information, which can influence subsequent movement in information space.

17.8 Formulation of a Browsing Strategy

Notwithstanding any element of opportunism (Tweedie, 1995), a user may decide, from their interpretation of a current display (but additionally influenced by whatever internal models are deemed to be relevant to the task at hand), that a new region of information space should be browsed. As already pointed out, that browsing will be characterised by three components: location, scan and attention.[6]

It seems clear that the available movement in information space should be matched to the sort of movement likely to be required by a user. Thus, if the engineering designer has decided, from inspection of Figure 17.2, that movement to higher values of X1 is desirable, then the means of achieving such movement might well be a mouse click at the position where the new image centre should be, rather than the keyboard entry of new numerical X1 and X2 coordinates. Furthermore, as with any interaction design, the *actual* control affordance should be identical, if at all possible, with the *perceived affordance*. There is always the danger that a desired browsing strategy that is difficult to execute may be ignored in favour of a less desirable one which is not.

The human user is not the only agent determining the location component of browsing. For example, in automated design (Colgan et al., 1995) the movement in information space may be determined by an algorithm which is seeking to improve a design, and the human partner may simply be observing some representation of successive designs ready, if appropriate, to halt the algorithm and redirect it. Another example is the "autoscan" control on a CD player, the operation of which causes a sequence of very brief segments of the music to be played, thereby giving the user a feeling for the CD's content. This control also determines the scan component of browsing; only the listener determines the attention component, perhaps unconsciously.

In view of the above discussion we offer a definition:

formulation of browsing strategy: *on the basis of an interpretation regarding potentially useful movement in information space and an awareness – possibly incomplete – of available means of executing the browsing activity, the selection of a browsing mechanism.*

---

[6] Perhaps usefully though informally summarised as Where?, How? and What?

17.9 Navigation

We use the term *navigation* to describe iteration around the loop shown in Figure 17.4. Most importantly, we do not try to ascribe to the user any underlying intention in so doing. Thus, the user may be exploring information space merely to acquire an internal model, or cognitive map,[7] of part or the whole of that space; a good analogy might be the sightseeing trip that a first visitor to Paris might take, prior to a decision to spend an afternoon in the Louvre and the Tuilleries Gardens. On the other hand, the sole objective might be to move towards and eventually reach a specific goal, with no concern whatsoever for the acquisition of an internal model other than that required to suggest local movement. Movement through the pages of a dictionary to reach a specific word would be a good example. Often, however, the movement in information space will be a mixture of the two, determined by some higher cognitive activity. With these considerations in mind, navigation might usefully be defined as:

navigation: *the concurrent creation of an internal model of parts of information space and intentional movement towards a target (however precisely or loosely defined), the content of each at any instant of time being controlled by a strategy formulated by the user.*

Again, the above definition differs radically from a commonly held view that navigation is the activity of working out which direction to move in while one is moving through information space.

17.9.1 Exploration, Querying and Search

Other terms have been used in the context of information space navigation, and can usefully be defined and differentiated from the activities already discussed.

The term *exploration* could be assigned to that part of the navigational activity associated with the formation of an internal model. To call it "information seeking" is to use too vague a term. Thus, a useful definition might be:

exploration: *movement in information space with the specific and sole aim of creating or enhancing an internal model of a part of information space.*

Thus, exploration does not exclude the revisitation of a location previously visited.

---

[7] Tversky (1993) makes the point that, instead of a continuous cognitive model, there is usually formed a "cognitive collage".

The act of querying has been defined as the act of exploration with a specific target in mind, but this activity falls firmly under the heading of navigation. Rather, the essence of querying is *automatic movement* of some kind: a useful physical analogy might be the hailing of a taxi and the announcement of a desired destination, with no subsequent attempt to learn anything about the route taken to that destination. An appropriate definition might therefore be:

querying: *the description of a specific or general target, and the subsequent automatic, and often invisible, translation in information space to the location of the target or to a region of information space wherein the target is likely to be found.*

In Waterworth and Chignell's (1991) view, the use of querying would be classed as a *descriptive* method of interaction, whereas others would be termed "*referential*". Increasingly available are facilities for query-initiated navigation, often termed query-initiated browsing (Furnas, 1997) in which an automatic process places a user within a limited environment offering the probability that subsequent navigation will be successful, whether the outcome is arrival at a specific target or the acquisition of insight as to how to proceed further.

The term "search" can cover so many activities that a definition may not prove useful in the context of our study of navigation. If search is defined as the collection of activities that take place following the conscious formulation of a target (however precise or vague) and either arrival at that target or a revised target or, perhaps, the abandonment of the search, then a combination of querying and navigation may well be involved.

17.10 Display Design

Not surprisingly, different guidelines apply to the design of a display to support browsing, interpretation and the formulation of a browsing strategy. However, there is only one display, so the interaction designer, in choosing what to display, must balance these three requirements. In what follows, however, we consider the three activities separately.

For all the activities involved in navigation, the range of tasks, users and available data are such that no precise step-by-step method is available to influence design. It is for this reason that we provide, below, illustrative examples. Design for each activity is also complicated by the choice of media (visual, aural, tactile or olfactory) and the ability to have any specific activity under the user's control, determined by default, or determined by some algorithm or software agent. The examples below are chosen to illustrate the wide variety of approaches to the design of a display to support browsing, interpretation and the formulation of

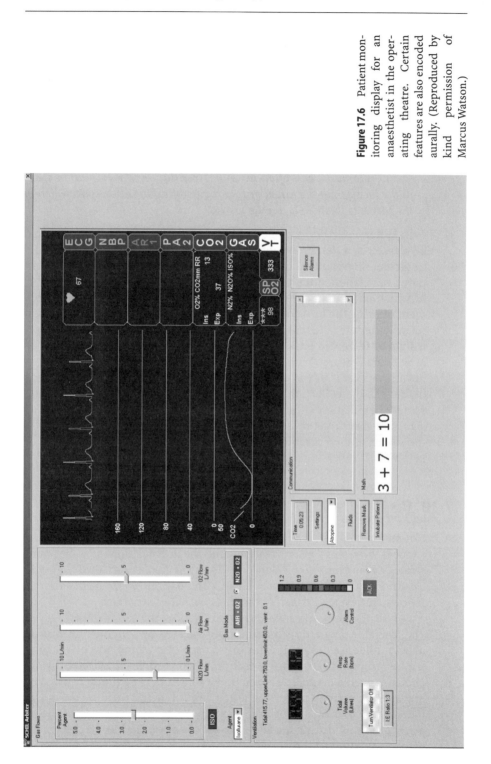

Figure 17.6 Patient monitoring display for an anaesthetist in the operating theatre. Certain features are also encoded aurally. (Reproduced by kind permission of Marcus Watson.)

browsing activity, and in this way to provide concepts and techniques that might be added to the interaction designer's "palette" for use where deemed appropriate.

17.11 Design for Browsing

What is common to all forms of browsing are its three basic components – location, scan and attention.

17.11.1 CD Autoscan

With the CD "autoscan" feature (see section 17.8), location is determined by the user when selecting the CD, scan is by default (i.e., chosen by the interaction designer) and attention is usually unconsciously determined by the user's mood.

17.11.2 Anaesthetist's Display

Figure 17.6 shows a display designed to inform an anaesthetist in the operating theatre about the condition of the patient (Watson et al., 2000). What cannot be shown in the figure is the *aural* display of critical parameters such as blood pressure. The aural display is provided in case the anaesthetist's attention is for some reason diverted from the visual display (perhaps by an urgent telephone conversation), and takes the form of a "beep" repeated at intervals of a few seconds: a change in the beep's pitch, and especially its cessation, immediately alerts the anaesthetist. Here, location is by default, scan is by default, and attention is unconsciously determined.

17.11.3 Document Visualisation

It was pointed out (Jul and Furnas, 1997) that three levels of structure are involved in any consideration of data visualisation: the inherent structure of the data, a (designable) imposed and externalised (i.e., displayed) structure, and the user's cognitive map[8] (Figure 17.7). Design for browsing must therefore acknowledge the fact that there may be more than one possible imposed structure (i.e., location) for a given body of data. In document visualisation, for example, it may be helpful for the user to be

---

[8] The activity of modelling appears to resemble the action which Carmel et al. (1992) call "review browse" and which integrates the content. As navigation proceeds the internal model, as well as the interpretation, thereby generated may become a collage (Tversky, 1993).

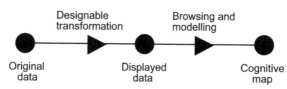

Figure 17.7 Transformation of an inherent data structure into an imposed structure with a view to influencing the formation of a mental model.

able to request the result of a clustering operation (in other words, a new imposed structure, or location) in order better to interpret certain properties of the data.[9] Thus, location is user selected.

17.11.4 Opportunistic Browsing

Human beings do not always view data with a specific information processing task consciously in mind, especially within a ubiquitous computing environment (Norman, 2000). An example is provided by the Coffee Table resulting from the EC Living Memory project (Living Memory, 2000). The primary function of the table (Figure 17.8) is to support conventional social interaction, and to this end functions correctly even when hot coffee cups, plates of donuts and books are placed on it. However, the table top is an LCD display: around its periphery is a continuous slow movement of images related to activities in the community within which the table is situated. On occasion, an item will catch the eye of the person sitting at the table, whereupon further information may easily and rapidly be archived for later study before social interaction is resumed with minimal interruption. Here, the browsing is referred to as opportunistic browsing (de Bruijn and Spence, 2001). With the table, location is not under the user's control: indeed, the information displayed might well be influenced (Mamdani et al., 1999) by software agents.

17.11.5 House Purchase: Attribute Explorer and Neighbourhood Explorer

The purchase of objects such as cars or houses can be facilitated by visualisation tools. If the original database contains many objects, for example

---

[9] Relevant to the concept illustrated in Figure 17.7 is the recent work of Chi (2000) who presents a model showing the transformations involved in proceeding from "value" (in other words, the original data) to "view" (what the user sees on a display). It is a model which encompasses a wide range of information visualisation tools.

Figure 17.8 Coffee table incorporating display to support opportunistic browsing. (Reproduced by permission of Philips Design, Eindhoven, The Netherlands.)

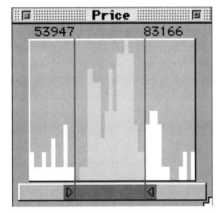

Figure 17.9 A histogram of the Attribute Explorer showing the selection of a subset of houses by the positioning of attribute limits.

more than 1000, a process of "whittling down" that number to a much smaller collection (e.g. 100) is probably a first objective. For this purpose the most appropriate data display might involve aggregate data and selectable attribute limits, as with the Attribute Explorer (Figure 17.9). Perhaps following an intermediate stage based on bargrams (Apperley et al., 2001), the Neighbourhood Explorer (Apperley et al., 1999) is appropriate to a smaller (e.g. 15) number of objects, and offers two advantages. Objects (here, houses) can be compared with their near "neighbours", using that term not in the geographic sense but with reference to various important attributes (Figure 17.10). As with many objects for sale, the non-quantitative attribute of appearance can be handled in view of the small number of objects involved. In this example the user is specifying location in information space by means of a sequence of "whittling down" actions.

419

Figure 17.10 The interface of the Neighbourhood Explorer, allowing the comparison of a "reference" house (centre) with its "neighbours" with respect to attributes such as price and number of bedrooms which are arranged radially.

17.11.6 Inhabited Information Spaces

The architect of a rich information space populated by StarCursors representing real human users is faced with a very complex task, and it is difficult to provide more than a few guidelines. There may, for example, be much to recommend a fairly densely populated view of that space so that a user can rapidly become aware of its content as well as any relevant cues. Nevertheless, there will be many difficult design decisions: should, for example, similar services be grouped together to facilitate navigation, or spread apart to provide a source of adventure? Here, location is determined, by a user, by their StarCurser's orientation and position in space.

17.11.7 Agents and Recommender Systems

It is not only the system designer who determines the content which is browsed. In a recommender system such as that incorporated within Amazon.com it is the collective actions of individual purchasers which determine messages to the effect that "people who bought this book also bought ..." (Lieberman et al., 2001).

17.11.8 On-line Shopping

A common approach to the design of a web site for on-line shopping is to expose the shopper to a representative array of products, notwithstanding any previous selection of a category to identify a subset of reasonable size. A high density "broad" (Larson and Czerwinski, 1998) presentation can allow a rapid movement of eye gaze to assess the user's interest in any given object, and minimise the need to make selections. Here, location is chosen by the web site designer. An interesting variation arises with the use of Rapid Serial Visual Presentation (RSVP). In some of the RSVP modes (Wittenburg et al., 2000) the designer not only selects the location but has considerable influence over scan as well, since the user is encouraged or forced to view items sequentially.

17.11.9 Tagging

The ability of a user to recall the intermediate results of some information space activity is limited, suggesting that certain intermediate results of especial interest might be "tagged" and appear suitably encoded in a display. Here, the user is adding to the information space.

17.12 Design for Interpretation

As discussed above, the need for movement in information space will largely be determined following an interpretation of the current display, an interpretation which can be gained from encoded sensitivity information. Again, as with the browsing activity, there is no step-by-step procedure suited to all situations and we therefore present illustrative examples.

17.12.1 The Attribute Explorer

The Attribute Explorer (Spence and Tweedie, 1998; Smith and Moore, 2000) is a visualisation tool designed to facilitate a user's exploration of a collection of objects, each defined by the values of a number of attributes.

To support the purchase of a house, for example, each of a number of attributes is associated with a histogram (Figure 17.11 – see also colour plate 15) for which attribute limits can be positioned by a user. The combination of limits on many different attributes modifies the histogram by colour-coding. Whereas green indicates houses that satisfy all attribute limits, black indicates houses that fail one limit. The sensitivity information encoded black therefore indicates those attribute limits that can be

421

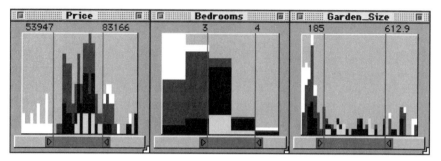

Figure 17.11 The colour-coding of individual houses in the Attribute Explorer histograms provides sensitivity information. Black houses lying outside a limit will turn green if that limit is extended to encompass them. (See also colour plate 15.)

Number of Bedrooms

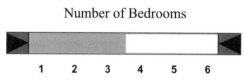

Figure 17.12 The colour-coding indicates that object selection will be unaffected while the lower limit stays within the grey region. When a limit moves into the yellow region selection will be affected. (See also colour plate 16.)

modified to result in more acceptable (green) houses, a feature especially valuable when a "no hit" situation is encountered.

17.12.2 The Prosection

For the engineering designer, a prosection such as that shown in Figure 17.2 could be said to be very rich in sensitivity information: it may not only suggest where large green areas are available but indicate areas with closely spaced boundaries where tolerances on components may lead to very variable product behaviour. Since the data embodied within a prosection may be expensive to generate, the implementation of a design system based on prosections may require consideration of a trade-off between the granularity of the image and the interpretation of sensitivity information.

17.12.3 Slider Sensitivity

Within the Spotfire visualisation tool a remarkably simple but very effective display of sensitivity information is contained within the sliders by means of which attribute value limits are positioned by a user (Figure 17.12 – see also colour plate 16). The yellow section of the slider indicates the region within which variation of a limit will cause a change in the selection of objects to be displayed. Such a technique can probably usefully be generalised to many other applications.

17.13 Design for the Formulation of a Browsing Strategy

One or more of the three aspects of browsing (*location, scan, attention*) are chosen by the user and, where appropriate, executed by interaction with some control. Where such a control is involved it should, as far as practical, be chosen to be compatible with whatever browsing activity appears most desirable to the user. Indeed, when formulating a desirable browsing action the user will normally be influenced not only by the interpretation of displayed data but additionally by knowledge of available controls and their ease of use. Thus, without careful interaction design, a desirable browsing strategy that is awkward to execute may be ignored in favour of a less desirable one which is not.

Depending upon the application, each of the three aspects of browsing may variously be under user control, defined algorithmically, available by default or (for scan and attention) determined cognitively, either consciously or unconsciously. Since many combinations are possible and will be chosen to suit a given application, we group the illustrations presented below according to the browsing feature.

17.13.1 Location

User Selection

A design engineer viewing the image of Figure 17.2 will almost certainly wish to explore the hypothesis that there is a large green region to be revealed at higher values of X1. Some form of direct engagement may be most suitable for specifying the new location, for example a mouse click offset from the centre of the image in the direction in which the designer wishes to explore, the degree of offset indicating the desired extent of movement in information space. Such a control mechanism would usually be preferable to the keyboard entry of precise numerical ranges of X1 and X2, especially during the qualitative aspects of early stages of design. In this example, the scan and attention features of browsing will be cognitively determined on the basis of the engineer's experience.

Automated Selection

In the CoCo system for the human guidance of automated design (Colgan et al., 1995) the browsable location in information space is determined by

Figure 17.13   The "cockpit" of the CoCo system for the human guidance of automated design. Bars indicate the current values of components and the sensitivity of artefact performance to those components. Circles indicate the discrepancy between desired and achieved performance at different levels of detail.

a free-running optimisation algorithm which presents a new view as often as twice a second.

Moreover, the view presented (Figure 17.13) is quite rich, involving both a tree-structured display of artefact performance, a series of bars indicating parameter values (like the X1 and X2 of the prosection of Figure 17.2) and another set of bars indicating the sensitivity of artefact performance to changes in those parameters. Because the display is changing so rapidly, and because only qualitative information is of interest, no numerical values are displayed: rather, circle size and bar length have been chosen to encode the numerical data. In the event that the user wishes to return for any reason to an earlier iteration it is common to provide some indication of the "success" of each iteration and ensure that a click on an iteration bar is all that is needed to achieve that change in location.

Here, location is determined algorithmically, though the user can retreat to a previously visited iteration and can certainly provide the algorithm with a new starting condition. A design engineer using the CoCo system will determine scan and attention according to the progress of the automated design and the designer's experience.

17.13.2 Scan

The method of presentation known as Rapid Serial Visual Presentation (Spence, 2002) can exert a strong influence upon the scan feature of browsing. With keyhole-mode RSVP, the user views, at high speed, a predetermined sequence of images relating to some content (i.e. location) previously selected by the user, all within the same "window" of the display screen. While the nature of the scan component of browsing is therefore predetermined, the user can nevertheless control the speed of the scan and, most importantly, can halt the sequence.

17.13.3 Attention

Solso (1998) introduces the subject of attention with the definition:

attention: the concentration of mental effort on sensory or mental events.

The complex consequences of such concentration began to be studied about 50 years ago through elegant experiments conducted by Cherry (1953) and Broadbent (1958) and, later, by Treisman (1964) and others. As a result, information processing models were proposed to characterise observed behaviour. Nevertheless, the complexity of the phenomenon of attention, coupled with current understanding, is such that little if any direct and concise guidance can be offered to the interaction designer concerned with the browsing activity within navigation. In circumstances where attention is a critical parameter the introduction by Solso (1998) offers a route to the relevant literature.

17.14 Design for Social Navigation

The navigation framework of Figure 17.4 has been presented, explained and illustrated with a view to providing a tool for the interaction designer. It is hoped that this material will form a useful basis for organised thought about the design of spaces to support social navigation.

17.15 Conclusions

Interaction design is as much an art as any other branch of engineering design, and has to be concerned with many aspects of human–computer interaction. Only one of these is the navigation of information spaces. Design to facilitate navigation is also largely an art, so that a detailed prescriptive approach is unavailable. It is within this context that this paper has presented what is hoped will be a useful framework to inform design for information space navigation, as well as concepts and techniques that might well be added to the "palette" of the interaction designer.

References

Abowd, G., Atkeson, C., Hong, J., Long, S., Kooper, R. and Pinkerton, M. (1997) Cyberguide: A mobile context-aware tour guide. *Wireless Networks*, 3: 421–433.

Abu-Ghazzeh, T.M. (1996) Movement and wayfinding strategies in the King Saud University. Built environment: A look at freshmen orientation and environmental information. *Journal of Environmental Psychology*, 16: 305–318.

Abu-Ghazzeh, T.M. (1997) Signs advertising and the imagability of buildings: A perceptual selection in the view from the street in Amman Jordan. *Habitat International*, 21 (2): 255–267.

Ackerman, M.S. (1994) Augmenting the organizational memory: A field study of Answer Garden. *Proceedings of the Conference on Computer-Supported Cooperative Work (CSCW '94), Chapel Hill, NC*. New York: ACM Press, pp. 243–252.

Ackerman, M.S. (1996) Answer Garden 2: Merging organizational memory with collaborative help. *Proceedings of the Conference on Computer-Supported Cooperative Work (CSCW '96)*. Boston, MA: ACM Press, pp. 97–105.

Ackerman, M.S. and Starr, B. (1995) Social activity indicators: Interface components for CSCW systems. *Proceedings of the ACM Symposium on User Interface Software and Technology (UIST '95)*. New York: ACM, pp. 159–168.

Aiello, J.R. (1987) Human spatial behavior. In D. Stokols and I. Altman (eds), *Handbook of environmental psychology: Volume 1*. New York: Wiley & Sons, pp. 389–504.

Alexander, C., Ishikawa, S. and Silverstein, M. (1977) *A pattern language: Towns, buildings, construction*. New York: Oxford University Press.

Alexander, C., Ishikawa, S., Silverstein, M., Jacobson, M., Fiksdahl-King, I. and Angel, S. (1997) *A Pattern Language*. New York: Oxford University Press.

Altman, I. (1975) *The environment and social behavior*. Wadsworth, Monterey.

Altman, I. and Vinsel, A.M. (1977) Personal space: An analysis of ET Hall's proxemics framework. In I. Altman and J.F. Wohlwill (eds), *Human behaviour and the environment: Vol. 2. Advances in theory and research*. New York: Plenum, pp. 181–259.

Altman, I. and Zube, E.H. (1989) *Public places and spaces*. New York: Plenum.

Anderson, B. and McGrath, A. (1997) Strategies for mutability in virtual environments. *BCS Conference: Virtual environments on the Internet, WWW and Networks, Bradford*.

Anderson, J.R. (1980) *Cognitive psychology and its implications*. San Francisco, CA: Freeman.

Ang, S.H., Leong, S.M. and Lin, S. (1997) The mediating influence of pleasure arousal on layout and signage effects: Comparing more and less customised retail services. *Journal of Retailing and Consumer Services*, 4 (1): 13–24.

Apperley, M.D., Spence, R. and Gutwin, C. (1999) *The neighbourhood explorer*. Working Paper 99/15, Department of Computer Science, University of Waikato, New Zealand.

Apperley, M.D., Spence, R. and Wittenburg, K. (2001) Selecting one from many: The development of a scalable visualization tool. *ACM Proceedings (HCC '01)*, pp. 366–372.

427

Arnheim, R. (1984) *Art and visual perception. A psychology of the creative eye.* Berkeley: University of California Press.

Arnheim, R. (1996) *Die Macht der Mitte. Eine Kompositionslehre für die bildenden Künste.* Cologne: Dumont.

Bacon, E.N. (1974) *Design of cities.* London: Thomas Hudson.

Baecker, R., Nastos, D., Posner, I. and Mawby, K. (1993) The user-centered iterative design of collaborative writing systems. *Proceedings of the ACM Conference on Human Factors in Computing Systems (InterCHI '93).* New York: ACM Press, pp. 399–405.

Balabanovic, M. and Shoham, Y. (1997) Fab: Content-based, collaborative recommendation. *Communications of the ACM,* **40** (3): 66–72.

Balling, J.D. and Falk, J.H. (1982) Development of visual preference for natural environments. *Environment and Behavior,* **14** (1): 5–28.

Bannon, L. and Bødker, S. (1997) Constructing common information spaces. In J. Hughes, T. Rodden, W. Prinz and K. Schmidt (eds), *Proceedings of the 5th European Conference on Computer-Supported Cooperative Work (ECSCW '97).* Dordrecht: Kluwer Academic Publishers, pp. 81–96.

Barker, R.G. (1968) *Ecological psychology: Concepts and methods for studying the environment of human behaviour.* Stanford, CA: Stanford University Press.

Barrett, R. and Maglio, P.P. (1998) Intermediaries: New places for producing and manipulating web content. *Computer Networks and ISDN Systems,* **30**: 509–518.

Barrett, R. and Maglio, P.P. (1999) Intermediaries: An approach to manipulating information streams. *IBM Systems Journal,* **38**.

Barrett, R., Maglio, P.P. and Kellem, D.C. (1997) How to personalize the web. *Proceedings of the ACM Conference on Human Factors in Computing Systems (CHI '97).* New York: ACM Press, pp. 75–82.

Baudisch, P. (1998) Recommending TV programs on the Web: How far can we get at zero user effort? *Recommender Systems: Papers from the 1998 Workshop.* AAAI Press, Technical Report WS-98-08, pp. 16–18.

Baym, N. (1995) The performance of humor in computer-mediated communication. *Journal of Computer-Mediated Communication,* **1** (2).

Becker, B. and Mark, G. (1998) Social conventions in collaborative virtual environments. In D. Snowdon and E. Churchill (eds), *Proceedings CVE '98, University of Manchester, Manchester, UK,* 17–19 June, pp. 47–55.

Becker, B. and Mark, G. (1999) Constructing social systems through computer-mediated communication. *Virtual Reality,* **4**: 60–73.

Bellotti, V. (1997) Design for privacy in multimedia computing and communications environments. In P.E. Agre and M. Rotenberg (eds), *Technology and privacy: The new landscape.* Cambridge, MA: MIT Press, pp. 63–98.

Bellotti, V. and Bly, S. (1996) Walking away from the desktop computer: Distributed collaboration in a product design team. *Proceedings of the ACM Conference on Computer-Supported Cooperative Work (CSCW '96).* Boston, MA: ACM Press, pp. 209–218.

Bellotti, V. and Sellen, A. (1993) Design for privacy in ubiquitous computing environments. *Proceedings Third European Conference on Computer-Supported Cooperative Work (ECSCW '93).* Dordrecht: Kluwer, pp. 77–92.

Benedikt, M. (1992) *Cyberspace.* Cambridge, MA: MIT Press.

Benford, S. and Fahlen, L. (1993) A spatial model of interaction for large virtual environments. *Proceedings of the European Conference on Computer-Supported Cooperative Work (ECSCW '93).* Dordrecht: Kluwer.

Benford, S., Bowers, J., Fahlen, L., Greenhalgh, C. and Snowdon, D. (1995) User embodiment in collaborative virtual environments. *Proceedings of the ACM Conference on Human Factors in Computing Systems (CHI '95).* New York: ACM Press, pp. 242–249

Benford, S., Bowers, J., Fahlen, L., Mariani, J. and Rodden, T. (1994) Supporting co-operative work in virtual environments. *The Computer Journal*, 37: 8.

Benford, S., Brown, C., Reynard, G. and Greenhalgh, C. (1996) Shared spaces: Transportation, artificiality and spatiality. In M. Ackerman (ed.), *Proceedings of ACM Conference on Human Factors in Computing (CSCW '96)*. Boston, MA: ACM Press, pp. 77–86.

Benford, S., Greenhalgh, C. and Lloyd, D. (1997) Crowded collaborative virtual environments. *Proceedings of the ACM Conference on Human Factors in Computing Systems (CHI '97)*. New York: ACM Press, pp. 59–66.

Benford, S., Ingram, R. and Bowers, J. (1996) Building virtual cities: Applying urban planning principles to the design of virtual environments. *Proceedings of the ACM Conference on Virtual Reality Software and Technology (VRST '96)*, Hong Kong. New York: ACM Press.

Benford, S., Snowdon, D. et al. (1997a) Informing the design of collaborative environments. *Proceedings GROUP '97 (Phoenix, Arizona, 16–19 Nov.)*. ACM Press, pp. 71–79.

Benford, S., Snowdon, D., Brown, C., Reynard, G. and Ingram, R. (1997b) The populated web: Browsing, searching and inhabiting the WWW using collaborative virtual environments. *Proceedings of INTERACT '97*. Sydney: Chapman and Hall, pp. 539–546.

Bentley, I., Alcock, A., Murrain, P., McGlynn, S. and Smith, G. (1985) *Responsive environments a manual for designers*. London: Architectural Press.

Benyon, D.R. (1998a) Beyond navigation as metaphor. In N. Dahlbäck (ed.), *Exploring navigation: Towards a framework for design and evaluation of navigation in electronic spaces*. SICS Technical Report 98–01, pp. 31–43.

Benyon, D.R. (1998b) Cognitive ergonomics as navigation in information space. *Ergonomics*, 41 (2): 153–156.

Benyon, D. and Höök, K. (1997) Navigation in information spaces: Supporting the individual. *INTERACT '97*. Sydney: Chapman and Hall.

Benyon, D.R. (2001) The New HCI? Navigation of information space. *Knowledge-Based Systems*, 14 (8): 425–430.

Berners-Lee, T. (1997) World-wide computer. *Communications of the ACM*, 40 (2): 57–58.

Bharat, K., Kamba, T. and Albers, M. (1998) Personalized, interactive news on the web. *Multimedia Systems*, 6 (5): 349–358.

Bird, G. (1996) The International Monetary Fund and developing countries: A review of the evidence and policy options. *International Organisation*, 50: 477–511.

Bittner, M.J. (1992) Servicespaces: The impact of physical surroundings on customer and employee responses. *Journal of Marketing*, 56 (April): 57–71.

Bly, S., Harrison, S. and Irwin, S. (1993) Media spaces: Bringing people together in a video, audio and computing environment. *Communications of the ACM*, 36 (1): 28–47.

Boden, D. and Molotch, H.L. (1994) The compulsion of proximity. In D. Boden and R. Friedland (eds), *NowHere: Space, time and modernity*. Berkeley, CA: University of California Press.

Borghoff, U.M. and Schlichter, J. (2000) *Computer-supported cooperative work*. Berlin, Heidelberg, New York: Springer Verlag.

Bowers, J. (1995) The social logic of cyberspace. In *COMIC Deliverable 4.3*. Lancaster University. [This report is available via anonymous FTP from ftp.comp.lancs.ac.uk.]

Box, G.E.P. and Draper, N.R. (1987) *Empirical model-building and response surfaces*. New York: Wiley.

Bradner, E., Kellogg, W.A. and Erickson, T. (1999) The adoption and use of Babble: A field study of chat in the workplace. *Proceedings of the European Conference on Computer-Supported Cooperative Work (ECSCW '99)*, pp. 139–158.

429

Brand, Stuart (1994) *How buildings learn: What happens after they're built.* Penguin Books.

Breese, J.S., Heckerman, D. and Kadie, C. (1998) Empirical analysis of predictive algorithms for collaborative filtering. *Proceedings of the Fourteenth Conference on Uncertainty in Artificial Intelligence.* Madison, WI.

Bridges, A. and Dimitrios, D. (1997) On architectural design in virtual environments. *Design Studies*, 18: 143–154.

Broadbent, D.E. (1958) *Perception and communication.* London and New York: Pergamon Press.

Broadbent, G., Bunt, R. and Jencks, C. (eds) (1980) *Signs, symbols and architecture.* Chichester: Wiley.

Broadbent, G., Bunt, R. and Llorens, T. (eds) (1980) *Meaning and behaviour in the built environment.* Chichester: Wiley.

Broadbent, J. and Marti, P. (1997) Location aware mobile interactive guides: Usability issues. *Proceedings of the Fourth International Conference on Hypermedia and Interactivity in Museums (ICHIM '97).*

Brodbeck, D., Chalmers, M., Lunzer, A., Cotture, P. (1997) Domesticating bead: Adapting an information visualization system to a financial institution. *Proceedings IEEE Information Visualization*, 97: 73–80.

Bruckman, A. (1992) *Identity workshop: Emergent social and psychological phenomena in text-based virtual reality.* Technical report, MIT Media Laboratory.

Bruckman, A. and Resnick, M. (1995) virtual professional community: Results from the MediaMOO project. *Convergence*, 1: 1.

Bruckman, A. (1997) MOOSE Crossing: Construction, Community, and Learning in a Networked Virtual World for Kids. PhD dissertation, Massachusetts Institute of Technology.

Burrell, J. and Gay, G. (2001) Collectively defining context in a mobile, networked computing environment. *Extended Abstracts: Proceedings of the ACM Conference on Human Factors in Computing Systems (CHI '01).* New York: ACM Press.

Büscher, M., O'Brien, J., Rodden, T. and Trevor, J. (2001) He's behind you: The experience of presence in shared virtual environments. In E. Churchill, D. Snowdon and A. Munro (eds), *Collaborative virtual environments. Digital places and spaces for interaction.* London: Springer, pp. 77–98.

Bush, Vannevar (1945) As we may think. *Atlantic Monthly*, July.

Button, G. and Dourish, P. (1996) Technomethodology: Paradoxes and possibilities. *Proceedings of the ACM Conference on Human Factors in Computing Systems (CHI '96)*, Vancouver. New York: ACM, pp. 19–26.

Button, G. and Harper, R. (1996) The relevance of 'work-practice' for design. *Computer-Supported Cooperative Work*, 4: 263–280.

CACM (1998) Special issue on recommender systems. *Communications of the ACM.*

Cadiz, J.J., Gupta, A. and Grudin, J. (2000) Using web annotations for asynchronous collaboration around documents. *Proceedings of the ACM Conference on Computer-Supported Collaborative Work (CSCW 2000).* New York: ACM Press.

Campbell, C.S. and Maglio, P.P. (submitted) Facilitating navigation in information spaces: Road signs on the World Wide Web. To appear in *International Journal of Human-Computer Studies.*

Canter, D. and Kenny, ?. (1975) Spatial environments.. In D. Canter and P. Stringer (eds), *Environmental interaction: Psychological approaches to our physical surroundings.* London: Surrey University Press, p. 374.

Carlsson, C. and Hagsand, O. (1993) DIVE: A platform for multi-user virtual environments. *Computers and Graphics*, 17 (6), 663–669.

Carmel, E., Crawford, S. and Chen, H. (1992) Browsing in Hypertext: A cognitive study. *IEEE Transactions on Systems, Man and Cybernetics*, 22: 865–884.

Carroll, J.M., Mack, R.L. and Kellogg, W.A. (1988) Interface metaphors and user interface design. In M. Helander (ed.), *Handbook of human–computer interaction*. New York: Elsevier, pp. 67–85.

Carroll, J.M. and Thomas, J.C. (1982) Metaphors and the cognitive representation of computing systems. *IEEE Transactions on System, Man and Cybernetics*, **12** (2).

Carroll, J.M. (2000) *Making Use: Scenario-Based Design of Human-Computer Interactions*. Cambridge, MA: MIT Press.

Castro, P., Chiu, P., Kremenek, T. and Munz, R.R. (2001) A probabilistic room location service for wireless networked environments. In G. Abowd, B. Brumitt and S. Shafer (eds), *Ubicomp 2001: International Conference on Ubiquitous Computing. Atlanta, Georgia*, 30 September–2 October. Berlin: Springer, pp. 18–34.

Caswell, D. and Debaty, P. (2000) Creating web representations for places. *Proceedings of HUC 2000, Bristol, England*, pp. 114–126.

Catedra, M. (1991) Through the door: A view of space from an anthropological perspective. In D.M. Mark and A.U. Frank (eds), *Cognitive and linguistic aspects of geographic space*. Dordrecht: Kluwer, pp. 53–63.

Catledge, L. and Pitkow, J. (1995) Characterizing browsing in the World Wide Web. *Proceedings of the Third International World Wide Web Conference*.

Chalmers, M. (1996) A linear iteration time layout algorithm for visualising high-dimensional data. *Proceedings IEEE Visualization*, pp. 127–132.

Chalmers, M. (1999) Comparing information access approaches. *J. American Society for Information Science (JASIS)*, 50th Anniversary Issue, **50** (12), 1108–1118.

Chalmers, M. and Chitson, P. (1992) Bead: Explorations in information visualization. *Proceedings of the Fifteenth Annual ACM SIGIR Conference on Research and Development in Information Retrieval*. New York: ACM Press.

Chalmers, M., Ingram, R. and Pfranger, C. (1996) Adding imageability features to information displays. *Proceedings of the ACM Symp. User Interface Software and Technology (UIST '96)*. New York: ACM Press, pp. 33–39.

Chalmers, M., Rodden, K. and Brodbeck, D. (1998) The order of things: Activity-centered information access. *Computer Networks and ISDN Systems*, **30**.

Chase, W.G. (1983) Spatial representations of taxi drivers. In R. Rogers and J.A. Sloboda (eds), *Acquisition of symbolic skills*. New York: Plenum Press.

Chau, P.Y.K., Au, G. and Tam, K.Y. (1996) User interface design of interactive multimedia services (IMS) applications: An empirical evaluation. *Proceedings of the 3rd Pacific Workshop on Distributed Multimedia Systems (Hong Kong, June)*, pp. 25–28.

Cherny, L. (1995) *The MUD Register: Conversational modes of action in a text-based virtual reality*. Unpublished PhD dissertation. Palo Alto: Stanford University.

Cherny, L. (1999) *Conversation and community: Chat in a virtual world*. Stanford, CA: CSLI Publications.

Cherry, C. (1953) Some experiments on the recognition of speech with one and with two ears, *Journal of the Acoustic Society of America*, **25**: 975–979.

Cheverst, K., Davies, N., Mitchell, K., Friday, A. and Efstratiou, C. (2000) Developing a context-aware electronic tourist guide: some issues and experiences. *Proceedings of the ACM Conference on Human Factors in Computing Systems (CHI 2000)*. New York: ACM Press, pp. 17–24.

Chi, E., Pirolli, P. and Pitkow, J. (2000) The scent of a site: A system for analyzing and predicting information scent, usage and usability of a Web site. *Proceedings of the ACM Conference on Human Factors in Computing Systems (CHI 2000)*. New York: ACM Press, pp. 161–168.

Chi, E.H. (2000) A taxonomy of visualization techniques using data state reference model. *IEEE Proceedings of Information Visualization (Info Vis '00)*. IEEE, pp. 69–75.

Chi, E.H., Pirolli, P., Chen, K. and Pitkow, J. (2001) Using information scent to model user information needs and actions on the Web. *Proceedings of the ACM Conference on Human Factors in Computing Systems (CHI '01)*. New York: ACM Press, pp. 490–497.

431

Churchland, P. (1998) Folk psychology. In P.M. Churchland and P.S. Churchland, *On the contrary: Critical essays 1987-1997*. Cambridge, MA: MIT Press, pp. 3–15.

Ciolek, T.M., and Kendon, A. (1980) Environment and the Spatial Arrangement of Conversational Encounters. In: Sociological Inquiry Nos 3-4, 50, pp. 237-271.

Citera, M. (1998) Distributed Teamwork: The impact of communication media on influence and decision quality. *Journal of the American Society for Information Science*, **49** (9): 792–800.

Claypool, M. Gokhale, A., Miranda, T., Murnikov, P., Netes, D. and Sartin, M. (1999) Combining content-based and collaborative filters in an online newspaper. *Proceedings of the SIGIR Workshop on Recommender Systems: Algorithms and Evaluation*.

Cohen, D., Jacovi, M., Maarek, Y. and Soroka, V. (2000) Collection awareness on the web via Livemaps. *Proceedings of the International Workshop on Awareness on the WWW at CSCW*.

Cohen, J. (1994) Monitoring background activities. In G. Kramer (ed.), *Auditory display*. New York: Addison-Wesley, pp. 439–531.

Colgan, L., Spence, R. and Rankin, P.R. (1995) The cockpit metaphor. *Behaviour and Information Technology*, **14** (4): 251–263.

Colomina, B. (1996) *Privacy and publicity: Modern architecture as mass media*. Cambridge, MA: MIT Press.

Coulclelis, H., Golledge, G., Gale, N. and Tobler, W. (1987) Exploring the anchor-point hypothesis of spatial cognition. *Journal of Environmental Psychology*, 7: 99–122.

Coulson, S. (1996a) *Semantic leaps: The role of frame-shifting and conceptual blending in menaing construction*. Unpublished PhD dissertation. San Diego: University of California.

Coulson, S. (1996b) The Menendez brothers virus. In A. Goldberg (ed.), *Conceptual structure, discourse and language*. Cambridge, England: Cambridge University Press.

Coulter, J., and Parsons, E.D. (1991) The praxiology of perception: visual orientations and practical action. *Inquiry*, **33**: 251-72.

COVEN (1997) *Guidelines for building CVE applications*, p. 60.

Coyne, R. (1995) *Designing information technology in the postmodern age: From method to metaphor*. Cambridge, MA: MIT Press.

Cubbit, S. (1998) *Digital aesthetics*. London: Sage.

Curtis, P. (1996) MUDding: Social phenomena in text-based virtual realities. In P. Ludlow (ed.), *High noon on the electronic frontier: Conceptual issues in cyberspace*. Cambridge, MA: MIT Press, pp. 347–373.

Cybertown: http://ww.w.c.ybertown.com/.

Dahlbäck, Nils (ed.) (1998) *Exploring navigation: Towards a framework for design and evaluation of navigation in electronic spaces*. Swedish Institute of Computer Science, TR 98:01.

Danet, B., Ruedenberg, L. and Rosenbaum-Tamari, Y. (1998) Hmmm... where's that smoke coming from? Writing, play and performance on Internet Relay Chat. In F. Sudweeks, M. McLaughlin and Rafaeli (eds), *Network and netplay: Virtual groups on the internet*. Menlo Park, CA: AAAI Press, pp. 41–76.

Darken, R.P. (1997) A simple model of navigation in large-scale virtual spaces, Position paper for the Workshop on Navigation in Electronic Worlds (see Jul and Furnas, 1997)

Darken, R.P. and Sibert, J.L. (1996a) Navigating in large virtual worlds. *International Journal of Human Computer Interaction*, 8: 49–72.

Darken, R.P. and Sibert, J.L. (1996b) Wayfinding strategies and behaviors in large virtual worlds. *Proceedings of the ACM Conference on Human Factors in Computing Systems (CHI'96), Vancouver, BC*. New York: ACM Press, pp. 142–149.

Davies, N.J. et al. (1996) Using clustering in a WWW information agent. *Eighteenth BCS Information Reterieval Colloquium*. British Computer Society.

Davies, N.J., Weeks, R. and Revett, M.C. (1995) An information agent for WWW. *Fourth International Conference on World Wide Web, Boston, MA*.

de Bruijn, O. and Spence, R. (2001) Serendipity within a ubiquitous computing environment: A case for opportunistic browsing. In G.D. Abowd, B. Brumitt and S. Shafer (eds), *Ubicomp 2001: Ubiquitous computing*. Springer, LNCS 2201, pp. 362–369.

de Saussure, F. (1959) *Course in general linguistics* (trans. Wade Baskin). New York: McGraw-Hill.

Deming, W.E. (1986) *Out of the crisis: Quality, productivity and competitive position*. New York: McGraw-Hill.

Dieberger, A. (1995a) On magic features, in (spatial) metaphors. *SigLink Newsletter*, 4 (3): 8–10.

Dieberger, A. (1995b) Providing spatial navigation for the World Wide Web. In A.U. Frank and W. Kuhn (eds), *Spatial Information Theory: Proceedings of COSIT '95*. LNCS 988. Semmering, Austria: Springer, pp. 93–106.

Dieberger, A. (1996) Browsing the WWW by interacting with a textual virtual environment: A framework for experimenting with navigational metaphors. *Proceedings Hypertext '96, Washington DC*, pp. 170–179.

Dieberger, A. (1997a) A city metaphor to support navigation in complex information spaces. In S.C. Hirtle and A.U. Frank (eds), *Spatial information theory: A theoretical basis for GIS (COSIT '97)*. Berlin: Springer-Verlag.

Dieberger, A. (1997b) Supporting social navigation on the World-Wide Web. *International Journal of Human-Computer Studies* (special issue on innovative applications of the Web), **46**: 805–825.

Dieberger, A. (1999) Social connotations of space in the design for virtual communities and social navigation. In A.J. Munro, K. Höök and D. Benyon (eds), *Social navigation of information space*. London: Springer, pp. 35–54.

Dieberger, A. (2000) Where did all the people go? A collaborative Web space with social navigation information. *Proceedings of the Ninth International World Wide Web Conference*. Reston VA: Foretec Seminars Inc.

Dieberger, A. and Frank, A.U. (1998) A city metaphor for supporting navigation in complex information spaces. *Journal of Visual Languages and Computing*, 597–622.

Dieberger, A., Dourish, P., Höök, K. and Wexelblat, A. (2000) Social navigation: Techniques for building more usable systems. *Interactions*, 7 (6): 36–45.

Dillon, A., McKnight, C. and Richardson, J. (1990) Navigation in hypertext: A critical review of the concept. *Proceedings INTERACT '90*. Amsterdam: Elsevier, pp. 587–592.

Dix, A.J., Finlay, J.E., Abowd, G.D. and Beale, R. (1998) *Human–computer interaction* (2nd edn). Hertfordshire, UK: Prentice Hall Europe.

Donath, J. (1995) Visual who: Animating the affinities and activities of an electronic community. *Proceedings of the ACM International Multimedia Conference*. New York: ACM Press, pp. 99–107.

Donath, J., Karahalios, K. and Viegas, F. (1999) Visualizing conversation. In J.F. Nunamaker, Jr and R.H. Sprague, Jr (eds), *Proceedings of the Thirty-Second Hawai'i International Conference on Systems Science*.

Dourish, P. (1999) Where the footprints lead: Tracking down other roles for social navigation. In A.J. Munro, K. Höök and D. Benyon (eds), *Social navigation of information space*. London: Springer-Verlag.

Dourish, P. (ed.) (1998) Interaction and collaboration in MUDs. Special issue of *Computer Supported Cooperative Work*, 7 (1–2).

Dourish, P. (2001) *Where The Action Is. The Foundations of Embodied Interaction*. MIT Press.

Dourish, P. and Bellotti, V. (1992) Awareness and coordination in shared workspaces. *Proceedings of the ACM Conference on Computer-Supported Cooperative Work (CSCW '92)*. New York: ACM Press, pp. 107–114.

Dourish, P. and Bly, S. (1992) Portholes: Supporting awareness in a distributed work group. *Proceedings of the ACM Conference on Human Factors in Computing Systems (CHI '92)*. New York: ACM Press, pp. 541–547.

Dourish, P. and Chalmers, M. (1994) Running out of space: Models of information navigation. Short paper presented at HCI '94 (Glasgow, Scotland).

Downs, R. and Stea, D. (1973) Cognitive representations. In *Image and the environment*. Chicago: Aldine, pp. 79–86.

Downs, R. and Stea, D. (1977) *Image and the environment*. Chicago: Aldine.

Downs, R.M. (1979) Mazes, minds and maps. In D. Pollet and P.C. Haskell (eds), *Sign systems for libraries*. New York: Bowker, pp. 17–32.

Drozd, A., Bowers, J., Benford, S., Greenhalgh, C. and Fraser, M. (2001) Collaboratively improvising magic: An approach to managing participation in an on-line drama. *Proceedings of the Seventh European Conference on Computer-Supported Cooperative Work*, pp. 159–178.

Egan, D. (1988) Individual differences. In M. Helander (ed.), *Handbook of human–computer interaction*. New York: Elsevier.

Engelbart, D. and English, W. (1968) A research center for augmenting human intellect. *Proceedings of the Fall Joint Computer Conference (San Francisco, CA)*. Reston, VA: AFIPS, pp. 393–410.

Engeström, Y., Brown, K., Engeström, R. and Koistinen, K. (1990) Organizational forgetting: An activity-theoretical perspective. In D. Middleton and D. Edwards (eds), *Collective remembering*. Sage Publications.

Erickson, T. (1990) Working with interface metaphors. In B. Laurel (ed.), *The art of HCI design*. Menlo Park, USA: Addison-Wesley.

Erickson, T. (1993) From interface to interplace: The spatial environment as a medium of interaction. In A.U. Frank and I. Campari (eds), *Spatial information theory: A theoretical basis for GIS*. Berlin: Springer-Verlag.

Erickson, T. (1999) Rhyme and punishment: The creation and enforcement of conventions in an on-line participatory limerick genre. In J.F. Nunamaker Jr and R.H. Sprague Jr (eds), *Proceedings of the Thirty-Second Hawai'i International Conference on Systems Science*.

Erickson, T. and Kellogg, W. (2000) Social translucence: An approach to designing systems that support social processes. *ACM Transactions on Computer–Human Interaction*, 7 (1): 59–83.

Erickson, T. and Kellogg, W.A. (2002) Knowledge communities: Online environments for supporting knowledge management and its social context. To appear in: M.A. Ackerman, V. Pipek and W. Wolf (eds), *Beyond knowledge management: Sharing expertise*. Cambridge, MA: MIT Press.

Erickson, T. and Laff, M.R. (2001) The design of the 'Babble' timeline: A social proxy for visualizing group activity over time. *Extended Abstracts: Proceedings of the ACM Conference on Human Factors in Computing Systems (CHI 2001)*. New York: ACM Press, pp. 329–220.

Erickson, T., Smith, D.N., Kellogg, W.A., Laff, M., Richards, J.T. and Bradner, E.A. (1999) Sociotechnical approach to design: Social proxies, persistent conversations and the design of Babble. *Proceedings of the ACM Conference on Human Factors in Computing Systems (CHI '99)*. New York: ACM Press, pp. 72–79.

Espinoza, F., Persson, P., Sandin, A., Nyström, H., Cacciatore, E. and Bylund, M. (2001) GeoNotes: Social and navigational aspects of location-based information systems. In G. Abowd, B. Brumitt and S. Shafer (eds), *Ubicomp 2001: Ubiquitous Computing, International Conference Atlanta, Georgia*, 30 September–2 October. Berlin: Springer, pp. 2–17.

Everitt, N. and Fisher, A. (1995) *Modern epistemology: A new introduction*. New York: McGraw-Hill.

Fahlén, L.E., Brown, C.G. Stahl, O. and Carlsson, C. (1993) A space based model for user interaction in shared synthetic environments. *Proceedings of the ACM Conference on Human Factors in Computing (InterCHI '93)*. New York: ACM Press.

Fällman, D. (2001) 'Where's the Interface?' Enhanced use models for mobile interaction [Doctoral Consortium Paper]. In *Proceedings of INTERACT '01, Eight IFIP TC.13 Conference on Human-Computer Interaction, Waseda University Conference Centre, Shinjuku, Tokyo, Japan*, 9–13 July.

Fauconnier, G. (1997) *Mappings in thought and language*. Cambridge England: Cambridge University Press.

Fauconnier, G. and Turner, M. (1994) *Conceptual projection and middle spaces*. Technical Report 9401, University of California, San Diego, Department of Cognitive Science.

Fauconnier, G. and Turner, M. (1996) Blending as a central process in grammar. In A. Goldberg (ed.), *Conceptual structure, discourse and language*. Cambridge, England: Cambridge University Press.

Fauconnier, G. and Turner, M. (1998) Conceptual integration networks. *Cognitive Science*, **22**: 133–187.

Feldman, D.C. (1984) The development and enforcement of group norms. *Academy of Management Review*, **9** (1), 47–53.

Field, G.E. and Apperley, M.D. (1990) Context and selective retreat in hierarchical menu structures. *Behaviour and Information Technology*, **9** (2): 133–146.

Field, R.H.G. and House, R.J. (1995) *Human behaviour in organizations: A Canadian perspective*. Scarborough, Canada: Prentice-Hall Canada.

Fielding, R., Gettys, J., Mogul, J., Frystyk, H., Masinter, L., Leach, P. and Berners-Lee, T. (1999) *Hypertext transfer protocol HTTP/1.1*. IETF Network Working Group, RFC-2616.

Finke, G.D. (1994) *City signs and innovative urban graphics*. New York: Madison Square Press.

Finn, K.E., Sellen, A.J. and Wilbur, S.B. (1997) *Video-mediated communication*. Mahwah, NJ: Lawrence Erlbaum Associates.

Fish, R., Kraut, R. and Chalfonte, B. (1990) The VideoWindow system in informal communication. *Proceedings of the ACM Conference on Computer-Supported Cooperative Work (CSCW '90)*. New York: ACM Press, pp. 1–11.

Fishkin, K. and Stone, M.C. (1995) Enhanced dynamic queries via movable filters. *Proceedings of the ACM Conference on Human Factors in Computing Systems (CHI '95)*. New York: ACM Press.

Fitzpatrick, G., Kaplan, S. and Mansfield, T. (1996) Physical spaces, virtual places and social worlds: A study of work in the virtual. *Proceedings of the Conference on Computer-Supported Cooperative Work (CSCW '96)*. Boston, MA: ACM Press, pp. 334–343.

Fletcher, A. (1997) The rhetoric of synthetic vs analytic truth on the internet as it relates to nonverbal communication. http://www.geocities.com/Paris/Metro/1022/nonverbl.htm.

Foucault, M. (1972) *The archaeology of knowledge* (trans. A.M. Sheridan Smith). London: Routledge.

Freedman, J.L., Heshka, S. and Levy A. (1975) Crowding as an intensifier of the effect of success and failure (abstract). In J.L. Freedman (ed.), *Crowding and behavior*. San Francisco: Freeman, pp. 151–152.

Frostling-Henningsson, M. (2000) *Dagligvaruhandel över nätet … vad innebär det? En kvalitativ studie av 22 svenska hushåll 1998–1999*. Licentiate Thesis, in Swedish, available from School of Business, Stockholm University, Sweden. ftp:media.mit.edu: /pub/asb/papers/ identity-workshopps.

Fuchs, L., Pankoke-Babatz, U. and Prinz, W. (1995) Supporting cooperative awareness with local event mechanisms: The GroupDesk System. *Proceedings of the European Conference Computer-Supported Cooperative Work (ECSCW '95).* Dordrecht: Kluwer, pp. 247–262.

Fuchs, L., Poltrock, S. and Wojcik, R. (1998) Business value of 3D virtual environments. *SIGGROUP Bulletin,* **19** (3): 25–29. New York: ACM Press.

Furnas, G.W. (1997) Effective view navigation. *Proceedings of the ACM Conference on Human Factors in Computing Systems (CHI '97).* NewYork: ACM Press, pp. 367–374.

Furuta et al. (1997) Hypertext paths and the World Wide Web: Experiences with Walden's Paths. *Hypertext '97 Proceedings.* New York: ACM Press.

Garfinkel, H. (1967) *Studies in ethnomethodology.* Cambridge: Polity.

Garfinkel, H. and Sacks, H. (1970) On formal structures of practical actions. In J.C. McKinney and E.A. Tiryakian (eds), *Theoretical sociology.* New York: Appleton Century Crofts, pp. 338–366.

Gehl, J. (1980) *Life between buildings: Using public space.* New York: Van Nostrand Reinhold.

Gentner, D. and Imai, M. (1992) Is the future always ahead? Evidence for system-mappings in understanding space-time metaphors. *Proceedings of the Fourteenth Annual Meeting of the Cognitive Science Society.* Hillsdale, NJ: LEA.

Gibbs, R.W. (1994) *The poetics of mind.* Cambridge, England: Cambridge University Press.

Gibbs, R.W. and Colston, H.L. (1995) The cognitive psychological reality of image schemas and their transformations. *Cognitive Linguistics,* **6**: 347–378.

Gibson, D., Kleinberg, J. and Raghavan, P. (1998) Inferring web communities from link topology. *Proceedings of the Ninth ACM Conference on Hypertext and Hypermedia.* New York: ACM Press.

Gibson, J.J. (1986) *The ecological approach to visual perception.* Hillsdale, NJ: Lawrence Erlbaum Associates.

Gibson, J.J. (1987) *The Ecological Approach to Visual Perception.* Lawrence Erlbaum Assoc; ISBN: 0898599598.

Gilbert, N. and Mulkay, N. (1984) *Opening Pandora's Box.* Cambridge: Cambridge University Press.

Goffman, E. (1963) *Behavior in public places. Notes on the social organization of gatherings.* New York: The Free Press.

Goldate, S. (1997) The 'Cyberflaneur' – Spaces and places on the internet. *Art Monthly Australia.* http://www.geocities.com/Paris/LeftBank/5696/flaneur.htm.

Goldberg, D., Nichols, D., Oki, B. and Terry, D. (1992) Using collaborative filtering to weave an information tapestry. *Communications of the ACM,* **35** (12): 61–70.

Gómez, E.J., Quiles, J.A., Sanz, M.F. and del Pozo, F. (1998) A user-centered cooperative information system for medical imaging diagnosis. *Journal of the American Society for Information Science,* **49** (9): 810–816.

Good, N., Schafer, J.B., Konstan, J.A., Borchers, A., Sarwar, B., Herlocker, J. and Riedl, J. (1999) Combining collaborative filtering with personal agents for better recommendations. *Proceedings of AAAI-99.* AAAI Press, pp. 439–446.

Goodman, P.S., Ravlin, E. and Schminke, M. (1987) Understanding groups in organizations. In L.L. Cummings and B.M. Staw (eds), *Research in organizational behavior,* Vol. 9, pp. 121–173.

Gottdiener, M. and Lagopoulou, A. (eds) (1986) *The city and the sign.* New York: Columbia University Press.

Grady, J., Taub, S. and Morgan, P. (1996) Primitive and compound metaphors. In A. Goldberg (ed.), *Conceptual structure, discourse and language.* Cambridge, England: Cambridge University Press.

Greenhalgh, C. and Benford, S. (1995a) Virtual reality tele-conferencing: Implementation and experience. *Proceedings of the European Conference on Computer-Supported Cooperative Work (ECSCW '95).* Dordrecht: Kluwer, pp. 165–180,

Greenhalgh, C. and Benford, S. (1995b) MASSIVE: A virtual reality system for tele-conferencing. *ACM Transactions on Computer Human Interfaces (TOCHI),* **2** (3): 239–261.

Grudin, J. (1989) Why groupware applications fail: Problems in design and evaluation. *Office, Technology and People,* **4** (3): 245–264.

Gruen, D. and Moody, P. (1998) Synchronous WebPath as a tool for leveraging expertise. Paper presented at *Human Computer Interaction Consortium Conference, Snow Mountain Ranch, CO.*

Gutwin, C. and Greenberg, S. (1998a) Design for individuals, design for groups: Tradeoffs between power and workspace awareness. *Proceedings of Conference on Computer-Supported Cooperative Work (CSCW '98).* Seattle, WA: ACM Press, pp. 207–216.

Gutwin, C. and Greenberg, S. (1998b) Effects of awareness support on groupware usability. *Proceedings of the ACM Conference on Human Factors in Computing Systems (CHI '98).* Los Angeles, CA: ACM Press, pp. 511–518.

Gutwin, C., Greenberg, S. and Roseman, M. (1996) Workspace awareness in real-time distributed groupware: Framework, widgets and evaluation. In R.J. Sasse, A. Cunningham and R. Winder (eds), *People and Computers, XI. Proceedings of HCI '96,* London: Springer, pp. 281–298.

Hall, E.T. (1966) *The hidden dimension.* New York: Anchor Books.

Hanson, J. (1994) 'Deconstructing' architects' houses. *Environment and Planning B: Planning and Design,* Vol. 21, pp. 675–704.

Hardin, G. (1977) The tragedy of the Commons. In G. Hardin and J. Baden (eds), *Managing the Commons.* San Francisco: Freeman, pp. 16–30.

Harper, R. (1998) Information that counts: Sociology, ethnography and work at the international monetary fund. *Proceedings of Workshop on Personalised and Social Navigation in Information Space, Roselagens Pärla.* Sweden Swedish Institute of Computer Science.

Harper, R. (1999) Information that counts: A sociological view of information navigation. In A. Munro, K. Höök and D. Benyon (eds), *Social navigation of information space.* London: Springer-Verlag.

Harper, R.H.R. (1998) Inside the IMF: *An ethnography of documents, technology and organizational action.* Computers and People Series. London: Academic Press.

Harper, R.H.R. (in press) The organisation, in ethnography. *CSCW: An International Journal.*

Harrison, J.D. and Howards, W.A. (1980) The role of meaning in the urban image. *Meaning and Behaviour in the Built Environment,* **1**: 163–182.

Harrison, S. and Dourish, P. (1996) Re-place-ing space: The roles of place and space in collaborative systems. *Proceedings of ACM Conference on Computer-Supported Cooperative Work (CSCW '96).* Boston, MA: ACM Press, pp. 67–76.

Heath, C. (1986) *Body Movement and Speech in Medical Interaction.* Cambridge, UK: Cambridge University Press.

Heath, C. and Luff, P. (1991) Collaborative activity and technological design: Task coordination in London Underground control rooms. *Proceedings of the European Conference on Computer-Supported Cooperative Work (ECSCW '91),* pp. 65–80.

Heath, C. and Luff, P. (1992a) Collaboration and control: Crisis management and multimedia technology in London Underground line control rooms. *Computer-Supported Cooperative Work. An International Journal,* **1**: 69–94.

Heath, C. and Luff, P. (1992b) Media space and communicative asymmetries: Preliminary observations of video mediated interaction. *Interacting with Computers*, 5 (2): 193–216.

Heath, C. and Luff, P. (2000) *Technology in action*. Cambridge: Cambridge University Press.

Heath, C.C., Jirotka, M., Luff, P. and Hindmarsh, J. (1994) Unpacking collaboration: The interactional organisation of trading in a city dealing room. *Computer-Supported Cooperative Work*, 3: 147–165.

Heath, C.C. et al. (1993) Unpacking collaboration: The interactional organisation of trading in a city dealing room. *Proceedings of the European Conference on Computer-Supported Cooperative Work (ECSCW '93) Milan.*

Heidegger, M. (1962) *Being and time* (trans. J. Macquarrie and E. Robinson). HarperCollins.

Heim, M. (1993) *The metaphysics of virtual reality*. Oxford: Oxford University Press.

Henderson, D.A. and Card, S. (1986) Rooms: The use of multiple virtual workspaces to reduce space contention in a Window-based graphical user interface. *ACM Transactions on Graphics*, 5 (3): 211–243.

Herlocker, J. (2000) *Understanding and improving automated collaborative filtering systems*. PhD Dissertation, University of Minnesota.

Herlocker, J., Konstan, J.A. and Riedl, J. (2000) Explaining collaborative filtering recommendations. *Proceedings of the ACM Conference on Computer-Supported Cooperative Work (CSCW 2000)*. New York: ACM Press, pp. 241–250.

Herlocker, J., Konstan, J.A., Borchers, A. and Riedl, J. (1999) An algorithmic framework for performing collaborative filtering. *Proceedings of SIGIR '99*, pp. 230–237.

Herzog, T. and Smith, G.A. (1988) Danger, mystery and environmental preference. *Environment and Behavior*, 20 (30): 320–344.

Hill, W. and Hollan, J. (1993) History-enriched digital objects. *Proceedings of Computers, Freedom and Privacy (CFP '93)*, available from http://www.cpsr.org/dox/ conferences/cfp93/hill-hollan.html.

Hill, W. and Terveen, L. (1996) Using frequency-of-mention in public conversations for social filtering. *Proceedings of the ACM Conference on Computer-Supported Cooperative Work (CSCW '96)*. Boston, MA: ACM Press, pp. 106–112.

Hill, W., Hollan, J.D., Wroblewski, D. and McCandless, T. (1992) Edit wear and read wear: Text and hypertext. *Proceedings of the ACM Conference on Human Factors in Computing Systems (CHI '92)*. New York: ACM Press, pp. 3–9.

Hill, W., Stead, L., Rosenstein, M. and Furnas, G. (1995) Recommending and evaluating choices in a virtual community of use. *Proceedings of the ACM Conference on Human Factors in Computing Systems (CHI '95)*. New York: ACM Press, pp. 194–201.

Hillier, B. (1996) *Space is the machine*. Cambridge University Press.

Hillier, B. and Hanson, J. (1984) *The social logic of space*. Cambridge, UK: Cambridge University Press.

Hillier, B. and Hanson, J. (1989) *The Social Logic of Space*. Cambridge University Press. pp.296.

Hindmarsh, J., Fraser, M., Heath, C., Benford, S. and Greenhalgh, C. (1998) Fragmented interaction: Establishing mutual orientation in virtual environments. *Proceedings of the ACM Conference on Computer-Supported Cooperative Work (CSCW '98)*. Seattle, WA: ACM Press, pp. 217–226.

Hinrichs, E. and Robinson, M. (1997) *Study on the supporting telecommunications services and applications for networks of local employment initiatives (TeleLEI project)*. GMD, German National Research Centre for Information Technology, Institute for Information Technology, Sankt Augustin.

Hirtle, S. (1997) Spatial knowledge and navigation in real and virtual environments. Position paper for the *CHI '97* Workshop on Navigation in Electronic Worlds.

Hollan, J., Hutchins, E. and Kirsh, D. (2002) Distributed cognition: Toward a new foundation for human–computer interaction research. In J.M. Carroll (ed.), *Human–computer interaction in the new millennium*. New York: ACM Press.

Höök, K., Dahlbäck, N. and Sjölinder, M. (1996) Individual differences and navigation in hypermedia. *ECCE 1996: European Conference on Cognitive Ergonomics, Spain.*

Hudson, S. and Smith, I. (1996) Techniques for addressing fundamental privacy and disruption tradeoffs in awareness support systems. *Proceedings of the ACM Conference on Computer-Supported Cooperative Work (CSCW '96).* Boston, MA: ACM Press, pp. 248–257.

Hunt, J.D. (1997) The garden as virtual reality. *Die Gartenkunst Magazine, 2.*

Hutchins, E. (1983) Understand Micronesian navigation. In D. Gentner and A. Stevens (eds), *Mental models.* Hillsdale, NJ: Erlbaum.

Hutchins, E. (1990) The technology of team navigation. In Galagher, Kraut and Egido (eds), *Intellectual teamwork: The social and technological foundations of cooperative work.* Hillsdale, NJ: Erlbaum, pp. 191–221.

Hutchins, E. (1995) *Cognition in the wild.* Cambridge, MA: MIT Press.

Huxor, A. (1998) An active worlds interface to BSCW to enhance chance encounters. *Proceedings of Collaborative Virtual Environments (CVE '98).* University of Manchester, UK, pp. 87–93.

Ihde, S., Maglio, P.P., Meyer, J. and Barrett, R. (2001) Intermediary-based transcoding framework. *IBM Systems Journal, 40:* 179–192.

Institute of Signs (1979) D. Pollet and C. Haskell (eds), *Effective library signage: A pictorial study.* New York: Bowker, pp. 203–228.

Isaacs, E.A., Tang, J.C. and Morris, T. (1996) Piazza: A desktop environment supporting impromptu and planned interactions. *Proceedings of the Conference on Computer-Supported Cooperative Work (CSCW '96).* Boston, MA: ACM Press, pp. 315–324.

Ishii, H. (1990) TeamWorkStation: Towards a seamless shared workspace. *Proceedings of the Conference on Computer-Supported Cooperative Work (CSCW '90).* New York: ACM Press, pp. 13–26.

Jackson, J.B. (1984) *The world itself: Discovering the vernacular landscape.* New Haven, CT: Yale University Press.

Jacobs, J. (1961) *The death and life of great American cities.* New York: Random House.

Jayyusi, L. (1991) Values and moral judgement: Communicative praxis as moral order. In G. Button (ed.), *Ethnomethodology and the human sciences.* Cambridge: Cambridge University Press, pp. 227–51.

Jeffrey, P. and Mark, G. (1998) Constructing social spaces in virtual environments: A study of navigation and interaction In K. Höök, A. Munro and D. Benyon (eds), *Workshop on Personalised and Social Navigation in Information Space.* SICS Technical Report 98:01, Stockholm, Sweden, pp. 24–38.

Jenison, R.L. and Zahorik, P. (1998) Presence as being-in-the-world. In *Presence, 7* (1): 78–89.

Joachim, S. et al. (1997) WebWatcher: A tour guide for the World Wide Web. *Proceedings of IJCAI '97.*

Johnson, M. (1987) *The body in the mind: The bodily basis of meaning imagination and reason.* Chicago, IL: University of Chicago Press.

Johnson, M. (1992) Philosophical implications of cognitive semantics. *Cognitive Linguistics, 3:* 345–366.

José, R. and Davies, N. (1999) Scalable and flexible location-based services for ubiquitous information access. *Handheld and Ubiquitous Computing, First International Symposium,* Karlsruhe, Germany, September.

Jul, S. and Furnas, G.W. (1997) Navigation in electronic worlds: A CHI workshop. New York: ACM. *SIGCHI Bulletin, 29:* 44–49.

Kalawsky, R.S. (1999) VRUSE – A computerised diagnostic tool: For usability evalua-tion of virtual/synthetic environment systems. *Applied Ergonomics*, **30**: 11–25.

Kaplan, R. and Kaplan, S. (1989) *The experience of nature*. Cambridge: Cambridge University Press.

Kaplan, S. (1987) Aesthetics, affect and cognition: Environmental preference from an evolutionary perspective. *Environment and Behavior*, **19** (1): 3–32.

Karatani, K. (1995) *Architecture as metaphor: Language, number, money*. MIT Press.

Karsenty, A. (1997) Easing interaction through user-awareness. *Proceedings of Intelligent User Interfaces '97*. Orlando, FL: ACM Press, pp. 225–228.

Kauppinen, K., Kivimäki, A., Era, T. and Robinson, M. (1998) Producing identity in collaborative virtual environments. *VRST '98: Symposium on Virtual Reality Software and Technology*. New York: ACM Press, pp. 35–42.

Kaur, K. (1998) *Designing virtual environments for Usability*. Centre for Human-Computer Interface Design. London, City University, p. 240.

Kautz, H., Selman, B. and Shah, M. (1997) Referral web: Combining social networks and collaborative filtering. *Communications of the ACM*, **40** (3): 63–65.

Kendon, A. (1990) *Conducting interaction: Patterns of behavior in focused encounters*. Cambridge, MA: Cambridge University Press.

Keshkin, C. and Vogelmann, V. (1997) Effective visualisation of hierarchical graphs with the Cityscape metaphor. *Proceedings of the Workshop on New Paradigms in Information Visualisation and Manipulation*. ACM Press, pp. 52–57.

Klein, N. (2000) *No logo: Taking aim at the Br and bullies*. Picador.

Knapp, M.L. (1978) *Nonverbal communication in human interaction*. New York: Holt.

Kollock, P. and Smith, M. (1996) Managing the virtual commons: Cooperation and conflict in computer communities. In S.C. Herring (ed.), *Computer-mediated communication. Linguistic, social and cross-cultural perspectives*. Philadelphia, PA: John Benjamins North America, pp. 109–128.

Konstan, J.A., Miller, B.N., Maltz, D., Herlocker, J.L., Gordon, L.R. and Riedl, J. (1997) GroupLens: Applying collaborative filtering to Usenet news. *Communications of the ACM*, **40** (3): 77–87.

Kraut, RPatterson, M., Lundmark, V., Kiesler, S., Mukophadhyay, T. and Scherlis, W. (1998) Internet paradox: A social technology that reduces social involvement and psychological well-being? *American Psychologist*, **53** (9): 1017–1031.

Kuhn, W. (1993) Metaphors create theories for users. In A.U. Frank and I. Campari (eds), *Spatial information theory: A theoretical basis for GIS (COSIT '93)*. Berlin: Springer-Verlag.

Lakoff, G. (1987) *Women, fire and dangerous things: What categories reveal about the mind*. Chicago, IL: University of Chicago Press.

Lakoff, G. and Johnson, M. (1980) *Metaphors we live by*. Chicago: University of Chicago Press.

Lakoff, G. and Johnson, M. (1999) *Philosophy in the flesh: The embodied mind and its challenge to western thought*. New York: Basic Books.

Lamping, ?., Rao, ?. and Pirolli, ?. (1995) A focus+context technique based on hyperbolic geometry for visualizing large hierarchies. *Proceedings of the ACM Conference on Human Factors in Computing Systems (CHI '95)*. New York: ACM Press.

Larson, K. and Czerwinski, M. (1998) Web Page design: Implications of memory, structure and scent for information retrieval. *Proceedings of the ACM Conference on Human Factors in Computing Systems (CHI '98)*. Los Angeles, CA: ACM Press, pp. 25–32.

Latour, B. (1987) *Science in action*. Cambridge, MA: Harvard University Press.

Laurel, B. (1991) *Computers as theatre*. Addison Wesley.

Lefebvre, H. (1991) *The production of space*. Oxford: Blackwell.

Leonhardi, A., Kubach, U., Rothermel, K. and Fritz, A. (1999) Virtual information tow-ers: A metaphor for intuitive, location-aware information access in a mobile environment. *Proceedings of the Third International Symposium on Wearable Computers (ISWC '99)*. San Fransisco, CA: IEEE Press.

Levy, R.M. (1995) Visualization of urban alternatives. In *Environment and Planning B: Planning and Design*, **22**: 343–358.

Lewis, D. (1994) *We, the voyagers*. Honolulu: University of Hawaii Press.

Lieberman, H. (1997) Autonomous interface agents. *Proceedings of the ACM Conference on Human Factors in Computing Systems (CHI '97)*. New York: ACM Press, pp. 67–74.

Lieberman, H., Fry, C. and Weitzman, L. (2001) Exploring the Web with reconnaissance aagents. *Communications of the ACM*, **44** (8): 69–75.

Linton, F., Joy, D., Schaefer, H.-P. and Charron, A. (2000) OWL: A recommender system for organization-wide learning. *Educational Technology and Society*, **3** (1): 62–76.

Living Memory (2000) see http://www.living-memory.org/.

Lönnqvist, P., Dieberger, A., Höök, K. and Dahlbäck, N. (2000) Usability studies of a socially enhanced web server. Short paper accepted to CHI 2000 Workshop on Social Navigation, Netherlands, The Hague.

Luff, P., Heath, C. and Greatbatch, D. (1992) Tasks-in-interaction: Paper- and screen-based documentation in collaborative activity. *Proceedings of the Conference on Computer-Supported Cooperative Work (CSCW '92)*. New York: ACM Press, pp. 163–170.

Luff, P., Hindmarsh, J. and Heath, C. (2000) *Workplace studies. Recovering work practice and informing system design*. Cambridge: Cambridge University Press.

Lund, A. and Waterworth, J.A. (1998) Experiential design: Reflecting embodiment at the interface. *Computation for Metaphors, Analogy and Agents: An International Workshop, University of Aizu, Japan*, April 1998.

Lund, A. and Wiberg, M. (2001) Situating events in RoamViz: Using spatio-temporal dimensions to visualize sustained and dynamic mobile projects. In S. Bjørnestad, R.E. Moe, A.I. Mørch and A.L. Opdahl (eds), *Proceedings of IRIS24, Ulvik, Norway*, Vol. II, pp. 99–114.

Lynch, K. (1960) *The image of the city*. Cambridge. MA: MIT Press.

Lynch, K. (1972) *What time is this place?* Cambridge, MA: MIT Press.

Lynch, K. (1981) *A theory of good city form*. Cambridge, MA: MIT Press.

Lynch, K. (1990) In T. Banerjee and M. Southworth (eds), *City sense and city design: Writings and projects of Kevin Lynch*. Cambridge, MA: MIT Press.

MacLean, A., Carter, K., Moran, T. and Lovstrand, L. (1990) User-tailorable systems: Pressing the issues with buttons. *Proceedings of the ACM Conference on Human Factors in Computing Systems (CHI '90)*. New York: ACM Press.

Maglio, P.P. and Barrett, R. (1997a) How build modeling agents to support web searchers. *Proceedings of the Sixth International Conference on User Modeling*. New York: Springer.

Maglio, P.P. and Barrett, R. (1997b) On the trail of information searchers. *Proceedings of the Nineteenth Annual Conference of the Cognitive Science Society*. Mahwah, NJ: Lawrence Erlbaum.

Maglio, P.P. and Barrett, R. (1998) Adaptive communities and web places. In P. Brusilovsky and P. De Bra (Chairs), *Proceedings of 2nd Workshop on Adaptive Hypertext and Hypermedia (Hypertext '98)*. Pittsburgh, PA.

Maglio, P.P. and Barrett, R. (1999) WebPlaces: Adding people to the Web. *Eighth International World Wide Web Conference (WWW8), Toronto, Canada*.

Maglio, P.P. and Barrett, R. (2000) Intermediaries personalize information streams. *Communications of the ACM*, **43** (8): 96–101.

Maglio, P.P. and Farrell, S. (2000) LiveInfo: Adapting web experience by customization and annotation. *Proceedings of the First International Conference on Adaptive Hypermedia and Adaptive Web-based Systems (AH 2000)*. Berlin: Springer, pp. 144–154.

441

Maglio, P.P. and Matlock, T. (1999) The conceptual structure of information space. In A.J. Munro, K. Höök and D. Benyon (eds), *Social navigation of information space*. London: Springer, pp. 155–173.

Maglio, P.P. and Matlock, T. (1998) Constructing social spaces in virtual environments: Metaphors we surf the web by. In K. Hook, A. Munro and D. Benyon (eds), *Workshop on Personalised and Social Navigation in Information space*. SICS Technical Report 98:01, Stockholm, Sweden, pp. 138–149.

Major, M. (1997) *Proceedings of 1st International Symposium on Space Syntax*. London: University College.

Maltz, D. and Ehrlich, E. (1995) Pointing the way: Active collaborative filtering. *Proceedings of the ACM Conference on Human Factors in Computing Systems (CHI '95)*. New York: ACM Press, pp. 202–209.

Mamdani, A., Pitt, J. and Stathis, K. (1999) Connected communities from the standpoint of multi-agent systems. *Journal of New Generation Computing*. Special issue on new challenges in intelligent systems (ed. Toyaki Nishida), **17** (4): 381–393. Springer-Verlag, August. ISSN 0288-3635.

Mandler, J.M. (1992) How to build a baby: II. Conceptual primitives. *Psychological Review*, **99**: 587–604.

Marks, B. (1979) The language of signs. In D. Pollet and P.C. Haskell (eds), *Sign systems for libraries*. New York: RR Bowker & Company, pp. 89–98.

Marmasse, N. and Schmandt, C. (2000) Location-aware information delivery with ComMotion. *Proceedings of HUC 2000, Bristol, England*, pp. 157–171.

Marshall, C.C. (1998) Toward an ecology of hypertext annotation. *Proceedings of Hypertext '98*. Pittsburgh, PA: ACM Press, pp. 40–49.

Masterson, J. (1996) *Nonverbal communication in text-based virtual realities*. MA Thesis. University of Montana. http://www.montana.com/john/thesis/.

Matlock, T. and Maglio, P.P. (1996) Apparent motion on the World Wide Web. *Proceedings of the Eighteenth Annual Conference of the Cognitive Science Society*. Mahwah, NJ: LEA.

Matlock, T. and Maglio, P.P. (1997) Untangling talk about the World-Wide Web. Unpublished manuscript. University of California, Santa Cruz, Psychology Department.

Maxwell, K. (2002) The maturation of HCI: Moving beyond usability toward Holistic interaction. In Carroll J. (ed) *Human Computer Interaction in the New Millennium*. New York: ACM Press.

McCall, R. and Benyon, D.R. (2000) Using ENIspace in designing 3D virtual environments. *UK VRSIG 2000*. Glasgow, UK:. British Computer Society.

McCarthy, J. and Anagnost, T. (1998) MusicFX: An arbiter of group preferences for computer supported collaborative workouts. *Proceedings of the ACM Conference on Computer-Supported Cooperative Work (CSCW '98)*. Seattle, WA: ACM Press, pp. 363–372.

McClosky, D.N. (1985) *The rhetoric of economics*. Madison, WI: University of Wisconsin Press.

McCormick, E.J. and Ilgen, D. (1987) *Industrial and organizational psychology* (8th edn). Englewood Cliffs, NJ: Prentice-Hall.

McDonald, D.W. and Ackerman, M.S. (1998) Just talk to me: A field study of expertise location. *Proceedings of the ACM Conference on Computer-Supported Cooperative Work (CSCW '98)*. Seattle, WA: ACM Press, pp. 315–324.

McKnight, C., Dillon, A. and Richardson, J. (1991) *Hypertext in context*. Cambridge, England: Cambridge University Press.

Meyrowitz, J. (1986) Television and interpersonal behaviour: Codes of perception and response. In G. Gumpert and R. Cathcart (eds), *Inter/Media: Interpersonal communication in a media world*. New York.

Miller, B., Riedl, J. and Konstan, J. (1997) Experiences with GroupLens: Making Usenet Useful Again. Proceedings of the 1997 Usenix Technical Conference.

Modjeska, D. (2000) *Hierarchical data visualization in desktop virtual reality*. PhD Thesis. University of Toronto.

Modjeska, D. and Waterworth, J.A. (2000) Effects of desktop 3D world design on user navigation and search performance. *Proceedings of IV2000, International Conference on Information Visualisation, London, England, July 2000*. IEEE Press.

Moran, T.P. and Anderson, R.J. (1990) The workaday world as a paradigm for CSCW design. *CSCW '90*. New York: ACM Press.

Morita, M. and Shinoda, Y. (1994) Information filtering based on user behavior analysis and best match text retrieval. *Proceedings of the 17th Annual International SIGIR Conference on Research and Development*, pp. 272–281.

Munro, A. (1998) Inhabiting information space: Work, artefacts and new realities. In N. Dahlbaeck (ed.), *Exploring navigation: Towards a framework for design and evaluation of navigation in electronic spaces*. Stockholm: SICS Technical Report, T98:01, pp. 91–114.

Munro, A. (1999) *Fringe benefits: An ethnographic study of social navigation at the Edinburgh Festival*. Deliverable 2.1.1 from the PERSONA project, available from SICS, Stockholm, Sweden.

Munro, A., Höök, K. and Benyon, D. (eds) (1999) Footprints in the snow. In *Social navigation of information space*. London: Springer-Verlag.

Murray, C. (1998) The Cityscape: Theory and empirical work. eSCAPE Working Paper.

Murray, J. (1997) *Hamlet on the Holodeck: The future of narrative in cyberspace*. Cambridge, MA: MIT Press.

Nagel, T. (1986) *The view from nowhere*. New York: Oxford University Press.

Nardi, B. (1996) *Context and consciousness: Activity theory and human–computer interaction*. MIT Press.

Nardi, B. and Barreau, D. (1997) 'Finding and reminding' revisited: Appropriate metaphors for file organization at the desktop. *ACM SIGCHI Bulletin*, **29** (1): 76–78.

Naughton, J. (1999) Internet column. *The Observer*, 17 January.

Neal, L. (1997) Virtual classrooms and communities. In S.C. Hayne and W. Prinz (eds), *Proceedings of ACM Group '97*. New York: ACM Press, pp. 81–90.

Nielsen, J. (1990) The art of navigating through hypertext. *Communications of the ACM*, **33**: 296–310.

Nielsen, J. (1999) Ten usability heuristics. Useit.com.

Nilan, M. (1995) Ease of user navigation through digital information spaces. *Proceedings of the 37 Allerton Institute, Monticello, Illinois*. On-line: http://edfu.lis.uiuc.edu/allerton/95/s4/nilan.html.

Norberg-Schultz, C. (1971) *Existence, space, architecture*. London: Studio Vista.

Nord, Synnes and Parnes (2002) An architecture for location-aware applications. *Proceedings of the Hawaii International Conference on System Sciences (HICSS-35)*. Big Island, Hawaii, USA.

Norman, D.A. (1983) Some observations on mental models. In D. Gentner and A. Stevens (eds), *Mental models*. Hillsdale, NJ: Lawrence Erlbaum Associates, pp. 7–14.

Norman, D.A. (1988) *The psychology of everyday things*. New York: Basic Books.

Norman, D.A. (1999) *The invisible computer*. Cambridge, MA: MIT Press.

Norman, D.A. (2000) *The Invisible Computer*. MIT Press.

Norman, D.A. and Draper, S. (1986) *User-centred systems design*. Hillsdale, NJ: LEA.

Nunberg, G. (ed.) (1996) Farewell to the information age. In *The future of the book*. University of California Press, pp. 103–138.

Oikarinen, J. and Reed, D. (1993) *Internet relay chat protocol*. IETF Network Working Group, RFC-1459.

443

Okada, K., Maeda, F., Ichikawaa, Y. and Matsushita Y. (1994) Multiparty videoconferencing at virtual social distance: MAJIC design. *Proceedings of the ACM Conference on Human Factors in Computing Systems (CHI '94)*. New York: ACM Press, pp. 385–393.

Orr, Julian (1996) *Talking about machines: An ethnography of a modern job*. Cornell University Press.

Osmond, H. (1957) Function as a basis of psychiatric ward design. *Mental Hospitals (Architectural Supplements)*, **83**: 235–245.

Ostrom, E. (1991) *Governing the Commons: The evolution of institutions for collective action*. Cambridge, UK: Cambridge University Press.

Palfreyman, K. and Rodden, T. (1996) A protocol for user awareness on the World Wide Web. *Proceedings of the ACM Conference on Computer-Supported Cooperative Work (CSCW '96)*. Boston, MA: ACM Press, pp. 130–139.

Pascoe, J. (1997) The Stick-e Note architecture: Extending the interface beyond the user. *Proceedings of IUI '97*, pp. 261–64.

Passini, R. (1984) *Wayfinding in architecture*. New York: Van Nostrand Reinhold.

Passini, R. (1996) Wayfinding design: Logic, application and some thoughts on universality. *Design Studies*, **17**: 319–331.

Passini, R. (2000) Signs-posting. In R. Jacobson (ed.), *Information design*. Cambridge, MA: MIT Press, pp. 83–98.

Pedersen, E.R. and Sokoler, T. (1997) AROMA: Abstract representation of presence supporting mutual awareness. *Proceedings of the ACM Conference on Human Factors in Computing Systems (CHI '97)*. New York: ACM Press, pp. 51–58.

Persson, P. (1998) Towards a psychological theory of close-ups: Experiencing intimacy and threat. *KINEMA: A Journal of History, Theory and Aesthetics of Film and Audiovisual Media*. Waterloo, Canada: University of Waterloo Press.

Persson, P., Espinoza, F. and Elenor, C. (2001) GeoNotes: Social enhancement of physical space. *Design-Expo at CHI 2001, Seattle*, April.

Perziosi, D. (1979) *The semiotics of the built environment: An introduction to architectonic analysis*. Bloomingsdale, London: Indiana University Press.

Picard, R. (1997) *Affective computing*. Cambridge, MA: MIT Press.

Pirolli, P. (1997) Computational models of information scent-following in a very large browsable text collec-tion. *Proceedings of the ACM Conference on Human Factors in Computing Systems (CHI '97)*. New York: ACM Press.

Pirolli, P. and Card, S. (1995) Information foraging in information access environments. *Proceedings of the ACM Conference on Human Factors in Computing Systems (CHI '95)*. New York: ACM Press.

Pollet, D. and Haskell, P.C. Eds. (1979) *Sign systems for libraries solving the wayfinding problem*. New York: Bowker, pp.271.

Polson, P., Lewis, C., Reiman, J. and Wharton, C. (1992) A method for theory-based evaluation of user interfaces. *International Journal of Man-Machine Studies*, **36**: 741–773.

Potter, M. (1993) Very short-term conceptual memory. *Memory and Cognition*, **21**: 156–161.

Potter, M. (1999) Understanding sentences and scenes: The role of conceptual short-term memory. In V. Coltheart (ed.), *Fleeting memories: Cognition of brief visual stimuli*. Cambridge, MA: MIT Press, pp. 13–46.

Puglia, S., Carter, R. and Jain, R. (2000) MultECommerce: A distributed architecture for collaborative shopping on the WWW. *Proceedings of the 2nd ACM Conference on Electronic Commerce*. Minneapolis, MN: ACM, pp. 215–224.

Radley, A. (1990) Artefacts, memory and a sense of the past. In D. Middleton and D. Edwards (eds), *Collective remembering*. Sage Publications.

Rankin, P. and Spence, R. (1999) A contrast between information navigation and social navigation in virtual worlds. In A. Munro, K. Höök and D. Benyon (eds), *Social navigation of information space.* London: Springer-Verlag.

Rankin, P.J., van Heerden, C., Mama, C., Nikolovska, L., Otter, R. and Rutgers, J. (1998) StarCursors in Contentspace: Abstractions of people and places. *Proceedings of SIGGRAPH '98.* ACM, p. 250.

Rankin, P.J. et al. (1998) StarCursors in Contentspace: Abstractions of people and places. *Workshop on Personalised and Social Navigation of Information Space.* Stockholm: Swedish Institute of Computer Science.

Rapoport, A. (1982) *The meaning of the built environment a nonverbal communication approach.* Beverly Hills: Sage.

Raubal, M., Egenhofer, M.J., Pfoser, D. and Tryfona, N. (1997) Structuring space with image schemata: Wayfinding in airports as a case study. In S.C. Hirtle and A.U. Frank (eds), *Spatial information theory: A theoretical basis for GIS (COSIT '97).* Berlin: Springer-Verlag.

Raybourn E. (1998) *An intercultural computer-based multi-user simulation supporting participant exploration of identity and power in a text-based networked virtual reality: DomeCity^{TM} MOO.* Unpublished dissertation. Department of Communication, University of New Mexico. Albuquerque, NM.

Reeves, B. and Nass, C. (1996) *The media equation: How people treat computers, television and new media like real people and places.* Cambridge, UK: Cambridge University Press.

Rekimoto, J. and Ayatsuka, Y. (1998) Augment-able reality: Situated communication through physical and digital spaces. *Proceedings of the 2nd International Symposium on Wearable Computers.* 19–21 October, Pittsburgh, Pennsylvania, USA.

Rennison, E. (1994) Galaxy of news: An approach to visualising and understanding expansive news landscapes. *Proceedings of UIST '94.* Marina Del Ray, CA: ACM Press, pp. 3–12.

Resnick, P. and Varian, H.R. (1997) Recommender systems. *Communications of the ACM,* **40** (3): 56–58.

Resnick, P., Iacovou, N., Suchak, M., Bergstrom, P. and Riedl, J. (1994) Grouplens: An open architecture for collaborative filtering of netnews. *Proceedings of the ACM Conference on Computer-Supported Cooperative Work (CSCW '94).* New York: ACM Press, pp. 175–186.

Resnick, P. and Miller, J. (1996) PICS: Internet access controls without censorship. *Communications of the ACM,* **39** (10), 87–93.

Richmond, A. (1996) Enticing online shoppers to buy – A human behaviour study. *Computer Networks and ISDN Systems,* **28**: 1469–1480.

Ricoeur, P. (1981) *Hermeneutics and human sciences: Essays on language, action and interpretation* (trans. J. Thompson). Cambridge: Cambridge University Press.

Robertson, T. (1997) Cooperative Work and Lived Cognition: A Taxonomy of Embodied Actions. In: Hughes, J.A., W. Prinz, T. Rodden, K. Schmidt 1997. ECSCW'97. Proceedings of the Fifth European Conference on Computer Supported Cooperative Work. London: Kluwer.

Rockwell, B. (1998) From chat to civilization: The evolution of online communities. http://www.blaxxun.com/company/vision/cmnty.html, 1998.

Rohrer, T. (1997) Conceptual blending on the information highway: How metaphorical inferences work. In *Discourse and perspective in cognitive linguistics.* Amsterdam: John Benjamins.

Rose, D.E., Borenstein, J.J. and Tiene, K. (1995) MessageWorld: A new approach to facilitating asynchronous group communication. *CIKM '95 (Conference on Information and Knowledge Management).* Baltimore, MD, pp. 266–273.

Rutter, D.R. (1987) *Communicating by telephone.* Oxford: Pergamon.

Sacks, H. (1992) *Lectures on conversations,* Vols 1 and 2. Blackwell, pp. 81–94.

Sarwar, B., Konstan, J.A., Borchers, A., Herlocker, J., Miller, B. and Riedl, J. (1998) Using filtering agents to improve prediction quality in the grouplens research collaborative filtering system. *Proceedings of the ACM Conference on Computer-Supported Collaborative Work (CSCW '98).* Seattle, WA: ACM Press.

Sarwar, B.M., Karypis, G., Konstan, J.A. and Riedl, J. (2000) Analysis of recommender algorithms for e-commerce. *Proceedings of the ACM E-Commerce 2000 Conference.* ACM Press.

Schafer, J.B., Konstan, J. and Riedl, J. (2001) Electronic commerce recommender applications. *Journal of Data Mining and Knowledge Discovery.* ??

Schiano, D.J. and White, S. (1998) The first noble truth of cyberspace: People are people (even when they MOO). *Proceedings of the ACM Conference on Human Factors in Computing Systems (CHI '98).* Los Angeles, CA: ACM Press, pp. 352–359.

Schmidt, K. (1997) Of maps and scripts: The status of formal constructs in cooperative work. *Proceedings ACM Group '97.* New York: ACM Press, pp. 38–147.

Schutz, A. (1962) *On phenomenology and social relations.* Chicago: University of Chicago Press.

Schwartz, M. (1997) *Transfiguration of the commonplace.* Washington, DC: Spacemakers Books.

Selfridge, K.M. (1979) Planning library signage systems. In D. Pollet and P.C. Haskell (eds), *Sign systems for libraries.* New York: Bowker, pp. 49–68.

Shardanand, U. and Maes, P. (1995) Social information filtering: Algorithms for automating 'Word of Mouth'. *Proceedings of the ACM Conference on Human Factors in Computing Systems (CHI '95).* New York: ACM Press, pp. 210–217

Shum, S.B. (1990) Real and virtual spaces: Mapping from spatial cognition to hypertext. *Hypermedia,* 2 (2): 133–158.

Siegel, A. and White, S.H. (1975) The development of spatial representations of large-scale environments. *Advances in Child Development,* 10: 10–55.

Silverman, D. (1998) *Harvey Sacks: Social science and conversation analysis.* Oxford: Polity.

Sjölinder, M., Höök, K. and Nilsson, L. (2000) Age differences in the use of an on-line grocery shop – implications for design. *Proceedings of the ACM Conference on Human Factors in Computing Systems (CHI 2000), The Hague.* New York: ACM Press, p. 135.

Slater, M., Steed, A., McCarthy, J. and Maringelli, F. (1998) The Influence of body movement on presence in virtual environments. *Human Factors.*

Smith, A.J. and Moore, S.E. (2000) http:// www.106.ibm.com/developerworks/library/us-atex

Smith, C.W. (1989) *Auctions: The social construction of value.* New York: Free Press.

Soininen, K. and Suikola, E. (2000) Information seeking is social. *Proceedings of the NordiCHI Conference, Stockholm (Stockholm, Sweden, October).*

Solomon, J. (1998) *The architectural sign: Semiotics and the human landscape.* New York: Harper & Row.

Solso, R.L. (1998) *Cognitive psychology* (5th edn). Boston: Allyn & Bacon.

Sorkin, M. (1993) *Local code: The constitution of a city at 42 degrees N latitude.* New York: Princeton Architectural Press.

Spence, R. (1997) Towards a framework for organised thought about navigation. Position paper for the Workshop on Navigation in Electronic Worlds (see Jul and Furnas, 1997).

Spence, R. (1999) A framework for navigation. *International Journal of Human–Computer Studies,* 51: 919–945.

Spence, R. (2001) *Information visualization.* Addison Wesley.

Spence, R. (2002a) Rapid, serial and visual: A presentation technique with potential. *Information Visualization,* 1: 13–19.

Spence, R. (2002b) *Sensitivity encoding to support information space navigation: A design guideline.* Internal Report.

Spence, R. and Tweedie, L.S. (1998) The attribute explorer: Information synthesis via exploration. *Interacting with Computers,* 11: 137–146.

Spencer, H. and Reynolds, L. (1977) *Directional signing in libraries and museums a review of current theory and practice.* London: Royal College of Art.

Sproull, L. and Kiesler, S. (1988) Reducing social context cues: Electronic mail in organisational communication. In *Computer-supported co-operative work: A book of readings.* San Mateo, CA: Morgan Kaufmann.

Star, S.L. and Ruhleder, K. (1994) Steps towards an ecology of infrastructure: Complex problems in design and access for large-scale collaborative systems. *Proceedings of the ACM Conference on Computer-Supported Collaborative Work (CSCW '94), Chapel Hill, NC.* New York: ACM Press.

Star, S.L., Bowker, G.C. and Neumann, L.J. (1997) *Transparency at different levels of scale: Convergence between information artifacts and social worlds.* Urbana-Champaign, IL: Library and Information Science, University of Illinois.

Stephenson, N. (1992) *Snow crash.* New York: Bantam Books.

Stevens, A. and Coupe, P. (1978) Distortions in judged spatial relations. *Cognitive Psychology,* 10: 422–437.

Stiny, G. (1981) Review–C. Alexander: The timeless way of building. *Environment and Planning B: Planning and Design,* Vol. 8, pp. 119–122.

Stiny, G. and Gips, J. (1978) *Algorithmic aesthetics: Computer models for criticism and design in the arts.* Berkeley, CA: University of California Press.

Stokols D. (1972) On the distinction between density and crowding: Some implications for future research. *Psychological Review,* 79 (3): 275–278.

Stokols, D. and Resnick, S.M. (1975) The generalization of residential crowding experiences to non-residential settings. *Annual Conference of the Environmental Design Research Association.* Kansas: Lawrence Earlbaum.

Strathclyde University and The Lighthouse (1999) *The Glasgow Directory.*

Streeter, L.A., Vitello, D. and Wonsiewicz, S.A. (1985) How to tell people where to go: Comparing navigational aids. *International Journal of Man–Machine Studies,* 22: 549–562.

Streitz, N., Hannemann, J. and Thuring, M. (1989) From ideas and arguments to hyperdocuments: Travelling through activity spaces. *Proceedings of the ACM Conference on Hypertext.* New York: ACM Press, pp. 343–364.

Strickland, D., Hodges, L., North, M. and Weghorst S. (1997) Overcoming phobias by virtual exposure. *Communications of the ACM,* 40 (8): 34–39.

Su, H., Nelder, J., Wolbert, P. and Spence, R. (1996) Application of generalised linear models to the design improvement of an engineering artifact. *Quality and Reliability Engineering International,* 12: 101–112.

Suchman, L. (1987) *Plans and situated actions: The problem of human–machine communication.* Cambridge: Cambridge University Press.

Suchman, L. (1995) Making work visible. *Communications of the ACM,* 38 (9): 56–65.

Suchman, Lucy A. (1987) *Plans and situated actions.* Cambridge: Cam-bridge University Press

Sudnow, D. (1972) Temporal parameters of interpersonal observation. In D. Sudnow (ed.), *Studies in social interaction.* New York: The Free Press.

Svensson, M. (2000) *Defining and designing social navigation.* Licentiate thesis, DSV report series 00–003. ISSN 1101–8526; available from Stockholm University.

Svensson, M., Höök, K., Laaksolahti, J. and Waern, A. (2001) Social navigation of food recipes. *Proceedings of the ACM Conference on Human Factors in Computing Systems (CHI 2001).* New York: ACM Press, pp. 341–348.

Sweetser, E. (1990) *From etymology to pragmatics: Metaphorical and cultural aspects of semantic structure.* Cambridge, England: Cambridge University Press.

447

Tang, J., Isaacs, E. and Rua, M. (1994) Supporting distributed groups with a montage of lightweight connections. *Proceedings of the ACM Conference on Computer-Supported Cooperative Work (CSCW '94), Chapel Hill, NC.* New York: ACM Press, pp. 23–34.

Tauscher, L. and Greenberg, S. (1997) Revisitation patterns in World Wide Web navigation. *Proceedings of the ACM Conference on Human Factors in Computing Systems (CHI '97).* New York: ACM Press.

Terry, D. (1993) A tour through tapestry. *Proceedings of the ACM Conference on Organisational Computing Systems (COOCS '93).* New York: ACM Press, pp. 21–30.

Terveen, L. and Hill, W. (1998a) Evaluating emergent collaboration on the Web. *Proceedings of the ACM Conference on Computer-Supported Cooperative Work (CSCW '98).* Seattle, WA: ACM Press, pp. 355–362.

Terveen, L. and Hill, W. (1998b) Finding and visualizing inter-site clan graphs. *Proceedings of the ACM Conference on Human Factors in Computing Systems (CHI '98).* New York: ACM Press, pp. 448–455.

Terveen, L., Hill, W., Amento, B., McDonald, D. and Creter, J. (1997) PHOAKS: A system for sharing recommendations. *Communications of the ACM,* **40** (3): 59–62.

Thomas, J.C., Kellogg, W.A. and Erickson, T. (2001) The knowledge management puzzle: Human and social factors in knowledge management. *IBM Systems Journal,* **40** (4): 863–884.

Thorndyke, P.W. and Hayes-Roth, B. (1982) Differences in spatial knowledge acquired from maps and navigation. *Cognitive Psychology,* **14**: 560–598.

Timpka, T. and Hallberg N. (1996) Talking at work – professional advice-seeking at primary healthcare centers. *Scandinavian Journal of Primary Health Care,* **14**: 130–135.

Treisman, A.M. (1964) Selective attention in man. *British Medical Bulletin,* **20**: 12–16.

Trevor, J., Palfreyman, K. and Rodden, T. (1998) Open support for shared spaces based on e-scapes. *eSCAPE Deliverable 1.1.* Lancaster University. ISBN: 1–862220–052–1. This report is available from http://escape.lancs.ac.uk, pp. 161–181.

Tuan, Y. (1997) *Space and place: The perspective of experience.* Minneapolis, MN: University of Minnesota Press.

Turkle, S. (1997) *Life on the screen: Identity in the age of the Internet.* New York: Touchstone.

Turner, M. (1987) *Death is the mother of beauty. Mind, metaphor, criticism.* Chicago, IL: University of Chicago Press,

Turner, M. and Fauconnier, G. (1995) Conceptual integration and formal expression. *Metaphor and Symbolic Activity,* **10**: 183–204.

Tversky, B. (1993) Cognitive maps, cognitive collages and spatial mental models. In *Spatial information theory – A theoretical basis for GIS. Proceedings of the European Conference COSIT '93.* Springer-Verlag, Lecture Notes on Computer Science, pp. 14–24.

Tversky, B. (1996) Spatial perspective in descriptions. In P. Bloom, M.A. Peterson, L. Nadel and M.F. Garrett (eds), *Language and space. Language, speech and communication.* Cambridge, MA: MIT Press.

Tweedie, L. (1995) Interactive visualisation artifacts: How can abstractions inform design? In *People and Computers X, Proceedings of HCI '95,* pp. 247–265.

Tweedie, L.A., Spence, R., Dawkes, H. and Su, H. (1996) Externalising abstract mathematical models. *Proceedings of the ACM Conference on Human Factors in Computing Systems (CHI '96).* New York: ACM Press, pp. 406–412.

Vecchio, R.P. (1991) *Organizational behavior* (2nd edn). Orlando, FL: Dryden.

Vincente, K.J. and Williges, R.C. (1988) Accommodating individual differences in searching a hierarchical file system. *International Journal of Man–Machine Studies,* **29**: 647–668.

Waterworth, J.A. (1995) *Viewing others and others' views: Presence and concealment in shared hyperspace*. Presented at Workshop on Social Contexts of Hypermedia, 16–17 February 1995, Department of Informatics, Umeå University, Sweden.

Waterworth, J.A. (1996) A pattern of islands: Exploring public information space in a private vehicle. In P. Brusilovsky, P. Kommers and N. Streitz (eds), *Multimedia, hypermedia and virtual reality*. Springer Verlag Lecture Notes in Computer Science.

Waterworth, J.A. (1997) Personal spaces: 3D spatial worlds for information exploration, organisation and communication. In R. Earnshaw and J. Vince (eds), *The Internet in 3D: Information, images and interaction*. New York: Academic Press.

Waterworth, J. (1998) Experiential design of shared information spaces. *Workshop on Personalised and Social Navigation of Information Space*. Stockholm: Swedish Institute of Computer Science.

Waterworth, J. and Chignell, M.H. (1991) A model for information exploration. *Hypermedia*, 3 (1): 35–58.

Waterworth, J.A. and Singh, G. (1994) Information islands: Private views of public places. *Proceedings of MHVR '94 East–West International Conference on Multimedia, Hypermedia and Virtual Reality*. Moscow, September 14–16.

Watson, M., Russell, W.J. and Sanderson, P. (2000) Anesthesia monitoring, alarm proliferation and ecological interface design. *Australian Journal of Information Systems*, 7 (2): 109–114.

Wechsler, S. (1979) Perceiving the visual message. In D. Pollet and P.C. Haskell (eds), *Sign systems for libraries*. New York: Bowker & Company, pp. 33–46.

Wegner, P. (1997) Why interaction is more powerful than algorithms. *Communications of the ACM*, 40 (5): 80-91.

Westin, A. (1970) *Privacy and freedom*. New York: Atheneum.

Wexelblat, A. (1998a) History-rich tools for social navigation. *Proceedings of the ACM Conference on Human Factors in Computing Systems (CHI '98). Conference Summary*. Los Angeles, CA: ACM Press, pp. 359–360.

Wexelblat, A. (1998b) Communities through time: Using history for social navigation. In Toru Ishida (ed.), *Community computing and support systems*. Lecture Notes in Computer Science, Volume 1519, Springer Verlag.

Wexelblat, A. (1999a) *Footprints: Interaction history for digital objects*. PhD Thesis, MIT Program in Media Arts and Sciences.

Wexelblat, A. (1999b) History-based tools for navigation. *Proceedings of the 32nd Hawaii International Conference on Systems Sciences (HICSS-32)*, IEEE Computer Society Press.

Wexelblat, A. and Maes, P. (1997) Visualizing histories for web browsing. *RIAO '97: Computer-Assisted Infor-mation Retrieval on the Internet*. Montreal.

Wexelblat, A. and Maes, P. (1999) Footprints: History-rich tools for information foraging. *Proceedings of the ACM Conference on Human Factors in Computing Systems (CHI '99)*. New York: ACM Press, pp. 270–277.

Wheeler (1971) Social interaction and urban spaces. *Journal of Geography*, 70: 200–203.

Whyte, W.H. (1980) *The social life of small urban spaces*. Washington DC: The Conservation Foundation.

Whyte, W. (1988a) *City: Rediscovering the center*. New York: Doubleday.

Whyte, W.H. (1988b) *City: Return to the center*. New York: Anchor Books.

Wickens, C.D. (1984) *Engineering psychology and human performance*. Columbus: Charles Merrill.

Willis, P. (1990) *Common culture. Symbolic work at play in the everyday cultures of the young*. Boulder: Westview Press.

Winograd, T. (1996) *Bringing Design to software*. Addison-Wesley.

Wittaker, S. et al. (1998) The dynamics of mass interaction. *Proceedings of the ACM Conference on Computer-Supported Cooperative Work (CSCW '98)*. Seattle, WA: ACM Press, pp. 257–264.

Witten, I.H., Moffat, A. and Bell, T.C. (1999) *Managing gigabytes: Compressing and indexing documents and images* (2nd edn). San Francisco, CA: Morgan Kaufmann.

Wittenburg, K. (1997) Navigation and search – what's the difference? Position paper for the Workshop on Navigation in Electronic Worlds (see Jul and Furnas, 1997).

Wittenburg, K., Chiyoda, C., Heinrichs, M. and Lanning, T. (2000) Browsing though rapid-fire imaging: Requirements and industry initiatives. *Proceedings Electronic Imaging 2000*.

Wittgenstein, L. (1953/1997) *Philosophical investigations.* Oxford: Blackwell.

Wittgenstein, L. (1958) *Philosophical investigations* (3rd edn; trans. G.E.M. Anscombe). Oxford: Oxford University Press.

Wolf, J., Aggarwal, C., Wu, K.-L. and Yu, P. (1999) Horting hatches an egg: A new graph-theoretic approach to collaborative filtering. *Proceedings of ACM SIGKDD International Conference on Knowledge Discovery and Data Mining*. San Diego, CA.

Wood, D. (1992) *The power of maps.* New York: The Guilford Press.

Woolgar, S. (1988) *Science: The very idea.* London: Routledge.

Youll, J. and Krikorian, R. (2000) Wherehoo Server: An interactive location service for software agents and intelligent systems. Workshop on Infrastructure for Smart Devices – How to Make Ubiquity an Actuality. *The 2nd International Symposium on Handheld and Ubiquitous Computing, Bristol (UK)*, September 27.

Zellweger and Polle (1989) Scripted documents: A hypermedia path mechanism. *Hypertext '89 Proceedings.* ACM Press.

Zube, E.H., Sell, J.L. and Taylor, J.G. (1982) Landscape perception: Research, application and theory. *Landscape Planning*, **9**: 1–33.

Zuberec, S. (1994) *Visualization of text based information.* Master's Thesis. University of Toronto.

Index

453